Marc M

IRISH LAW OF

IRISH LAW OF DEFAMATION

Second Edition

Marc McDonald
BCL, MLitt, Barrister-at-Law

WITH A FOREWORD BY

The Hon. Thomas A. Finlay
Chief Justice of Ireland

THE ROUND HALL PRESS
in association with
IRISH ACADEMIC PRESS

The typesetting of this book was input by
Gilbert Gough Typesetting, Dublin
and output by Computer Graphics Ltd, Dublin
for The Round Hall Press, Kill Lane, Blackrock, Co. Dublin

First edition 1987
Second edition 1989

BRITISH LIBRARY CATALOGUING IN PUBLICATION DATA

McDonald, Marc
Irish law of defamation, 2nd ed.
1. Ireland. (Republic). Defamation. Law
I. Title
344.17063'4

ISBN 0-947686-49-5 pbk
ISBN 0-947686-33-9

Printed by Antony Rowe Ltd, Chippenham, Wiltshire

Contents

'Give me a hint, dear sir, a taste merely, of that stream of calumny, which, according to the Bishop of Meath, rolls down the streets of our favourite towns, taking a little fresh venom at every house it passes.'

Mrs Piozzi in a letter to an unnamed friend, quoted in J. Healy, *History of the Diocese of Meath,* III (Dublin, 1908).

Foreword

An Irish textbook on the law of defamation was greatly overdue. I, therefore, warmly welcome the repair of this omission and, in particular, the way in which this book has done it.

The author has, I believe, grasped clearly the fact that the provisions of our Constitution probably merit a much greater examination by lawyers than they have so far received in relation to the law of defamation.

This book, in which are to be found carefully examined and accurately set out the leading Irish authorities on defamation as well as the leading English authorities which have been from time to time cited here with approval, also contains critical but constructive comment on the state of the law of defamation in Ireland at present.

Not only, therefore, does it constitute a valuable reference book both for the student and for the practising lawyer, but it should in addition, in my opinion, help to create further discussions and consideration which is almost certainly overdue of methods of reforming the laws of defamation so as to resolve the conflicting interests with which in many instances it is concerned.

I welcome this book and trust that it will have the success which I believe it deserves.

Thomas A. Finlay
Chief Justice of Ireland,
Four Courts,
Dublin 7.

Pour Frédérique et Maxime Santiago

Preface

This book grew out of a thesis for the MLitt degree in Trinity College Dublin under the supervision of Professor Nial Osborough, whose valuable tutelage I would like to acknowledge. Since then it has been re-written as a text suitable for practising lawyers and journalists and students of those professions.

I should also like to thank a number of people who have helped me in the writing of this book. I owe a particular debt of gratitude to William Binchy, Cyril Cawley, Jim Farrelly, Nial Fennelly and Justin MacCarthy, and also to Michael Adams, Eileen Colgan and Tony Farmar — all of whom gave generously of their time and energy. I would like to thank the Chief Justice for having so kindly writtin a foreword; and finally I must thank Frédérique for having endured my singlemindedness while working on this project.

The prospect of statutory reform of the law of defamation has received a boost as a result of two recent events. The first was the launch of *A Report on Press Freedom and Libel* by Professor Kevin Boyle and Marie McGonagle. Although commissioned by newspaper interests, and adopting a decidedly free speech perspective on reform matters, the report makes a number of interesting reform recommendations and contains some very welcome research findings about the operation of defamation law in practice. It has, unfortunately, not been possible to incorporate a consideration of the report into the text. The second event was the request made by the Attorney General, John Murray, to the Law Reform Commission to examing defamation law with a view to providing reform proposals. Such a request does seem to imply some official concern about the present state of the law.

It has also not been possible to incorporate into the text the recent Supreme Court decision in *Hynes-O'Sullivan v O'Driscoll*, 21 July 1988. This was a non-media qualified privilege case in which the court reversed a High Court trial judge's ruling that 1) a solicitor who made a complaint about a doctor to the wrong medical authorities acted on a privileged occasion, and 2) that there was insufficient evidence of malice, on other privileged occasions, for the issue to be left to the jury.

Three points may be briefly made about the Supreme Court decision.

Firstly, the court declined the defendant's 'attractive' invitation to re-model the basis of the qualified privilege defence by adding — to the requirement that the statement is made to a recipient interested in receiving it — the further possibility that the occasion could be privileged if the defendant honestly, or honestly and reasonably, believed that the recipient had an interest in receiving it. This reluctance was based, it seems, on uncertainty about the wider ramifications of such a change.

Secondly, the court judgments contain some statements on the relationship between the Constitution and the defamation action, and so add to the build-up of judicial observations in this area. Two of the judgments — those of Henchy and McCarthy JJ — cited constitutional provisions in support of their rejection of a change in the common law position; and Henchy J stated that 'the law as to qualified privilege must reflect a due balancing of the constitutional right to freedom of expression and the constitutional protection of every citizen's good name'. However, in context these references were really only 'called-in-aid' type of arguments, like indeed previous court pronouncements. We still await 1) clear and authoritative declarations that the common law protection of reputation is based on the constitutional protection of good name, 2) some generalised court prognostications on the significance of this, and 3) pointers to the continued propriety of using a pro-reputation title like 'Law of Defamation', when the law is really cataloguing a huge number of different situations where speech and reputation are, alternately, preferred.

Thirdly, when the Supreme Court reversed the trial judge's ruling that there was not sufficient evidence of malice for the issue to be left to the jury, it seems to have taken a slightly different, and somewhat broader, view of whether individual acts can, if taken together, constitute sufficient evidence of malice for the issue to be left to the jury. Although it is difficult to criticise Supreme Court subjectivism on such fine points as the weight to be given to items of evidence of malice, the view of the trial judge, and even of precedent, may well be preferable, since it is a prudent safeguard against findings of malice where malice could be too easily found.

For this second edition minor corrections of style and typography have been made and the text of the Defamation Act 1961 has been added as an appendix.

Table of Cases

Other Tables

Table of Articles of the Constitution

Statutes

Statutes in other jurisdictions

Table of Rules of Superior Courts

1

Introduction

The need for an Irish text on defamation arises because there has been no monographic treatment of this important area of law in Ireland before now, general Irish texts do not consider the subject in sufficient detail, and English defamation texts, while occasionally generous in references to Irish cases, do not, amongst other things, deal with the indigenous legal environment of Irish defamation law and its potentialities.

There are also some other significant reasons for such a text. In general, the absence of a text on an area of national law can hinder the proper development of that law. Insufficient attention may be given to indigenous case law and legislation, and sometimes even none at all if a particular decision has been forgotten about.[1] There may be little or no academic writing.[2] Lawyers cite foreign texts and cases. The judiciary follow suit,[3] and the legislature likewise when it comes to statutory reform. The pattern is easily set. The judiciary can become detached from its own roots, and display insufficient awareness of its national legal identity. The possibility of separate development of rules is reduced, and judicial creativity, in the sense of being a consequence of national identity and existence, is negligible. The Irish law of defamation in both the nineteenth and twentieth centuries has displayed many of these symptoms of legal underdevelopment.

Not surprisingly in this situation, the law in the English and Irish jurisdictions has become perceived as being identical. In 1874, Barry J stated 'The law of libel in England and the law of libel in Ireland

1 For example, the decision in *Cassidy v Kincaid* (1865) 10 IJ NS 176 — see p. 153 — post would have been of interest in *Curneen v Sweeney* (1969) 103 ILTR 29 where a defendant was held not to have had a sufficient interest in another's welfare to have acted on a privileged occasion when defaming the plaintiff. Another example concerns pleading the defence of fair comment — see p. 225 post.

2 Most, though not all, academic writing here on defamation law has concerned English developments.

3 The judgement of Black J in *Pyke v Hibernian Bank* [1950] IR 195, and that of Gibson J in *Crawford and Frame v Vance* [1903] 2 IR 521 illustrate this in varying degrees.

are the same — the same in principle and in practice'.[4] The reason why it was the same in principle is that nineteenth century Irish judges saw themselves as applying the English common law in Ireland, and not an Irish common law. Nonetheless, because of the nature of the common law system, some indigenous developments occurred [5] if only because no particular English precedent existed at that time. [6] Further, some differences may have arisen because later English reforming decisions reversed previous English precedents which had in the meantime been followed in Ireland.[7]

Barry J's remark was not entirely correct for the area of procedural law. Some noticeable differences existed here between Irish and English law, and in the nineteenth century when procedure was, for a long time, as important as substance, this was significant. And, indeed, some sense of the distinctiveness of Irish practice, and a desire to retain it is evident.[8] However, the predominant and almost embarrassing desire of Irish judges to emphasise and achieve uniformity counteracted any such tendency. On one occasion where legislation not only permitted but even required an existing difference of practice to be recognised, the English practice was preferred;[9] and, on others, this desire for uniformity could be shown in an unflattering light when a later English reform adopted the practice followed earlier here. Some differences in practice here appear simply to have been forgotten about;[10] and while reasons of space prevent this text from dealing with procedural law, such things would not have occurred so readily if a textbook had existed which highlighted them.

At present, there are some but not many differences between Irish and English statutory and common law rules of substantive defamation

4 *Stannus v Finlay* [1874] IR 8 CL 264, 290.

5 An example of this occurred in relation to the occasion of qualified privilege that allowed a defensive response to a public attack to be made in public — see p. 146 post

6 Judicial creativity in the nineteenth century is most evident in the impressive contribution of Chief Justice Monahan of Common Pleas to the development of the defence of qualified privilege. In a century marked by a striking expansion of the occasions of qualified privilege, at least ten reported cases between 1856 and 1869 involving claims of privileged occasion were heard by him. In only two instances the claim was not upheld, and in most of the other cases there was either no precedent in point or judgement was delivered without citing any.

7 An English case which may have caused some differences is *Munster v Lamb* (1883) 11 QBD 588. See p. 135 post

8 See, for example, the remarks in the High Court, of Johnson J in *Fisher v Nation Newspaper and Rooney* [1901] 2 IR 465, 477. See p. 49 post.

9 This occurred in Fisher's case above where the Court of Appeal reversed the High Court decision.

10 An example of this concerns the pleading of the defence of fair comment. See p. 225 post

law.[11] What is considered defamatory is likely to be broadly similar — despite the different social circumstances of both countries, and the possible predominance here of the judicial rather than the community view of what is defamatory[12] — because standards of opinion which do not consist of those of all reasonable minded people are now recognised by the law. However, in addition to the differences that now exist, there are significant divergent pressures working on defamation law here which seem likely to produce a quite different Irish defamation law from the English one. Firstly, statutory reform here is unlikely any longer slavishly to follow the English pattern. English reform reports are not now the only ones on which we can act. There are other often different, and often better reports, although the general idea of establishing reform bodies and using their reports as a means of effecting change in defamation law is open to question, and is considered in Chapter 13. Secondly, an increasing reliance here on constitutional provisions is likely to alter radically many of the familiar common law concepts of defamation law and while the impact of these provisions is considered at various points in the text, the general relationship between the common law action and the Constitution will be examined shortly.

A number of difficulties face a writer of a text on Irish defamation law, and it may be helpful to allude briefly to some of these. This text has a traditional title and a traditional format of presentation, since an important function of the work is to describe through Irish sources the common law and statutory content of the law. There are, however, as has been suggested, influences from reform bodies, the Constitution, and even the European Community for change in that law which necessitate some comment and analysis. Both these and other issues considered in the text will raise serious questions about which common law rules remain valid.

Furthermore, the common law rules do not constitute by any means a homogeneous entity. They suffer from varying degrees of inconsistency in the estimation of values and in the balancing of rights. The text writer in this context faces diverging demands of orientation whose reconciliation is not easy. Reform suggestions cause particular difficulties, since in addition to describing and assessing them, one must try to evaluate their implications, and see how they might affect other rules. Unfortunately, space in a general text does not allow the kind of assessment which periodic literature

11 These concern infectious malice, slander limitation periods, the defence of unintentional defamation, concurrent wrongdoers, and the extent of certain media privileges contained in s. 24 of the Defamation Act 1961. There are also some clear and express constitutional differences relating to reports of Oireachtas proceedings — see p. 123 post.

12 See p. 15 post

permits. The general approach adopted has been to consider the reform of various rules as they arise in the text, with certain topics being left to the end of chapters, and a more comprehensive look at possible future developments is contained in the last chapter.

THE CONSTITUTION AND THE COMMON LAW

Central to any consideration of the common law of defamation in Ireland is an appreciation of the effect which the Constitution of 1937 has on that law. Constitutional provisions are also of crucial importance in determining whether the recommendations of foreign reform bodies can be acted on here, or indeed, in determining the general legislative capacity to effect change in defamation law.

Article 40.3 (2) of the Constitution refers to the state's guarantee to 'protect as best it may from unjust attack and, in the case of injustice done, vindicate the .. good name... of every citizen'. This reference has received little judicial recognition,[13] and its operation is one of the remaining enigmas of constitutional law. If the reference actually constitutes the foundation of the common law protection of reputation in Ireland then much of defamation law is brought into the realm of constitutional law. It opens up all the common law concepts, balances and rules to constitutional scrutiny. And since good name is not an absolute right, to judge from the constitutional text, it particularly entitles judges and litigants to test the constitutional protection of good name against other constitutional protections such as freedom of expression, equality of treatment, the protection of the media, and other rights. The common law rules, posited on balances struck in earlier times by judges and legislators, are therefore vulnerable to constitutional action, and the judiciary is clearly entitled, should it see fit, to move those balances to accord better with constitutional requirements. There is much in the present law which one may suspect to be of doubtful constitutionality.[14] Certainly that

13 The various non defamation references are collected in Kelly, *The Irish Constitution* (2nd ed) 471 et seq. The only major use made so far of this right by the Supreme Court in *Re Haughey* [1971] IR 217 to entitle a witness before a parliamentary committee to defend himself was, it is suggested, a peculiar one. The court's objective in that case could more satisfactorily have been attained by the use of accepted doctrines of natural justice and self defence rather than an opportune reliance on good name.

14 Questions are raised in the text concerning the constitutionality of many rules, including the denial of individual actionability of group defamation, many aspects of the libel/slander dichotomy, aggravated damages arising from certain unsuccessful justifications, the exclusive emphasis in justification on truth, the denial of a wider media public interest privilege, the references to Northern Ireland and certain detailed media privileges contained in the Defamation Act

has been the experience in the US, mainly since 1964, where radical changes have been made in the common law by constitutional interpretation.

There are a number of reasons for suggesting that the constitutional phrase 'good name' implies reputation, and would therefore form the basis of the common law action in defamation. Firstly, it is quite clear that the general legal usage in defamation cases in different common law jurisdictions takes the terms good name and reputation to refer to the same thing. Secondly, an increasing number of judges here have mentioned the Constitution in defamation actions, plainly on the assumption that the common law action is based on the constitutional reference.[15] Thirdly, the Irish translation of the title of the Defamation Act 1961 refers to 'Chlúmhilleadh' and good name is described in the Irish text of the Constitution as 'dea-chlú'. This suggests that the statutory enactment addresses the same concept as the constitutional provision. Fourthly, if the view that the common law action is based entirely on the constitutional right is not correct, and that good name does not include reputation, then it is difficult to see what adequate meaning good name can have. A question may also be raised about how the common law action survived the adoption of the 1937 Constitution.[16] Any response which refuses to accept the logic of the view argued for above — and one commentator has recoiled at the thought that the Constitution might impose a font of tort law [17] — comes close to treating the constitutional reference as empty.

While the basis for the constitutional interpretation of defamation law may appear sound, it should nonetheless be appreciated that there is an element of speculative comment in the detailed criticisms contained in this text of a number of common law rules for appearing to conflict with various provisions of the Constitution. The judiciary has not, by and large, given an indication of its view in this area. One can, however, be reassured in making such comments partly

1961, aspects of the defence of fair comment such as the infectious malice rule, the non availability of correction remedies, and the use of certain interlocutory injunctions.

15 See McLoughlin J in *Berry v Irish Times* [1973] IR 368,382; Hamilton J in *Penny Bentley v Sunday World,* The Irish Times, 18 November 1976; Hamilton P in *De Valera v Independent Newspapers,* The Irish Times, 14 December 1984; McCarthy J in *Barrett v Independent Newspapers,* [1986] ILRM 601, 616.

16 While doubts may exist over whether the word 'laws' in Article 50 of the Constitution — which continued pre-1937 law in the new era — refers to all law or just legislation — see Kelly, *The Irish Constitution* p. 709f — no matter what way these are finally resolved, the constitutional reference to good name would still, at its least, form an important basis for the common law action.

17 Heuston, 'Personal Rights under the Irish Constitution' [1976] IJ NS 205, 222.

because a failure to make them may result in an incomplete picture of defamation law being given, partly because of comparable American constitutional developments which are mentioned in the text, and partly because the judiciary here has, on occasion, shown itself receptive to informed and reasoned, if novel, argument in the area of constitutional protection of fundamental rights.

AN OVERVIEW OF DEFAMATION LAW

The law of defamation regulates the numerous and varied occasions of human activity when individuals have reason to speak unpleasantly of one another. The resulting web of legal rules identifies the social and legal perception of when and in what detail it is legally permissible to speak, and when it is not, and what the consequences of either action are. The basic tenet of the law is that any statement, however made, and whether public or private, which is adversely reflective on the name or reputation of another is capable of being defamatory and of being sued upon. The law starts from the premise that the maker of a disparaging statement is liable. The defamed person has only to convince a jury, or judge as the case may be, that it is reasonable to consider that those who received the statement would view him less favourably. As a result, much defamation law is concerned with identifying the existence and scope of permissible excuses why liability should not then be imposed. The law starts, therefore, with an easily established and potentially immense range of liability which is not significantly reduced by the rule that if a statement is true, then liability will not be imposed. This is because the law assumes that a statement is untrue if it is defamatory, and the onus of showing it to be true is placed on the maker of the statement. He is unlikely to attempt this, because of the difficulty of proving to a jury that a statement is true, and because if he tries and fails to do it he could be penalised for appearing to have used the court hearing as an opportunity for repeating his claims.

Although the usual impact of a defamatory statement is to cause a general readjustment of one person's views of another, the constraints imposed by litigation require considerable exactitude in establishing one's case. Accordingly, the law places what has become a somewhat technical emphasis on ensuring that the defamed person was referred to by the statement and that the statement bears the meaning he complains about.

Another basic proof in a defamation action involves showing that at least one other person besides the defamer and the defamed became aware of the imputation. This process — known technically as publication — is often easily established, since the disparaging statement may have been made quite openly. However, both accidental and unforeseen publications can also occur, and a number of rules have been developed which show how liability is not found in these cases. Publication rules also describe, among other things, the position concerning the liability of the various parties involved in a publication, such as authors, editors, proprietors, printers and so on, both on their own accounts, and where they know that there will be a follow on publication, partly as a result of their efforts.

The jury has an important role in many aspects of a High Court defamation action. It is, however, subject to the control of the trial judge, and the respective functions of each throughout the action is traced in the text. As will be seen, the jury's involvement in defamation proceedings is often controversial, partly as a result of its unpredictability and partly on account of a tendency to make excessive awards. Its use stems from the general use of juries in tort actions, and also from the view that, since it is community reaction which determines defamatory effect, the jury drawn from the community is a suitable instrument for determining a response to the statement. How true this latter view can be is, however, doubtful, as will be seen.

A great deal of defamation law consists of rules for the avoidance of liability. Some of these involve technical refinements, such as distinguishing between defamatory and other unpleasant statements, or between actionable and non actionable publications, or in denying that individuals can be defamed by group defamations, or in a number of blatant and anachronistic slander rules. In most cases some sound policy basis for a denial of liability is evident, as with innocent and careful distributors of media publications. Most liability avoidance rules come under the defamation defences properly so called. One of these — involving proving that the statement was true (known technically as the defence of justification) has already been mentioned. Another class of permissible excuse for untrue statements is called privilege, and can be either absolute or qualified. This differentiation reflects the different status which the law accords each type of excuse. On the occasions of absolute privilege — which broadly involves statements made in parliament, the courts, and by the executive — the law values the necessity for uninhibited speech so much over any damage caused to reputation that liability is altogether prohibited, at least in the courts. On the occasions of qualified privilege — which relate mostly to the legitimate necessity for unpleasant statements in everyday and public life — the law still values the occasion of the speaking highly, but not so highly as to protect those who use the opportunity for the wrong reasons. Determining whether this was the case involves an examination of the defendant's state of mind for the (technically defined) motive of malice, and if it is found the privilege is lost. So complete is the operation of both types of privilege when properly established that care has to be taken to identify correctly the limits of these privileges. A great number of defamation rules are concerned with this. Indeed, the identification of occasions of qualified privilege constitutes the largest single group of defamation rules.

The law of defamation generally disregards any element of culpability or moral blameworthiness in determining whether a person should be liable for making a defamatory statement, except with the defence of qualified privilege and a narrow category of closely defined unintentional defamation. On that account defamation law is more protective of its ideal of reputation than many other areas of civil law where fault of one type or another is used to adjust competing interests. Whether this is a constitutionally permissible feature of the law is a matter that is examined at various points in the text.

Damages and injunctions are the main remedies for defamation, as for other torts. The rules governing the assessment of damages are of their nature different from the case of personal injuries, and refer mainly to the nature of the reputation damaged, the extent of the damage caused and any mitigating or aggravating circumstances.

The possibility of an award of compensatory damages has had a profound influence on the evolution of defamation law. It has concentrated attention on the development of defences whereby monetary liability is avoided, without considering whether anything else could or should be required of a defendant. Successfully raising such a defence gives the impression that the statement complained of was justified (ie true), although the statement may have been both untrue and defamatory. Whether other remedies could be devised which would prevent this false impression being given is considered in the text.

There is a possibly greater recourse to aggravated or punitive damages in defamation cases than in other tort actions because the nature of some defences involves a focus on malice, and because juries may sometimes be encouraged to hit defendants, especially media defendants, hard. Whether it is proper to continue to allow such awards to be made in civil proceedings is another matter which is examined. Injunctions, although not often used in defamation proceedings, are a particularly drastic defamation remedy. Because of the totally prohibitive effect which they have, the validity of their use also calls for examination in addition to the circumstances of their use.

In its present form the law of defamation is very much the product of its historical development, and may be criticised for being the worse for that. But even in a more adapted form, recourse to law can only achieve a certain amount in vindication of reputation, because of the human tendency for people to think the worst of their neighbours. There are always other non-litigious ways open to people to protect their reputations. Perhaps no method can ever fully clear a person's name. Yet the minimum which the law of defamation can do it should do, and do effectively, because its existence represents the state's formal concern with the protection of reputation. It seems especially important that the law should, so far as it can, encourage people to be charitable in their reactions to disparaging statements and not to be credulous. It is also important that the law should never be seen to deny a claim, or refuse redress, if there is any merit in it. In reality, however, the substantive law as it stands does not much reflect these concerns. It is a civil law — as the following chapters will testify — which one can say has been sidetracked from its inception by the remedy of damages, guided by legal intellect, and led into areas of complexity and detail far removed from the simple necessity of speedily enabling people to protect their reputations.

2

The Nature of a Defamatory Statement

The action in defamation is a common law action which exists to protect a person's reputation against defamatory statements. Reputation is the estimation in which a person is held by others. In legal terms it is assumed to be a good one. 'Every person has some reputation to protect, howbeit small, unless there is overwhelming and convincing evidence to the contrary'.[1]

Three elements must be present before a person's reputation will be recognised by the law. The person must exist, he must be capable of interacting with others, and he must actively interact with others. Existence here refers to human existence, and also to the existence of non-human entities like all incorporated bodies and such unincorporated bodies as partnerships, friendly societies, and trade unions. The latter two elements of capacity and activity can, collectively, be called personality. They suppose the existence of a conscious intelligence.

Most unincorporated associations, like residents' associations and sports clubs, are both capable, and active, but the law has refused — for doubtful reasons which are referred to later[2] — to recognise that they possess any legal existence. A foetus, or a baby, is alive, but is neither capable nor active, except in a very limited sense, and thus its personality and reputation is of little significance. As its personality develops, its reputation will grow in turn, so that an adult is accorded a presumption of reputation arising from the personality he is assumed to possess. The presumption of reputation relates only to the normal range of activities of which a person is capable in given circumstances. For matters clearly beyond one's range of capacity and activity, there will be no reputation. Further, while the protection which the law offers to reputation consists of compensation for damage already done, the protection is also directed towards ensuring that the future life of a defamed person is free from the taint of disgrace. This aspect of the protection of reputation is, again, signified by the rule that you cannot defame the dead. This is because, although the

1 *Ajala v Adelagun* (1979) 3 LRN 28, 30 per Desalu J.
2 See p. 176 post.

memory of a dead person may cause others to react, he is not alive, and his memory is not able in an active sense to interact with others. An artificial intelligence or a robot may possess both capacity and activity, but it is not human and the law has not yet recognised its existence.

A reputation is neither an invariable, uniform, nor constant thing. It can vary with the conduct and circumstances of a person. One can have a good reputation for one type of activity and a bad reputation for another type. A reputation can also vary with time. A good reputation can quickly become a bad one, while a change in the other direction may also occur, though perhaps with less alacrity. A reputation may be great or little because it is related to personality, and that may vary greatly depending on whether a person is, say, widely involved with others or not, or whether he possesses a large or small amount of material wealth;[3] and while a small reputation suggests a small injury — which may yet be aggravated by the circumstances[4] — the courts also recognise, that reputation is a valuable thing no matter which stratum of society a person belongs to.[5] The legislature has not, however, shown a similar regard for the small man's reputation: it refused, against the recommendations of the Committee on Civil Legal Aid and Advice, to include defamation actions within the scope of the Scheme of Civil Legal Aid,[6] and because defamation actions cannot be brought in the District Court.

DEFAMATORY EFFECT AND STATEMENTS IN GENERAL

In order for a statement to damage reputation, it must possess defamatory effect. An effect can usually be shown to have occurred, but because it might not be possible to show a defamatory effect, the law allows this to be presumed from the tendency of a statement.

3 E.g. *Barton v Doran* (1932) LJ Ir 124.

4 E.g. *Higgins v Monaghan and O'Reilly* (1939) 74 ILTR 56. See also 'the poor man's reputation is as important as is the rich man's' *Report of the Committee on Civil Legal Aid*, 1977, 45-6.

5 *Fleming and Lyons v Aer Lingus*, CCt, Irish Independent, 16 January 1980.

6 See the Committee Report supra; also *Dáil Debates*, vol 319, cols 1787/1958. Defamation actions were excluded because of fears that there might be a proliferation of such actions, even though the Committee had recommended that only meritorious cases should be aided. There are some limited circumstances involving defending counterclaims for defamation in which aid may be given — *Scheme of Civil Legal Aid and Advice*, 38. In practice the exclusion of defamation does not appear to have caused injustice, which might suggest that the fears of a flood of cases being unleashed are unreal, though it might also be that people do not enquire about aid for defamation cases because they already know it will not be given.

The effect has been variously described over the years, and covers a number of unrelated ideas which by their nature have proved difficult, and perhaps impossible, to encompass in a single proposition.[7] Definitions propounded in the last century tended to emphasise the strength of the hostile feelings aroused by the statement about the plaintiff, with sometimes such terms of excessive disapproval as execration and odium being used, though these were not the more usual terms. In 1835, Joy CB referred to 'public hatred, contempt or ridicule';[8] in 1840 Brady CB considered that 'whatever tends to vilify a man, to render him odious in the eyes of his fellow-men, or lower him in their estimation is in law a libel'.[9] Another Irish judge, Burton J in 1845, described the effect as an exposure to the 'ill-will, derision and contempt of the public';[10] and in 1873 it was described as exposing another to 'obloquy or censure or to the contempt or dislike of his fellow men'.[11] Defamatory effect, however, cannot always be so narrowly defined for it also includes statements not affecting a person's character at all such as 'a libel upon a trader affecting his credit, affecting his property',[12] for example 'that which is most of all calculated to defame the plaintiff [trader] in society viz. a want of respectability in himself or his [business] house'.[13] There is a further kind of defamatory effect, not to be found in the Irish cases, and which also need not excite feelings of hostility at all, as where others simply avoid and shun a person because he is stated to possess a contagious disease.

Defamatory effect has also been described in more detached and broader terms, as in 1869, 'to lower a person ... in the estimation

7 In view of this, the *Report of the Committee on Defamation* in New Zealand 1979 (afterwards referred to as the NZ Committee Report) did not favour enacting any definition in proposed legislation — para 61. The *Report of the Committee on Defamation* in England, 1975 (afterwards referred to as the Faulks Committee Report), on the other hand, did, though with dissent and its definition has been criticised. The report titled *Unfair Publication,* 1979 by the Australian Law Reform Commission (afterwards referred to as the ALCR Report) also recommended a statutory definition — para 84 — though that was because of the perceived need to create a national law there. The recommended definition was: 'defamatory matter is published matter concerning a person which tends:
(a) to affect adversely the reputation of that person in the estimation of ordinary persons;
(b) to deter ordinary persons from associating or dealing with that person ; or
(c) to injure that person in his occupation, trade, office or financial credit'
This is more of a description, than a definition and both parts (b) and (c) may be cast in terms which are too broad.

8 *Crotty v McMahon* (1835) 1 Jones 465, 479.

9 *Ahearne v Maguire* (1840) Arm Mac Og 39, 43.

10 *Barrett v Long* (1846) 8 ILRC 331, 373.

11 *Stannus v Finlay* (1874) IR 8 CL 264, 294 per Whiteside CJ.

12 *McNally v Oldham* (1863) 16 ICLR 298, 310 per Lefroy CJ.

13 *Barrett v Long* supra, 343, per Lefroy B.

of society' or 'right-thinking men',[14] or more recently by Walsh J in 1971, 'in the eyes of the average right-thinking man'.[15] This definition however might not include defamatory statements about business people or sufferers from contagious diseases which do not necessarily reflect on their individual personalities. Perhaps the statement which best encompasses all of these ideas of character failing, occupational discredit, and social ostracism is that of Powell J in 1920, when he described as defamatory whatever 'disparages the plaintiff or tends to bring him into ridicule or contempt',[16] though even this is not entirely satisfactory for a disparagement might include an injurious falsehood and that might not be defamatory at all.[17]

A wide variety of statements are capable of producing these described effects and a list of these is given later.[18] These statements can be placed into three categories according as they concern (1) the character or personality of the individual in itself, (2) the individual's character in financial matters, or (3) the individual's character as he seeks to earn a livelihood. Statements in the first category can range from suggestions of specific misconduct, such as sexual misconduct, or more generally to a lacking in any of the virtues of the character, such as honesty or tolerance, and even to a lacking in any of the human faculties, such as sanity, which cannot be attributed to any character failing. Also included in this category would be suggestions of criminal or civil wrongdoing. Statements in the second category can include suggestions of indebtedness, disinclination or inability to pay debts, or that a debtor is absconding. Statements in the third category concern expressions of dissatisfaction with an individual in his employment, such as the absence of essential qualities, or of laziness or misconduct, whether the individual is employed or self-employed, and whether in a commercial context or otherwise.

THE REASONABLE MAN

The defamatory effect of a statement must be shown to work on that person termed the reasonable man. At this stage, one is concerned with how he thinks and reacts to a statement which might be construed as being defamatory. The separate question of whether this person

14 *Mawe v Pigott* (1869) IR 4 CL 54, 59-62 per Lawson J. General references to society and or to right thinking people generally are misleading nowadays since minority groups can constitute standards of opinion. See p. 17 post.

15 *Quigley v Creation Ltd* [1971] 1 IR 269, 272.

16 *Dunlop v Dunlop Rubber* [1920] 1 IR 280, 290.

17 See p. 23 post

18 See p. 31 post

can be a solitary individual or whether he must belong to a group, large or small, or whether he will only be found in the midst of the general community is considered shortly.[19] The manner in which this person reasons may be relevant at three stages in the hearing — when the trial judge determines if a statement is reasonably capable of defamatory meaning, when the jury decides if it is defamatory, and when an appelate court reviews either finding. The judicial view of this person will be the predominant one for a number of reasons. Firstly, in jury trials the trial judge may in certain cases decide that a reasonable person could only react in a particular way. Secondly, appelate courts can and do reverse the findings of juries. Thirdly, there is probably constitutional support for judicial intervention in the requirement in the Preamble to the Constitution that the ideal of charity should inform constitutional principles. This may mean as a matter of law, that the judical recognition of a reasonable reaction to a defamatory statement should be a charitable one. Fourthly increasingly in this country due to the enlarged jurisdiction of the Circuit Court, defamation actions will be heard by judges sitting alone.

The criterion of defamatory effect has been variously described — whether a person is affected as a reasonable,[20] or fair-minded[21] or common,[22] or ordinary[23] man — and although these terms have, on occasion, been used interchangeably, they do denote different ideas, and it is clear from the cases that there are actually two fundamentally opposed views. On the one hand, courts will not recognise the reactions of one who is possessed of a 'morbid or suspicious mind',[24] and who is prone to a "non-natural, unreasonable and farfetched construction';[25] while on the other, one English judge has stated that 'he can and does read between the lines',[26] and another, Lord Devlin, has stated that 'The layman reads in an implication much more freely [than the lawyer]; and unfortunately, as the law of defamation has to take into account, is especially prone to do so when it is derogatory'.[27] The same judge also provided a good example of how lawyers and lay persons can reason differently — if it was said that a man was seen going into a brothel, nine men

19 See p. 16 post
20 *Kavanagh v The Leader*, SCt, unreported, 4 March 1955, Ó Dálaigh J at p. 6 of his judgement.
21 *Keogh v Incorporated Dental Hospital* [1910] 2 IR 577, 586.
22 *Power v Haydn* (1824) Sm & Bat 386, 393.
23 *O'Hea v Guardians, Cork Union* (1892) 32 LR Ir 629, 642.
24 *Keogh v Incorporated Dental Hospital 586,* per O'Brien LCJ.
25 *O'Hea v Guardians, Cork Union*, 642 per Johnson J.
26 *Lewis v Daily Telegraph* [1964] AC 234, 258 per Lord Reid. See also *Evening Post v Singh* (1978) 26 WIR 75. In *Mirror Newspapers v World Hosts* (1978-79) 141 CLR 632 the High Court of Australia applied the 'loose thinking' criterion.
27 Supra 277.

out of ten would assume that he was going to fornicate, but the lawyer would say that a man might go to a brothel for an innocent purpose.[28] These differing understandings of how the reasonable person may think has resulted in one of the most remarkable features of the law of defamation. Judges, and at the highest levels, have differed, sometimes sharply, on what they consider to be a reasonable reaction to a statement.[29] As regards which of the two views is in the ascendant in Ireland at the moment, it is difficult to be certain. In a recent Supreme Court case some judges reiterated that it was the ordinary person's, or the community view of the reasonable person's reaction that is the criterion of defamatory effect.[30] But how this can be, given the accepted powers of trial judges, appelate courts, and Circuit Court judges in this matter is difficult to see.

It may be that, considering both nineteenth and twentieth century cases together, the better supported view of the reasonable man here,[31] and the more logical in the circumstances, is the judicial view. This results in a picture of a reasonable person who tends not to draw damaging conclusions impulsively, and instead shows some reasoning ability and restraint, and gives full weight to any doubts he might have. He has in some cases, been able to find as many as three,[32] or even six,[33] innocent meanings to one defamatory one. It is hardly difficult to see why the judicial view of the reasonable person should be different from that of the ordinary man's. Many judges are not able to discard their legal conditioning when reacting to a statement, and that conditioning is set by a lifetime's practice in the virtues of reason, analysis and restraint. The courts have not openly

28 Supra 278.

29 *McCann v Edinburgh Roperie* (1889) LR Ir 24 — 2 to 1, *Crawford and Frame v Vance* [1908] 2 IR 521 — HCt, 2 to 1, Ct A unanimous; *Pyke v Hibernian Bank* [1950] IR 195 — 2 to 2; *Berry v Irish Times* [1973] IR 368 — 3 to 2. See also *Lewis v Daily Telegraph* supra. 'The opinions of juries — and of judges — are notoriously subjective and unpredictable in deciding what is defamatory' — *Barrett v Independent Newspapers* [1986] ILRM 601, 615 per Hederman J.

30 *Barrett by Independent Newspapers* supra, Henchy and Hederman JJ. A case consistent with this view is *Latham and Byrne v Independent Newspapers*, The Irish Times, 9 May 1986 where a false report that two persons were charged in the District Court with possession of firearms was held defamatory.

31 E.g. *O'Hea v Guardians, Cork Union* supra, *Keogh v Incorporated Dental Hospital* supra, *Berry v Irish Times* supra, *Connors v Irish Press* post.

32 *Keogh v Incorporated Dental Hospital.*

33 *O'Hea v Guardians, Cork Union* He, apparently, does not react as McLoughlin J in *Berry v Irish Times* supra, 379: 'When I got the book of appeal the first document I saw was a photograph of a man carrying a placard.. The impresssion this conveyed to me was that the publication was so clearly defamatory of the plaintiff that it was beyond all argument. It is important that I should state my first impression because it could well be, in my view, the first impression of others seeing no more than was seen by me in the photograph'.

admitted that the common terminology used when referring to the criterion of defamatory effect masks the existence of the two separate views of what is a reasonable reaction to a statement.[34] Dissent in the cases has invariably occurred when the exceptional judge attempts to break that mould.

STANDARD OF OPINION

A statement will only be held to be defamatory if its effect works upon reasonable or right thinking people, as they constitute a standard of opinion recognised by law, by which the effect can be judged. Such people may know the defamed person personally, or even not at all since the law's protection also seeks to ensure the future treatment of a person at the hands of those who may not know him yet. Certain groups, such as those engaging in or supporting illegal activities, cannot constitute a recognisable standard of opinion.[35] A standard of opinion refers to the view of a distinct number of reasonable people of a like mind on a particular issue. In the many judicial references to the right-thinking person there has been an unspoken assumption by the courts that there is such a thing as a uniform set of values or priorities in society, which do not take account of minority priorities unshared by the rest. Thus, in some English cases, the employer of a domestic servant was unable to establish as defamatory a statement that he had borrowed money from his servant,[36] and, similarly, the physician who was said to associate with unregistered practitioners,[37] and the miller who was said to have broken an agreement among certain millers and to have sold flour to a baker,[38] were also unable to establish defamation. There could never, however, have been any validity in the view that there existed a uniform set of values which all reasonable people shared, except perhaps some minimum code of Christian morality, recognised as such for the convenience of society. There are so many other issues and matters in which everybody, in one way or another, interest or involve themselves, of great or little importance, that it would be

34 Hints that the judicial view is different have been given on occasion. O'Brien J stated in *Bolton v O'Brien* (1885) 16 LR Ir 97, 113 'in determining what the libel is we have to place ourselves as near as can be to the sense of the community'. The clearest hint was that of Bushe CJ in *Power v Haydn* (1824) Sm & Bat 386, 393 who stated that judges 'are to look at the words in their ordinary sense, such as they would put upon them out of court'. Of course, the average judge does not leave his legal skills behind him when he goes home after his day's work.

35 See p. 18 post

36 *Sim v Stretch* (1936) 52 TLR 669.

37 *Clay v Roberts* (1863) 8 LT 397.

38 *Leetham v Rank* (1912) 57 SJ 111.

blinkered for the law to ignore that the devotees of a minority interest could constitute a standard of opinion. It would be wrong, as well, because in each instance where the law takes the view that a group cannot constitute a standard of opinion, it is effectively making a value judgement on the worth of the group. Prosser writes that 'this seems clearly wrong, since the court cannot be called upon to make a definitive pronouncement upon whether the views of different segments of the community are right or wrong, sound or morally justifiable'.[39] Judges risk criticism if they purport to say that no reasonable person would belong to this or that group, or would take such a view.

Fortunately, the courts nowadays more realistically accept that some reasonable persons may be concerned with one matter while other reasonable persons may not, and thus that standards of opinion short of every right thinking member of the community, may be recognised by the law. As Walsh J stated in *Quigley v Creation Ltd* in 1971 '... words are defamatory if they impute conduct which would tend to lower that person in the eyes of a considerable and respectable class of the community, though not in the eyes of the community as a whole',[40] and in Quigley's case the group was those interested in the development of the theatre in Ireland. Beyond, however, considerable and respectable classes it is not clear how far the law will go in recognising small groups as standards of opinion. In Quigley's case Walsh J in an obiter comment seemed to suggest that a particular class or section of society might not constitute a standard.[41] In contrast to this, there was the clear remark of McLoughlin J in another case on what is meant by the phrase 'right-thinking people'. He stated 'it does not mean all such people but only some such people, perhaps even only one, because if a plaintiff loses the respect for his reputation of some or even one right-thinking person he suffers some injury'.[42]

The latter view seems the better one. It is certainly the more logical. The reasoning which recognises that reasonable people can have opposing views, or even none at all, and that either can constitute a standard of opinion, cannot be stopped short of small groups and even individuals without the intrusion of illogical and external considerations; nor would there be any difficulty if this were to lead to a statement and its antithesis being both held defamatory, for that is only an aspersion, if that, on humanity and not on the law. The law already lives with a similar difficulty where the same statement can, in different cases, be held both defamatory and not so. There

39 *Prosser and Keaton on Torts* 5th ed, 777. See also Tommaney,'Community Standards of Defamation' (1970) 34 Albany L Rev 634.

40 [1971] IR 269, 272.

41 Supra.

42 *Berry v Irish Times* supra 380.

is also the constitutional point that the view that a minority group cannot constitute a standard of opinion may amount to a denial to defamed members of that group of rights to a good name for no better reason than that they belong to a minority group.

Inadmissible standard of opinion

The prevailing view is that the opinions of those who engage in or approve of criminal or other activities of which the law disapproves, or who hold opinions which the law cannot countenance, cannot be a criterion by which the defamatory nature of a statement is determined. The standard of opinion must be one which the court can recognise and which is consistent with wider conceptions of legal policy. Thus a mere reduction in popularity as a result of a statement is not enough to establish that a statement is defamatory. So, the law would not regard with contempt, though it would not either allow an action to be brought by, the school sneak who splits to the head, despite what his fellows might think;[43] and in a recent Circuit Court action it was held that it was not actionable for a newspaper to wrongly imply that a family were itinerants by reporting that a deceased child was an itinerant.[44] The propositions governing the disallowance of the views of supporters of criminal activities are based, on the decisions in two well known cases, *Mawe v Piggott* in 1869,[45] and *Berry v Irish Times* in 1973.[46] In the first case where a newspaper printed an article quoting a parish priest as stating, inter alia 'I will watch them, I will denounce them' — to which was ascribed by innuendo 'that the plaintiff would watch certain persons and would become an informer against them so as to have them prosecuted for a political offence' — the court upheld the defendant's claim that the words were not capable of a defamatory meaning. Lawton J stated that it has been 'argued that amongst certain classes who were either

43 Unlike the view expressed by McLoughlin J in *Berry v Irish Times* supra.
44 *Connors v Irish Press, Wicklow People*, 22 February 1985. By contrast, in the US, according to Eldredge *The Law of Defamation*, 37/38 a charge of poverty might be actionable.
45 (1869) IR 4 CL 54.
46 [1973] IR 368. See also *McKiernan v Coulson* (1920) 54 ILT & SJ 305.

themselves criminal or who sympathised with crime it would expose a person to great odium to represent him as an informer or prosecutor....; that is quite true, but we cannot be called upon to adopt that standard.... We can only regard the estimation in which a man is held by society generally'.[47]

In Berry's case, similar reasoning was relied upon by a majority of the Supreme Court judges, with two dissenting,[48] where the defendants published in their newspaper a photograph which showed a placard stating 'Peter Berry — 20th Century Felon Setter. Helped Jail Republicans in England'. Ó Dálaigh CJ, in delivering the majority judgement, considered that it was 'perhaps surprising that the Supreme Court should be asked to hold, as a matter of law, that it is necessarily defamatory to say of one of the citizens of this country that he assisted in the bringing to justice in another country of a fellow countryman who broke the laws of that country and who was tried and convicted for that offence in the ordinary course of the administration of criminal justice'.[49]

It should be noted, however, that Ó Dálaigh CJ did not entirely exclude the possibility that an allegation of informing could be defamatory. He pointed out the absence of any innuendo and suggested that the words meant informer rather than informant — which would not be defamatory. He also stated that, unlike the case before him, words which suggested informing in disregard of official instructions could be defamatory.

Berry's case was also concerned with the actionability of imputations of informing on crimes committed abroad and although the imputation there was held not actionable, it is clear from the judgement of Ó Dálaigh CJ that such imputations could be defamatory in some circumstances, as where the offence imputed is repugnant to our concepts of law and justice, or where the trial procedure could only be regarded as a travesty of justice.

There is some judicial and academic support for the minority view here that if an imputation suggests disloyalty to an idea or group which the plaintiff was thought to espouse, then, though the group be engaged in or approve of an unlawful activity, it may nonetheless constitute a standard of opinion, and the statement may be capable of defamatory meaning. In two nineteenth century Scottish cases,[50] it was held capable of defamatory meaning to accuse a person of being an informer; and in one of the cases, where the plaintiff was accused of informing on a distiller to the officers of Excise, one of the judges

47 Supra 62.
48 Fitzgerald and McLoughlin JJ.
49 Supra 375. See also *Stapleton v Macartney* (1794) ITR 90.
50 *Graham v Roy* (1851) 13 D 634; *Wran v Quillan* (1899) 375 LR 38.

stated 'It maybe perfectly legitimate to give information but an informer is by no means a popular character'.[51] So also of the two dissenting judgements in Berry's case, one in particular — that of McLoughlin J emphasised the narrow question of reduction in popularity. Fleming supports this emphasis, because, in his view, to do otherwise is to ignore that it is community attitudes that determine defamatory effect and also because the action exists only to protect reputation and not to enforce other legal policy.[52]

It seems clear that these two contrasting views represent fundamentally opposite conceptions of the relation between the defamation action — one might say any action — and the general and wider trends of legal policy. An interesting, though unsuccessful, attempt to find middle ground between them was made in the English case *Byrne v Deane*[53] where a member of a golf club was accused of informing the police of the illegal presence of gambling machines on the club's premises. A distinction was sought to be made between more and less serious or trivial offences, so that in the latter case an accusation of reporting the offence to the police could be defamatory. However, the court could not see any basis for such a distinction. Greene LJ stated 'It seems to me that no distinction can be drawn between various categories of crime ... [and] if the argument is to be accepted it would involve the Court in this position; that it would have to differentiate between different kinds of crime and put in one category crimes which are of so bad a character as to call for universal reprobation ... and in another category crimes which many people think are stupid and ought never to have been made crimes at all'.[54] The idea, however, might not be without merit.[55] If it is desirable to attempt to coalesce decisions in cases with what people actually think, it does seem possible to make some distinction between wrongful acts involving a minimum public morality, and the many prohibitions that exist for administrative, financial or public convenience reasons only.[56] On the other hand, any distinction would involve treating unequally those suffering a reduction in popularity by recognising a right to good name only where an

51 *Graham v Roy* supra 626 per Lord Fullerton. See also the dissenting judgement of Greer LJ in *Byrne v Deane* supra 827; and the apparently non-committal reference to Mawe's case by Wright J at [1903] 2 IR 347, 383.

52 *The Law of Torts*, 5th ed, 530.

53 [1937] 1 KB 818.

54 Supra 840; also Slesser LJ at 834.

55 It should be noted that the non actionability of imputations of informing about such serious crime only applies to the defamation action. Where reputation is not in issue, the action in injurious falsehood is available..

56 The fact that imputations of informing about such crimes might involve only small damage to reputation would not be an argument against the distinction, but only in favour of small damages.

imputation involving a less serious crime is made. This could render the distinction constitutionally invalid. What may ultimately rule the matter, however, is the succinct remark of Ó Dálaigh CJ in Berry's case. 'This Court is bound to uphold the rule of law and its decisions must be conditioned by this duty'.[57] In basing his view on the judicial duty under the Constitution to administer justice, or so it seems, Ó Dálaigh CJ seems to have foreclosed the constitutional dimension to this area of law. Whatever about Fleming's view of the situation in Australia,[58] it is unlikely that here the defamation action can be viewed as succouring the victims of prejudice. Their only resort is to the action for injurious falsehood.

RELEVANCE OF THE DEFENDANT'S INTENTION

The issue of a defamer's intent arises in two contexts. The first, which concerns the effect of the intent on whether the statement is defamatory, is dealt with here. The second, which concerns the relevance of intent to a finding of liability against a defendant, is considered later.[59] The intention with which a person makes a defamatory statement is of no relevance in determining whether the statement is defamatory. Whilst in some early English authorities this was not always so,[60] there are, in the reports, a number of affirmations of this present rule. In 1856, Monahan CJ stated that it had by then been 'firmly established that in actions [for libel]... the intent of the party was altogether immaterial .... and that the question was not what the writer intended, but what effect they were likely to produce on the person who read or heard them'.[61]

More recently Ó Dálaigh CJ stated, in 1972, 'The intent of the author or the publisher of a libel ... does not determine the question whether the material complained of is or is not defamatory'.[62] So that, if a defendant claims to have uttered words only in jest, it will not prevent a finding of defamation, unless his listeners could also have reasonably thought so. In *Donoghue v Hayes* in 1831,[63] the defendant had accused the plaintiff of being a bodysnatcher, and claimed that the words were spoken jocularly. A verdict for the defendant was set aside on appeal, it appearing that the trial judge's charge could have been understood as meaning that jocularity in the

57 Supra 375.
58 Supra.
59 See p. 229 post
60 *King v Waring* (1803) 5 Esp 13; *King v Hoare* (1844) 13 M & W 494.
61 *White v Tyrrell* (1856) 5 ICLR 477, 487; *Bolton v O'Brien* (1855) 32 LR Ir 97, 108, 118; *Campbell v Irish Press* (1955) 90 ILTR 105, 111.
62 *Berry v Irish Times* at 374.
63 (1831) Hayes 265.

mind of the defendant alone, as opposed to being shared by the bystanders, was a sufficient defence. Similarly, if a person defames another by mistake that, too, affords no defence to a finding of defamation. In *Doyle v Irish Press*[64] a newspaper which mistakenly published the plaintiff's photograph under the headline 'Irishman guilty of huge fraud' was held liable in defamation. And in a number of English cases, findings of defamation were not prevented by a defendant intending to refer to a fictitious character,[65] when in fact 'out of the wilds of North Wales appeared' a real person;[66] nor by a statement intending to refer to one person when there was another matching the description used,[67] nor by a statement apparently innocent and yet defamatory because of facts unknown to its maker.[68]

The defendant's intention is irrelevant to a finding of defamation because defamation is pre-eminently concerned with the effect of the statement on the standard of opinion, and thus the damage to the plaintiff's reputation. In concentrating on this effect, no account can be taken of something which, remaining in the speaker's mind, cannot influence those who hear the statement. The effect of the statement being thus so important, at least to the barring of evidence of the defendants' intent, one might expect that this focus would also allow in evidence the actual response of those to whom the statement was made[69] — which evidence is not now admissible;[70] and also that it would require proof of actual damage to reputation, rather than the current presumption of damage.

Though the rule is clear, it operates at the expense of a degree of reality, because most obviously a defendant's intent is very much in issue on the finding of a defamation. In fact, the whole action is taken because of it. For it is the defendant who has chosen the words alleged to be defamatory; that is to say, the words were chosen to give expression to his intention. What the law then actually means when it says that intent is irrelevant is that, if a defendant wishes to claim a desire or meaning for the words — which is different from what they would reasonably be understood to mean — he will not be allowed to do so. Of course, where a plaintiff ascribes by innuendo a particular meaning to words that are ambiguous or capable of more than one meaning, a defendant remains free to argue against the particular meaning.

Furthermore, there are some instances where the defendant's

64 The Irish Times, 6 December 1984. See also *Craig v Faloon* (1859) 4 IJ NS 202.
65 *Hulton v Jones* [1910] AC 20.
66 Prosser 808.
67 *Newstead v London Express* [1940] 1 KB 377.
68 *Cassidy v Daily Mirror* [1929] 2 KB 331.
69 *Slim v Daily Telegraph* [1968] 2 WLR 599.

intention may be relevant at various stages in the action. It may prevent a finding, even of defamation, if the very act of publication was neither voluntary or intentional; such as when one is forced to publish against one's will. It may prevent the innocent distributor of defamatory material being found liable if he can establish that he did not know, nor ought he to have known, that the material was defamatory.[71] It may also prevent a finding of liability, as opposed to a finding of defamation, where, on the issue of malice, a defendant produces evidence of honest intent in response to a plaintiff's efforts to prove the contrary.[72] It may allow reliance on the statutory defence contained in section 21 of the Defamation Act 1961.[73] Finally, the intention of a defendant may be relevant, after liability is found, in deciding whether to award aggravated or exemplary damages.[74]

DEFAMATION AND INJURIOUS FALSEHOOD

The action in defamation exists to protect reputation. The action for an injurious falsehood exists to protect any other interest which suffers actual loss as a result of an untrue statement which is made maliciously. It is important to distinguish between the two actions, though it is often not easy to do so and were lawyers to reason as ordinary people, the distinction might in many cases be thought unreal.[75] Injurious falsehood is a much less advantageous action than defamation. The plaintiff must prove the statements untrue, and that he suffered loss, and that the defendant acted maliciously, whereas in defamation, once a defamatory effect is established, both untruth and damage to reputation are presumed.

The distinction, so far as it is valid, is between statements which reflect only on tangibles or services, and are merely injurious, and statements which reflect dishonesty or fraud or some dishonourable conduct, which are defamatory. Examples of injurious falsehoods are slander of title, slander of goods, slander of credit and 'an action on the case for false representation of ....a trader, in respect of his trade, from which injury has resulted'.[76] These are all untruths directed

70 See p. 50 post
71 See p. 65 post
72 See p. 205 post
73 See p. 229 post
74 See p. 256 post
75 Though most common law jurisdictions appear to acknowledge this distinction, according to Fleming *The Law of Torts*, 5th ed, 501, several Australian jurisdictions treat all imputations affecting a person in his trade or profession as defamatory, except slanders of title.
76 *McNally v Oldham* (1863) 16 ICLR 298, 310 per Lefroy CJ.

at aspects of a person's interests that can, supposedly, be clearly separated from any reflection on reputation. It is in this question of whether it is possible to separate some injurious falsehoods from, say, an adverse comment on the person who sells goods or asserts title to property, that the difficulty lies.

In some cases where the distinction has been applied, disparagements of the quality of a trader's goods,[77] or a person's entitlement to property,[78] or an assertion that a trader has ceased business — his 'disused toy factory'[79] — and possibly also that his business has been taken over,[80] have all been held injurious falsehoods. On this view, the following statement by counsel for the plaintiff in *Jones v McGovern* (1867),[81] well states the distinction 'Suppose it was written or spoken of an eminent physician that he had given up his practice and gone to London to devote himself to the care of cholera patients there, whereby he suffered damage, there the thing written or spoken would not amount to libel or slander, yet it would inflict a very serious injury'. But in other cases the statement has been held to be both an injurious falsehood and a defamation. In *McNally v Oldham* (1863),[82] and in *Jones v McGovern*,[83] assertions that a judgement was still outstanding against a person and that a judgement had been recovered against another, were, respectively, held both defamatory and injurious. Prosser, also, considers that many statements are both.[84] In still more cases, where, in light of this distinction, a statement might have been thought injurious only, courts here have found them defamatory. In *Foster v Hood* (1873),[85] where it was said of a guano merchant that people in the area had been robbed by the sale of bad guano, the plaintiff succeeded in an action in defamation, although the defendant argued that the words imputed no fraud to the plaintiff; and in *Towell v Fallon* (1912),[86] where it was alleged that a suit sold by a tailor who specialised in manufactured Irish goods was not Irish made, the statement was considered to convey a defamatory imputation, although it was also held to have been privileged. From the reports it seems clear that both actions were laid and treated as

77 *Western Counties Manure v Lawes Manure* (1874) LR 9 Ex 218.
78 *Loudon v Ryder (No 2)* (1953) Ch 423. See the facts of *Roche v Meyler* [1896] 2 IR 35.
79 *Irish Toys & Utilities v Irish Times* [1937] IR 298. See also *Ratcliffe v Evans* [1892] 2 QB 524.
80 *Hall-Gibbs v Dunn* (1910) 12 CLR 92,93.
81 (1867) IR 1 CL 1 ,103.
82 Supra.
83 (1867) IR 1 CL 681.
84 4th ed., 918.
85 (1873) 7 ILTR 92.
86 (1912) 47 ILTR 176.

being in defamation. The correctness of this view is further emphasised in the fact that in each case doubts were expressed by some judges about whether the words were actually defamatory.[87] It can be argued that these cases merely involve the recognition, acknowledged by Prosser, that 'It might be possible to imply some accusation of personal inefficiency or incompetency in nearly every imputation directed against a business or its product'.[88] In this regard there is the oft-quoted dictum of an English judge[89] — that to impute to a trader that his wine was bad when all of the vintage was also bad would be only an injurious falsehood, whereas to impute that his judgement was bad for having selected the wine would be defamatory. This assertion is false in its first premise for it is surely a reflection on him for choosing to sell bad wine, even though the whole vintage was bad. This reasoning is more than a little akin to the unreal legal reasoning described earlier in Lord Devlin's brothel example.

The distinction between defamatory and injurious falsehoods will not be applied to a criticism of a professional person, for, in a relatively recent English case,[90] an action for a criticism of the professional technique of a dentist was held properly laid in defamation, because the technique was part of him as a professional person and could not be criticised without implicitly reflecting on him in his professional capacity.[91]

A statement which may appear actionable only as an injurious falsehood, may yet, by the pleading of an innuendo and the averring and establishing of extrinsic facts, be shown to be defamatory. An innuendo was pleaded in Foster's case, and it is interesting that the dissenting judge in the English case, referred to above, pointed out the lack of any ascribed innuendo meaning.[92]

Both causes of action may be pleaded in the alternative, and even where a claim is laid, say in libel, the other action may be raised as well, as happened in one case,[93] where the judge went on to consider whether the statement was an injurious falsehood after holding that it was not capable of defamatory meaning. But, this is

87 In Foster's case, see Monahan CJ at 93; in Towell's case, see Gibson J at 178 and the reported remark of Holmes LJ at 179 on appeal.

88 4th ed., 918. A similar view is expressed by Hubschman, 'Defamation or Disparagement'(1942) 24 Minn L Rev 625. What may reinforce this view is that such statements may often be made between traders whose reactions probably constitute a valid standard of opinion.

89 Lord Esher MR in *South Hetton Coal v North Eastern News* [1894] 1 QB 133,139.

90 *Drummond-Jackson v BMA* [1970] 1 WLR 688.

91 Supra 698.

92 Lord Denning MR 694.

93 *Irish Toys & Utilities v Irish Times* supra. See also *Ratcliffe v Evans* supra.

a matter of discretion for the judge, depending on the course adopted by the plaintiff at the hearing, and whether the defence acquiesced in it. Thus Fitzgibbon J remarked in one case 'I had supposed at first that the present verdict might be sustained upon the authority of *Ratcliffe v Evans...* , but it is clear that the trial was fought as one for slander only; the point was specifically taken by the defendant's counsel, no amendment was asked for or made, and the President in charging the jury directed their attention to the distinction'.[94]

DEFAMATION AND ABUSE

Defamatory statements are to be distinguished from abusive statements. The former are actionable, the latter are not. The defamatory statement is able by itself, in the circumstances, to lower reputation; whereas the abusive statement merely makes others aware of its maker's low opinion of his subject, but does not succeed thereby in inducing others to lower their opinion. Shortly put, defamation may hurt reputation, dignity and pride. Abuse hurts only the latter two.

The circumstances in which the statement is made — particularly a predictable or customary usage of words or terms of accusation in an argument — will determine whether a statement is defamatory or abusive. Various terms, that were originally potent, may, due to an imprecise and excessive usage, become denuded of any real force for altering opinions. Thus an accusation by a local councillor that a contractor had used bribery and corruption to obtain a contract was held in *Crawford v Vance* (1908),[95] not to be defamatory; the jury concluded that its usage in the circumstances did not suggest any criminal wrongdoing. Holmes LJ agreed 'Acts are often described as bribery which are not only not indictible, but comparatively harmless', and added that 'Candidates at parliamentary elections are often charged by their political opponents with bribery and corruption when they promise that their party will support a generous contribution from the ... Exchequer for the benefit of a class of electors ...'[96] A Nigerian judge was able to state that 'It is a matter of common knowledge ... that people in this country, particularly women, call each other "ex-convict, prostitute" in their heated arguments quarrels, and/or altercations, which often lead to blows or fights and which words no-one takes seriously as they were words

94 *McMullan v Mulhall* [1929] IR 470,481.
95 [1908] 2 IR 521 and 581.
96 Supra 588.

of anger'.[97] In this country, rather robust methods of electioneering may well prevail,[98] in addition to tasteless rhetorical flourishes by local councillors about jobs,[99] but to all this 'However tolerant juries may be of strong language used in the heat of a political struggle, there is a point beyond which such language ought not to go'.[1] Such a point was reached, and passed, in *Fisher v Nation Newspaper and Rooney* in 1900 where an accusation of religious bigotry made against a candidate in an election address, which also stated, inter alia, that 'if he had power he would trample your religion and you who belong to it in the dust', was held defamatory.[2]

Another reason why a statement might fail to alter opinion is that it is used in a context so different from its ordinary one that any comparison or analogy between the two is so unlikely that no reasonable person would allow his opinion to be influenced by it. So, in a New Zealand case where those involved in a protest march in a dispute over wages at a local factory were called 'Hitler's fascist people' or 'Hitler's puppets', it was held, that the comparison being pointless and unlikely, the words were incapable of defamatory meaning.[3]

Where a newspaper reports mere verbal abuse, it may be that the report might fail to convey how a reasonable listener might not have considered it defamatory. That could, in the circumstances, cause the reasonable reader to read the report as being defamatory. But, it seems too much to suggest, as a Nigerian judge has done,[4] that spoken abuse as reported is automatically actionable.

Whether an innuendo has been pleaded and extrinsic facts averred and proved can be of considerable importance in having a prima facie abusive statement held to be defamatory. Thus Pigot CJ stated in one case 'There is nothing in the pleadings to indicate that the word 'vagabond' was used in the defamatory sense of imputing an offence within the Vagrancy Acts; it is used as an adjective, and commonly as an abusive term; it should therefore be shown by the pleading that it was used in a defamatory or actionable sense'.[5]

97 *Ajala v Adelagun* (1979) 3 LRN 28, 34 per Desalu J.
98 *Fisher v Nation Newspaper and Rooney* [1901] 2 IR 465, 482.
99 *Crawford and Frame v Vance* supra 580. For accusations of swindling or theft, see p. 82 post
1 *Fisher v Nation Newspaper and Rooney* supra 483 per Holmes LJ.
2 Supra. A more recent case where the point was passed and the defendant found liable is Keating v Stephen's Green Publications, The Irish Times, 17 December 1985.
3 *Gwynne v Wairarapa Times-Age* [1972] NZLR 586.
4 *Benson v West African Pilot* [1965] 2 All NLR 161.
5 *Campbell v White* (1856) 5 ICLR 312, 315.

The publishing of anything that renders a man ridiculous is defamatory and so, actionable. Joy CB stated in 1831 'The principle is clear, that a person shall not be allowed to murder another's reputation in jest',[6] and, of course, as we have seen, it is no defence to say that one only meant to joke and not to defame, if one's wit is so sublime that that is not how it appeared to the reasonable listener.[7] Ridicule usually consists of the expression of opinion and comment, and when a statement is clearly defamatory a defamer's main defence is likely to be fair comment. Depending on how strong the ridicule is, and whether it is of too personal a nature, rather than relating to the person's work or activities, the defence might not succeed.[8]

Originally, it seems that statements rendering a man ridiculous were actionable because their effect was to induce others to cease their dealings with him or to avoid him.[9] In time, however, the idea became extended to statements which caused one to become the butt of another's humour; the general principle being seemingly that, so long as the statement resulted in a lowered opinion or diminished respect, it did not matter that it was evidenced passively through avoidance, or actively through name calling, derision or jeering.

No general rule can be laid down defining absolutely when a statement will render a person ridiculous. It depends to a great extent on the position in society of the person, and on the nature of the statement. As Powell J stated in *Dunlop v Dunlop Rubber* in 1920,

> A gentleman, for example, who had adopted the stage for his profession could not, I take it, reasonably object that in advertisement by way of poster of a theatrical performance in which he takes a part he is depicted in the garb proper to the part which he plays, whereas an ordinary citizen who does not aspire to histrionic fame might legitimately object to notoriety of such a kind even although he were made to represent a person of some fame and distinction in history, because it would make him merely ridiculous. Again ... if a man is a public character in respect to whom it might be said that his public life or his great position was calculated to create an interest, it would be unreasonable to

6 *Donoghue v Hayes* (1831) Hayes 265, 266.

7 *Donoghue v Hayes* supra.

8 See Naughton and Gilbertson 'Libellous Ridicule by Journalists' (1969) 18 Clev St L Rev 450.

9 *Mason v Jennings* (1680) Sir Thos Raym 401; *Villers v Monsley* (1769) 2 Wilson 403.

suppose that his portrayal in exaggerated form would tend to injure his reputation in the sense of making him an object of ridicule.[10]

If the public figure is, say, a politician, and has another occupation as well, then the cartoonist should take care that the politician is not thereby injured in his other capacity; otherwise the statement may be defamatory.[11] There is therefore scope for the political cartoonist to lampoon public men,but at the same time he 'has no special immunity ... and in the matter of comment [is] in no better or worse position than any other citizen'.[12] The ridiculer should also take care to mask any anger or irritation he feels since such a mood is not the usual occasion for jocularity.[13] In *Kenny v Freemans Journal* (1892),[14] a Catholic doctor and member of parliament was depicted in a cartoon 'with a stethoscope as a penny-whistle', alongside three other members of parliament; written aside the plaintiff's likeness was 'Down with Priests', and underneath a caption read 'Unholy Alliance: shake hands brothers, you're a Priest hunter and I'm another'. This was held defamatory. In *Dunlop v. Dunlop Rubber*[15] a caricature of the appearance of a plain and ordinary citizen of Dublin in which he was portrayed 'as dressed in a very exaggerated foppish manner wearing a tall white hat, white waist-coat and carrying a cane and eye glass' was held defamatory. In another case *Kavanagh v The Leader* (1955),[16] it was suggested in a literary article that, inter alia, a poet and literary figure was wont to hunker on a bar stool surrounded by adoring young poets and painters who hung upon his words, and thought that nothing like him was to be found on the Left Bank of the Seine; in the Supreme Court, Kingsmill Moore J considered this defamatory.[17]

According to some of the authorities, a distinction must be drawn between defamatory ridicule and whatever induces merely innocuous humour at a person's expense, or good natured chaff,[18] or a joke[19]

10 *Dunlop v Dunlop Rubber* [1920] 1 IR 280, 291.
11 E.g. *Kenny v Freemans Journal* (1892) 27 ILTR 8.
12 *Vander Zalm v Times Publishers* (1979) 96 DLR (3d) 172, 174 per Monroe J. For the interesting way one American judge decided whether a caricature caused actionable ridicule, see Eldredge *The Law of Defamation* 39.
13 *Bankole-Bright v Crompton* (1920-36) ALR SL 159.
14 Supra.
15 Supra.
16 SCt, unreported, 4 March 1955. See also *Fullam v Ass. Newspapers* (1955) IJR 79 and *Long v Byrne*, The Irish Times 27 November 1984. A case of, unspecified, ridicule was *Sinclair v Gogarty* [1937] IR 377.
17 At 1. The Supreme Court upheld by three to one the plaintiff's appeal against the jury's verdict, and ordered a new trial.
18 *Blennerhassett v Novelty Sales* (1933) 175 LTJ 393, 394.
19 *McInerney v Clareman Printing and Publishing* [1903] 2 IR 347, 372 per Kenny J.

which would not be considered defamatory. 'But if words be so spoken that it is obvious to every bystander that only a jest is meant, no injury is done and consequently no action would lie'.[20] In an English case[21] a bridegroom unsuccessfully sued on a statement that he had married the day before the scheduled date, which resulted in such ridicule that he was unable to work the next morning.

It is difficult, however, to identify the grounds on which this distinction is supposed to rest. To render a person ridiculous can either involve making him appear absurd, or less than that, merely making light mockery of him. In one case, a judge explicitly considered that mild ridicule could be defamatory,[22] so merely making another into an object of fun seems likely to constitute ridicule. Thus no distinction between actionable and non actionable ridicule can be based on the fact of fun being caused. Further, no distinction can be based on the culpability or otherwise of the conduct of the maker of the statement. There have been suggestions in some of the cases that — whether a defendant knew beforehand of the existence of the plaintiff,[23] or whether he made an innocent mistake in making the statement,[24] or whether he was infringing confidences in making the statement,[25] or whether he had earlier received poor service from the plaintiff[26] — can influence whether the statement is defamatory or not. It is submitted, however, that these views cannot be correct. The essential criterion for determining defamatory effect is whether the statement diminishes the view of those who constitute the standard of opinion. Matter which remains in the mind of the maker of the statement and is neither known nor is obvious to the others cannot influence their view. The ambit of the publication cannot, either, mark the distinction because, though in all the Irish cases the statement was made to a number of persons, yet in some of the English cases,[27] where the same applied, the statement was still held to be only non-actionable fun. The only other ground upon which any distinction can be made between making one into an object of defamatory as opposed to non-defamatory fun, is whether the fun once generated will be forgotten or whether it is likely to recur in the future. Certainly, in some of the cases, the fear that a nickname once given will persist probably to the end of a person's life has

20 Per Joy CB supra.
21 *Emerson v Grimsby Times* (1926) 42 TLR 238.
22 *Kavanagh v The Leader* supra per Kingsmill Moore J at 1.
23 *Blennerhassett v Novelty Sales* supra.
24 *Emerson v Grimsby Times* supra.
25 *Dolby v Newnes* (1887) 3 TLR 393; *Cook v Ward* (1830) 6 Bing 409.
26 *Thorpe and Lee v Ames*, The Irish Times, 23 November 1977, CCt.
27 E.g. *Blennerhassett v Novelty Sales, Emerson v Grimsby Times*.

induced him to bring an action,[28] and instances of repetition would, no doubt, be relevant on the assessment of damages. But the only way that anything in the future can be of relevance when deciding if a statement was defamatory when it was made, is by showing that the statement would be reasonably likely to be repeated in the future. Besides which, in some of the cases,[29] statements were sued upon, which occurred only once and there was no reference to the likelihood of repetition in the future.

From all of this it would seem correct to conclude that an actionable ridicule can be any untrue statement which turns another into an object of fun. Consistent with this would seem the decision in a recent Circuit Court action,[30] in which two barmen recovered damages for a statement in a local newspaper that 'One of the barmen looked like Lazarus before he came out of retirement. The other fellow was the reverse: he looked like him when he went back again'. If any statement could be thought to poke only innocuous fun, this might have been it.

EXAMPLES OF DEFAMATORY IMPUTATIONS

It is illustrative, and useful, to provide some examples of statements that have been held by the courts to be defamatory; though this does not mean that such statements would be so found again, for much depends on the surrounding circumstances of each case. Still, previous instances can assist a court in determining, as a matter of law, whether in the circumstances a statement is capable of defamatory meaning. Courts have occasionally looked to precedent on this question.[31]

In many of the examples given below, the plaintiff will have succeeded, in that the statement was found defamatory and no defence was established, or an injunction was granted: though in others a defence, say, of qualified privilege, may have succeeded but the case would still be authority that the statement was defamatory, because the defence is only raised if a defamation is found. In cases decided in the last century on a type of motion known as a demurrer — which allowed points of law to be decided before the hearing — the courts expressly or implicitly assumed for that purpose various statements to be defamatory. Some of these are cited on the assumption that if the statement was manifestly incapable of defamatory meaning this would have been adverted to.[32]

28 E.g. *Levi v Milne* (1827) 4 Bing 195.
29 E.g. *Donoghue v Hayes* supra.
30 *Thorpe and Lee v Ames* supra.
31 E.g. *Pyke v Hibernian Bank* [1950] IR 195.
32 For convenience it has been necessary to cite only one or some of the many imputations that are often contained in many cases.

It has been held defamatory to accuse a person of stealing,[33] or of being a rogue or vagabond,[34] or to report that the evidence of a witness at an inquest was described as 'nothing short of perjury'[35] or to say 'It would be worth your while to go and see the house that she burned herself and laid on the county'.[36]

It has been held defamatory to accuse a person of being in the IRA,[37] or of being guilty of a huge fraud,[38] or illegal fishing,[39] or of felony and vice of an unnatural kind,[40] or of being a white slave trafficker,[41] or of being a body snatcher,[42] or to pronounce a person excommunicated.[43] It has been held defamatory to say 'You are a bester; there are a lot of your sort coming in here',[44] or to accuse a person attending an auction of refusing to acknowledge a bid,[45] or to accuse a person of bringing a neighbourhood into turmoil by reprehensible conduct,[46] or to write of an intending bridegroom 'Why, if you inquire of Doctor Atkinson's character, I can only say it is a very bad one. He sticks at no foul means to get money. He treated his first wife extremely ill, and for some bad reason or other prosecuted her father and it is well known that money is his object in everything'.[47] It has been held defamatory to accuse a person of making his deceased brother cut his throat and to add that he would yet grace Botany Bay, or the front of Newgate.[48]

It might be defamatory to accuse a person of being the father of vicious offspring,[49] and it may be defamatory to accuse a mother of drunkeness and of preventing her husband from communicating with

33 *McFadden v Lynch* (1883) 17 ILTR 93, demurrer; *Coleman v Keanes Ltd* (1946) IJR 5 pl suc'ed; *Smith v Corr* [1937] IR 248, pl suc'd; *Kilbride v R J F Security, The Irish Times*, 24 July 1985, pl suc'd.
34 *Pope v Foy*, The Irish Times 27 November 1984, pl suc'd.
35 *Lynam v Gowing* (1880) 6 LR Ir 259 demurrer; see also *Joyce v Monaghan* (1890) 24 ILTR 100, def suc'd; *Keenan v Wallace* (1916) 51 ILTR 19, pl suc'd.
36 *Gillis v McDonnell* (1869) IR 4 CL 342, demurrer; *O'Connor v Lloyd* (1830) 2 Hud & Br 626, pl.suc'd.
37 *Kelly v Independent Newspapers,* The Irish Times, 5 December 1984, pl.suc'd.
38 *Doyle v Irish Press,* The Irish Times, 6 December 1984, pl.suc'd.
39 *Bennett v Barry* (1863) 8 IJ NS 167 demurrer.
40 *Bolton v O'Brien* (1885) 16 LR Ir 97, pl suc'd.
41 *Cooney v Wilson and Henderson* [1913] 2 IR 402.
42 *Donoghue v Hayes* (1831) Hayes 265, new trial.
43 *McLoughlin v Welsh* (1846) 10 ILR 19, pl suc'd.
44 *Barton v Doran* (1932) LJ Ir 124, pl. suc'd.
45 *Maxwell v Gavin Low* HCt, unreported, 11 January 1967, def. suc'd.
46 *Halloran v Thompson* (1863) 14 ICLR 335, demurrer.
47 *Atkinson v Congreve* (1857) 7 ICLR 109, demurrer.
48 *Ahern v Maguire* (1840) Arm Mac & Og 39, pl. suc'd.
49 *Kirwan v Tully* (1838) Cr & Dix, Ab Cas 388.

their child.[50] It has been held defamatory to accuse a person of religious intolerance and bigotry,[51] or to write that a person would seem to be tainted with insanity and that he was a 'most deceptive sneaking fellow who cannot be believed'.[52]

It has been held defamatory to impute prostitution to a woman,[53] or to state that a married woman has been caught in a certain shrubbery in a questionable position with a man,[54] or to accuse a man of seduction,[55] or of immorality with a married woman,[56] or to state of a man 'that he was guilty of the most abominable conversation and exposure of his person',[57] or to suggest that a couple had to get married quickly because the woman was pregnant.[58] It has been held defamatory to announce that an employer and his female employee were married and that she had recently given birth to a child,[59] or to state of a servant that she had been sent away by her employer after having a miscarriage,[60] or that she had a child by her master and was a wicked profligate and unfit to have charge of his daughters.[61]

Financial imputations

It has been held defamatory to write of a person that he has not paid off a judgement debt,[62] or to write that judgement has been obtained against him personally,[63] or to say 'you are a man of no punctuality in your money payments — your circumstances are bad — your credit is bad as a merchant',[64] or to threaten to 'again publicly expose' a debtor for non payment of debt,[65] or to state that a debtor was absconding from his creditors, that he was willing to pay a bribe to keep it secret and that he answered to a false name when the ship's passenger list was called,[66] or to say of a merchant 'Did you hear of Black? You will not long be troubled with him,

50 *McDermot v Eason & Son* (1913) 48 ILTR 1.
51 *Teacy v McKenna* (1869) IR 4 CL 374, demurrer.
52 *Fitzsimmons v Duncan, Kemp & Co* [1908] 2 IR 483, pl. suc'd.
53 *Corcoran v Corcoran* (1856) 7 ICLR 272, demurrer.
54 *Tait v Beggs* [1905] 2 IR 525, pl. suc'd.
55 *Cassidy v Kincaid* (1865) 10 IJ NS 176, def. suc'd.
56 *McCullough v Munn* [1908] 2 IR 194, def. suc'd.
57 *Torbitt v Clare* (1846) 9 ILR 86, demurrer.
58 *Kavanagh v Lowry*, Meath Chronicle, 19 February 1980.
59 *Bell v Northern Constitution* [1943] NI 108. adm. by def.
60 *Connors v Justice* (1862) 13 ICLR 451, demurrer.
61 *Quinn v Wilson* (1850) 13 ILR 381, demurrer.
62 *McNally v Oldham* (1863) 16 ICLR 298, demurrer.
63 *Annally v Trade Auxiliary* (1889) 26 LR Ir 11, 394, def. suc'd.
64 *Kirwan v Denman* (1828) 2 Hud & Br 628, demurrer.
65 *Jacob v Lawrence* (1879) 4 LR Ir 579, demurrer.
66 *Davis v Reeves* (1855) 5 ICLR 79, pl. suc'd.

he is off'.[67] It has been held defamatory to impute that a person was about to go to goal for insolvency and to write 'I know his position and that was my reason for urging you to look sharp',[68] or to say of applicant guarantors 'I know the three men...; they are men of straw, that is, they are not worth a farthing',[69] or for a bank to write on a customer's cheque 'Refer to Drawer. Present Again',[70] or to state that a firm is insolvent and unable to meet its commitments and that 'It is general opinion that Praegar & Co. will go down in a few days and I think they are clever people to have remained up for so long'.[71]

Particular imputations

Solicitors It has been held defamatory to impute that a solicitor is unreliable and unfit, dishonest and not to be trusted,[72] or that he had agreed to represent the defence but had then without notice changed his mind and taken up for the plaintiff,[73] or to say that 'He brought an action in Circuit Court instead of the District Court to get more costs for himself',[74] or to accuse a solicitor of forging a certificate of taxation and of obtaining a bill of costs by false pretences,[75] or to accuse a solicitor's apprentice of having wilfully suppressed the truth when swearing an affidavit.[76]

Barristers It has been held defamatory to accuse a barrister of instigating a riot in court, of being of ungentlemanly appearance and doubtful sobriety in court, and of having boasted beforehand 'that he was come there to humble the magistrates',[77] or to write of a barrister 'This poor creature, who says he is a barrister, and who may be so for aught we know, for he is sometimes seen walking about in a peruke in the hall the Four Courts. This poor creature ... begged (he often does that) to propose a resolution...'.[78]

67 *Black v Holmes* (1822) 1 Fox & Sm 28, def. suc'd.
68 *Owens v Roberts* (1856) 6 ICLR 386, demurrer.
69 *Little v Pomeroy* (1873) IR 7 CL 50, def. suc'd.
70 *Pyke v Hibernian Bank* [1950] IR 195, pl. suc'd. On hearing the bank's appeal the Supreme Court sitting exceptionally with four members divided evenly and thus the High Court verdict for the plaintiff was affirmed. *Ross Meats v Bank of Ireland,* The Irish Times, 10 May 1986, def.suc'd. See also *Smith v Commonwealth Trust* (1969) 10 DLR (3d) 181.
71 *Praeger & Co v Shaw* (1855) 4 ICLR 660, demurrer.
72 *Curneen v Sweeney* (1969)103 ILTR 29, pl. suc'd.
73 *Hamerton v Green* (1863) 16 ICLR 77, demurrer.
74 *Bennett v Quane* (1948) IJR 28, pl. suc'd.
75 *McCarthy v Maguire* [1899] 2 IR 802, pl. suc'd.
76 *Buckley v Kiernan* (1857) 7 ICLR 75, demurrer.
77 *Croke v O'Grady* (1830) 4 Law Rec 49, pl. suc'd.
78 *Power v Haydn* (1824) Sm & Bat 386, demurrer.

Judges, Gardaí and members of the Defence Forces It has been held defamatory to accuse a judge of conspiracy to subvert judicial independence and party bias,[79] or to state that a judge was not impartial and was a tool in the hands of others,[80] or to write that he had been appointed to office as a token Catholic,[81] or to state that a Garda had tortured detainees,[82] or had been sexually immoral,[83] or to suggest that Gardaí were incompetent and unfit for their duties,[84] or to accuse an army officer of theft,[85] or of being a coward, liar and swindler and offering to make the charge before the regiment.[86]

Clergyman It has been held defamatory to write of a clergyman that he was drunk during divine service,[87] or that he has been charged with improper and indecent conduct, including assault, towards a woman,[88] or that he had been convicted of drunken driving and assault and that he had appeared in court in mufti and had had his sentence altered on revealing his true identity,[89] or to write that he was an arch-schismatic who was a degraded wretch that had been excommunicated and that he was 'running all over the country like the spirit of darkness seeking whom he might devour',[90] or to announce that a priest was suspended from his office and all its benefits until he came to his right mind and that infringements of ecclesiastical law and papal authority had occurred almost daily,[91] or to accuse a bishop of contravening canon law by opposing the confirmation of Catholic children attending state schools.[92] It has also been held defamatory to accuse a churchwarden of conversion and dishonesty,[93] or to state that he diverted himself on Sunday when he ought to have been in the house of God.[94]

Teachers It has been held defamatory to write of a headmaster that he did not co-operate with the parents of the students or with the

79 *R v Justice Johnson* (1805) 29 ST 81, Crm libel.
80 *R v Kelly* (1838) 1 Jebb & Sym 216.
81 *Doyle v The Economist,* The Irish Times, 28 June 1980, pl. suc'd.
82 *Egan v BBC,* The Irish Times, 12 December 1980, HCt, pl suc'd.
83 *Devine v Keane* (1927) 61 ILTR 118, pl. suc'd.
84 *Corliss and Diggin v Ireland,* The Irish Times, 30 November 1984, def. suc'd.
85 *Bell v Parke* (1860) 11 ICLR 413, pl. suc'd.
86 *Mitchell v Kerr* (1801) reported (1825) Rowe Rep 537, def. suc'd.
87 *Hurst v Whaley* (1843) 5 ILR 429, def. suc'd.
88 *Little v Clements* (1851) 1 ICLR 194, new trial.
89 *Egan v Hibernia,* The Irish Times, 17 August 1980, pl. suc'd.
90 *Crotty v McMahon* (1835) 1 Jones 465, demurrer.
91 *O'Keefe v Cullen* (1873) IR 7 CL 319, demurrer.
92 *Philbin v Irish Times,* The Irish Times, 16 May 1981, pl. suc'd.
93 *Robinson v Chambers (No. 2)* [1946] NI 148, pl. suc'd.
94 *Moore v Bloxham* (1796) ITR 91.

board of management and that certain aspects of his personal life had been criticised,[95] or to accuse a teacher of having robbed banks and post offices and of shooting innocent people and to say 'You are nice people in the parish of Bekan that you have such a blackguard ... to train children',[96] or to accuse a student of obtaining a money order by false pretences.[97]

Doctors It has been held defamatory to write of a doctor that there was greater reason for complaint against him in the treatment of his patients than there was against a nurse,[98] or to write that he was unsuitable for a post because he lacked the necessary professional training and experience,[99] or to say of a doctor's report 'This report of yours is a lie' and also that 'It is a gross slander in my opinion ...'.[1]

Journalists and Artists It has been held defamatory to state of an article written by a journalist that it contained statements and accusations that were wholly unfounded,[2] or of an editor that he was biased, lacking in integrity, had attempted to frame a politician and was like an old dog urinating in a public place.[3] It has been held defamatory to state of an actor, who claimed to be interested in Irish theatre, that he was more interested in money,[4] or to impute that a poet was somewhat of a poseur, unsubtle, opinionated and overbearing,[5] or to state that an architect had wasted his architectural talents in drink.[6]

Business personnel It has been held defamatory to accuse a managing director of financial incompetence,[7] or a company director of knowingly issuing a false balance sheet,[8] or to state of a bank director that because of his political activities he was a dangerous person to be connected with a bank, that some customers had closed

95 *Coffey v Irish Times,* The Irish Times, 14 May 1977, pl. suc'd.
96 *McDonagh v Tarpey* [1933] IR 666, pl. suc'd.
97 *Kirkwood-Hacket v Tierney* [1952] IR 185, def. suc'd.
98 *McKeogh v O'Brien-Moran* [1927] IR 348, pl. suc'd.
99 *Lynch v Toland,* The Irish Times, 21 January 1984, def. suc'd.
1 *McCarthy v Morrissey* (1939) IJR 82, def. suc'd.
2 *Willis v Irish Press* (1938) 72 ILTR 238, def. suc'd.
3 *McConville v Kennelly,* The Irish Times, 27 January 1984, pl. suc'd.
4 *Quigley v Creation Ltd* [1971] IR 269, pl. suc'd.
5 *Kavanagh v The Leader*, SCt, unreported, 4 March 1955 per Kingsmill Moore J at 1, new trial.
6 *Scott v Eason & Son,* The Irish Times, 9 August 1980, inj. granted.
7 *Gallagher v Touhy* (1924) 58 ILTR 134, inj. ref'd.
8 *Waring v McCaldin* (1873) IR 7 CL 282, def. suc'd.

their accounts and others had threatened to do so because of his position, and that the board had considered removing him.[9]

It has been held defamatory to accuse an auctioneer of refusing to surrender the proceeds of a sale,[10] or of abetting fraud,[11] or to write that a coachmaker does not keep a respectable business house,[12] or that printer was not respectable,[13] or to accuse a tailor of selling shoddy goods and of pretending that they were Irish made when they were not,[14] or to accuse a butter buyer of fraudulently using his weights,[15] or a trader of short changing customers,[16] or to say of a wine merchant 'No matter what price is given for wine in Naas, it will be South African sherry',[17] or to write of one that 'as to his conduct, I did not say half enough, it more resembles that of a freebooter than of an honourable British merchant'.[18]

Land Agents and Tenants It has been held defamatory to accuse a land agent of mismanagement and of tyrannical conduct towards the tenants and to write that he had sided with a rival to the landlord's title,[19] or to accuse a land agent of harsh conduct towards his tenants resulting in the death of a former tenant and his son,[20] or to state of a bailiff that he had not drained a river as he had been directed to and which he had been paid for,[21] or to publish of a tenant 'I will continue to denounce the grabber until justice is done to his victims' and to write that he had become very notorious,[22] or to publish a notice that a tenant would be attached for impropriety in obtaining the tenancy,[23] or to accuse a tenant of having fraudulently deprived his sisters of monies due under their father's will and charged on the land.[24]

Employees It has been held defamatory to accuse an employee of theft of the employer's property,[25] or of property of which he has

9 *Jones v Sheehan* (1839) Smyth 205, pl. suc'd.
10 *Sayers v Bachelor* (1854) 7 IJ OS 257, demurrer.
11 *Murray v MacSwiney* (1876) IR 9 CL 545, demurrer.
12 *Barrett v Long* (1851) 3 HLC 395, pl. suc'd.
13 *Hobbs v Bryers* (1878) 2 LR Ir 496, demurrer.
14 *Towell v Fallon* (1912) 47 ILTR 176 def. suc'd.
15 *Hennessey v Morgan* (1859) 8 ICLR App lxix, demurrer.
16 *Dunne v O'Grady* (1856) 5 ICLR 450, demurrer.
17 *Murphy v Kellett* (1862) 13 ICLR 488, demurrer.
18 *MacDougall v Tyrrell* (1855) 1 IJ NS 465, demurrer.
19 *Stannus v Finlay* (1874) IR 8 CL 264, pl. suc'd.
20 *Morrow v McGaver* (1851) 1 ICLR 579, def. suc'd.
21 *Simmonds v Dunne* (1871) IR 5 CL 358, demurrer.
22 *McInerney v Clareman Printing and Publishing* [1903] 2 IR 347, pl. suc'd.
23 *Clarke v Roe* (1854) 4 ICLR 1, pl. suc'd.
24 *Dwyer v Esmonde* (1877) IR 11 CL 542, demurrer.
25 *Corcoran v W. & R. Jacob* [1945] IR 446, def. suc'd. *Hyland v Clery & Co*

charge,[26] or to impute incompetence to any employee as where it was written of one employed to maintain machinery 'It is a shame that thoroughly good class machinery should be allowed to get into the condition in which they now are',[27] or to accuse a former employee of blackmail,[28] or theft,[29] or to write that he had not accounted for money received from a customer while in his former employment.[30]

Office holders It has been held defamatory to accuse a public office holder of having committed crimes equal to those of any felon in history and to state that he will become immortalised for his crimes,[31] or to accuse a public servant of being biased towards Catholics,[32] or a civil servant of wrongfully disclosing official information,[33] or a rate collector of an illegal seizure.[34] It has been held defamatory to accuse the treasurer of a fundraising committee of misappropriating part of the funds to his own use,[35] or to state that the secretary and treasurer of a parochial relief committee 'is getting more money than he is acknowledging'.[36]

Sports activists It has been held defamatory to write of a promoter of billiards games that he had organised an exhibition match inefficiently and incompetently,[37] or to write of one who bets at racehorse meetings that his name be added to the list of defaulters,[38] or to write of the owner and jockey of a racehorse that he had been warned off courses for fraudulently concealing his true weight at a weighing in,[39] or to write of a professional soccer player that he never used his right foot for anything except balancing himself and that his club has unsuccessfully attempted to induce him to use his right foot by getting him to wear a slipper on his left foot at practise.[40]

HCt, unreported, 9 April 1964, def.suc'd. *Boland v Tara Mines,*The Irish Times, 3 March 1984, pl. suc'd. See also *Moore and Pine v Irish Press,* The Irish Times, 5 December 1986, pl. suc'd.

26 *Wallace v Carroll* (1860) 11 ICLR 485, demurrer.
27 *Denvir v Taylor* (1935) IJR 4, def. suc'd.
28 *Hartery v Welltrade,* HCt, unreported, 15 March 1978, def. suc'd.
29 *Dempsey v Wall & Co and Ryan* (1943) 78 ICLR 73, demurrer.
30 *Fox v Broderick* (1862) 14 ICLR 453, demurrer.
31 *R v Edgeworth* (1828) 1 Law Rec 304.
32 *Kearney v McCusker,* The Irish Times, 30 April 1983, def. suc'd.
33 *McDonnell v Preece,* The Irish Times, 21 November 1985, pl. suc'd.
34 *Pope v Coates* (1863) 16 ICLR 156, pl. suc'd.
35 *Clanchy v Cahill* (1825) Sm & Bat 232, demurrer.
36 *Currigan v Ryan* (1865) 11 IJ NS 406, demurrer.
37 *Campbell v Irish Press* (1955) 90 ILTR 105, new trial.
38 *Reilly v Gill* (1946) 85 ILTR 165, pl. suc'd.
39 *Green v Blake* [1948] IR 242, new trial.
40 *Fullam v Associated Newspapers* (1955) IJR 79, pl. suc'd.

Local Authority representatives It has been held defamatory to accuse a member of a local authority of not being independent, of being insolvent and unable to pay his debts,[41] or of being in arrears with his payment of rates,[42] or of being a religious bigot,[43] or to accuse him of making 'reckless allegations utterly devoid of foundation' and adding that he had displayed a 'perverted mentality and unqualified disregard for truth and public decency in debate',[44] or to accuse a lord mayor of criminal conspiracy that could result in a charge of murder and to say that 'you would never have been Town Councillor, Alderman or Lord Mayor of Belfast if the burgess roll had not been packed from year to year',[45] or to write of a lord mayor that he had solicited and obtained bribes,[46] or to accuse the members of a corporation of jobbery, to describe their proceedings as a travesty and exploitation of democracy and to state that they had acted unblushingly to the call of interests behind the scenes.[47]

Politicians It has been held defamatory to accuse a member of parliament of being an 'Invincible',[48] or of betraying his principles by promoting landlord instead of tenant interests and that while in the party had conspired to betray the party by disrupting it,[49] or of being involved in savage scenes outside Leinster House and of pulling a journalist's beard,[50] or to accuse a Labour member of parliament of advising the government that the unemployed should be shot down if they agitated for work, that the government should organise an army of scabs to break any strike or lockout and to write 'It is time Labour dealt with this English traitor. Months ago we told our readers that . . . was going over to capitalism, and by that we meant his services were in the market'.[51] It has been held defamatory to accuse a former Tanaiste of refusing to pay betting tax and of placing him in the same category as a public representative convicted of the same offence and another charged with homosexual offences,[52] or to publish the photograph of a current minister alongside that of a former President of the U.S.A. and to write 'Is this to be Irish

41 *Murphy v Halpin* (1874) IR 8 CL 127, demurrer.
42 *Keaveney v Geraghty* [1965] IR 551.
43 *Fisher v Nation Newspaper and Rooney* [1901] 2 IR 465, pl. suc'd.
44 *Nevin v Roddy and Carty* [1935] IR 397, def. suc'd.
45 *R v Rea* (1864) 17 ICLR 584, crim. libel.
46 *R v O'Brien* (1833) Cooke & Alc 128, crim. libel.
47 *Black v Northern Whig* (1942) 77 ILTR 5, pl. suc'd.
48 *Harris v Arnott* (1889) 26 LR Ir 55, adm. by def.
49 *O'Brien v Freemans Journal* (1907) 41 ILTR 35.
50 *Barrett v Independent Newspapers,* The Irish Times, 18 April 1985, pl. suc'd; appealed to SCt, new trial.
51 *Johnson v Larkin and Gaelic Press* [1926] IR 40, pl. suc'd.
52 *MacSharry v McCormick,* The Irish Times, 1 May 1985, pl. suc'd.

Watergate?',[53] or to state that a former minister had had a fight with an official of a state company,[54] or had given £10 million of state money to four people tax free for effectively nothing.[55] It has been stated that to accuse a constitutional politician with strong republican views of being a supporter of violence is defamatory.[56] To accuse a Labour candidate at an election of having previously been a scab has been held defamatory,[57] as also was a charge of personation made against an elector when voting in an election.[58]

JUDGE AND JURY

There are numerous judicial statements describing the division of function between judge and jury when deciding the question whether a statement is defamatory. The formal position can be readily stated. Where a judge sits with a jury, the determination of whether the statement was, in the circumstances of the case, defamatory rests with the jury. But before the matter may go to the jury it is settled that the trial judge must be satisfied that the statement is reasonably capable of being found to be defamatory. If he is not, then the issue does not go to the jury. Whatever decision is made by either judge or jury is subject to review by an appellate court, and, in the case of the jury, can be overturned if it was one which no jury of twelve people could reasonably reach.[59] This almost trite law actually belies a surprising degree of confusion, uncertainty and illogicality concerning ideas of what trial judges and appellate courts may properly do, which has existed for a long time. The numerous judicial uttterances have, moreover, consistently overstated the longevity and uniformity of practice in the area.

The present role of the jury in determining whether a statement is defamatory developed in circumstances particularly unhelpful towards revealing a satisfactory rationale for that role. It was based on the deliberate misapplication by civil law judges of an eighteenth century statutory rule concerning the division of function between

53 *Cooney v Sunday World,* The Irish Times, 8 November 1978, pl. suc'd. A case where a jury found that the positioning of a politician's photograph alongside a report of a riot did not mean that she supported violence is *De Valera v Independent Newspapers,* The Irish Times, 14 December 1984.

54 *Lindsay v Amarach,* The Irish Times, *15 February 1983, pl. suc'd.*

55 *Keating v Stephen's Green Publications,* The Irish Times, 17 December 1985, pl. suc'd.

56 *De Valera v Independent Newspapers* supra.

57 *Cullen v Stanley* [1926] IR 73, inj. granted.

58 *Higgins v Monaghan and O'Reilly* (1939) 74 ILTR 56, pl. suc'd.

59 *Dunlop v Dunlop Rubber* (1920) 1 IR 280, 290 per Powell J. Also *Barrett v Independent Newspapers,* [1986] ILRM 601.

judge and jury in criminal libel;[60] a rule, too, which was never intended to affect the civil position. The change involved an odd turn of events since the statutory rule had been intended to remedy an earlier subversion of the criminal rule by the civil one, and it in turn succeeded in subverting the civil position.[61] The increased role of the jury in civil proceedings did not go unopposed,[62] and as late as the 1850's Perrin J in two cases disputed the practice.[63] What may, in part, have assisted the enhanced jury role in the civil action, was a greater appreciation of the suitability of the jury role in a cause of action dependant on determining community reaction to a statement.

If the jury was thus paramount in deciding this matter, that ought then to have raised questions about whether a trial judge could ever withhold the issue from the jury, and whether an appellate court could ever review a jury finding on this point. Yet strangely, the courts do not ever appear to have doubted that the trial judge could withdraw the issue from the jury if he felt the statement incapable of defamatory meaning; although from 1882 in England[64] and 1889 here,[65] serious confusion arose over whether the trial judge could withdraw the issue from the jury when both innocent and defamatory meanings could be taken from the statement. For a long time an assertive view of the power of withdrawal prevailed by which the judge could withdraw the issue if innocent meanings were possible. In time, however, this came to be perceived as a usurpation of the jury's role, so that now the trial judge must leave the issue to the jury if there is a possible defamatory meaning, regardless of any innocent ones.[66] Nor, surprisingly, do the courts appear to have doubted that appellate courts could reverse jury verdicts on this point, though, again, battles were fought over how rarely or less rarely the circumstances of review arose.[67] Most recently, dispute has developed on the seemingly novel point of whether the trial judge can withdraw from the jury the issue of whether the statement is defamatory, not because it might be incapable of defamatory meaning but on exactly the opposite point — because it might be incapable of innocent meaning. The Supreme

60 Contained in the English Libel Act 1792, and the Irish Libel Act 1793.

61 See generally Corbett's *Parliamentary History of England*, 1817, Vol 29, Cols 571, 578/579; also Napier, *Lecture on the Law of Defamation* (1840) 1 Leg Rep 132,133.

62 See Best CJ in *Levi v Milne* (1827) 4 Bing. 195.

63 *Spong v Fahy* (1855) 5 ICLR 351; *Pilson v Johnson* (1856) 6 ICLR 505.

64 *Capital and Counties Bank v Henty* (1882) 7 App Cas 741.

65 *McCann v Edinburgh Roperie* (1889) 28 LR Ir 24; *O'Hea v Guardians, Cork Union* (1893) 32 LR Ir 629; *Keogh v Incorporated Dental Hospital* [1910] 2 IR 166, 577.

66 *Pyke v Hibernian Bank* [1950] IR 195, especially O'Byrne J at 205.

67 E.g. see *McInerney v Clareman Printing and Publishing* [1903] 2 IR 347.

Court decided in a recent case by three to two that the trial judge cannot do this.[68] In none of these latter disputes, however, can one present those favouring a broader view of the judicial role as carrying the standard of such as Perrin J. That view seems now foreclosed no matter how unsatisfactory the origins of the present position are, and which the courts have shown no inclination to examine. Nor have they actually considered the policy and logic behind the present position. They have been more concerned to identify correct lines of authority and to follow them. Yet a review of the present situation is needed because there is much in the current law of defamation which contradicts the jury function and which, if anything, argues for a greater judicial role in this matter. Firstly, it is not clear how the power of a trial judge to withdraw the issue from the jury on grounds that the statement is incapable of of defamatory meaning is not inconsistent with the jury determining whether a statement is defamatory; it is also not clear how the power of appellate courts to review jury findings of innocent or defamatory meaning is consistent with that role; and lastly there is reason to suspect that the existence of both these judicial powers is inconsistent with the refusal to allow the trial judge to decide himself that a statement is incapable of innocent meaning.[69] Secondly, the number of reasons why a trial judge can prevent a jury from determining whether a statement is defamatory are great. He might decide the statement was only abusive, or ridiculous, or injurious or was a non actionable publication, or was fair comment or was made on any of a large number of privileged occasions. Can it not be stated that the refusal to let the jury decide whether the statement was defamatory in these instances is a denial of its role? Then, there is no jury in the Circuit Court. Does this mean that defamation in the Circuit Court is different from defamation in the High Court? Finally, juries play no role in the exercise of interlocutory injunction jurisdiction in defamation actions. If the jury's real role is to interpret community reaction — and is not just a mode of proceeding — then the less often the action reflects what the jury say the community really thought, the less is the justification for a jury role at all, and the greater is the case for

68 *Barrett v Independent Newspapers* supra. The majority consisted of Henchy, Griffin and Hederman JJ, and the minority was Finlay CJ and McCarthy J. In the US, according to Eldredge *The Law of Defamation*, 41 fn 46, the cases support the minority view in Barrett's case.

69 In Barrett's case Finlay CJ at 603 deduced the trial judge power of withdrawal from the appellate court power of review. In *Broome v Agar* (1928) 138 LT 698, Scrutton LJ at 699 stated that it was a long step to pass from a power to withdraw that the statement is incapable of defamatory meaning to a power to withdraw on grounds that the statement is incapable of innocent meaning. But he did not show how this is so, and it is not clear that it is.

a complete judicial determination of whether a statement was defamatory.

In conclusion, the present division of responsibilty in High Court actions between judge and jury reflects an uneasy accommodation between a formal jury role and a judicial assertiveness. It appears illogical and inconsistent in a number of ways. For as long as the trial judge can find ways to exclude the jury — mainly to avoid damages awards — the value of the jury as a supposed arbiter of community reaction is doubtful. On the other hand, the removal of damages, and the consequent necessity for matters to be kept from juries, and its replacement by rights of retraction and reply could allow an even greater scope for juries than at present, with the abolition of trial judge powers of withdrawal, and possibly even appellate court powers of review.

3

Interpretation and Identification

INTERPRETING THE MEANING

The law uses the concept of the reasonable person to discover the meaning of statements. It makes no assumption that the maker of the statement is such a reasonable person, and so neither the knowledge nor intent of that person when making the statement are of relevance in discovering its meaning. The reasonable person will construe not only the words or other media of expression used according to their natural meaning, but he will also consider the surrounding and relevant circumstances in which the statement was made to see what bearing, if any, they had on that meaning. As these circumstances can vary infinitely, it follows that no words or combination of words are in themselves necessarily defamatory, or for that matter, necessarily harmless. Findings on defamatory meaning in previous cases must therefore be used carefully. Indeed, this variability in circumstance can be such that, in different cases the same statement has been alternately held to be defamatory and to be harmless,[1] and also in some cases a statement has been made as a fact while in others it has been held to be a comment.[2] Surrounding circumstance may also work so that a statement, true on its face and so not defamatory, may yet be held untrue and so defamatory.[3] Conversely, a statement which is prima facie defamatory may actually be found not defamatory.[4]

Innuendoes

Statements may be expressed and understood in a wide variety of ways, and with varying degrees of clarity. Only the simplest of statements, for example, are incapable of more than one meaning.

1 See p. 82 post
2 See p. 213 post
3 *Irish People's Assurance v Dublin City Assurance* [1929] IR 25
4 *Crawford and Frame v Vance* [1908] 2 IR 521

It is also clear that, especially in the case of a derogatory statement, it is difficult to achieve a consensus view both on the question of its interpretation and on the appropriate degree of adverse reaction.

All this may be reason enough why a plaintiff — who rarely, if ever, suffers from difficulty in identifying the attack on his reputation — would not, or could not, risk granting the same aptitude to those who received the statement. From this lack of confidence in, or fear of, the appreciative qualities of others may spring a desire to point out or to explain the meaning of the statement for the benefit of the tribunal of fact in the hearing. An innuendo is a paragraph in a statement of claim which states this meaning. There can be two types of innuendo — true and false.

True innuendo

Where a plaintiff claims a meaning for a statement which on its face it is not capable of bearing, then he will need to plead a true innuendo in which he asserts that because of extrinsic facts, the statement had a libellous meaning. 'Innuendoes are alleged in order to give a libellous character to words which in their ordinary meaning they do not bear'.[5] In such a case, the plaintiff's fear of incomprehension by others is well justified, for to the ordinary recipient there will be an unbridgeable gap between the ordinary and the ascribed meanings. This gap can only be bridged, and the meaning in the innuendo established, by the averring and proving of extrinsic facts known to some or all of the recipients. There can be many reasons for such a gap, although it must be said that there are few enough clear examples in the cases of true innuendoes. One such example arose in *Bell v Northern Constitution*[6] in 1943 where a newspaper, in falsely announcing the birth of a baby to a couple was held liable since the couple were a widower and his unmarried employee.

At its farthest, a statement might not be in language at all. It might be a drawing, or a gesture, or a facial expression, or even an intonation of the voice — 'Take the case of an ironical libel "So-and-so is an honest man" meaning thereby that he was dishonest. No defamatory meaning can be proved save by extrinsic circumstances'.[7] The statement might be in a language other than English or Irish,[8] or it might be a slang or technical word which the jury or judge, as

5 *Daly v ITGWU* [1926] IR 118, 124 per O'Connor J
6 [1943] NI 108
7 *O'Hea v Guardians, Cork Union* (1893) 32 LR Ir 629, 640 per O'Brien J
8 A case where the defamatory statement was made in Irish is *Lindsay v Amarach*, The Irish Times, 15 February 1983

the case may be, would not be expected to be familiar with.[9] The statement may even be in English or Irish and possess a prima facie innocent meaning but in the circumstances be understood differently. Finally a statement might not indicate its subject, or may refer to a fictitious character[10] or to a group of individuals, so that 'by innuendo you may point out the particular individual to whom the words apply'.[11]

As the purpose of the true innuendo is merely to state the meaning which the statement possessed in light of the circumstances in which it was made, it follows that a proper innuendo is not an enlarging meaning. But if there is an improper meaning ascribed, that is to say, where an innuendo varies, enlarges, adds or changes the statement, then it is a bad innuendo, and a defamatory imputation cannot be found on foot of it.[12] All this means that when a true innuendo is found the statement is actually, on its own and in the circumstances, defamatory, so 'you cannot have a libellous innuendo without a libellous publication'.[13] A variety of bad innuendoes have been found in the cases. Thus, it has been held that the statement that a person was a judgement debtor was enlarged by the meaning that any customers of his ran the risk of being defrauded by him,[14] or that the statement that a priest was unruly was enlarged by the suggestion that he was unchristian,[15] or to write of a supplier of billiards equipment who had organised an exhibition match that 'The table told lies' was enlarged by the meaning that he was incompetent in his business of supplying equipment, as opposed to that of organising an exhibition.[16]

Where the meaning ascribed by the innuendo to the statement made consists of more than one imputation, and one or some of these imputations vary the meaning of the statement but others do not, then if the imputations are divisible and not linked so that one part does not affect or influence the other, the former part may be rejected and the latter part relied upon.[17]

9 *Kavanagh v The Leader* SCt, unreported, 4 March 1955, per Kingsmill-Moore J at 5
10 As in *Sinclair v Gogarty* [1937] IR 377
11 *Lefanu v Malcolmson* (1848) 1 HLC 637, 669 per Lord Campbell
12 *McManus v McEnroe* (1851) 1 ICLR 332, 341, per Monahan CJ
13 *Daly v ITGWU* supra
14 *Cosgrave v Trade Auxiliary* (1874) IR 8 CL 349
15 *Lavelle v Oranmore* (1861) 7 IJ NS 55
16 *Campbell v Irish Press* (1955) 90 ILTR 105. For other examples see *Barrett v Long* (1851) 3 HLC 395, *Maguire v Knox* (1871) IR 5 CL 408, *Pyke v Hibernian Bank* [1950] IR 195
17 *Barrett v Long* (1846) 8 ILR 331 Exch Cham

Averring and proving extrinsic facts

The true innuendo states the meaning the plaintiff wishes to put on the words used and which as they stand they do not bear. He can only prove this meaning by reference to factual evidence extrinsic to the statement and which shows that the statement was understood in the sense which he claims. The pleading and proving of extrinsic evidence is thus crucial to succeeding with the true innuendo. In 1892 Johnson J remarked on the importance of this type of evidence 'in order to establish the non-natural meaning imputed by innuendo, as I have said in a former case, "it was necessary for the plaintiff to prove by extrinsic evidence the surrounding circumstances which would lead an ordinary reader to the inference that the publication had the peculiar character and meaning imputed to it, and to place the jury as near as possible in the position of such a reader"'.[18] Failure to adduce such evidence will entitle a trial judge to decide himself that the statement is not capable of bearing the meaning in question, and so prevent the matter from being left to the jury.[19]

While it has always been necessary, where a true innuendo is pleaded, to prove in evidence the extrinsic facts supporting the innuendo meaning, it has not always been necessary to plead those facts in the statement of claim. Until 1853 material extrinsic facts had to be pleaded in the introductory matter, or prefatory averments, or colloquium to the various counts and innuendoes in the plaintiff's claim. By s 65 of the Common Law Procedure Amendment Act (Ireland) 1853, prefatory averments showing how the defamatory matter was used in the sense alleged by the innuendo were abolished. Thenceforth, and even after the repeal of this Act, in true innuendo cases only the innuendo meanings had to be pleaded, though it was of course still necessary to prove the supporting facts at the hearing. Although not compulsory, it remained open and was often done, at least in England, to plead those facts anyway.[20] The position there however, has now been changed back to the pre-1852 position,[21] since a reform committee recommended the change because it considered that ignorance of extrinsic facts could disadvantage and take by surprise a defendant.[22] No comparable change has been made here, and according to Lavery J in 1955 the position here is

18 *O'Hea v Guardians, Cork Union* (1892) 32 LR Ir 629, 643; see also [1929] IR 25, 36

19 As it happened in O'Hea's case, McCann's case and Keogh's case. It is doubtful, however, since Pyke's case, whether a trial judge could now withhold statements such as in these cases from the jury.

20 Porter Committee Report para 165

21 English Rules, O. 82 r. 3 (1)

22 Porter Committee Report supra

still the same,[23] regardless, it appears of any general requirements in the Rules of the Superior Courts that there be a disclosure of material facts in the pleadings.[24] Whether the new O.19 r.5 (1) requiring particulars of the wrong alleged to be pleaded in the statement of claim will affect this remains to be seen. In any case, it is now customary in practice to plead the necessary extrinsic facts in the statement of claim.

Where the innuendo is rejected

Where it is pleaded that the statement was defamatory in both an innuendo sense and in the natural meaning of the statement, and the innuendo meaning is rejected, it is, of course, open to the plaintiff to rely on the meaning of the words themselves. Where only an innuendo meaning is pleaded and this meaning is negatived, the law has varied in its approach to whether it will allow a plaintiff to fall back and rely on the natural meaning. For a long time during the last century, and until the beginning of this century, different rules were applied in Ireland and in England. Here, the 'certain' rule was applied that 'when a libel is capable of several senses, and a plaintiff takes one sense in particular, he puts his case on that sense, that ... he is "pinned down" to that sense; and, if he fails to make out that sense, cannot reject it and fall back upon some other sense, or upon the words themselves',[25] even if the words were actionable in themselves. So that in *Maguire v Knox*,[26] where the defendant published that 'The soldiers of the garrison are strictly prohibited from entering the house 180, North King Street kept by Mr P Maguire' and the jury rejected the suggested innuendo meanings, inter alia, that 'the said house was an unfit and improper resort' for the soldiers of the garrison and for the public, the plaintiff was not allowed rely on the natural meaning of the words themselves as he had not pleaded it. The Irish practice certainly dated from 1822, where in *Black v Holmes*, a case similar to Maguire's, Bushe CJ explained the reason for the rule '... a plaintiff shall not be at liberty to take

23 *Kavanagh v The Leader* at 4. Another jurisdiction where the position is the same is Ontario — s 21 Libel and Slander Act RSO 1980

24 Some English authority — considered by Symmons, 'The Problem of Hidden Reference in Defamation' (1974) Anglo-Am L Rev 98 — suggests that before 1949 in England their equivalent of s 65 applied only to meaning innuendo cases and not to identity innuendo ones, so that with the latter type there remained an obligation to plead the facts showing how the identification was made. The express terms of s 65 however, did not refer to such a distinction, and Lavery J did not either.

25 *Bolton v O'Brien* (1885) 16 LR Ir 97, 114 per O'Brien J

26 (1870) IR 5 CL 408

his adversary by surprise by imputing one meaning to words by his declaration and then at the trial insisting upon a distinct meaning altogether; and supporting his argument by an attack upon his own pleading'.[27] The House of Lords, in an Irish appeal in 1851,[28] actually purported to change the Irish rule and allow reliance on the words where the innuendo meaning was rejected, but this ruling was not successfully relied on in the Irish courts because 'in that case the difference in the English and Irish practice was not brought to the notice of the judges or of the House of Lords'.[29] In England, at least since s 61 of the Common Law Procedure Act 1852, if not before, the plaintiff was allowed treat his claim as being twofold in character — one cause being the meaning assigned by innuendo,and a second cause being the meaning of the words themselves.

The Irish Common Law Procedure Act of the following year contained no equivalent to the relevant English section, and it was subsequently decided in a number of cases in the Irish courts that this meant that no change had been made in the Irish rule, and so that it differed from the English one.[30] This situation continued despite the repeal of both acts, until the case of *Fisher v Nation Newspaper and Rooney,*[31] where the Court of Appeal, in 1901, reversed a unanimous Queen's Bench decision that refused to allow a fall back on the natural meaning of the words, which had not been specifically pleaded, after the innuendo meaning had been negatived. Since then the matter has not arisen in the reports except that, in 1955, Lavery J adverted to the decision in Fisher's case, and considered that it was still established law.[32] The judgement of the Court of Appeal in Fisher's case was delivered by Holmes L J and its basis rests more upon convenience, as that judge saw it, rather than, one submits, upon law. Holmes L J stressed the statutory imperative in the Judicature Act 1877 for similarity in the Rules of Court of Ireland and England, although this point was not referred to in either. He ignored however, or at least gave insufficient weight to, an equally explicit imperative contained in the Act that conformity was to be subject to any existing differences of practice, of which this was most clearly one. It can be further argued that there is not much justice in allowing a fall back for a plaintiff who, though entitled

27 (1822) 1 Fox & Sm 28
28 *Barrett v Long* (1851) 3 HLC 395
29 *Fisher v Nation Newspaper and Rooney* [1901] 2 IR 465, 477 per Johnson J
30 *Maguire v Knox* (1870) IR 5 CL 408, *Hort v Reade* (1873) IR 7 CL 551; *Hewson v Sheehy* (1876) 10 ILTR 173; *Godfrey v Walsh* unreported 1885, referred to [1901] 2 IR at 477
31 [1901] 2 IR 465
32 *Kavanagh v The Leader* supra

to, has chosen not to plead the natural meaning of the words as well. Accommodating a plaintiff here is surely a point at which he is being over favoured.

Assuming that Fisher's decision still stands, and that the previous rule has been reversed, it follows, as a perhaps undesirable consequence, that if there are then two causes of action, the issue must go to the jury as such, with the possibility of separate awards of damages. Such an eventuality has however been criticised in England as 'absurd' because the idea of separate causes of action is only a 'technicality'[33] 'of dubious value',[34] and that 'If you look at the substance of the claim, apart from any technicality, it ... is but one cause of action;' [35] and all the more so where there is 'one plaintiff, one defendant company, one publication and one subject matter'.[36] As well 'there is a risk that two separate awards may introduce an element of double counting',[37] which is not allowable. On these accounts, it has been recommended that there should be a statutory provision allowing only a single right of action for the same publication, irrespective of the number of imputations it contains and giving rise to just one award of damages.[38]

Permitting only one action to be taken in respect of the same statement maybe a good suggestion,[39] but one may criticize the idea of preventing a jury from making different awards for different imputations. It assumes that different imputations can be treated as one when they may clearly differ in the degree of adverse reaction which they provoke. In any case, if only one award were allowed a jury would still, when computing damages, have to treat, to some extent, the different imputations separately, and the risk of double counting may still exist.

Admissibility of opinion evidence of defamatory meaning

Ordinarily, neither the plaintiff nor any witness, including even the recipients of the statement, may be asked what effect the statement had on them with a view to establishing that the statement was defamatory. Such evidence is, however, admissible when it is tendered as proof of the statement's impact on the plaintiff and the recipients

33 *Pedley v Cambridge Newspapers* [1964] 1 WLR 988, 992 per Lord Denning MR
34 *Lewis v Daily Telegraph* [1964] AC 234, 279 per Lord Devlin
35 *Pedley v Cambridge Newspapers* at 991, per Lord Denning MR
36 At 993, per Danckwerts LJ
37 Faulks Committee Report at para 104
38 Faulks supra; ALRC Report at para 91
39 There is already authority to the effect that only one action can be taken — *Walkinshaw v Drew* (1936) 4 DLR 685

of the statement in assessing the amount of damages. The trial judge should be careful when admitting such evidence to instruct the jury that it is admitted for the latter purpose only; although so frequently is such evidence tendered and admitted that one cannot be sure that juries are always as alert, as the rule requires, to the distinction.

Palles CB stated the general exclusionary rule in 1892 'When the libel is entirely expressed in language, the rule of law is that a witness cannot be asked what impression was produced on him by the words, because the jury are the proper tribunal, and the witness would be usurping their province by doing so'.[40] The rule, however, is not a satisfactory one, and there are a number of reasons for suggesting that it should be discarded, and be replaced by an admonition to the jury from the trial judge against attaching too much weight to witness' opinions, and that they are to make their own decision on the matter. Firstly, the prohibition produces some odd consequences. To permit opinion evidence in the assessing of damages it to assume that a jury, aided by a judge, can distinguish between its admissibility for that purpose, and for proving defamatory effect. Yet, no similar assumption is made on the less difficult task of distinguishing between witness' views and making up their own minds as to the defamatory nature of the statement. Secondly, the prohibition seems to imply that witness' expressing views about their reactions to defamatory statements are as likely as not to be unreasonable in the views they express, and that the jury needs to be protected against this. This can have some bizarre consequences. The law assumes, on the one hand, that a plaintiff has a good reputation, yet, on the other hand, it assumes that he is more likely than not to be unreasonable in his fear that his reputation has been damaged. Similarly with the recipients of the statement, how can the assumption of responsibility implicit in the admissibility of their evidence on the extent of the damage to the plaintiff's reputation square with the assumption of unreasonableness on the issue of opinion evidence of defamatory meaning? Thirdly, the prohibition is probably not very effective anyway, partly because, as already indicated, juries may not always appreciate the true reason why such evidence can be admitted, and partly because a jury will be well aware of the views of the plaintiff and his witnesses about the statement, since the case has been taken, the witnesses are all ready to testify, the pleadings state that the statement is defamatory, and the efforts of the plaintiff's counsel to win the case will be obvious. All that the rule does is to occasionally prevent a witness from expressing his view of the statement directly from the witness box.[41]

40 *Kenny v Freemans Journal* (1892) 27 ILTR 8

41 Both the Faulks Committee Report para 103 and the NZ Committee Report paras 81/82 accepted that the present exclusionary rule can be criticised, but

The exceptional instance where opinion evidence of defamatory meaning is admissible is where a meaning that is different from the natural meaning of the statement is ascribed to the statement by means of a true innuendo. Then, once the plaintiff has given evidence of this meaning, and also of the special extrinsic circumstances supporting this meaning, he may prove that persons who received the statement knew the meaning and the circumstances, and understood the statement in the sense which has been attributed to them.[42] To quote again from Palles CB 'The one exception to the rule is that you may prove a special fact the effect of which is to show that the words were used in a different sense from their ordinary meaning, having proved which you may then ask the witness how did you understand the words used?'.[43] However, where no extrinsic evidence has been adduced to give a defamatory meaning to words innocent in themselves, then, as was stated by Johnson J in one case, 'the plaintiff could not legally put the newspaper into the hands of a witness and ask what meaning do you attach to the publication'.[44] An illustrative example of the admission of opinion evidence arose in *Kenny v Freeman's Journal,* where opinion evidence of the meaning of 'Priest-Hunter' was admitted because 'it is a compound word whose meaning is wholly different in collocation'.[45] Also admitted was opinion evidence of the meaning of a cartoon to which words were attached.

It is not clear — due to the absence of judicial explanation — why the exception, as such, is recognised, although it maybe that opinion evidence should always be admissible. Probably the exception exists because how otherwise could a plaintiff convince a judge and jury of the plausibility of a meaning which the statement on its face does not bear. In fact, however, once the judge and jury have been acquainted with the extrinsic circumstances, and the knowledge that the recipients were aware of the latter, they are as well positioned as any recipient was to judge whether the innuendo was so understood. Thus, there may actually be no greater reason for allowing in opinion evidence in this exception than in non innuendo situations.

they still favoured its retention because of fears that its removal might add to the expense and length of a trial, and might also cause confusion to the tribunal of fact.

42 *Kavanagh v The Leader* SCt, unreported, 4 March 1955, per Kingsmill Moore J at p 5

43 *Kenny v Freemans Journal* supra

44 *O'Hea v Guardians, Cork Union* (1893) 32 LR Ir 629, at 643; see also the same judge in Bolton v O'Brien (1885) 16 LR Ir 97 at 124

45 At 9 per Palles CB

False innuendo

A false innuendo meaning is pleaded where there is no gap or distance between the natural meaning of the statement and the one which the plaintiff will rely upon — thus the designation false. The plaintiff will be fearful that other, possibly less defamatory, or even innocent meanings will be found in the statement; or that his interpretation of the statement is not a clear one, and so he will wish the particular meaning or meanings he will rely upon to be emphasised by stating them in an innuendo in the statement of claim. Another reason why a false innuendo may be pleaded is that the defamatory statement may be quite lengthy and contain a great number of imputations, and a plaintiff may wish to facilitate and convenience the hearing by grouping related imputations into categories, and pleading their general meaning in an innuendo. Where a plaintiff relies upon the natural meaning of a statement, there is no question, unlike the true innuendo, of averring and proving any extrinsic evidence to fix that meaning on the statement. It is always a matter of degree whether there is a need for a plaintiff to highlight, explain or clarify a meaning he will rely upon. Pleaders very often think there is. Judges less so. Kingsmill-Moore J thought, in 1955, that 'This second class of innuendo may sometimes be necessary but can be much abused. It is rare to find any statement of claim which does not carry one or more innuendoes by which words, which in their ordinary sense are clearly defamatory, are given a variety of particularised meanings'.[46] A false innuendo may be appropriate where a bank refuses to honour a customer's cheque,[47] or a creditor threatens a debtor with a solicitor,[48] or where a school announces that an application for a course has been rejected, [49] or where an advertisement for solicitors states that those solicitors lately employed by the advertiser need not apply,[50] although a false innuendo might not have been needed where a notice was posted up forbidding soldiers from entering a certain business premises.[51]

There is no particular obligation on a plaintiff to specify in his pleadings the false innuendo that he will rely upon, unless he is asked for better particulars of his claim. On this, the Irish and English rules are similar. However, in England, there has been a judicial addition to the rules by Lord Denning MR in the Court of Appeal, after the House of Lords declined to do so,[52] whereby 'in most cases it is not

46 *Kavanagh v The Leader* supra
47 See *Pyke v Hibernian Bank* [1950] IR 195
48 See *McCann v Edinburgh Roperie* (1891) 28 LR Ir24
49 See *Keogh v Incorporated Dental Hospital* [1910] 2 IR 166, 577
50 See *O'Hea v Guardians, Cork Union* (1893) 32 LR Ir 629
51 *Maguire v Knox* (1870) IR 5 CL 408
52 *Lewis v Daily Telegraph* [196] AC 234

only desirable but absolutely necessary for the plaintiff to set in his pleading the meaning which he says the words bear. At any rate, he should do so when there are two or more meanings which the words bear. The only exception is when there is only one meaning which is clear and explicit'.[53] It is likely that a similar rule could be found here in the court's duty to administer justice if, on suitable facts where particulars of the meaning to be relied upon were not requested, injustice would be done to a defendant who is taken by surprise.

IDENTIFICATION OF THE PERSON DEFAMED

In order to maintain an action in defamation a plaintiff must establish that he is the person referred to in the defamatory statement. He does this when he satisfies the trial judge that he is reasonably capable of being identified from the statement; and when he satisfies the jury that he was in fact the person referred to. He need not show that everyone who received the statement so understood it. It is enough to show that some, even one,[54] so understood it, and if necessary by virtue of facts known only to them. A statement may, on its face, enable identification of a person. It may, for instance, use his name, all[55] or part[56] of it, or his photograph[57] or likeness in a drawing[58], or effigy.[59] Even without these clear indications of reference, there can be an obvious identification from the fact that a statement of, say, accusation is made directly to the person who is defamed.[60]

In many instances, however, where there are none of the obvious *indicia* of identification in the statement, and the statement is not made directly to the person defamed,then identification is only possible by the proof of extrinsic circumstances which coincide, to the necessary degree of proof, with whatever less obvious *indicia* are actually used in the statement and which lead to the conclusion that the statement referred to the person in question. So in *Le Fanu v Malcolmson,*[61] in 1848, where a newspaper article referred to alleged cruelties and abuses in some factories in County Waterford, the owners of factories there were allowed establish by extrinsic evidence that the factories referred to were theirs; in another case,[62] a

53 *Allsop v Church of England Newspaper* [1972] 2 QB 161, 167
54 As in *Sinclair v Gogarty* [1937] IR 377
55 *Currigan v Ryan* (1866) 11 IJ NS 406
56 *Curneen v Sweeney* (1969) 103 ILTR 29
57 *Cooney v Sunday World, The Irish Times,* 8 November 1978
58 *Dunlop v Dunlop Rubber* [1920] 1 IR 280
59 *Edwards v Harding* (1787) Vern & Scriv 99
60 *Maxwell v Gavin Low* SCt, unreported, 11 January 1967
61 (1846) 8 ILR 418; (1848) 1 HLC 637
62 *Campbell v Irish Press* (1956) 90 ILTR 105

journalist was able to establish that an apology printed by his paper, for untruths contained in an article, referred to him by proving that he had written the article. In a Nigerian case,[63] a newspaper article imputed corruption to a recently retired public engineer who had been a government employee for nearly twenty years and who was said to have worked on a particular job and to have owned property in London. This article was held to have referred to the plaintiff when he established that he was the only such recently retired official to fit this description. On the other hand, in a recent action here,[64] a reference in a letter to a newspaper citing another case as an example of a number of lawyers and judges scheming and plotting against the Constitution and family life, was, somehow, found by a jury not to refer to the solicitors who had acted for the plaintiff in that case.

Beyond the types of statement considered so far, there may be other statements which contain no description or any kind of *indicia* of a plaintiff, but which may yet be understood by inference to refer to a person, as where a person could be identified from a statement that a girl was kidnapped last week, by showing that he was seen with her at that time. Although some judges have expressed disquiet that the law would go so far,[65] and have attempted to restrict such a use of extrinsic circumstances to require some real 'key or pointer' in the statement indicating the plaintiff,[66] yet the law has in fact gone so far as to recognise a sufficient identification from such circumstances,[67] regardless of how a reasonable man would react, or at least on a broader view of how he would react.

A defamer who attempts to disguise the direction of his attack by altering some, though of course not all, of the *indicia* of identification will not however escape liability if an identification can still be made from the *indicia* that are unchanged. Thus, in *Sinclair v Gogarty*, in 1937, Hanna J thought of a purported work of fiction 'that there are sufficient *indicia* in the passages to give anyone who knew the

63 *Ukpoma v Daily Times of Nigeria* (1979) 2 LRN 357. See also *East Africa Standard v Gitan* [1970] EA 678, and *Long v Byrne*, The Irish Times, 27 November 1984

64 *Gallagher and Shatter v Independent Newspapers*, The Irish Times, 10 May 1980

65 *Morgan v Odhams Press* [1971] 1 WLR 1239, 1262 per Lord Guest. For a detailed consideration of the identity and innuendo issues raised in this case, see Symmons, 'The Problem of Hidden Reference in Defamation' (1974) Anglo-Am L Rev 98

66 *Morgan v Odhams Press* [1970] 1 WLR 820, 828 per Lord Denning MR in the Court of Appeal. In the US the requirements of the controversial libel per quod rule necessitated proof of special damage in an extrinsic evidence case — Prosser, 'Libel per Quod'(1960) 46 Va L Rev 839. Eldredge 151-176 has, however, doubted the existence and origins of this rule. It appears now to be largely superseded by a constitutional rule requiring proof of actual loss in all media defendant cases. See p. 95 post

67 *Morgan v Odhams Press* [1971] 1 WLR 1239 at 1245 per Lord Reid, 1269 per Lord Pearson

family the necessary clue to their identity. The author, by giving their business place as Sackville Street instead of Grafton Street or Nassau Street, and referring to the Jewish grandfather as a usurer instead of an antique dealer, has only resorted to the usual devices of those who lampoon others and seek to escape liability'.[68] However, too easy a finding of plaintiff identification in works of fiction may be unfair to authors since they all, to some extent,draw on real life for their material. [69] Besides this, an author can claim that a statement was not defamatory of some real person because a reasonable reader would accept that it was written as fiction.

Individual identifiability in a group context

If a statement is made which is defamatory of a group, there are a number of legal consequences that may follow. Firstly, the group itself might sue, but whether it can do so depends on it being either incorporated or being one of that narrowly defined type of unincorporated association that is legally recognised. Secondly, a representative action might be taken by some members of the group on behalf of the rest; or else, all of the members might take separate actions which could be consolidated in one hearing; or further all of the members might sue as joint plaintiffs for a joint tort; finally, an individual member may bring an action on his own behalf. This last consequence is the crucial one because the actionability of each of the variations outlined in the second possibility above depends on this last one.

Whether an individual can bring an action on the basis of a group defamation is a question of fact for a jury to decide after considering the evidence of identification adduced, including the size of the group and the specificity of the charge. But, before the issue can be left to a jury, the trial judge has to decide whether the statement is capable of referring to the individual.

The general rule is that an individual cannot bring an action unless he can establish that there is also, in the circumstances of the case, a reference in the statement to himself. If there is nothing explicitly pointing to the individual, then, in Ireland anyway, the courts have

68 At 380

69 A useful article on this issue is Wilson 'The Law of Libel and the Art of Fiction' (1981) 44 Law & Contemp Problems 27; also Kirby 'Books Bookselling and the Law' (1982) NZLJ 222. In order to protect authors better, and to further society's interest in the benefit to art and culture stemming from fiction, Wilson (at 42) suggests as a test of plaintiff identification — would a reasonable reader consider the plaintiff identified? was the work fiction? and was the characterization intended to defame the plaintiff?

refused to find any such pointer in the mere fact of a group defamation. In *O'Brien v Eason & Son*[70] in 1912, an action by one member of an organisation — the Ancient Order of Hibernians, whose membership 'could be counted, certainly in towns in tens of thousands, probably in hundreds of thousands' — was based on newspaper accusations that members of the organisation had committed crimes and had a rule that they would not talk to Protestants. The action was dismissed. Cherry LJ queried 'How could anybody suspect ... that a general statement that crimes had been committed ... pointed to a certain individual carrying on business as a saddler in Abbey Street, Dublin? There is not the slightest reference to any one individual and not in the most distant way is the plaintiff pointed out'.[71] Many statements derogatory of large groups might also not be actionable because they could only be regarded as being abusive and not defamatory. The decision in O'Briens's case was, of course, based on the assumption that a group defamation does not in itself reflect on the individual members of the group. That is a questionable assumption, both in logic and because there are Scottish,[72] English,[73], American,[74] Canadian,[75] and African[76] cases in which single members of groups of varying size from 'sixty or seventy'[77] down to four have been able to succeed on the basis of group defamation. What distinguished O'Brien's case is the large membership of the group, and the fear of 'probably, 100,000 actions'.[78] Yet some organisations representing thousands of people, like trade unions and public limited companies, are permitted to maintain actions.[79] The only relevant difference between a trade union and an organisation like the AOH is the pseudo corporate status enjoyed by the former by virtue of statutory control. Looked at from the point of view of the average person who may regard each as an identifiable entity, it is questionable whether

70 (1913) 47 ILTR 266. Of the considerable literature on group defamation, see Reisman 'Democracy and Defamation; Control of Group Libel' (1942) Colum L Rev 727; Tannenhaus 'Group Libel' (1950) 35 Corn L Q 261; Fryer 'Group Defamation in England' (1964) 13 Clev-Mar L Rev 51. Only the civil law dimension to the group libel problem is considered in the text. The law of criminal libel is another response to the problem, and is dealt with in the first two articles cited.

71 At 268

72 *Browne v Thomson* (1912) SC 359

73 *Foxcroft v Lacey* (1614) Hobart 89

74 For a list of cases, see Eldredge 60-61, Prosser 784

75 *Ortenburg v Plamondon* (1914) 24 Quebec KB 69; *MacKay v Southam* (1955) I DLR (2d) 1

76 *Dasani v Uganda African Newspapers* [1971] EA 450

77 See Prosser 784

78 Supra, 267 per Holmes LJ

79 See pp. 274, 278 post

such a distinction is a fair basis for denying a right of action to some unincorporated associations but not to others.

Where a group is not inordinately large it may be that a court now would accept that there could be individual reference in a group defamation. That seems to be implied in the unreported *ex tempore* decision against Independent Newspapers in 1975.[80] In that case a newspaper article had suggested that a number of companies in the meat processing industry were falsifying returns in order to claim EC intervention money. All twenty four companies in the industry took an action as joint plaintiffs against the newspaper, and on a preliminary motion relating to discovery of documents, Doyle J held in the High Court that each company had shown a prima facie claim.[81]

These may also be constitutional reasons favouring the acceptance of individual actionability of group defamation. The present rule might involve the denial of two constitutional rights — the right of access to the courts and the right to a good name simply because a defamer was crafty enough to attack only a large group or expressed himself only in the most general terms. It is true that the problem of multiplicity of actions could arise with a large group, and no constitutional policy could favour that. But that is not a sufficient reason to discard logic and attempt to say that individuals in small groups can sue, but not if they are in large ones. Rather, it would justify employing a different remedy where a person belonged to a large group, such as some form of declaratory judgement or correction order, or nominal damages, or even a criminal punishment that would be sought in a representative, joint or consolidated action. At least, the type of inequality which this would involve is probably constitutionally justified, and seems less invidious than the total denial of rights which members of large organisations or groups may suffer.

There are two final points that may be made in this area. Firstly, an apparent exception has already been recognised to the general prohibition on individual actionability of group defamation, and this arises where terms such as each or every are used, and which show a particular reference to all the individuals in the group. It can be argued, however, that this is only a tautology since even without these

80 *The Irish Times*, 8 October1975; *The Irish Times*, 2 December 1975

81 The motion for discovery was taken presumably to determine which companies the defendant's article had referred to. On appeal, the Supreme Court reversed the order of Doyle J for discovery on the ground that the order was not relevant to the plaintiff (the appeal was taken against only one plaintiff) convincing a jury that they had been referred to. The court did not specifically deal with Doyle J's ruling that a prima facie claim had been made but it did seem to indicate that a trial judge could be reasonably satisfied that there was sufficient evidence for the issue of identification to be left to a jury

terms individuals can be defamed by group defamations. Secondly, a statement may refer to only some members of a group and not to all of the group, but without indicating which members are being referred to. In such a case, it has been thought that whether an action may be brought depends on how many were included in or excluded by the statement.[82] If all but one were included, then all could sue, but if just one of many were referred to then none could sue. However, in the case mentioned above, Doyle J in arriving at his conclusion seemed to contravert this view of the law when he stated that if words claimed that A, B, C or D, or some or one of them had stolen a watch, that would give rise to an action by any of the four. This seems the better view because it recognises that although only one person may have taken the watch, suspicion would still attach to them all.[83] The actual damage to reputation, though, might not be so great because of the uncertainty about who is being accused.

82 Prosser supra.
83 Eldredge 61.

4

Publication

It is a fundamental requirement in an action for defamation that a plaintiff establish that there was a publication of the defamatory statement to persons other than himself. This is because 'the cause of action is the publication of the defamatory statement'.[1] The necessity for persons other than the plaintiff to become aware of the statement was stated by Brady CB in a charge to a jury in 1840,

> If a letter..., however slanderous, is received only by the person to whom it is addressed, and does not go beyond him, there is no publication of it in law to support an action for libel'.[2]

So, simply to make up or compose a defamatory statement is not actionable. As Metge B remarked in 1787, in a case concerning publication by effigy, 'The making [of] an effigy is in itself none; a man may make one in his closet for his own amusement, it is the *publishing* that makes the offence'.[3]

The requirement of a publication follows from the fact that reputation consists of the estimation in which others hold a particular person, and not some personal sense of honour, so it can only be as those others become aware of the statement, and react in a reasonable fashion, that damage to reputation can be ascertained. In this emphasis on the knowledge and understanding, though not usually the actual reaction of others, the law uses the term publication

1 *Johnson v Larkin and Gaelic Press* [1926] IR 40, 46 per Fitzgibbon J. In some jurisdictions, such as Scotland — see Norrie, 'Hurts to Character, Honour and Reputation'(1984) Juridical Rev 163 — where the defamation action embraces hurts to dignity, in addition to reputation, there can be an actionable publication to the defamed person alone. With the development of the action for intentional or negligent infliction of emotional distress, our rule of defamation law requiring publication to at least another person, besides the defamed person, could, in time, become redundant. See p. 287 post

2 *Ahern v Maguire* (1840) Arm Mac & Og 39, 42. If, however, the receiver of a letter is blind or illiterate, and the sender should have realised that it would have to be read by some one else, then the sender will be liable for the publication to the reader — see Prosser 802.

3 *Edwards v Harding* (1787) Vern & Scriv 99, 103

in a wider, and older, sense than the layman's usage of the term, which merely refers to the production of printed matter. Confusingly, however, the term is sometimes used in both these senses, and reliance will need to be placed on the context to determine which is the appropriate sense.

There are opposing tendencies in how the law regards an actionable publication. On the one hand, there is the narrow emphasis on the question of persons other than the plaintiff becoming aware of the statement. Thus, the law ignores the actual reaction of the recipients of the statement, except for some exceptional instances referred to later. It also requires, at its lowest, merely a single other person to become aware of the statement,[4] and it does not matter whether the statement is made to the plaintiff or to another, whether in his presence or absence, and whether he appreciates the damage done to his reputation sooner or later. Nor does it matter whether the statement was made in confidence or not, or that it concerns a person's private life, though it may be that the increasing recognition of a general right of privacy will offer an additional cause of action for breach of privacy. Another example of the narrow tendency arises where an employer is held liable for a publication that consists of a communication made by him or by one of his employees, to another employee, regardless of whether the statement is to be passed on, or to be typed or copied and returned.[5] It was argued in an English case that 'the act of one servant in making the report would be the act of the master: and the act of the servant in receiving it and reading it would also be the act of the master. So it would be in law the master making a publication to himself. No one can be made liable for a libel published only to himself'.[6] This, however, was only a minority view, and the majority position was that an employer could be liable for an actionable publication by one employee to another.[7] Thus emphasis was placed only on the fact of publication.

On the other hand, there are certain instances where, although others are made aware of the statement, yet the law will also consider the actual reaction of the recipient of the statement, or the intent or care with which the publisher of the statement acted, with the possible result that no actionable publication will be found despite the fact that there is a publication. These instances, which do not appear to constitute a closed category, reflect a variety of views, such

4 E.g. *Curneen v Sweeney* (1969) 103 ILTR 29
5 E.g. *Pullman v Hill* [1891] 1 QB 524
6 *Riddick v Thames Board Mills* [1977] QB 881, 893, per Lord Denning MR
7 For an account of the authorities, see Stephenson LJ at 898. A similar difference of opinion is evident in the American cases — Prosser 798-9 — with the majority holding that, for example, dictation to an employee is an actionable publication.

as that there should be no liability for uncomprehended or mistaken publication, or for publication by mere distributors unconcerned with actual content.

THE IMPORTANCE OF THE RECIPIENT'S REACTION

In order for a publication to be actionable, it must possess the effect of reducing the recipient's estimation of the subject of the statement. Surprisingly, perhaps, this effect cannot be established by allowing the recipient state his actual reaction because of the fear that in doing this he will usurp the function of the judge or jury.[8] Instead, the recipient may testify that he received the statement, that he understood and believed it, and that he reacted to it, and then the tribunal of fact will decide whether as a reasonable person the recipient actually lowered his opinion of the plaintiff as a result. If, however, it is suggested that the recipient's acceptance of the statement was lacking in any of the respects just mentioned, then evidence of his actual reaction on that point may be admitted. A person may be blind and so not be able to read a libel, or deaf and so not be able to hear a slander. The statement may be made in a foreign language which he does not understand,[9] or a child may be too young to understand words in his own language.[10] A person might not believe a statement that is made to him, though, as a general proposition, defamation law assumes that recipients do believe statements which are made to them. All of such evidence may prevent a publication being held actionable. Another example would arise where the recipient had heard the statement previously, and its present receipt only coincides with, or leaves unchanged his earlier reaction. Where a recipient of a statement was its original author and was merely receiving it back from his typist or copier, that too would not be an actionable publication. In *Eglantine Inn v Smith* in 1947,[11] Andrews LCJ, in the Northern Ireland High Court, refused to regard as actionable the return by printers of handbills to the person who had given them the contract and also the text of the message. 'Were the law otherwise', he remarked, 'a clerk or typist to whom a defamatory statement was handed by his or her employer to be copied would be liable to damages in an action of libel when he handed it back to the employer'.[12]

There does not appear to be any rule requiring the publication

8 See p. 51 supra
9 *Jones v Davies* (1597) Cro Eliz 496; *Price v Jenkins* (1601) Cro Eliz 865
10 See Prosser 798 fn 11
11 [1948] NI 29
12 At 33

to a recipient to be contemporaneous with his alteration of opinion. Time may elapse because the statement was made in a foreign language and needs to be translated, or because when first received, the recipient was performing a mechanical function, such as shorthand note taking, and it would only be afterwards when writing up the notes that the significance of the meaning would be appreciated. The actionable publication in such a case would seem to occur when the recipient appreciated the meaning of the statement, and not when he received it.

THE IMPORTANCE OF THE PUBLISHER'S STATE OF MIND

Unforeseen publication

Where a person directs a defamatory statement towards its subject so that, in the normal course of events, no one else should become aware of it — unless subsequently at the hand of the plaintiff — and, for whatever reason, a third person does become aware of it, then whether the publisher will be held responsible for the unforeseen publication depends on whether he ought to have anticipated what happened. If he ought not to have anticipated it, then he will not be responsible because there is no liability for an accidental and unforeseeable publication. Initially, the trial judge will decide whether the defendant could at all have anticipated the outcome. If he finds that the defendant could have anticipated it, then he will leave it to the jury to decide whether the defendant should have anticipated what happened.

There can be an unforeseen publication for a variety of reasons, such as where a remark is overheard by bystanders, or passers-by, or where the statement is contained in a letter addressed to a named person and which is opened and read by the addressee's employee, or by a member of his family. In the former situation, there is less difficulty in deciding whether a speaker knew or ought to have known that others were sufficiently close that he could be overheard, or whether his voice was louder that it need have been.[13] In the latter situation, however, where there might be no direct evidence as to a publisher's knowledge about who might open his letter, the law decides on what that person ought to have known by allowing inferences to be drawn from his presumed knowledge of certain facts which are held to be common knowledge. One such clear fact of common knowledge is that where a letter is addressed to a business concern — say in the form of 'X & Co'- a defendant will be held

13 E.g. *Maxwell v Gavin Low* HCt, unreported, 11 January 1967

to have appreciated the possibility that the letter may be opened by some employee deputed to do so. In *McCann v Edinburgh Roperie* in 1891,[14] a postcard addressed to 'McCann & Co., Dublin' was delivered to the firm's premises and was read by the firm's manager before he gave it to the plaintiff. An actionable publication to the manager was found; and although the court did not explain its reasoning, in an English case with similar facts,[15] Lord Esher MR explained that 'mercantile firms and large tradesmen generally depute some clerk to open business letters addressed to them. [Here] [t]he sender of the letter ... had directed it in such a manner that it might possibly be opened by a clerk of the firm to which it was addressed'.[16] However, the recognition of this particular fact as a matter of common knowledge depends on how widespread the practice of deputing employees to open mail is in an industry or service. Amongst those that practised dentistry in Dublin in 1908, there was no such presumption applied by the court in *Keogh v Incorporated Dental Hospital.*[17] In that case, a dental school sent a letter rejecting an application to enrol in the school to a person who had practised dentistry for fifteen years, although not a qualified dentist. The letter was opened by a clerk employed by the applicant, and it was attempted to sue for this publication. In rejecting the claim, O'Brien LCJ stated 'No doubt they might have known that the plaintiff practised dentistry work, but they did not know, nor might they have known, nor was there any presumption that they knew, that the plaintiff had a clerk who, in his absence, was authorised to open letters addressed to him'.[18]

Another presumed fact of common knowledge, which was applied in an English case,[19] is that where a woman is known to be married and living with her husband, the husband will open any sealed and unstamped envelopes addressed to her that resemble election literature. This is, however, a questionable presumption.[20] In the US 'it is not reasonable to assume that the father or mother of a 17- or 18 year old girl living with her parents would open and read her letters unless she had authorized them to do so'.[21]

The need to rely on presumed facts like these only arises where there is no direct evidence of the publisher's knowledge that someone else might become aware of the statement.[22] Such direct evidence

14 (1891) 28 LR Ir 24
15 *Pullman v Hill* [1891] 1 QB 524
16 At 528
17 [1910] IR 166, 577
18 At 587
19 *Theaker v Richardson* [1962] 1 WLR 151
20 See the dissent of Ormrod LJ in this case.
21 Stevens, 'The Reputation Rights of Infants' (1975) 9 Family LQ 435, 439
22 *Delacroix v Thevenot* (1817) 2 Stark 63 is a case where there was direct evidence

may be found in the manner in which the letter is addressed, as where, to his disadvantage, the publisher addresses a letter to one brother knowing that it might also refer to another brother,[23] or where, to his advantage, the publisher marks the letter private to prevent its being opened by a clerk.[24] If such a letter was then opened by a clerk, that might well be an unforseen publication for which the sender of the letter would not be liable. Evidence to the advantage of a defamed person can also be found in the manner in which the communication is made, such as by post. Thus, in *Robinson v Jones* in 1879,[25] where an open postcard was sent through the post, Palles CB remarked 'We are bound to take notice of the course of post, and of the stamps of post-offices upon letters; and I cannot see why we are to shut our eyes to a postcard being an unclosed document the writing wherein in necessarily visible to every person through whose hands it passes'.[26]

Distribution of defamatory statements

Since at least 1885,[27] if not before then, in England,[28] and since 1910, in Ireland,[29] the law has recognised that, in the case of distributors of defamatory material who are not the first publishers of it, there is an exception to the general rule that each time another person becomes aware of a defamatory statement there is an actionable publication.

Both the rule and the circumstances which must be established in order to come within the exception were described by Madden J in *Fitzgibbon v Eason & Son* when he stated '... the vendor of a newspaper who, in the ordinary course of business sells or distributes a paper containing a libel, is *prima facie* liable, but can escape liability by showing that he did not know and had no grounds for thinking that the matter was libellous, and that his ignorance was not due to negligence'.[30] Thus, in the leading English decision which established this exception — *Emmens v Pottle* — a plaintiff, who

that the publisher knew that letters were opened by the addressee's employee.

23 *Paul v Holt* (1935) 69 ILTR 157

24 *Pullman v Hill* [1891] 1 QB 524, 529 per Lopez LJ

25 (1879) 4 LR Ir 391

26 Supra 395, 396. According to Prosser 798, most American authority disagrees with this view expressed by Palles CB, and requires some proof that the message was read.

27 *Emmens v Pottle* (1885) 16 QBD 354

28 *Ridgeway v Smith & Son* (1889) 6 TLR 275, 276

29 *Fitzgibbon v Eason & Son* (1910) 45 ILTR 91

30 Supra 91, also *Cooney v Wilson and Henderson* [1913] 2 IR 402, 408 per Holmes LJ; *McCartan v Houlton* (1922) 56 ILTR 131, 133 per Molony LCJ

claimed to have been defamed in a newspaper which the defendant news vendors had sold, failed in his action because the jury found that there was neither knowledge nor carelessness attributable to the defendant's act.

The exception has developed narrowly so far. Print and broadcast media when reporting the statements of others are not regarded as distributors. Printers, whose work is preparatory to distribution, are not usually considered to be within the exception, although, interestingly a New Zealand judge has recently suggested that they may be.[31] Telephone and telegraph companies might be within the exception, but there is little case law on the matter, or indeed on the general subject of the liability of such companies for defamatory publications made by users of their services. These latter instances, particularly, raise difficult legal issues concerning the innocent person or utility who assists, either actively or passively, the distribution of defamatory matter through electronic or other means. While common sense might suggest that there should not be liability in such cases, it is not clear whether that would be because there is no publication by the utility, or if there is, that it is absolutely privileged, or that it comes within the distributor's exception, or is protected by a qualified privilege — which, in the last two cases would mean that liability could be found on some occasions.[32]

Because the defence is an exception to a general rule, the distributor is considered to be prima facie liable; the onus rests on him to produce evidence which brings him within the exception. Palles CB stated that 'the onus lies upon the defendant of convincing the jury that he is within the exceptions....'.[33] There is therefore no legal onus,

31 Prichard J in *Jensen v Clarke* [1982] 2 NZLR 268; this would, however, contrary to the judges view, represent a considerable extension to the exception. It seems that at present printers are often indemnified against liability by their clients.

32 Telegraph companies have been held liable in the US — see Smith, 'Liability of a Telegraph Company for Transmitting a Defamatory Message' (1920) 20 Colum L Rev 30, 369; Eldredge 233-6 — because a message is read when transmitted and there is thus an opportunity to see if it is defamatory However, even if a message appears defamatory some later American authority suggests that if there is some legal duty on the utility to transmit, then there should only be liability if the utility knew that the sender was not acting on a privileged occasion. On a similar basis of liability a telephone company has avoided liability, on appeal, for passively providing a recording facility on which it had been warned a customer was making defamatory statements — see Note 'Must the Telephone Company Censor to Avoid Liability for Libel': *Anderson v New York Telephone* (1974) 38 Albany L Rev 317; Eldredge 440-3. The Second Restatement of Torts s 612 (2) describes the position as follows 'a public utility under a duty to transmit messages is privileged to do so, even though it knows the message to be false and defamatory, unless (a) the sender of the message is not privileged to send it, and (b) the agent who transmits the message knows or has reason to know that the sender is not privileged to publish it' — Eldredge 442

33 *Ross v Eason & Son and The Winning Post* (1911) 45 ILTR 89, 92.

at least initially, on a plaintiff to show evidence of knowledge or carelessness. So, when a judge states that he can find no evidence of carelessness what he actually means is that the defendant has produced evidence of a carefulness which has not been shaken by the plaintiff. Where a distributor seeks to have an action against him stayed on the ground that it is frivolous or vexatious the onus is also on him to produce evidence of ignorance and carefulness, and where no such evidence is adduced, then '[the defendant] is *prima facie* liable. I consider that is enough, and do not go into the point raised by [counsel for the plaintiff] that there were reasons why Eason & Son should in this case have known that the Saturday Review contained a libel'.[34] Where, however, a defendant does adduce evidence of carefulness, the plaintiff may rebut this with evidence of carelessness, as he did, successfully, in *McDermott v Eason & Son*[35] where to the defendant's affidavit evidence that they did not know nor ought they to have know of the libel, the plaintiff was able to adduce evidence showing that the defendant ought to have known of it.

To succeed in the defence, it must be established by the distributor that there was nothing in the work itself, or in the type of work it was, or in the reputation of the author in question, or that there was nothing in the circumstances in which the distributor received or disseminated it, or even more generally, which should have caused him to inspect the publication to see if it contained a libel. It would seem in logic that the distributor may also establish that even if he had inspected the work that he would not have discovered the defamatory statement because it was defamatory only be reference to extrinsic facts which were unknown to him. It is clearly a difficult task for a distributor to know when he should inspect. On the one hand, it does not seem that periodic checks of specimen issues of a work is, without more, either necessary or useful. As was stated by an English judge 'If Messrs. Woolworth had in fact examined specimen magazines that would have no effect unless the libel was contained in the actual magazine which was examined. How would a periodic examination of specimen magazines show that the magazine in question contained a libel?'.[36] A failure to note that the table of contents of a magazine refers to an article that is probably defamatory does not constitute evidence of carelessness unless there was carelessness in not inspecting the magazine in the first place, and the former failure is not evidence of such carelessness.[37] On the other hand, it may be carelessness to never make any checks, and to knowingly run the risk of publishing libels and being sued for

34 *Fitzgibbon v Eason & Son* (1910) 45 ILTR 91 per Madden J
35 (1914) 48 ILTR 1
36 *Bottomley v Woolworth* (1932) 48 TLR 521, 521 per Scrutton LJ
37 *Bottomley v Woolworth* supra

it; in an English case,[38], distributors who admitted to this because the cost of checking was too great were held to have been careless. This particular judgement, however, is not as satisfactory as it might be for it does not state, as in logic it should do, that the libel in question was one which a reasonable inspection would have uncovered.

On balance, the reasonable distributor will be influenced to a considerable extent in deciding whether to inspect by the character of the publication and of its author. Concerning books, an English judge stated 'There were some books as to which there might be a duty on distributing agents to examine them carefully because of their titles or the recognised propensity of their authors to scatter libels abroad', though it does not seem that simply because a book is of the biographical type, and therefore to be expected to contain personal remarks about other persons, that it should therefore be inspected, especially if the work is by 'authors of high character'.[39] Concerning newspapers, Holmes L J stated in 1911, after emphasising the importance of the newspaper's character and reputation, 'I could name newspapers that once flourished but have now ceased to exist, whose circulation depended on the fact that they were to a considerable extent composed of matter what was *prima facie* libellous. A news vendor who sold such papers cannot in my opinion excuse himself on the grounds that he exercised all reasonable care. If he desires to be safe, he ought not to sell them at all'.[40]

Other matters, as well, will influence the reasonable distributor in deciding whether to distribute the work. It may be that the newspaper had published the libel before, and that it was a matter of general knowledge and so the distributor might easily have known about it.[41] It may be that the defamed person had informed the distributor that the paper had previously made an accusation against him and that it was likely to be repeated.[42] It may be that the distributor received the publication accompanied by a circular requesting prominent exposure and 'booming' the story.[43] Finally, it may be that there is a trade magazine in which notices are carried requesting the return of publications that are the subject of defamation

38 *Vizetelly v Mudie's Select Library* [1900] 2 QB 170

39 *Weldon v Times Book* (1911) 28 TLR 143, 144 per Cozens-Hardy MR

40 *Ross v Eason and The Winning Post* at 93; some newsagents have refused to carry particular books because of an apprehended libel content, and have also been reported, on occasion, to require a favourable opinion from counsel, paid for by the publisher, before carrying a work.

41 *Fitzgibbon v Eason & Son* (1910) 45 ILTR 91 per Kenny J

42 *McDermott v Eason & Co* (1914) 48 ILTR 1

43 *McDermott v Eason & Son* supra

allegations or proceedings. Failure to read this — receiving it is not enough — may constitute evidence of carelessness.[44]

PROOF OF PUBLICATION

The publication of a defamatory statement may be established in evidence by proof that, say, words were spoken within earshot of others,[45] or that a document was read aloud,[46] or handed out to passers-by,[47] or that a letter was posted and read,[48] or that a postcard or telegram was posted,[49] or that newspaper was published and read or bought,[50] or that a programme was broadcast and received.[51] On their own, such facts would not establish, what must have been the case, that the recipient of the statement was actually aware of, and understood, the statement. However, in most cases of ordinary facts, it will be likely that the recipient does possess average faculties, and was both aware of and understood the statement. To reflect this likelihood, the law allows a presumption to be drawn, which may be rebutted, so that establishing the factual circumstances of publication will suffice to establish an awareness of the meaning of the statement. Publication may also be established by failure in the defendant's pleadings to deny the assertion of publication in the statement of claim. In practise publication is almost always admitted by media defendants.

It is not clear whether the law recognises any presumption of an actionable publication merely from the fact that an edition of a paper was printed on a particular day, or that a programme was broadcast, although some American courts have recognised such a presumption in the case of newspapers.[52] It might be that, in time, our courts will also recognise a presumption of publication from the fact that an edition of a paper was produced on the day in question, or that a programme was broadcast, since no other inference can seriously be drawn from that fact. There was in the past a statutory procedure, which has since been repealed, which was intended to facilitate proof

44 *Vizetelly v Mudie's Select Library* [1900] 2 QB 170
45 *Wallace v Carroll* (1860) 11 ICLR 485
46 *Robinson v Chambers (No. 2)* [1946] NI 148
47 *Eglantine Inn v Smith* [1948] NI 29
48 *Warren v Warren* (1834) 1 CM & R 250
49 *Robinson v Jones* (1879) 4 LR Ir 391
50 *Duke of Brunswick v Harmer* (1849) 19 LJ QB 20, *R v Harrington* (1889) Judg'ts Sup Cts 211, 220
51 A case of broadcast defamation is *Egan v BBC,* The Irish Times, 12 December 1980
52 E.g. *Witcher v Jones* (1892) 43 NY St Rep 151 See also, Note 'The Single Publication Rule in Libel: A Fiction Misapplied' (1949) 62 Harv L Rev 1041

of publication by newspapers, under which the paper lodged in the Stamp Office a declaration containing its name and other relevant details, and on production at the trial a copy of this declaration together with a copy of the edition of the paper answering to the details in the declaration, it was not necessary for a plaintiff to show that the paper was purchased.[53]

Liability for publication, and for republication by others

Anyone who publishes an actionable defamatory statement, and any non-exempt distributor who assists its circulation, is liable for the damage which is caused by it. In the case of, say, the print media this can render liable the journalist, the letter writer, press or advertising agency, editor, media proprietor, printer and various wholesale and retail distributors. The media proprietor is often the main target of an action, although journalists, editors and printers are also sued. Besides his personal liability, the media proprietor is additionally subject to vicarious liability for the acts of his employees and agents, and probably also any contributors whose remarks are carried by the medium,[54] in the same way as any employer or principal is liable for defamatory remarks made by their employees or agents in the course of their employment.[55] 'If [the proprietor] be satisfied to pocket the profits of the establishment ... and employs others to compose articles for his paper, he must be content to be answerable for the conduct of those to whom he confides the management of his establishment'.[56]

The media proprietor's liability, both personal and vicarious, or that of any media defendant, is a strict one, which takes no account of any degree of fault, or lack of it, on his part, aside that is from the restrictive circumstances in which the defence of unintentional defamation applies.[57] This is a somewhat onerous liability, and there may be some grounds for doubting whether it is a valid one. During live broadcasts the controllers have little control over what the contributors say; the analogy between the broadcasting station's role and that of newsagents is sufficiently close that to deny the defence of innocent publication in the former instance and to allow its use in the latter could be unconstitutionally unequal treatment. A more general constitutional point can also be made. The special reference

53 See *R v Cavendish* (1832) Alc & Nap 76, and *Kirwan v Tully* (1839) Cr & Dix Ab Cas 388
54 See p. 270 post
55 E.g. *Fitzsimmons v Duncan and Kemp & Co* [1908] 2 IR 483, 513, Ct A
56 *R v Edgeworth* (1828) 1 Law Rec 304, 305 per Bushe CJ
57 See p. 229 post

to media rights contained in Article 40. 6 (1) of the Constitution reflects an evaluation of media importance such that any legal rule affecting the media which does not give proper weight to that importance might not be consistent with the constitutional requirement. There is good reason to suspect that this may be so with the strict liability rule since with interests less explicitly, or less favourably, treated by the Constitution — such as many of those balanced by the tort of negligence — a more lenient fault liability is adopted. Media liability should not rest on any basis less favourable than that. This is already the case in the U S, where constitutional protection of the media prevents liability in the absence of some kind of fault.[58]

There is a further instance in which a publisher will be personally liable for the acts of others, and which can consequently greatly increase the number of publications for which may be liable. Holmes LJ stated the position in 1911 'If it is the intention of the person that first promulgates a libel or slander that the publication should be repeated to a particular person, in a particular way, I hold the law to be now settled that such repetition is the joint act of both the original promulgator and the person who repeats'.[59] Although Holmes LJ considered only the liability of the first publisher, it seems reasonable to conclude that in fact the rule would also place a liability on later publishers for publications subsequent to theirs. This would follow from the duty in negligence that a person will be liable for whatever loss results from his failure, as a reasonable person, to foresee the likely outcome of his act. Proof of carelessness by the later, say, media publisher would however be necessary to render him liable for publications subsequent to his own. It may also be noted that for a joint wrongful publication, each of the concurrent wrongdoers is individually liable for the whole of the damage which is caused,[60] in addition to being jointly liable.[61]

As liability only arises for the subsequent acts of publication that were within the publisher's contemplation at the time of the publication, considerable importance attaches to what he intended or knew or ought to have known at that time. An act of republication is clearly within a person's contemplation when he actually requests or authorises it, either expressly, or implicitly. 'A written communication sent to the editor of a periodical, or a statement made to the reporter of a newspaper *with the knowledge in either case that they will be sure to be published,* would be evidence from which a jury

58 See p. 143 post

59 *Ross v Eason and Son and The Winning Post* (1911) 45 ILTR 89, 93

60 Civil Liability Act 1961, s 12(1)

61 The rules on the joinder of defendants, and some other instances of concurrent wrongdoing, are referred to later. See p. 268 post

might infer ... a request to publish it'.[62] Thus, in *Pierce v Ellis* in 1856,[63] a member of a local authority who, after making a speech at a meeting of the body, gave a copy of the speech to a reporter who had asked him for it, was held liable for a publication by the newspaper of a part of his speech.[64] So also a person who makes a complaint to a person in authority about a public official will be taken to have appreciated that in order to investigate the matter it will be necessary for the investigator to show the complaint to others.[65] For these other publications the complainant may be liable. Another example of an implicit authorisation to republish arose in *Fitzsimmons v Duncan and Kemp & Co*,[66] where a form used by credit assessors for obtaining reports from their agents stated: 'The purport of your reply will be communicated to our subscribers only who give us an undertaking to receive same in strict confidence'. The Court of Appeal regarded 'sending information in reply to an inquiry in this form, and for reward, not merely as clear authority to publish .. but as an acceptance of responsibility for the publication when made for the purpose for which the information has been required'.[67]

The original publisher of a defamatory statement will not be liable where the repetition is the voluntary act of a free agent over whom he has no control, and for whose acts he is not responsible, as where other papers, of their own volition pick up a defamatory item carried by the first publisher.[68] Where the republication was also neither requested nor intended nor expected, there will again be no liability. The case of *Coates v Pope*, in 1863,[69] illustrates this well. The defendant wrote a letter of complaint about a rate collector to the Poor Law Commissioners who sanctioned the appointment of rate collectors, although the local authority actually appointed them. After investigation, the Commissioners informed the local authority that they would not sanction the reappointment of the rate collector, who had in the meantime resigned, and they enclosed a copy of the defendant's letter. At the next meeting of the authority, the clerk read out this letter, and the defendant was subsequently held liable in defamation for this publication. However, at another meeting of the authority which could not, although it purported to, deal with

62 *Fitzsimmons v Duncan and Kemp & Co* at 504 per Johnson J, H Ct
63 (1856) 6 ICLR 65
64 See also *Lukidi v Lalobo* [1971] EA 87 where it was stated that authorisation for republication should very readily be implied where a person has agreed to give an interview to a press reporter.
65 *Black v Holmes* (1822) 1 Fox & Sm 28; *Coates v Pope* (1863) 16 ICLR 156
66 [1908] 2 IR 483
67 At 515 per Fitzgibbon LJ
68 *Basse v Toronto Star Newspapers* (1984) 4 DLR (4d) 381
69 (1863) 16 ICLR 156

this matter, the letter was read out again at the request of a member who had not been present at the first reading. An attempt to make the defendant liable for this publication was rejected on appeal because the investigation that has been caused by the letter had been completed. The Commissioners had stated that they would not sanction a re-appointment. 'That second reading became thereupon a new and different publication, connected neither directly nor indirectly with any act of the defendant'.[70]

Where a republication is not identical with the previous publication then whether the earlier publisher continues liable for the republication is a question depending in whether the earlier meaning is largely maintained. If it is, the earlier publisher will be liable. Johnson J stated in Fitzsimmons' case that 'so long as the sense and substance of the defendant's communication by writing or conduct is preserved in the published libel, it is not necessary for the plaintiff ... to prove that the published libel is verbally and literally the identical communication which originated with the defendant'.[71] In that case, though the republication was expressed in different terms from the original and omitted some of the damaging parts of it, it was found to convey the meaning of the original publication, and the original publisher was held liable for it. In Pierce's case,[72] too, the fact that the newspaper printed only parts of the defendant's speech did not prevent the defendant being liable for the republication. Where, however, the part omitted alters the sense of the original statement, then the original publisher might not be liable for the republication.[73]

INDUCED PUBLICATION

On occasion, a person conceiving himself to have been defamed will have no actual proof that the statement was published to others. He may wish then, for the purpose of obtaining such proof, to send an agent to the suspected defamer in order to induce the latter to make the statement to the agent. The question whether proof of publication obtained in this way can constitute evidence upon which an action can be successfully brought, has been differently answered in different jurisdictions.[74] In the USA[75] and Canada, it has been held that where a publication is obtained in this way the defence of consent to publication by the plaintiff can be raised against it. However, this

70 At 166 per Lefroy CJ
71 At 503
72 Supra
73 *Pierce v Ellis* at 67
74 Gatley para 853
75 Eldredge 319-320, Prosser 823

depends on the motive with which the plaintiff instigated the publication. If it was done in order to genuinely discover what was said, then there is a publication to which the defence of consent is not thereby raised. But, if it was done merely for evidential purposes, then the defence may be validly established. So, in the Canadian case of Jones v Brookes[76] in 1974, no actionable publication was found, when a solicitor hired two private detectives to 'check out the slanders' which he believed had been stated of him, because 'The plaintiff had good reason when he sent the detectives to anticipate that the response by the defendants to the inquiries might be defamatory'.[77] It seems harsh indeed that such a view is taken, and that a person, who would only wish to vindicate his good name, should instead find himself further damning the name he seeks to protect.

In Ireland, the law does not regard the inducing of a publication, where otherwise there would be no provable publication, as a consent to the publication, and so no defence can be raised on that ground. This was first established by the Supreme Court in 1929 in *Irish People's Assurance v City of Dublin Assurance*,[78] where, to the defendant's argument that the plaintiff, with knowledge of the likely response, had sent his agents to procure publication, Fitzgibbon J stated 'If this were the law, it would in many cases be impossible for a plaintiff to prove publication at all; and the practice of sending an agent to purchase a copy of a libellous document in order to give formal proof of publication is so notorious and universal, and well recognised, that it would not be surprising if no one had thought it worthwhile to report a case on the point'.[79] Since 1961, the law here would also be based on s.34 of the Civil Liability Act of that year, which has been interpreted to mean that a waiver by a person of a legal right to sue, and constituting a complete defence to an action, only arises where there is an express statement to that effect actually communicated before the wrongful act.[80] An implicit communication, such as an induced publication, would not then appear to raise the statutory defence.

It may, nonetheless, be undesirable for the law to sanction the use of induced publication since it involves playing a trick, or deceiving another, even if it is done for understandable reasons. This could be reflected in the size of a jury award,[81] or in whether a court ought to grant an injunction in lieu of damages. A defendant might

76 (1974) 45 DLR (3d) 413; See also Linden, *Canadian Tort Law* 3rd Ed, 716
77 Supra 420 per MacPherson J
78 [1929] IR 25
79 Supra 37. For the defence of consent see p. 227 post
80 *O'Hanlon v ESB* [1969] IR 75; *McComiskey v McDermott* [1974] IR 75
81 *Irish People's Assurance v City of Dublin Assurance* at 40, Murnaghan J, dissenting

even argue that the agent sent to encourage the publication could not consider it defamatory, or had heard it before from the plaintiff, so that his only reaction to the induced publication was either disbelief, or coincided with, and did not differ from, his earlier opinion. A possible solution to the problem would be the recognition of a rebuttable presumption of publication to operate in cases where a person cannot reasonably establish the fact of publication, but can reasonably establish the liklehood of it from all the circumstances, including the existence of rumours, ostracism, or actual loss.

MULTIPLE PUBLICATION

Every time a defamatory statement is published to another person, a new cause of action arises in respect of that publication.[82] Because of the number of people who may buy or read a newspaper, or who receive a broadcast, the number of actions that could result from the issue of a single edition of a newspaper, or a single broadcast, could be great indeed. This could be further increased due to the fact that some newspapers carry stories published by others. When one adds to this the liklihood of future repetition, particularly of broadcasts, plays and books, the action in defamation would see a young man grow old, passing his time in litigation! Plainly, such an absurdity would not be allowed. At present, however there is nothing in the formal elements of the defamation action which would prevent this, aside, that is, from the practice whereby plaintiffs who are defamed in the media are content in single completed proceedings to recover compensation for all foreseeable present and future damage caused by an entire edition or a broadcast. What would have to be relied on is the common law doctrine of abuse of legal process, which would stop a multiplicity of litigation,[83] eventually, and it would do so because a time would come when the enforcement of a person's right to a good name would begin to unjustly burden the time, resources and contentment of the wrongdoer. A wrongdoer is entitled to the security of knowing that at some point he will have finished paying for his wrong, and so can conduct his lawful business without uncertainty and worry. The point at which litigation begins to become an abuse of process must depend on the facts of each case, and the more damaging, widely circulated and likely to be repeated a charge is, the more likely it is that the point will be reached later rather

82 E.g. *McDonagh v Tarpey* [1933] IR 666; *Duke of Brunswick v Harmer* (1849) 9 LJQB 20

83 *Goldsmith v Sperrings* [1977] 1 WLR 478. For another method, that of unanticipated republication, see *Coates v Pope* (1869) 16 ICLR 156

than sooner. It does not seem that, in Ireland or England,[84] the possibility of numerous actions resulting from multiple publication has produced especial difficulties for the media, although it does happen that actions are taken against different media for publishing the same statement.[85] In multi state jurisdictions, such as Australia and the US, the problem can become acute because individual states can have different defamation rules with the possible result that there may be liability for the same statement in one jurisdiction, but not in another.[86] There is the potential for a similar problem within the European Community, where there is already a considerable trans-national trade in news and information — and it may be that in the long term an EC directive may be needed to standardize, amongst other things, publication liability rules.

For the present, the media may still unhappily face the possibility of a multiplicity of proceedings stemming from a single person, and can rely only on that person choosing to be satisfied with a single action, or on the subjective decision of a judge whether the litigation has become excessive. There is a considerable consensus of opinion that the media deserve some formal protection, and a variety of different responses have been suggested. In the US a number of jurisdictions have adopted a single publication rule, under which the entire edition of a newspaper, book, or magazine, or a single broadcast may be treated as a single publication giving rise to one action only.[87] All of the reform bodies are agreed in also recommending a single action for an entire edition or broadcast,[88] and on the inclusion in that action of liability for future publications of the statement.[89] They also agree, however, that some leeway — involving preliminary court approval — for future actions ought still to be allowed to cater for unforeseen existing or future publications. In contrast to this, some jurisdictions operate short and inflexible

84 Faulks Committee Report para 290

85 E.g. See the newspaper report of *Lindsay v Maher*, The Irish Times, 3 February 1984; a procedural rule which attempts to indirectly make it less attractive to launch a miltiplicity of proceedings against one or more parties stemming from the same defamatory statement is s 26 Defamation Act 1961, which allows in mitigation of damages evidence of other damages recovered. See p. 253 post.

86 See ALRC Report para 109. The closest to the problem that arises here is when, as has happened, a newspaper is sued in both Northern Ireland and the Republic for the same defamatory statement. See *Deighan v Sunday Newspapers*, HCt (N.I.), 15 May 1987.

87 Eldredge 209-217; Prosser 800-801, Note 'The Single Publication Rule in Libel; A Fiction Misapplied'(1949) 62 Harv L Rev 1041. A similar rule also exists in some Canadian jurisdictions — *Thomson v Lambert* (1938) 2 DLR 545

88 Faulks Committee Report para 290; NZ Committee Report 320; ALRC Report para 113

89 Despite the difficulty that exists in estimating the extent of future publication and in measuring damages for it — see Note supra 1046

limitation periods as a means of ensuring media security. In Ontario, for example, actions must not only be started within three months of the person becoming aware of the publication, but must be preceded by a written notice of complaint to the medium delivered within six weeks of that date.[90] As regards multiple publication by other media, New Zealand has operated a rule since 1954 whereby when an action is taken against a newspaper there is a prohibition on any other actions being taken against other newspapers for the same statement more than thirty days after the first action is started.[91]

In Ireland it seems likely that constitutional protection of the media may have some bearing on the common law rule which gives rise to the media's problems with multiple publication. The common law rule is not only clearly inimical to various media entitlements, it even exists as though those entitlements are of no greater account than they are with the average person. This is clearly fallacious. The explicit constitutional recognition of the importance of the media in Irish society suggests that special account should be taken of those entitlements, and a rule like the present which is overly threatening to them might not do that.

90 Ss 5 (1), 6 Libel and Slander Act 1980 RSO. See also Linden 692 fn 138, Note supra 1045

91 S 9 Defamation Act 1954; NZ Committee Report para 316.

5

Slander and Libel

A defamatory statement may be either a slander or a libel. These are two distinct causes of action, even where the same statement is published as a slander and as a libel.[1] If a statement is a slander, then, depending on the circumstances, it can either be actionable per se — that is to say, a plaintiff will not need to show any particular loss resulting from the publication to succeed in his claim; or it can be such that a plaintiff will need to show special damage in order to succeed. A libel, on the other hand, never requires the proof of any particular loss in order to be actionable. Thus, it may happen that an expression, which if spoken, would not be actionable, yet, if contained in a written document, would be.[2] The existence of these differences, both between the various slanders and as between slander and libel, is not based on any particular logic other than that which results from the historical development of the law.

In this situation any attempt to describe the distinction will be a difficult and unsatisfactory one. Hopefully, in the future, it may also be unnecessary, for the reform bodies in the jurisdictions where the distinction still remains have recommended its abolition and have suggested that instead all slanders should become actionable in themselves.[3] But, though the distinction may be likely to go, it is still the law and can have important consequences in respect of proof of damage and the starting point and length of the limitation period. It needs therefore to be considered. Similar considerations apply to the distinction between slanders actionable per se and those not so.

DISTINGUISHING BETWEEN SLANDER AND LIBEL

The distinction between slander and libel is the product of history and expediency.[4] Ever since a law of libel was purposively and

1 *Smith v Corr* [1937] IR 248.
2 *Crotty v McMahon* (1834) 1 Jones 465, 478 per Joy CB.
3 See p. 94 post.
4 For an account of the development of the law see Holdsworth, *History of English*

inelegantly introduced into English law in the early seventeenth century, and was later matched up with an existing jurisdiction for slander, there has not been a single or constant meaning accorded to the terms slander and libel. A slander could be both oral and written,[5] and so could a libel.[6] Prior to the end of the nineteenth century, the distinction was sometimes perceived to rest in a greater capacity for damage in a libel, or in a lesser malignity of purpose in a slander. For example, as late as 1848, an Irish commentator put it thus '[Slander] passes away with the storm that gives it birth. Written calumny is different: it implies cool design and is therefore the more deliberately malicious'.[7] The use of the two terms did become more settled towards the latter half of the nineteenth century, and it is mainly by relying on decisions in the last hundred years or so that one can determine the meaning of these terms.

In the cases in which a person has been libelled many of the media by which the statements were published were both permanent and visible in form. Thus libels have been contained in books,[8] newspapers,[9] magazines,[10] advertisements,[11] leaflets,[12] pamphlets and posters,[13] photographs,[14] cartoons,[15] caricatures,[16] and effigies.[17] It has also been stated that defamation by statute would be a libel.[18] Most slanders, being spoken were ephemeral and audible. Gestures, however, were considered to be slander,[19] even though visible. In one Circuit Court action,[20] a plaintiff succeeded in a claim for slander for words suggesting that she had married because she was pregnant and for a gesture made by the defendant at the time of speaking indicating pregnancy. Furthermore, the artificial definition

Law Vol 8, 333-379; Veeder, 'The History of the Law of Defamation' (1909) *Select Essays in Anglo-American Legal History* Vol 3, 440; Carr 'The Engish Law of Defamation with especial reference to the distinction between Libel and Slander' (1902) 18 LQR 255; Kaye 'Libel and Slander — Two Torts or One?' (1975) 91 LQR 524.

5 *Crotty v McMahon* (1834) 1 Jones 465, 478 per Joy CB; *Barrett v Long* (1846) 8 ILR 331, 335 per Jackson J.

6 See Kaye 530.

7 Napier 'Lecture on the Law of Defamation' (1840) 1 Leg Rep 129, 131.

8 E.g. *Sinclair v Gogarty* [1937] IR 377.

9 E.g. *Bolton v O'Brien* (1885) 16 LR Ir 97, 483.

10 E.g. *Quigley v Creation Ltd* [1971] IR 269.

11 E.g. *Tolley v Fry* [1931] AC 333.

12 E.g. *Eglantine Inn v Smith* [1948] NI 29.

13 E.g. *Cooney v Wilson and Henderson* [1913] 2 IR 402.

14 E.g. *Berry v Irish Times* [1973] IR 368.

15 E.g. *Kenny v Freemans Journal* (1892) 27 ILTR 8.

16 E.g. *Dunlop v Dunlop Rubber* [1920] 1 IR 280.

17 E.g. *Edwards v Harding* (1787) Vern & Scriv 99.

18 *Dunlop v Dunlop Rubber* at 290 per Powell J.

19 Gatley para 142.

20 *Kavanagh v Lowry*, Meath Chronicle, 19 February 1980.

of 'words' used in s 14 (2) of the Defamation Act 1961 for the purposes of Part II of that Act includes gestures. A defamatory act or action, while it will normally require an innuendo to make it actionable, is also regarded as slander, or of the nature of slander, though it is unusual not to find some printed or spoken words accompanying the act which can be fixed on to base an action.[21] So, the permanency of the means of commmunication rather than its visibility is the criterion of a libel, and transitoriness rather than audibility is the criterion of slander.

This distinction was satisfactory, as far as it went. The development of electronic media of communication posed, however, new difficulties for the distinction between libel and slander, and necessitated a more acute analysis of the manner in which a person may be defamed. Hitherto, the law did not need to make any distinction between the form of a statement and the means by which it was communicated because with spoken and printed words they were the same; nor had the law to consider which of these two features of a statement was the crucial one for legal purposes. The new electronic media did, however, require some distinction to be made between the two since in the case of say, films and records, the form of the statement could be permanent but the means of communicating it could be transitory. If the law maintained a simple focus on the latter aspect — as in logic it might have done — the possibly greater degree of damage to reputation caused by a film would have had to be litigated through the less advantageous slander action. It was to avoid such a result that both judiciary and legislature adopted the pragmatic view that with the new media emphasis should be laid on the form of the statement, and not on the means of communication.

The result was that in the English case of *Youssoupoff v MGM* (1933)[22] defamation by moving film was treated as a libel, and the Oireachtas, when following English legislation based on the Porter Committee Report, enacted in s.15 of the Defamation Act 1961 that 'For the purposes of the law of libel and slander the broadcasting of words by means of wireless telegraphy shall be treated as publication in permanent form'.[23] This peculiar approach towards ensuring that

21 *Corliss and Diggin v Ireland*, HCt, unreported, 23 July 1984 is a recent case where the act of transferring a Garda from one section to another was held to be of the nature of a slander. The act of an electronic security system in a shop erroneously going off might also be actionable as slander.

22 (1933) 50 TLR 581; while the statement in that case might not have included the sound track, American authority is clear that defamation by 'talking picture' is a libel — Prosser 787.

23 'Wireless telegraphy' is defined by the Broadcasting Act 1926 as, essentially, involving communication by radiated electromagnetic waves. This suggests that defamatory radio messages involving taxis, gardaí, airplanes and ships are libels. Defamatory communication by telegram and telephone, which may involve

broadcast defamation is libel has at least the merit of avoiding the uncertainty of the bewildering American state response to broadcast defamation[24] and has become so accepted that a Ugandan court in 1972 was able, without any statutory equivalent to s.15 to hold that the broadcasting of a defamatory song was a libel.[25] Other forms of defamatory information transfer, such as a statement on a computer visual display unit, are likely to be treated as a libel.[26] Even in the non electronic area the emphasis on form prevails. A Northern Ireland court in 1946[27] held that reading aloud a defamatory document was a libel and not a slander.

SLANDER

Ever since the middle of the sixteenth century when the common law courts started hearing slander actions to protect reputation, it has been established that, within this area, a distinction is drawn between slanders which are actionable because they were spoken, and slanders which are actionable because they also caused special damage. The special damage required was, and is, some real material loss and not just a loss of society or friendship. In its original distinction just three types of slander were actionable in themselves. These were (1) words which imputed the commission of a criminal offence, (2) words which imputed the possession of a contagious disease, and (3) words which tended to cause injury in the way of one's office, profession, calling, trade or business. A fourth type of slander was added by statute in 1891, and re-enacted in s 16 of the Defamation Act 1961, and concerns words which impute adultery or unchastity in a woman or girl.

One cannot be sure how the distinction between the various slanders came to be established.[28] Not enough is known about that formative period in the sixteenth century. The requirement of special damage may have originated from the assumption by the common law courts

communication by wires, may also be regarded as libel by virtue of s 14 (3) of the 1961 Act, which seems to equate telegraphy with wireless telegraphy for the purposes of the Act. S 14 (3) also appears to suggest that where a telephone system is purely internal and requires no statutory licence a defamatory communication might be slander, and not libel.

24 Described by Eldredge 81-90; Prosser 787; a new term 'defamacast' has even been coined to meet the problem.

25 *Olowo v AG* [1972] EA 311, 312 per Russel Ag J. In light of this trend, doubts whether the sound track of a film, record, or tape is a libel do not seem justified.

26 Scott *Computer Law* 724.

27 *Robinson v Chambers* [1946] NI 148.

28 See Holdsworth 'Defamation in the Sixteenth and Seventeenth Centuries' (1924) 40 LQR 397; Veeder supra 457; Kaye supra 527.

of a slander jurisdiction from ecclesiastical courts, with a consequent need for temporal loss to be shown to succeed in an action. The fact that new actions, at that time, had also to be laid as actions on the case, and not trespass, may have contributed to this. The more numerous slanders actionable in themselves may have pre-dated the other type in the secular courts, and may have been too well recognised as capable of causing loss to require any formal proof.

Words imputing a criminal offence

Where words are spoken which impute the commission of a criminal offence which is punishable corporally, as by a term of imprisonment, they are actionable in themselves. The most frequently imputed offence is that of stealing.[29] Other offences which have been imputed are atttempted stealing,[30] receiving stolen property,[31] obtaining money[32] or goods[33] by false pretences, blackmail,[34] indecent exposure,[35] perjury,[36] and arson.[37].

Whether an accusation of wrongdoing amounts to a criminal offence or not depends to a considerable extent on the circumstances in which the statement was made, and on the state of the changeable criminal law at the time of speaking. Words which prima facie might impute a crime might not be held actionable if, on a consideration of all the circumstances, no reasonable person could conclude that criminal wrongdoing was intended.[38] A statement might only be abusive, so an accusation that a woman was a whore and a vagabond was held not actionable and only abusive.[39] Differing conclusions can be reached on differing facts. On its own, an imputation of swindling may well not impute a criminal offence. 'If a man gives you a verbal promise that he will repay you money he borrows on a certain day, and he does not, he may be a "swindler", yet he has not been guilty of an ... offence'.[40] But if the accusation is allied with circumstances

29 *McFadden v Lynch* (1883) 17 ILTR 93; *Ede v Scott* (1858) 7 ICLR 607; *Wallace v Carroll* (1860) 11 ICLR 485; *Corcoran v W & R Jacob* [1945] IR 446; *Boland v Tara Mines* The Irish Times, 3 March 1984.
30 *Bell v Parke* (1859) 10 ICLR 279; *Dempsey v Wall & Co and Ryan* (1943) 78 ILTR 73.
31 *Sevenoaks v Latimer* (1919) 54 ILTR 11.
32 *Kirkwood-Hackett v Tierney* [1952] IR 158.
33 *Barton v Doran* (1932) LJ Ir 124.
34 *Hartery v Welltrade* HCt, unreported, 15 March 1978.
35 *Torbitt v Clare* (1846) 9 ILR 86.
36 *Keenan v Wallace* (1916) 51 ILTR 19.
37 *O'Connor v Lloyd* (1830) 2 Hud & Br 626.
38 *Campbell v White* (1856) 5 ICLR 312, per Pigott CB; *Torbitt v Clare* supra.
39 *Campbell v White* supra.
40 *Black v Hunt* (1878) 2 LR Ir 10 per Fitzgerald J.

more clearly suggesting criminal wrongdoing, then the accused may be guilty of the offence of obtaining by false pretences.[41] Another example concerns accusations of theft. In one case an accusation of theft was held not actionable because 'the word thief is ambiguous' and because it 'does not necessarily imply an act punishable by law'.[42] But, in another,[43] where a person was accused of being a pickpocket, and it was pleaded that this meant that he was a thief, the court held the words actionable in themselves after discovering a statutory reference to a felony of theft. Lefroy CJ stated 'as we are to interpret the words in their ordinary sense, the word pickpocket is equivalent to the word thief; and the word thief is equivalent to a person who steals money ...'.[44] Nowadays courts might more easily be satisfied that theft suggests larceny, when for example, a customer is wrongly accused of stealing from a shop.[45] A statement might also not be actionable because the act imputed has ceased to be criminal. Thus reputed thieves who loiter would no longer be criminal vagabonds.[46]

The words used by the defendant do not have to name the criminal offence in its terms. It is enough that a reasonable person could consider that they imputed either particular[47] or general[48] criminal wrongdoing. A plaintiff may, if he wishes, by innuendo, state in his pleadings what the offence was. But, according to Keogh J in 1877, he does not have to identify the particular offence in his pleading if he does not wish to, 'The practice is now long established that it is sufficient to charge that the words impute an ... offence'.[49] However it may still be that if a refusal to supply such information would prejudice a defendant in conducting his defence, he might well be entitled to this information under O 19 of the Rules of the Superior Courts.

It is the function of the judge to decide whether the words used, and the innuendo if any, are capable of imputing the offence, and it is the function of the jury to determine whether the words actually did impute the offence.[50]

41 *Kinahan v McCullough* (1877) 11 CL 1.
42 *Sayers v Bachelor* (1855) 7 IJ OS 257.
43 *Henderson v Boyd* (1857) 3 IJ NS 27.
44 At 28; see also *Paris v George* (1939-49) ALR SL 57.
45 E.g. *Kilbride v R J F Security,* The Irish Times, 24 July 1985.
46 *King v AG* [1981] IR 233.
47 *Odongkara v Asltes* [1970] EA 374.
48 *Gray v Jones* [1939] 1 AER 798; cf *Conyd v Brekelamans* (1971) 18 DLR (3d) 366. Where the act is alleged to have been committed abroad, its criminal character is to be determined by local law — Prosser 789.
49 *Kinahan v McCullagh* (1877) IR 11 CL 1, 3.
50 E.g. *Kinahan v McCullagh.*

The imputed offence must carry with it the possibility that, if charged and convicted, a person could be imprisoned or hanged or suffer some other form of corporal punishment. If the only punishment is a fine, or where imprisonment may be imposed but only in default of paying a fine — 'if the offender has the right by the payment of money to escape imprisonment'[51] — then, the words are not actionable per se and special damage is needed to make them actionable. In *McCabe v Foot* in 1865,[52] an action for the words 'I heard that Daniel McCabe and Timothy Callaghan drew the River Blackwater with a net at night' was dismissed because conviction for the statutory offence imputed by these words could only result in a fine and confiscation of the offending implements, but not imprisonment.

Conflicting views have been expressed about the theory which underlies the actionability in itself of slanders imputing crimes punishable by imprisonment. On the one hand, it is said that such words are actionable because they place in jeopardy a person's freedom or physical wellbeing.[53] On the other hand, it has been said that the words are actionable because they leave a person open to the possibility of social ostracism.[54] It is only on the basis of the latter theory that statements that a person had in the past been convicted of an offence and served a term of imprisonment were held actionable in themselves.[55]

It was thought for a time, in the last century, that the offence imputed had to be an indictable one,[56] but there was no basis in the origins of the action for this view, and this was recognised by an English court, in 1883,[57] when it was held that the test was merely whether a person could be made to suffer corporally for the offence. As a result, the courts did not have to face the problem posed by statutory offences which can be tried either summarily or on indictment depending on the choice of the prosecution.

51 *Yasseen v Persaud* (1979) 24 WIR 242, 255 per Haynes C. In some US States, according to Prosser 789, 'moral turpitude' is the condition that must be met either alone, or in some cases as an alternative to 'infamous punishment'.

52 11 IJNS 287.

53 *Heming v Power* (1842) 10 M & W 564, *Carslake v Mapledoram* (1788) 2 TR 473; see also *Holt v Scholefield* (1796) 6 TR 691, *Onslow v Horne* (1771) 3 Wilson 177; also Holdsworth supra 398, 399; Carr supra 257.

54 *Fowler v Dowdney* (1838) 2 Moo & Rob 119, *Grey v Jones* supra, *Boston v Tatum* (1622) Cro Jac 623.

55 *Gainsford v Tuke* (1620) Cro Jac 536; or had been pardoned, or whose prosecution was time barred — Prosser 788.

56 Cases which referred to this test were *Currigan v Ryan* (1865) 11 IJ NS 406 and *Kinahan v McCullough* supra.

57 *Webb v Beavan* (1883) 11 QBD 609.

However, marginal enquiries may still be neccesary with some offences that do not carry the punishment of imprisonment on a first, or even a second, conviction but do so for a third or subsequent conviction.[58] In such a case, where the accusation expressly refers to the correct number of previous convictions, then it is clearly actionable in itself. But where, as in a West Indies case *Yasseen v Persaud*,[59] in 1979, an accusation only refers to the present offence and not to any previous convictions, then the accusation will not be actionable in itself. A court will not assume that the necessary number of previous convictions were implied in the statement,[60] and nor will it either enlarge the category of statements actionable in themselves, so as to include the statement. When determining whether a statement imputed the necessary kind of offence, the court in Yasseen's case appeared to suggest that cognisance could only be taken of the actual statement itself without reference to the surrounding circumstances; so that where a plaintiff actually had the necessary number of convictions the statement might still not be actionable in itself because that fact was not mentioned in the statement. It is difficult to see how such a view could be correct. The existence of previous convictions is an objective matter of fact, and a defamer's knowledge of, or reference to them seems irrelevant. All that ought to be necessary, one suggests, is that the court determine whether the plaintiff had the necessary number of previous convictions, and if he had, to hold the statement actionable regardless of whether the defamer knew of this. Whether an action would still be brought is, however, problematic, since with his previous convictions the plaintiff would hardly have much of a reputation to protect in respect of that activity.

Words imputing an infectious disorder

Where words are spoken which impute a disease or disorder which is infectious and which could result in a person being shunned or avoided, then the words are actionable in themselves. There have been no reported Irish cases on this, although the actionability here of these words has been acknowledged.[61] In some old English cases,

58 An example of an offence allowing imprisonment only on a third or subsequent conviction is contained in s 27 (1) (a) of the Misuse of Drugs Act 1977, as ammended by s 6 of the Misuse of Drugs Act 1984.

59 (1979) 24 WIR 242.

60 *Ormiston v Great Western Rly* [1917] 1 KB 598, 601.

61 *Barrett v Long* (1846) 8 ILR 331, 335 per Jackson J.

accusations of French pox,[62] and leprosy,[63] but not small pox,[64] were held actionable in themselves. There is little modern authority for this action,[65] perhaps because, as Prosser comments,[66] the advance of medical science has tended to limit the incidence of contagious disease. The present category of slander actionable per se seems however suited to protect those wrongly accused of having the presently incurable AIDS from the serious ostracism that can occur as a result of the accusation. Conflicting views have also been expressed concerning the basis on which accusations of these diseases are actionable in themselves — whether it is the reflection, if any, caused by possession of the disease on the moral character of the accused,[67] or whether it is the undesirable consequences of being avoided and outcast through fear of infection.[68] Although some authority supports the first view, it seems more likely that the second is the true basis of the action, particularly since imputations that a person had had the pox in the past are not considered actionable in themselves.[69] The old view — that an imputation of the plague was actionable in itself — suggests[70] that imputations of contagious skin complaints caused by personal uncleanliness are also actionable in themselves. Indeed, it would seem that the imputation of any contagious infection — however curable and transitory the illness — is actionable in itself. The more restrictive view that it was the 'permanent lingering and incurable' nature of a disease that rendered an imputation actionable[71] does not seem valid now, not least because of the continued acceptance that imputations of venereal disease are actionable in themselves, although venereal disease need not be either permanent, lingering or incurable.

Words injurious of a person in his office, etc

Where words are spoken which tend to injure a person in the course of his office, profession, calling, trade or business, they are actionable

62 *Crittal v Horner* (1614) Hobart 219, *Smith v Hodson* (1791) 4 TR 211, *Bloodworth v Gray* (1844) 7 M & Gr 334, *Grimes v Lovell* (1699) 1 Ld Ray 446.
63 *Taylor v Perkins* (1607) Cro Jac 144.
64 *James v Rutlech* (1599) 4 Co Rep 17.
65 One case is *Houseman v Coulson* (1948) 2 DLR 62.
66 Prosser 790.
67 Holdsworth supra 400, fn 3.
68 *Crittal v Horner* supra, *Taylor v Hall* (1743) 2 Strange 1189, *Carslake v Mapledoram* supra.
69 Carslake's case, supra; Taylor's case supra. See also March *Actions for slander* 105.
70 Porter Committee Report para 45.
71 Prosser 790.

in themselves. So provides s.19 of the Defamation Act 1961, which altered significantly the previous rule. Until then, a plaintiff had to establish two things in order to succeed in a claim for words which injured him in his occupation: firstly that the words were spoken of him in the way or context of his position and, secondly, that the words were likely to injure him in that position. Under the first proof, a plaintiff would show that, in being spoken, the words suggested the lack of a requisite for a particular occupation, and this, of course, required the courts to identify whether a particular trait or skill was necessary for the occupation. Thus, a state of chastity was found necessary for a female domestic servant,[72] and for a member of the Garda Siochana;[73] a solicitor needed to be honest and to be able to identify what court to bring a claim,[74] and an auctioneer would need to hand over the proceeds of a sale to a seller.[75] On the other hand, although words might be damaging generally, they were not actionable if they did not suggest the absence of qualities essential to the occupation. Courts held, effectively, that a cabinet maker, while needing to be skilled and able, did not apparently need to be honest;[76] a religious novice would not necessarily be affected by an imputation of unchastity while outside her convent;[77] a public works contractor did not need to be absolutely worthy for he could be corrupt, short of being criminally corrupt;[78] and a painter did not have to be in a trade union for 'how can it be said that they imply the want of any of those qualities which a house painter ought to possess?'[79].

In reasoning so particularly the courts were not unaware that this first requirement was not based on reason[80] — for to focus only on imputations relating to matters essential to a position was to ignore that the public would judge by these, it is true, but also by more as well, such as a person's general character of fitness or conduct. However, the essentially English view was taken that the artificiality of the rule was only a reason not to allow it be extended, though still to apply it, and to leave it to the legislature to make any desired changes. The Porter Committee observing the 'serious injustice'[81]

72 *Connors v Justice* (1862) 13 ICLR 451; 'Can anyone doubt that chastity is an essential requisite in a female domestic servant?' per Monahan CJ at 454.
73 *Devine v Keane* (1927) 61 ILTR 118.
74 *Bennett v Quane* (1947) IJR 28.
75 *McDougall v Tyrrell* (1855) 1 IJ NS 465.
76 *Sayers v Bachelor* (1855) 7 IJ OS 257.
77 *Dwyer v Meehan* (1886) 18 LR Ir 138.
78 *Crawford and Frame v Vance* [1908] 2 IR 521.
79 *McMullan v Mulhall* [1929] IR 470, 484 per Fitzgibbon J.
80 *Alexander v Jenkins* [1892] 1 QB 797, 801, per Lord Herschell; McMullan's case, supra, 482 pre Fitzgibbon,J; 485 per Murnaghan J.
81 Para 48.

caused by the rule, recommended that it be abolished. This was given effect to here, in s 19 of the Defamation Act 1961 which states: 'In an action for slander in respect of words calculated to disparage the plaintiff in any office, profession, calling, trade or business held or carried on by him at the time of the publication, it shall not be necessary to allege or prove special damage, whether or not the words are spoken of the plaintiff in the way of his office, profession, calling, trade or business'.

Under the law at present only the second proof referred to above need be established. If it is a consequence of the speaking of words that they could reasonably damage a person's position of employment, then the words are actionable in themselves. Thus, in addition to the imputations already referred to and held actionable, it is actionable to state that a nursery governess was unfit to attend on young ladies,[82] or that a solicitor was dishonest and untrustworthy,[83] or that a wine merchant would supply sherry of an inferior quality instead of the agreed wine,[84] or that a guano merchant robbed farmers by selling bad guano,[85] or that a company was insolvent and unworthy of trust and on the brink of bankruptcy.[86]

A distinction has been made between imputations against the holders of offices for profit, and the holders of offices of honour or credit. If the former kind of office were involved, then the imputation was actionable and it did not matter whether the words imputed misconduct or mere unfitness. With the latter kind of office, however, it was held that the words must impute misconduct, and that to impute unfitness did not render the words actionable in themselves.[87] This further distinction, it was admitted, was not based on 'any satisfactory principle',[88] and was designed only to prevent actions for words damaging a person in his office from becoming 'innumerable'.[89].

In Ireland, while imputations against holders of offices of profit seemed to have been actionable in themselves, it is not clear that this distinction between different imputations affecting offices of honour was recognised. However, a related but stricter distinction appears to have been applied here, which was that where the holder of an office of honour could show the likelihood of temporal loss, the words were actionable in themselves, but where he could only show the likelihood of removal from the office, without any temporal loss, then

82 *Quinn v Wilson* (1850) 13 ILR 381.
83 *Curneen v Sweeney* (1969) 103 ILTR 29.
84 *Murphy v Kellett* (1862) 13 ICLR 488.
85 *Foster v Hood* (1873) 7 ILTR 92.
86 *Praegar & Co v Shaw* (1855) 4 ICLR 660.
87 *Alexander v Jenkins* [1892] 1 QB 797.
88 Supra at 802 per Lord Herschell.
89 *Gallwey v Marshall* (1853) 9 Ex 294, 298 per Pollock CB.

the words were not actionable in themselves. In *Currigan v Ryan*,[90] in 1866, the secretary and treasurer of a voluntary committee for the relief of poverty was unable to recover for a slander imputing dishonesty in his use of the funds raised because his office was not one of profit, and because he would not have suffered any temporal loss by being removed from it. This emphasis was repeated by Murphy J, in 1886, when he stated 'It has always been held that the office, trade or business must be some employment or occupation from which the injured party derives profit or emolument and that the loss likely to be caused must be temporal loss or profit...'.[91] According to this view, a plaintiff will also need to establish that he possessed some legal entitlement to the temporal profit.[92] While, in most cases of employment, this will not be difficult, yet a member, or a prospective member, of a religious order who takes a vow of poverty and is judged by the rules of the society, may not have a legal right to such temporal benefit as she receives.[93] Temporal profit need not be limited to money, but can also include food and clothing.

Since the enactment of s.19 of the Defamation Act 1961, it is uncertain whether the decision in Currigan's case still represents the law and whether proof of a likelihood of temporal loss is still necessary. In England the requirement merely to show a likelihood of removal from an office of honour has been held to have survived the enactment of the equivalent of s.19.[94] It seems likely that here, regardless of s.19, the distinction may have gone since 1937 because of the effect of various constitutional provisions which are referred to later.

A person must enjoy the full status of a particular office before he can be injured in it. If he is undergoing a period of training and needs to pass various stages and to obtain the consent of others before assuming the position, or, one assumes, if he is a probationer in his employment, then he does not enjoy the full status of the office, and so cannot be injured in it.[95]

An employment does not end merely because the employee is absent from it. Dismissal and resignation would obviously end it. A short temporary absence is unlikely to disturb a person's continuity of service, while a prolonged absence over years would.[96] A self-employed person does not cease his trade or profession merely by being absent from his business.[97].

90 (1865) 11 IJ NS 406, which followed Gallwey's case — an English decision.
91 *Dwyer v Meehan* (1886) 18 LR Ir 138, 157.
92 Supra 149.
93 Supra 149.
94 Gatley para 174.
95 *Dwyer v Meehan* at 149 per Harrison J.
96 At 152 per Harrison J.
97 *R v Armagh JJ* [1897] 2 IR 57, 68.

Words imputing unchastity to a female

Where words are spoken which impute unchastity or adultery in a woman or girl, then they are actionable in themselves and do not require special damage to make them actionable. This is provided for in s 16 of the Defamation Act 1961, which re-enacted an identical provision[98] contained in the Slander of Women Act 1891. Before 1891, the rule was that imputations of unchastity against a female were not, without more, actionable. Special damage was required. Thus, statements calling a woman a whore,[99] or accusing her of incontinence,[1] or saying that she had left her home because she was with illegitimate child, and had gone to London falsely pretending to enter a convent,[2] were held not actionable on their own. On the other hand, if the woman could have shown that the words affected her in the way of her employment then they would be actionable under the previous cause of action. The decisions where a woman was denied redress were not reached without accumulating judicial criticism[3] by which the prohibition was called unsatisfactory,[4] and, barbarous;[5] and in *Dwyer v Meehan*, in 1886, Murphy J joined with Harrison J 'in sincere expression of regret that we feel compelled to give judgement against the plaintiff in this action'.[6] When introducing the bill in the House of Lords, the Lord Chancellor acknowledged that it was being moved in response to strong judicial criticism of the prohibition.[7]

The 1891 Act, then, rendered actionable in themselves imputations of unchastity or adultery to a female, and, since then, females have recovered in respect of imputations of unchaste behaviour.[8] In each case, there is an onus placed on the judge to decide, as a matter of law, whether a particular act constitutes an unchaste act. It seems that, of the two terms — unchastity or adultery — the former has the wider meaning[9] — adultery being but one instance of

98 In fact a minor change — applying the general rules governing the awarding of costs — was made, see Dáil Debates vol 191 col 1933-5.
99 *Campbell v White* (1856) 5 ICLR 312.
1 *Corcoran v Corcoran* (1856) 7 ICLR 272.
2 *Dwyer v Meehan* (1886) 18 LR Ir 138.
3 *Connors v Justice* at 455 per Monahan CJ.
4 *Lynch v Knight* (1861) 9 HLC 577, 593 per Lord Campbell.
5 At 594 per Lord Brougham, quoted by Harrison J in Dwyer's case at 147.
6 (1886) 18 LR Ir 138, 157.
7 Hansard's Debates, 3rd series, vol 354, col 1704-5.
8 E.g. *Tait v Beggs* [1905] 2 IR 525; *Kavanagh v Lowry* Meath Chronicle, 19 February 1980.
9 See the various dictionary definitions referred to by counsel at 410 in *Kerr v Kennedy* [1942] 1 KB 409.

unchastity. In an English case,[10] lesbianism was held to be included, and in an Irish case[11] Fitzgibbon L J used the phrases 'immorality', and 'conduct inconsistent with her chastity' interchangeably. One statement, however, which might not be within s 16 is an imputation of a likelihood to be unchaste, because the terms of the section appear to comprehend only imputed acts of unchastity, although it may be that a court would always find in such a charge an inference of alleged previous unchastity, which would be within the section. An imputation that a female had involuntarily engaged in unchaste activity does not appear to be included in the range of imputations covered by the section. But even if the section was construed as applying to such imputations, or even if special damage were shown, it must be doubtful that an Irish court, unlike an English one,[12] could find that such an imputation was defamatory. This would be because a trial judge might hold, as a matter of law, that either no reasonable person would shun, or think less of, say, a raped woman, or because the Christian bias of the Constitution would not allow the law to take cognisance of such a reaction.

The action is limited by the section to women or girls only. It does not apply to men or boys, and so, at common law, the position would be as stated by Monahan CJ when describing the law in 1862 '... it is now perfectly established, as a general rule, that the imputation of want of chastity of either man or woman is not actionable',[13] and this was quoted approvingly in 1886.[14] It may be noted that in a Circuit Court action in 1926, *Devine v Keane*,[15] when a garda brought an action for an imputation of indecent behaviour, he rested his claim on the effect of the statement of his employment; it, apparently, being accepted that the imputation of indecency was not actionable in itself.

Slander requiring proof of special damage

Where words are spoken which do not come within the preceding categories of slanders actionable in themselves, then it is necessary

10 *Kerr v Kennedy* supra.
11 *Tait v Beggs* at 532.
12 As in *Youssoupoff v Metro-Goldwyn-Mayer* (1933) 50 TLR 581.
13 *Connors v Justice* (1862) 13 ICLR 451.
14 *Dwyer v Meehan* at 147 per Harrison J. This does not mean that an accusation of homosexual behaviour is not actionable per se, and it is ironic that the Supreme Court in upholding in *Norris v AG* [1984] IR 36 the constitutionality of the criminal law on homosexuality should make it easier to sue in slander for such an accusation; had male homosexuality been decriminalised, it could only be sued for as slander actionable on proof of special damage.
15 (1926) 61 ILTR 118.

for a plaintiff, in order to succeed, to establish that he suffered special damage as a result of the speaking of the words. Here, it is the special damage that gives the entitlement to the action, unlike the other slanders where the speaking alone does so. With all slanders, it is of course necessary that the words are defamatory, so that even where special damage is alleged there will be no action in defamation if the words are not defamatory,[16] though of course other actions may lie.

Special damage is peculiarly and narrowly defined. On the one hand, it can be the loss of a trader's customers or goodwill, as in *McLoughlin v Welsh*,[17] in 1846, where corn-sellers refused to sell any longer to the plaintiff corn-miller; or it can be the loss of the supply of the material needs of a member of a religious community who is expelled as a consequence of the speaking of the words,[18] or it might be the loss to a wife of the company of her husband;[19] and in *Corcoran v Corcoran*, in 1856, Pennefather B held that the retraction of a promise to supply the plaintiff with the means to emigrate to Australia was sufficient special damage, 'This is a thing which the promisor has promised and engaged to do and upon a retraction of that promise, even for ever so short a time, there is damage'.[20] On the other hand, the loss of the society and companionship of others is not sufficient special damage.[21] Harrison J stated in 1886 'it is clearly settled that although the loss of substantial hospitality, which had been a permanent addition to a person's income, is a good ground of special damage ... mere loss of the society of acquaintances is not, nor even illness resulting from the slander'.[22] Nor is the fear that damage will result in the future sufficient damage.[23] It also seems that the loss of an entitlement to apply for membership of a group is not sufficient damage.[24]

The special damage must be the natural and probable consequence of the speaking of the words, or, where the damage consists of the act of a third party, the act must be such as 'any reasonable man'[25] would have done. One may have regard to the tendency of the

16 *Sheehan v Aherne* (1875) IR 9 CL 412.
17 (1846) 10 ILR 19.
18 *Dwyer v Meehan* (1886) 18 LR Ir 138, 157 per Murphy J.
19 *Lynch v Knight* (1861) 9 HLC 577, 591.
20 (1856) 7 ICLR 272.
21 *Currigan v Ryan* (1865) 11 IJ NS 406; *Dwyer v Meehan* supra.
22 *Dwyer v Meehan* supra 154. Even mental illness seems excluded, although the courts here had earlier recognised in *Byrne v GS & Rly*, unreported February 1884, considered at (1890) 26 LR Ir 428, 441 that mental illness was a recoverable tort injury.
23 *Corcoran v Corcoran* (1856) 7 ICLR 272, 275 per Pennefather B.
24 *Dwyer v Meehan* at 155 et seq.
25 *Lynch v Knight* at 592 per Lord Campbell.

words,[26] and also to the speaker's intention,[27] remembering that one is assumed to have intended the natural consequences of one's act, when considering what was predictable. However, the consequence must not be too remote,[28] and, while there has been disagreement on the point, it is clearly established that it is too much to say that 'consequence must be such as, taking human nature as it is with its infirmities, and having regard to the relationship the parties concerned, might fairly and reasonably have been anticipated ...'.[29] In ruling by a majority of three to one against this wider test of causation, the House of Lords in *Lynch v Knight* in 1861, overruled the majority opinion of the Court of the Exchequor Chamber in Ireland, and held that a refusal by a husband to live with his wife because of an imputation that she was likely to be unchaste was an excessive reaction, and not such a reasonable consequence that would constitute special damage.

As a rule a plaintiff must allege and prove the facts which constitute the special damage he relies upon. In McLoughlin's case, Blackburne CJ stated 'if the words are not actionable in themselves but by reason of the special damage they produce, the facts constituting that damage must be stated in pleading and proved in evidence'.[30] The same rule also applies where a plaintiff chooses to establish some special damage, although he does not have to. Where the special damage consists of loss of business or an actionable loss of society, the plaintiff should supply in his pleading the names of those no longer dealing with him. However, an exception is recognised to this, which is based on necessity and practical justice, in cases where it is impossible for a plaintiff to produce such evidence. To quote Blackburne CJ again 'The nature of the slander complained of in the present case renders these rules inapplicable, for the plaintiff complains of an act ... the object and effect of which were to put him out of the pale of society, and to interdict all intercourse with him ... He might be unable to produce a single person who in consequence of them had refused to deal with him in his trade and so be unable to prove any particular or special damage ...'.[31] In that case evidence of loss of business was admitted although it had not been pleaded..

REFORM

The existence of the various distinctions between slander and libel,

26 *McLoughlin v Welsh* (1846) 10 ILR 19.
27 See references by Blackburne CJ at 25, and Burton J at 26 in McLoughlin's case.
28 *Dwyer v Meehan* at 155.
29 *Lynch v Knight* at 600 per Lord Wenselydale.
30 *McLoughlin v Welsh* (1846) 10 ILR 19.
31 At 25.

between slanders actionable in themselves and those requiring proof of special damage, and within the various kinds of slanders, has been the subject of sustained criticism over the years.[32] The law has been criticised for being 'arbitrary and illogical',[33] unsatisfactory, and intended as much to stop actions being brought, as to protect and vindicate a citizen's rights. Only partial reforms were made by the Defamation Act 1961, because the Porter Committee in England in 1948 did not recommend the abolition of the distinction between slander and libel, although it did criticise it. The Committee preferred retaining the status quo more or less because of the fear that abolishing the distinction could unleash a flood of frivolous slander actions. This sort of reasoning is the worst ground for resisting change in the law, since it is very close to admitting that the law is not doing justice now, and what is more that it should not want to do so in the future either. When New Zealand and other jurisdictions abolished the distinction between slander and libel,[34] the flood did not materialise.[35] Recently, reform bodies in England,[36] and Australia[37] have recommended that the distinction be abolished, and that all slanders should be actionable in themselves. So far as this country is concerned, the question of reform is not merely a matter of changing by statute the distinctions that have been criticised, it is also a matter of whether these distinctions are in fact lawful now, or whether they infringe the provisions of the Constitution.

The key distinction in this area of law is between slanders requiring proof of special damage, and slanders and all libels which are actionable in themselves. If the distinction were found to be unconstitutional, and all defamatory imputations were henceforth to be actionable in themselves, then the several distinctions within the various slanders would go too. There are a number of grounds for suspecting that the basic distinction may offend the Constitution. Firstly, the distinction is shown at its most acute where the same statement is written and spoken, and, in its first form is actionable per se but in its second requires proof of special damage. It seems next to impossible to identify any sufficient contemporary and relevant ground for treating so unequally the two which would prevent the distinction from infringing the constitutional guarantee of equal treatment. Secondly, the law's hard-nosed emphasis on material loss

32 For a list of the criticisms see Faulks Committee Report para 80 et seq; ALRC Report paras 75, 76.
33 Porter Committee Report para 38.
34 For a list of these, see the ALRC Report para 76; also Fleming 517; Williams *The Law of Defamation in Canada* 1976, 57.
35 NZ Committee Report para 69.
36 Faulks Committee Report para 91.
37 ALRC Report para 76.

in the definition of special damage is so at odds with the ideas of ostracism, loss of standing and embarrassment, which are central to the law's concern with reputation that it is hard to see what connection it has with the action. The proof of material loss is a quite extrinsic factor which, unless there is some valid countervailing justification for it, seems a clear unconstitutional restriction on the protection of good name. Thirdly, the victim of a slander who cannot prove special damage, when he has to, might have no other legal redress open to him. A declaratory action might not be open to him since his cause of action would still depend on what he cannot prove. A claim for injurious falsehood would not be available to him for the same reason. This leaves a defamed person with a wrong without any legal redress, which is something that the Constitution does not appear to permit.

The foregoing criticism of the present use of proving special damage to distinguish between some slanders and all other defamatory statements is not, however, intended to suggest that a distinction in defamation law could never be based on such a requirement. In contrast to the strong support that now exists in most of the common law world for presuming damage with all defamatory statements, regardless of type, the US Supreme Court has chosen proof of actual loss — which is close to but not exactly the same as special damage — as the basis of defamation liability for media, and possibly non media, defendants as well, except where a plaintiff can establish a narrow kind of fault akin to deceit.[38] This was justified by the American constitutional protection of media rights and no doubt, by the excessive impact which damages and the possibility of them can have on the operations of the media. Given the comparable constitutional dimension to defamation law in Ireland, and in the context of the common law's present selection of damages as the primary defamation remedy, such a development might not be without significance here. But the American development is not a coercive one. It is just one possible reaction to the problem of damages awards. Another solution, which is suggested later,[39] is to relegate damages to being a secondary, or exceptional, defamation remedy. The greater plaintiff difficulty in getting to that point could then mandate an entitlement to a presumption of damage.

The remaining distinctions affecting the various slanders actionable in themselves can also be criticised on constitutional grounds. Insofar as the common law refusal to treat imputations of crime, punishable only by fine, as actionable in themselves was originally intended to

38 Eldredge 193-204; Prosser 793-797. See also p. 242 post.
39 See p. 265 post.

deter actions from being taken and this still remains the reason, the rule appears to be an unjustified denial of the right of access to the courts. It also seems unlikely that the distinction between fine and imprisonment can offer a satisfactory basis for the unfavourable treatment of those accused of crimes punishable by fine only, since many crimes carry both punishments in the alternative or the aggregate. The need for the holder of an office of credit to establish the likelihood of temporal loss before the words are actionable in themselves is another rule of doubtful validity. Such a loss seems irrelevant to whether a person actually suffers reputational damage, and might only be justified by some valid reason related to reputation for distinguishing between the two types of office in this way. It is hard to see any. Indeed, the selflessness of voluntary office holders could hardly be less graciously rewarded by such a litigation hurdle, especially when the damage caused by an imputation against the reputation of a voluntary office holder could be greater than to that of a professional office holder. The restriction of the actionability in themselves of words imputing unchastity to women and girls and the exclusion of men and boys on grounds of sex appears unrelated to any single sex function or capacity. There does not seem to be any reason for protecting female chastity which might not also apply to male chastity. This restriction too might be unconstitutional.[40]

40 A similar view, and for similar reasons, is taken by the *Second Restatement of Torts* s 574, of the many US state rules which still discriminate in the way the law does here — Eldredge 123.

6

The Defence of Justification

It is a rule of long standing[1] that a 'true statement cannot be actionable in a civil claim for damages'.[2] The fact that the statement concerns a private matter which is of no public interest or was made from malicious motives does not, according to the common law, affect this matter.

Whether these aspects of the defence will survive the constitutional recognition of a right to privacy and other rights is considered later. On the other hand, if a charge of previous, and private, misbehaviour is made, with the implication that the charge is still true, then a defendant will need to show not only that the charge was true in the past, but also, what may be more difficult, that the charge is still true.[3] The reason why the truth of a statement operates as a complete defence to an action in defamation is that 'the law will not permit a man to recover damages in respect of an injury to a character which he does not or ought not to possess';[4] although there is no reason why the pursuit of truth as a self evident ideal in a Christian democracy should not also provide a basis for the defence.[5] It is up to a defendant to establish that the imputation is true. A plaintiff does not, at least initially, have to prove that the statement is, untrue, because the law presumes any statement to be false if it is

1 *In re O'Brien* (1883) 12 LR Ir 29, 32 per May CJ.

2 *Keaveney v Geraghty* [1965] IR 551, 560 per Lavery J. Two cases where this defence was successfully established are *Hewson v Cleeve* [1904] 2 IR 536, and *Deighan v Sunday Newspapers*, The Irish Times, 16 February 1982; SCt, 28 March 1984.

3 *Sutherland v Stopes* [1925] AC 47, 74 per Lord Shaw.

4 *McPherson v Daniels* (1829) reported in (1829) 10 B & C 263, per Littledale J.

5 Among other suggested reasons for this rule are that the defendant has not, unlike the plaintiff, misled the public about the true situation and that the community benefits by the exposure of anti-social elements. A more contemporary suggestion bases the rule on the importance of free speech in society. See generally Ray 'Truth: A Defence to Libel' (1931) 16 Minn L Rev 43; Franklin 'The Origins and Constitutionality of Limitations on Truth as a Defence in Tort Law' (1964) 16 Stan L Rev 784.

defamatory.[6] This follows from the assumption made by the law that a person enjoys a reputation until the contrary is established.[7].

The term justification is a curious term by which to refer to proving the truth of a statement, and, as will be seen later, this has been the subject of recommendations by the reform bodies. As late as the early nineteenth century, when the law was still developing and such defences as qualified privilege and fair comment had not yet clearly evolved as separate entities, the term justification was used when describing the entirety of the defences available to an action — whether by showing the truth of the statement or by showing good cause for making it. As the occasions of qualified privilege and fair comment come to be recognised as such, the term ceased to be applied to them, but continued through habit in its present usage. Throughout this chapter, the term justification is used in this sense except in one instance — when considering whether repetition is a defence to an action. This is because during the nineteenth century newspaper defendants attempted unsuccessfully to justify a statement by showing that it was a true report of what someone else had said. As is seen shortly, the kernel of such a defence could be revived under certain reform body proposals.

A defendant who seeks to raise this defence must be careful that what he justifies, or proves true, is the exact imputation relied upon by the plaintiff. A defendant does not have to justify an imputation which there is no suggestion he made.[8] No difficulty is likely to arise on this in the rare instance where no innuendo is pleaded, or where an innuendo is negatived, and a defendant has only to meet the statement alleged. But where a plaintiff relies on an innuendo, a defendant has to plead to that meaning, and if he pleads only to the natural meaning of the words, then the defence will be inadequate. It was stated in 1873 that 'to answer the words of the libel without including the innuendoes is to leave the cause of action unanswered'.[9] In *Irish People's Assurance v City of Dublin Assurance*[10] in 1929 a business rival published accurate but selective details of the plaintiff company's balance sheet suggesting that the plaintiff was in debt. The plaintiff pleaded by innuendo that this meant that the company was insolvent and that it was unsafe for policy holders to insure with it. Having held that this was a proper meaning, the Supreme Court also held that it was no justification to show the 'verbal accuracy of each item', and that in the case of extracts from

6 *Campbell v Irish Press* (1955) 90 ILTR 105, 109 per Kingsmill-Moore J.
7 See p. 10 supra.
8 *O'Connell v Mansfield* (1846) 9 ILR 179.
9 *Hort v Reade* (1873) IR 7 CL 551, 555 per Whiteside CJ.
10 [1929] IR 25.

documents 'mere accuracy of extraction is not *per se* conclusive of the truth of the statement made by the collected extracts'.[11].

JUSTIFYING THE SUBSTANCE OF AN IMPUTATION

In order for a defendant to succeed in a plea of justification, it is not necessary that he should meet every part of the statement or meaning in question. It is sufficient if he establishes the truth of the substance of the imputation, and it does not matter if a minor detail not affecting an imputation is not met. It is a separate question from this, and one that is shortly examined, whether a defendant must justify all of the imputations in the statement or whether he need only justify substantial imputations. The courts have for a long time been attracted by the metaphor of extracting the sting of a libel. Thus, Lefroy B put it in 1846 'The rule laid down ... is, that the justification is sufficient if the sting of the libel is answered'.[12] In *O'Connor v Wallen*[13] in 1856, the libel stated of the plaintiff 'How he next appeared in Buncrana as curate and tutor; how he gave out while there that he was a Captain of Dragoons, a graduate of Oxford, and attempted to pawn the poetry of American and British poets on the public as his own'. The plaintiff pleaded by innuendo that this meant that he was a habitual misrepresenter of facts. The justification sought to meet all of these facts, except that it claimed he called himself a surgeon in the Navy rather than a Captain of Dragoons. It was held that the plea did not fail because of this difference.

At the trial, the task of identifying the substance of an imputation for the purpose of justifying it is performed at the same time as the task of deciding whether a statement is defamatory or not. So, the judge will decide what meaning is capable of forming the substance of an imputation, and whether the proof of justification is capable of meeting that; and the jury will decide what the substance of the imputation is, and whether the justification actually meets it. In deciding what the substance is both judge and jury will rely upon logic and their common sense. Sometimes difficult facts can arise, as in *Lavell v Oranmore*[14] in 1861, where the statement referred to the more disorderly character of one priest in comparison to another priest, as being the reason why the latter was chosen to replace the former, for a certain task. On a demurrer two of the judges[15] considered that the imputation was that one priest was more disorderly

11 At 36 per Fitzgibbon J.
12 *O'Connell v Mansfield* at 196.
13 (1856) 6 ICLR 378.
14 (1861) 7 IJ NS 55.
15 Lefroy CJ, Fitzgerald J.

than another, while a third[16] felt that the imputation was merely that the priest was a disorderly person. When an appellate court decides what the substance of an imputation is, it relies not only on logic and common sense, but also on the manner in which the pleadings have been stated and the trial conducted by each side. In one case,[17] a plaintiff was not allowed to argue that the statement possessed a certain meaning because he had only raised the suggestion on an appeal; and in another case,[18] where a plaintiff had attached a particular imputation — amongst others — to the statement, and the trial was conducted on these grounds, he was not allowed on appeal to treat that imputation as surplusage and irrelevant to the meaning of the statement, although in fact the imputation might have been unnecessary.

PARTIAL JUSTIFICATION OF AN IMPUTATION

A defendant cannot justify the whole of a defamatory imputation by proving the truth of only a part of it. In *Crotty v McMahon* (1834),[19] the defendant sought to prove the truth of a statement that a person had been excommunicated from all social contact by showing that he had been excommunicated from contact with his Church; and in *Morrow v McGaver*[20] (1851) the defendant attempted to prove the truth of an accusation that a land agent had ill-treated tenants for personal or selfish reasons by showing that he had harshly treated his tenants. In each case the justification was held insufficient. The defendant does not, of course, have to prove all of what is contained in the imputation. Minor variations of detail, it has already been noted, may be ignored; and, as will be seen, minor imputations may also be ignored.

The prohibition on proving the truth of the entire imputation by proving only a part of it, does not however prevent a defendant from justifying a part of the imputation for its own sake, so long as in doing so he does not purport to show that the whole of the imputation is true. Thus 'if a man says that a certain neighbour of his was guilty of manslaughter and was also a thief, it is perfectly open to take a plea in justification of either charge only'.[21] It is uncertain whether a partial justification as such, can, in Ireland, possess much value

16 Hayes J.
17 *O'Connell v Mansfield* (1846) 9 ILR 179.
18 *Crawford v Todd* (1941) 75 ILTR 233.
19 (1834) 1 Jones 465.
20 (1851) 1 ICLR 579.
21 *Sutherland v Stopes* [1925] AC 47, 78 per Lord Shaw; for an example of partial justification, see *Goody v Odhams Press* [1967] 1 QB 333.

in a case where no other defence is available for the unjustified part. A defendant might in such a case wish to admit liability for the rest and to make a payment into court. But O 22 r 1(3) of the Rules of the Superior Courts prohibits, in actions for libel or slander, the payment of money into court unless liability is admitted in the defence; and it is not clear whether only a partial admission of liability will suffice to allow payment into court. It is also not clear why this prohibition in defamation actions of both a denial of liability and a payment into court exists. The English predecessor of this rule was enacted in order to reverse a decision that allowed for a denial of liability and a payment into court, as in other tort actions. [22] Defamation was said to merit this exceptional treatment because a question of character was involved, though it is not clear how this follows.[23] It is interesting that in England the significance of this reasoning has ceased to be apparent for, under a further change made in the English rules, one can again deny liability and pay into court.[24]

There may also be grounds for doubting the constitutional probity of O 22 r 1(3). It is difficult to identify any especial feature of the defamation action, in contrast to other tort actions, that would necessitate the kind of blanket prohibition on a denial of liability that is involved here. If the prohibition related only to the defence of justification, the rule might possess some meagre validity. Yet even in that case if the intention were to stop a defendant from attacking a plaintiff's character, and paying in beforehand, the present rule does not even do that since after liability might be admitted, a defendant could still attack a plaintiff's character on the assessment of damages.

A partial justification of an imputation is different from showing the truth of an imputation by proof of a less serious form of the imputation. A defendant may not prove the whole or part of the truth of the occurrence of one wrong by showing that a less serious one occurred. In *White v Tyrrell* in 1856, where the statement imputed fraudulent dealings and the justification pleaded alleged only breach of contract, it was held that this was a bad justification.[25] More recently, however, the opposite view has been argued for,[26] so as to allow an imputation that a man was a convicted rapist to be partly

22 *Hawkesley v Bradshaw* (1880) 5 QBD 302.

23 *Fleming v Dollar* (1889) 23 QBD 388, 391 per Coleridge CJ.

24 See Gatley para 1188.

25 (1856) 5 ICLR 477, 498; American authority is to the same effect, according to Prosser 841, who states 'if the accusation is stealing a watch from A, it is not enough to show a different offence, even though it be a more serious one, such as stealing a clock from A, or six watches from B'.

26 Duncan & Neill *Defamation* para 11,10; see also Gatley para 354 fn 13.

proved true by showing that he had been convicted of indecent assault. One of the reform bodies,[27] in seeking to permit this, has even recommended that a defence of truth should not fail simply because the charge proved true is different from the charge imputed, provided the difference between the two is not a material one. These views are, it is submitted, unsound and ought not to be accepted. They imply that one wrong can be a milder or more severe form of another. That is untrue. A serious wrong does not consist of a less serious one plus the difference between them. If it did the criminal law would not have needed to distinguish between them and create two separate offences. The two wrongs are separate entities, and the proof of one ought not to be viewed as even a partial proof of the other.

SEVERANCE

Where more than one statement is made against a person, the question arises whether he may pick and choose between what he will complain of, or whether he is bound to sue for all statements which belong to a clearly identifiable context. The reason why a person might wish to sever the statements he will sue upon from some others is that the latter might be proved true, but the former might not be. The question of severability can also arise in a second context in the defence of justification, that of dividing up sued-upon statements into major and minor imputations in order to avail of the benefit of s 22 of the Defamation Act 1961. This latter context is considered shortly, but, first, the severance of statements will be examined.

Severance of statements

The law recognises that a plaintiff may sever the statements he will sue upon from those which he will not sue upon, but it only allows him to do this when the statements are clearly severable. Lord Denning MR has said that 'unless the parts are clearly severable I do not think it is open to the plaintiff to pick and choose'.[28] A court needs to be careful when either allowing or denying severance because of the conflicting interests involved. On the one hand, every person has the right to redress for an infringement of his right to a good name. This implies that he can choose what to complain about and what to ignore. On the other hand, the right of defence implies that a defendant may show that the plaintiff does not possess the reputation

27 NZ Committee Report para 114.
28 *S & K Holdings v Throgmorton Publications* [1972] 1 WLR 1036.

which he claims to possess by showing that related, but different, statements about him are true. If a plaintiff is permitted to sever too much, then he might obtain a verdict which he does not deserve. But, if too little is allowed to be severed, a court may end up conducting a number of other defamation actions, in addition to the plaintiff's complaint. The plaintiff could be forced into putting a considerable portion of his life on the line with a great increase in the complexity, expense and length of the hearing. Where severance is allowed, a defendant may still tender proof of the other statements in mitigation of damages as relevant to the kind of reputation a plaintiff has, if they are admissable reputation evidence.

There is little enough guidance in the cases to show how a relationship between statements for the purposes of severance is determined. A lot may depend on whether some general innuendo meaning is placed by a plaintiff on the sued-on allegation. If there is, then the severed allegations may be used to justify the charge, if relevant to it. Where there is, in essence, just one charge contained in one statement made on one occasion relating to the one subject matter, a court will not allow severance.[29] But the fact that the two alleged imputations are made in the same statement and concern the same general type of wrongdoing — say, criminal wrongdoing — does not mean that severance will not be allowed if the imputations are substantially different. Thus 'The Glasgow Police are searching for a bogus Scotland Yard detective inspector on several charges including one of carrying a revolver without a licence...' was held to contain two distinct charges, one of being a bogus detective, and the second of being wanted on several charges.[30] In a New Zealand case a plaintiff was allowed to sue only for an allegation that he despised jews, though the statement also claimed that he despised bureaucrats, politicians, women and professionals.[31] Where there are charges of different acts involving the same misconduct but occurring on different dates and places then these are different charges and severance will be allowed.[32] Whether the misconduct imputed in different statements is sufficiently similar so as to prevent severance can be a matter of difficulty. In *Plato Films v Speidel* (1961),[33] the House of Lords did not prevent a plaintiff, ex-German army officer, from suing for an imputation in a film suggesting that he was privy to murder in 1934, and had betrayed Rommel in 1944, although there were other imputations in the same film that he had been guilty of

29 *Davis v Billing* (1891) 8 TLR 58.
30 *O'Callaghan v Thomson* (1928) SC 532.
31 *Templeton v Jones* [1984] 1 NZLR 448; see also *Polly Peck Holdings v Trelford* [1986] 2 WLR 845.
32 *Clarkson v Lawson* (1829) 6 Bing 266.
33 [1961] AC 1090.

war crimes and atrocities which were not sued upon. Whereas in *S & K Holdings v Throgmorton Publications*(1972),[34] two out of three judges felt that there was an inseparable connection between a statement that a company was trying to appoint tame auditors and was using improper pressure to remove the existing ones, and another statement that the chairman of the company had, ten years previously been involved in some accounting controversies, even though these were unrelated to appointing tame auditors.[35]

Severance of imputations

The second context in which the question of severance may arise concerns the division of the sued-upon statement into materially injurious and non materially injurious, or major and minor imputations. Where a statement contains more than one distinct imputation and a defendant wishes to raise the defence of justification, he does not have to prove the truth of all of the imputations in order to do so. He need only show that the major imputations are true. S 22 of the Defamation Act 1961 provides:'In an action for libel or slander in respect of words containing two or more distinct charges against the plaintiff, a defence of justification shall not fail by reason only that the truth of every charge is not proved if the words not proved to be true do not materially injure the plaintiff's reputation having regard to the truth of the remaining charges'. The task of distinguishing between what is a major and minor imputation is an 'unenviable one',[36] which, as a matter of law, would seem to be for the judge alone. The section does not apply where the imputations are not distinct, which since the section is a restrictive one, ought perhaps to be broadly interpreted. Nor does it apply when the imputations are all materially injurious; and finally it does not apply where the minor imputation is true but the major one is untrue.[37] The section gave effect to a recommendation of the Porter Committee in England in 1948. The recommendation was made for particular reasons, one of which had no relevance to Ireland, another of which

34 See p. 104 supra.

35 Lord Denning MR and Roskill CJ. The third, Edmund-Davies LJ had strong doubts, though not to the point of dissent, that the statements were connected. The finding that the statements were not severable led to the New Zealand Court of Appeal in Templeton's case describing this case as a difficult one of rather dubious authority.

36 McMahon & Binchy *The Irish Law of Torts* 356.

37 As may have been the case in *Latham and Byrne v Independent Newspapers*, The Irish Times, 9 May 1986, where a newspaper reported that two men were charged with robbing cigarettes and possession of firearms with intent to endanger life. The first charge was accurate, the second was not.

was mentioned without citing any supporting evidence, and a third of which was more related to the law on costs than to the law on justification. Besides these, the recommendation and, thus, s 22, amounted to an attack on the very idea of protecting reputation because it effectively asserted that minor defamations are of no account and can be ignored by the law. The section is a warning to potential plaintiffs not to bring proceedings unless they are able to obtain sizeable damages. It is not at all clear that the constitutional duty placed on the state to vindicate the citizen's good name or to treat him equally permits such legislation, especially when the reasons for it seem so inappropriate, and even allowing for a measure of regulation of good name in favour of other rights.[38]

In recent times, reform bodies in several jurisdictions have examined their equivalents of s 22, but in only one instance,[39] can it be said that their recommendations will clarify and simplify what is rapidly and unnecessarily becoming a very complicated area of law. In each case,[40] concern was expressed that a plaintiff might circumvent, indeed exploit, the present law by choosing to sue only for the minor imputation and thus prevent admission of evidence on the major one, at least until the issue of the size of the compensation to be awarded is considered. Of course, as was earlier stated, plaintiffs cannot do this unless the statements or imputations are clearly severable. But, despite this satisfactory position, two of the committees[41] still made recommendations that purported to meet the difficulty. They recommended[42] that a defendant should be able to rely on the truth of the major imputation, which the plaintiff does not sue upon at all, in order to raise the defence of justification to the minor imputation that is sued on. This is an extraordinary suggestion, which would only heighten the present unsatisfactory state of the law. Before 1961, the defence of truth was only raised by proving the truth of the statement. Now, the defence can be raised by proving, say, that three quarters of the statement is true. If these recommendations are implemented, the defence could even be raised by proving that something entirely different is true. Commenting on the recommendation, the Australian Law Reform Commission referred to a submission it had received which considered it 'illogical to say that the truth of other imputations has the effect of making the false

38 There might be indefeasible unequal treatment in cases where the same imputation was accompanied by a major imputation and where it was not. The latter would be actionable, the former not.

39 ALRC Report.

40 Faulks Committee Report para 133; the NZ Committee Report para, 108; and the ALRC Report para 121.

41 Faulks Committee and the NZ Committee.

42 Faulks Committee Report para 134; NZ Committee Report para 111.

imputation sued upon true'.[43] The Australian Commission itself recommended, essentially, a return to the pre-1961 position,[44] whereby the rules of severance would decide what could be sued on. The defence could only be made by showing the truth of all the imputations sued upon, and any relevant and true statements would be admitted in evidence when assessing damages. This would be a clear and straightforward solution, and one which, it is submitted, a constitutional invalidation of s 22 could well produce.

PROOF OF JUSTIFICATION OF CERTAIN IMPUTATIONS

Where a defamatory statement contains an accusation of wrongdoing and a defendant intends to prove the truth of the accusation by relying upon the pronouncement of a competent adjudicating body, the question arises whether the law will allow a defendant to raise the defence of justification in this way, or whether it will require him to prove that the event actually occurred and so retry the earlier case. There may be three such pronouncements — the decision of a court of law, the decision of a body functioning under Article 37 of the Constitution, and the decision of a private tribunal whose jurisdiction is based on consent. There are authorities on the first and third type of pronouncements, and only these will be examined. There does not appear to be clear authority on the status to be accorded the second type of pronouncement; but since a body functioning under Article 37 is not the same as a court, it seems likely that the status of its pronouncements would, at the very least, be the same as with domestic tribunals.

Pronouncements of courts of law

Where a defendant in an action proposes to prove the truth of an accusation of legal wrongdoing, usually a criminal wrong, by establishing in evidence the finding of a court in a trial or hearing, the authorities are divided on whether to allow him to raise the defence in this way. In *Hollington v Hewthorn*,[45] in 1943, the English Court of Appeal held that the decision of a court in a criminal action was inadmissible as evidence in a civil action where the same issues were raised for determination. Although Hollington's case was not a defamation action, it was held in later English cases that the rule

43 Para 121.
44 Para 122.
45 [1943] KB 587.

applied in this area as well.[46] So a defendant could not prove the truth of an accusation of a crime by showing that the plaintiff had previously been convicted of the offence. The door was, thus, open to challenging in a defamation action the correctness of a decision in a criminal court. The decision in Hollington's case was widely observed in Australia and New Zealand,[47] and, one assumes, here also.[48] But almost from the date of the judgement, the decision has been subjected to sustained criticism[49] on the grounds that the precedents did not in fact support the decision and because, in principle, the decision understated the status which is deserved by the opinion of a court in a criminal matter. Such a court is less likely to make a mistake than a civil court because the burden of proof is higher, and its verdicts are acted upon by the state to enforce them. The decision also implied that 'in the opinion of lawyers a conviction by a criminal court is as likely to be wrong as right'.[50] These criticisms led to the rule being abolished by statue in England in 1968,[51] and to the New Zealand Court of Appeal refusing to apply it in 1969. These jurisdictions have, however, differed in the weight to be accorded to evidence of conviction when proving the truth of an accusation. The English legislation deems the conviction to be conclusive evidence that the offence was committed, whereas the New Zealand decision views it as 'some evidence that the person convicted committed the crime charged against him....'.[52]

In spite of the absence of exact authority here, there is good reason, in addition to the rejection by other jurisdictions of the rule, to doubt that the rule in Hollington's case would now be followed by an Irish court. Firstly, in a recent false imprisonment case[53] O'Hanlon J identified two doctrines — evidential estoppel and abuse of process — by which a person may be prevented from having retried issues determined in earlier proceedings. Estoppel might be the less useful of the two because of certainty of issue and symmetry of parties

46 *Loughans v Odhams Press* [1963] QB 299; *Goody v Odhams Press* [1967] 1 QB 333; see also *Hinds v Sparks* [1964] Crim LR 717. But where a statement asserted that a person had been found guilty of crime, it may be justified by proof of the conviction — *Mack v North Hill News* (1964) 44 DLR (2d) 147.

47 *Jorgensen v News Media* [1969] NZLR 961, 982 per Turner J.

48 The 9th Interim Report of the Committee on Court Practice and Procedure, *Proof of Previous Convictions*, did not consider Hollington's case, except at para 8 to observe that it reflected the better view on the matter.

49 For an account of this criticism see Jorgensen's case, 987 et seq per North P and 994, 999 per Turner J.

50 15th Report of the UK Law Reform Committee on the Law of Evidence, para 3.

51 Civil Evidence Act 1968, s 13 (1). Several Australian states have also legislated against this rule — Fleming 526.

52 Jorgensen's case supra, 992 per Turner J.

53 *Kelly v Ireland* [1986] ILRM 318.

difficulties. Abuse of process seems more appropriate to the defamation context, although rather than allow a defendent tender evidence in justification it prevents a plaintiff from continuing with proceedings.[54] The second reason for doubting that the rule in Hollington's case would be followed is that with such a rule a judge would not be showing the comity or respect for the decisions of other judges required by his constitutional duty to administer justice and uphold the status of the courts.

Pronouncements of domestic tribunals

In Jorgensen's case, the New Zealand court regarded the position concerning the admissibility in evidence of the decisions of domestic tribunals so as to prove the truth of a statement as uncertain. However, there is Irish authority to suggest that this evidence is admissible. The rule seems to be that where a defendant proposes to prove the truth of a defamatory statement by establishing in evidence the findings and pronouncement of a domestic tribunal whose jurisdiction to hear the matter and announce a decision was based on the consent of the parties, then the court will allow the defendant to do this and so to raise the defence of justification, provided the proceedings of the tribunal were lawfully conducted, natural justice was observed and the rules of the association do not offend civil law. This appears to be the effect of the decision of the Court of Queen's Bench here in *O'Keefe v Cullen* (1873).[55] In this case a parish priest brought an action for libel against a cardinal who published a sentence of suspension of the priest from office. The punishment had been imposed after a proper investigation held in accordance with the church's rules. The priest brought the action to question the legality or justifiability of the sentence. The cardinal pleaded, amongst other things, defences of justification based on the finding of the tribunal. These defences, however, failed, although the cardinal did succeed on other grounds, because the church ordinance, under which the tribunal acted, was held illegal according to civil law. It was, however, clear from the judgements of two of the majority[56] that had it not

54 O'Hanlon J stated, at 330, that 'in the absence of special circumstances, an effort to challenge the correctness of a decision by a Court of competent jurisdiction against a party in the course of a criminal trial, by means of civil proceedings instituted by such person after that decision has been made, should normally be restrained on an abuse of the process of the Court'.

55 (1873) IR 7 CL 319 For a consideration of this case see, Anon *O'Keefe v Cardinal Cullen* (1873) 7 ILT & SJ 359 et seq.

56 Barry and Fitzgerald JJ The other judge in the majority on this point was Whiteside CJ, although he dissented from the majority — comprising Barry, Fitzgerald and O'Brien JJ — when they upheld defences of qualified privilege.

been for this particular illegality, the pleas of justification based on the validity of the decision of tribunal would have been upheld. The dissenting judge,[57] who found the ordinance lawful, upheld the pleas of justification. The basis on which the court regarded the decision of a domestic tribunal as capable, in the right circumstances, of establishing a defence of justification was the obvious sense and justice of the maxim *volenti non fit injuria*,[58] nowadays known as the defence whereby the party beforehand agreed to waive his rights in respect of the wrong.[59]

Once evidence of a previous finding by a tribunal, or for that matter by a court or body under Article 37, is admitted, the question arises as to whether such evidence is conclusive of the truth of the sued on statement, or whether it is only some evidence which the court may accept or reject. There are dicta in O'Keefe's case[60] which seem to imply that the evidence would be conclusive because of a judicial reluctance to retry the earlier issue, and the abuse of process doctrine seems to make the previous decision generally conclusive, subject to significant new evidence. However, the notion that a judge cannot be compelled by outside authority to find certain facts[61] suggests that the trial judge must still make up his own mind on the weight of the evidence before him. That could mean, as the New Zealand court found in Jorgensen's case, that the previous decision is only some evidence and is not conclusive.

JUSTIFICATION BY REPETITION

It was seen in an earlier chapter that every person who adds to the circulation of a defamatory statement — and so anyone who repeats it — is liable for that act. However, it was once thought that it was a valid defence to an action for the repetition of a defamatory statement for a defendant to show that he only repeated what someone else had said or written, and that he had given the name of his informant at the time of repeating the statement.[62] This latter requirement was to provide the plaintiff with a action against the informant originator of the statement, and a witness as well. But this view was never entirely accepted,[63] for it was limited to where there was just cause for the repetition, which qualification would nowadays show itself

57 O'Brien J at 398.
58 Barry J at 362, Fitzgerald J at 373; O'Brien J at 379, 380.
59 *O'Hanlon v ESB* [1969] IR 75.
60 E.g. Fitzgerald J at 374.
61 See Kelly *The Irish Constitution* 2nd ed 265.
62 *Lord Northampton's Case* (1613) 12 Co 132.
63 *Lewis v Walter* (1821) 4 B & Ald 605.

as an occasion of qualified privilege; and in *O'Shaughnessy v Haydn*(1825)[64] the Irish King's Bench expressly rejected the idea that a person could justify a statement by showing that someone else had made it earlier. In that case, one newspaper copied from another an article accusing a priest of purporting to canonize two executed felons, of calling down God's curse on the prosecutor and of burning bibles in the gaol. The paper prefaced its article by stating ' We copy the following from the Antidote of Saturday. We do so for the purpose (if it be not founded on fact) of our thereby leading to the contradiction of so extraordinary an occurrence and, if it be true, of holding up such conduct to general reprobation'. In holding that this did not relieve the defendants of liability, Bushe CJ remarked 'that if any man shall venture in this manner to slander another, he can only justify himself by pleading and proving the truth of the charges... [and], admitting them to be false... he cannot be permitted to defend himself by saying that he was bona fide exercising the right of judging and condemning others'.[65] In *Clanchy v Cahill*[66] in the same court in the following year, an appeal on the ground that a defendant had only repeated what another had said was given up because it was accepted this was bad as a plea of a justification. In *Cleary v Lenihan* (1874)[67] a newspaper carried an article stating that a petition was about to be presented to a court against the election of a mayor on grounds of intimidation and undue influence during the election. No petition was in fact presented. It was held that no defence could be based merely on the fact of repetition.

Although the fact of repetition is irrelevant to a defence of truth, it may constitute an occasion of qualified privilege. It may also be relevant where on the assessment of damages the existence of repeated statements are, as rumours, admitted as character evidence in mitigation of damages.[68]

While the above common law rule seems firmly set against allowing the media justify by accurate reporting, there are persistent pressures from the media — which have been accepted to some extent — for variants of such a defence to be recognised. S 24 of the Defamation Act 1961, considered in Chapter 8, is one response. A broader response has been recommended by the Australian Law Reform Commission in the form of a defence of fair report of attributed statement, subject to a number of conditions such as public interest,

64 (1825) 2 Fox & Sm 208.
65 Supra.
66 (1825) Sm & Bat 232.
67 (1874) 8 ILTR 146.
68 See p. 250 post.

reasonableness of publication, and right of reply.[69] A US federal Court of Appeals has recognised a far ranging and controversial constitutional privilege for accurate and neutral reporting of newsworthy and serious charges against public figures, even where the reporter had serious doubts about the accuracy of the statement.[70]

AGGRAVATED DAMAGES

An unsuccessful attempt to prove the truth of a defamatory statement may be evidence on which a jury may award aggravated damages to a plaintiff. So, 'The adoption of this line of defence is a very serious step ...'.[71] In deciding whether such an attempt was made the jury are entitled to look at the whole conduct of the defendant from the time the libel was published down to the time they give their verdict. They may consider what his conduct has been before and after the trial and in court during the trial. This is the larger principle of which the undisputed law that a plea of justification, persisted in at the trial and not accepted by the jury, may be grounds for an award of increased damages, is but one example. Another is the conduct of the defendants in putting forward a witness who re-asserts the defamatory statement as true.[72] So it is not only by an unsuccessful defence of justification that aggravated damages may be awarded, but also where the truth of the statement is asserted in any other way, such as by the defence of fair comment.

It should be noted, however, that vigour in attempting to raise the defence may, on its own, suggest sincerity of belief as much as baseness of intent. The unsuccessful assertion of the truth of the statement does not necessarily lead to aggravated damages. A jury might take the view that an insertion of a plea of justification was evidence of the good faith of the publisher.[73] One commentator has suggested that the possibility that a jury may too readily award aggravated damages for an unsubstantiated justification might suggest the necessity for some statutory provision on the matter.[74] The American attitude in this area has, according to Prosser, been to limit the grounds for aggravated damages to 'cases where it appears that

69 ALRC Report para 174/180.
70 *Edwards v National Audubon* (1977) 556 F 2d 113; also Note, 'The Developing Privilege of Neutral Reportage' (1982) 69 Va L Rev 853; Eldredge 258/260.
71 *Gallagher v Touhy* (1924) 58 ILTR 134 per Murnaghan J.
72 *Campbell v Irish Press* (1955) 90 ILTR 105, 112 per Kingsmill-Moore J.
73 Supra.
74 Hayes 'The Jury Verdict in Defamation: Commonsense or Conniption'(1973) 11 West Aust LJ 140, 165/6.

the defence was entered in bad faith, without evidence to support it'.[75]

The original reason for the rule was that an unsuccessful defence could be evidence of actual malice, and that implied a relation between the extent of persistence with an unsuccessful assertion of truth and the sense of injury or outrage thereby occasioned the plaintiff.[76] More recently, some judges have described the reason for awarding aggravated damages in these circumstances as being the increase in circulation which is given to a statement by the case coming to trial and being reported by the news media.[77] This latter explanation might not be valid for two reasons. Firstly, every defamation action, whatever the defence, which is reported by the media may increase the circulation of a libel, but defeat does not necessarily lead to aggravated damages. Of course, justification is different in that the continued assertion of truth may influence the views of some of the new audience. But this new audience will abide, or should do, the result of the hearing and the rejection of the defence of truth. There should then, be no reason to single out an unsuccessful justification for aggravated damages. Secondly, if this explanation were correct, then it would follow that any unsuccessful justification must always result in aggravated damages being awarded, because all such justifications will involve a wider circulation. However no one has suggested that this should be so.

The entitlement to award aggravated damages for any unsuccessful assertions of truth made at any time is well established. However, it is submitted that the entitlement to make the awards on certain occasions — those which allow the pleadings and the course of the trial to be used as a ground for the damages — should give rise to concern, for two reasons. Firstly, the idea of awarding damages for the exercise of a right which the law confers is offensive. As an Australian judge remarked 'How can a defendant be mulcted in damages for merely exercising his right of defence?'.[78] Secondly, and this seems to be the more obvious point although there appears to be little enough awareness of it in the reports,[79] the awarding of aggravated damages because of the manner in which a defendant phrases his pleadings or conducts his case during the hearing appears to be in direct conflict with the immunity from any action which the law accords to relevant statements that are made as a result of,

75 At 842.

76 *Warwick v Foulkes* (1844) 12 M & W 507.

77 *Cassell v Broome* [1972] AC 1027, 1125 per Lord Diplock; see also *Herald & Weekly Times v McGregor* (1928) 41 CLR 255, 263.

78 *Herald & Weekly Times v McGregor* at 272 per Higgins J.

79 Both Isaacs and Higgins JJ showed an awareness of it in the Herald & Weekly Times case.

or in the course of, legal proceedings.[80] Further, unsuccessful attempts at justification in this way could not be the cause of a separate action. The suggestion that the pleadings could be sued on was made in one case, but it was rejected dismissively.[81] So, if it cannot be the subject of a separate action, it should surely follow that it cannot be tacked on to some other action. Nor, one considers, is this power to award aggravated damages validated by describing the damages as more retribution than compensation,[82] or by stating that this power is based on the principle *ut sit finis litium*.[83].

It is interesting to note that one reform body has accepted the undesireability of making an award of aggravated damages in these circumstances, and has recommended that no enlargement of damages be allowed for the way in which proceedings are conducted.[84]

REFORM

Two particular issues of fundamental concern to the defence deserve special consideration. The first concerns whether the law should switch the burden of proving truth in relation to the statement from the defendant to the plaintiff, and the second concerns whether truth alone should continue to constitute the defence, or whether some additional qualifying factor, such as public benefit or non malicious motive, should be attached to the defence.

When a defendant is required to prove that a statement is true an exceptional burden is placed on him. The general rule in tort is that when liability is imposed for untrue statements — whether negligently, intentionally or innocently made — the burden of proof in each case rests on the plaintiff to prove what he asserts i.e. that the statement is untrue. In defamation the reverse is the case. It is hard to see why a statement which damages a person's health or financial interests should be, effectively, presumed true and a statement which damages a person's reputation be presumed untrue. Reputation is, in its nature, different from other interests, but in its importance cannot be said to be of demonstrably greater account than an individual's other vital interests. It cannot either be said that because the law says a person

80 For the immunity in relation to defamation actions, see following chapter. For the immunity in relation to other tort actions, see *Saif Ali v Mitchell* [1980] AC 198.
81 *Warwick v Foulkes* at 508 per Parke B, referred to by Higgins J in the Herald & Weekly Times case at 273.
82 Herald & Weekly Times case at 266 per Isaacs J.
83 Herald & Weekly Times case at 274 per Higgins J.
84 That was the report of the New South Wales Law Reform Commission on Defamation, whose views on this are referred to by Hayes supra, 167.

is entitled to a good name that therefore the evidential burden of proof should be placed on the defendant. If this followed, then the same should be said of other tort actions where plaintiffs similarly sue on the basis of entitlements which the law says they have.

It is one of the curious features of the defamation action how seldom the defence of justification is actually raised given the importance of the truth or otherwise of the published statement. Allowing for circumstances where simple errors are made, there are still many cases where quite specific accusations are made, and a case is litigated, or settled without the defendant ever attempting to justify the statement, although he believed, and still does, that the statement is true. The issue of truth is therefore not in the case at all, when it should have been. The observer is left puzzled by how wrong the defendant got it, or appeared to get it. The untruth of the statement is established by default, and even plaintiffs must find this an unsatisfactory way to uphold their reputation, since many observers will appreciate this. Fear of an award of aggravated damages may be a contributory factor to a defendant's reluctance to make truth an issue in a case. But even if that power was abolished the present situation would still allow truth to be established by default when what is needed is a way to make truth an issue. If the burden of proof was switched and a plaintiff was obliged to prove untruth, it would not weaken his position. He could not object to proving untruth since, even now, no genuine plaintiff would take a case without being happy that he could prove untruth if he had to. He would also be in an equal, if not better, position than the defendant to be able to know and show what the real situation about the statement was. The reform bodies have reacted negatively to the idea of switching the burden of proof,[85] one of them arguing that it would severely upset the present balance in the law.[86] Interestingly in the US, where much of defamation law has been shifted on to a fault liability basis as a result particularly of constitutional protection of the media, a number of commentators have suggested that this effectively requires a plaintiff to prove untruth;[87] because when proving that the defendant knew the statement was untrue, or was reckless or careless about it, as the case may be, a plaintiff would also actually have to prove that the statement was untrue. Already, such a situation can arise here when

85 Faulks Committee Report para 141; NZ Committee Report paras 129-131.
86 Faulks Committee Report, supra.
87 See Eldredge 323-4, *Second Restatement of Torts* s 613, Comments. Prosser on the other hand is not convinced tha this is so, 639-64. See also Keeton 'Defamation and the Freedom of the Press' (1976) 54 Tex L Rev 1211, 1235 et seq, who argues that with intentional defamation the burden of proving untruth should be placed on the plaintiff because it is a logical corollary of the need to prove the defendant's state of mind.

malice is alleged in order to defeat defences like qualified privilege and fair comment. It is possible that the constitutional imposition of fault liability for media defendants here could lead to the same results as in the US.[88]

A second issue of reform concerns whether truth on its own should constitute the defence of justification. It does not do so with criminal libel, and in some Australian states an additional requirement,that the publication was for public benefit, must be satisfied.[89] In the US a minority of states have also attached conditions like proper motives, justifiable ends and public benefit to the defence, although the majority have retained the common law rule.[90] Since 1964, the US Supreme Court's emphasis on the media's constitutional rights to free speech has lead some to believe that attaching any qualification to the defence of justification might in media cases infringe the First Amendment to the Constitution,[91] although the court has so far spoken only in the media/public interest context; and in one state case a court upheld qualifications where the case did not concern media statements about public figures.[92] Both the English and New Zealand reform bodies recommended retaining the defence in its present form because, essentially, they viewed the suggested qualification of public benefit as being too vague and unworkable.[93] The credibility of this view is, however, rendered suspect by the fact that defamation law already uses such a criterion in s 24 of the Defamation Act 1961.[94] The Australian Law Reform Commission did accept that the law should be changed to require an element of public benefit, but recommended that this be achieved by a separate action for the protection of privacy, which would in appropriate cases be taken simultaneously with an action for defamation.[95]

In Ireland it is difficult to know what the constitutional position of the present exclusive emphasis on truth is. The law currently ignores

88 The applicability of American constitutional developments to Irish defamation law is considered more fully at pp. 143, 167 post.

89 See ALRC Report para 123.

90 Ray 'Truth: A Defence to Libel' (1931) 16 Minn L Rev 43; Franklin 'The Origins and Constitutionality of Limitations on Truth as a Defense in Tort Law' (1964) 16 Stan L Rev 784; Eldredge 324-9; Prosser 840-41.

91 See Eldredge supra.

92 *Welch v Chicago Tribune* (1969) 340 NE (2d) 539.

93 Porter Committee Report para 78; Faulks Committee Report para 138; NZ Committee Report para 122; the particular difficulties which authors, journalists and lawyers would face with such a test were also cited.

94 See p. 191 post.

95 Paras 123-5. The report's acceptance of a public benefit requirement was not based only on the need to achieve uniformity in the law throughout Australia, where some states already had the test but others had not. See Kirby 'The Purest Treasure? — National Defamation Law Reform in Australia' (1977) 8 Fed Law Rev 113, 128-130.

the distress and intrusion on privacy caused by the publication of past or irrelevant details about a person's life, and the Constitution probably endorses the pursuit of truth as a valuable Christian and democratic ideal, though it probably also recognises that the single minded pursuit of truth is not a practical idea in human affairs. For example, with the present defences of qualified privilege and fair comment, good name is sacrificed both to falsehood and free speech. The right of individual privacy is not given expression in the present law, or even put into the balance; and, while historically the common law was tardy about protecting privacy and emotional distress, these possibly enjoy constitutional support now. The recognition of these values could render any balance which is struck in their absence — such as the present one — a false one. If that is so, and one judge has suggested, extra-judicially, that the right to a good name does protect the individual against the exposure of non relevant personal details,[96] then the matter resolves itself to whether the defence of justification is modified by some public benefit test, or whether a simultaneous action for privacy or emotional distress is taken. Until the nature of privacy protection is better understood, it may be that the Constitution will require a public interest, or even public benefit test to be incorporated into the defence.

Whether malice is a constitutionally compelled element in the defence of justification seems doubtful. Its use as a balancing mechanism in the defences of qualified privilege and fair comment is understandable given that the issue is whether an untrue statement should be protected or not. When justification is pleaded and the statement is true, motive does not seem an appropriate pivot on which to make the defence stand. However, it may be that the Constitution does not coerce a conclusion either way on this issue, except perhaps with media publishers it might not be permissible to test their motives when they publish true statements.

96 Walsh J 'The Judicial Power and the Protection of the Right to Privacy' (1977) DULJ 3, 8.

7

The Defence of Absolute Privilege

The law of defamation recognises a variety of occasions on which a person who makes a defamatory statement enjoys a complete immunity from liability. These occasions concern statements made in connection with various proceedings in the Houses of the Oireachtas, with the administration of justice in courts and by bodies functioning under Article 37 of the Constitution, and with the activities of the executive. The uniform ground of exercising the powers of state justifies these absolute immunities, although curiously this has not resulted in all persons involved with each power being similarly protected. Lower judges and bodies under Article 37 are absolutely protected, but lower legislative bodies, such as local authorities in certain instances and lower executive officers, enjoy only a qualified protection.

The President is immune from any criminal or civil liability for acts done by him in the course of his office. This is provided for in Article 13.8(1) of the Constitution, which states 'The President shall not be answerable to either House of the Oireachtas or to any court for the exercise and performance of the powers and functions of his office or for any act done or purporting to be done by him in the exercise and performance of these powers and functions.' This immunity seems clearly to include the making of defamatory statements. When the President is not acting or purporting to act in his official capacity, then it seems that he is as liable as anyone else for a defamatory statement made by him. Proceedings of, and statements by, the Council of State and the presidential Commission are probably also absolutely privileged.

Extensive immunities and privileges of an absolute nature are enjoyed under European Community law by a wide variety of bodies and individuals connected with the working of the European Community, including officials and servants of the Community working in Ireland.[1] The protections confer an immunity against

1. The protections are set out in Article 28 of the Merger Treaty 1965, and in the Protocol on the Privilges and Immunities of the European Communities

liability under national law[2], and possibly even under community law, since although the latter is not directly protective of good name, if damage to good name is a consequence of a community tort there might be liability.[3] The protections exist to ensure the performance by the Community of its tasks, and there are a number of interesting waiver provisions under which officials and employees may be deprived of their protections unless the relevant institution considers that waiver would be contrary to the Community's interests.[4] The extent of Community protections seems broadly comparable to domestic protections, although the Community protection of assembly members, judges, and pre-trial communications may be more widely cast.[5]

It is sometimes stated that statements made between a client and a solicitor which are not essential to the course of a legal proceeding enjoy an absolute privilege from liability. Although there is an English authority[6] to this effect, the soundness of this view has been doubted,[7] and most academic opinion is against the recognition of such a privilege.[8] If recognised, it would be based on an extreme view of the importance of solicitors. For, outside of the area of legal proceedings where solicitors enjoy an absolute privilege it is difficult to see how the solicitor is so important that the victim of defamatory statements made by or to him should be denied a right to a good name, while the victim of defamatory statements involving other professional or business persons is not denied his right to a good name.

1965 dealing mainly with assembly and Commission members, officials and servants. See also the Protocol on the Statute of the Court of Justice 1957 dealing with judges, lawyers, agents and advisers; Article 21 of the 1965 Protocol and Article 32, Rules of Procedure. See generally Parry and Hardy *EEC Law* 2nd ed. pp. 63-7; *Hasselblad v Orbinson* [1985] 1 AER 173.

2 *Wagner v Fohrmann* [1964] ECR 195; *Wybot v Faure,* Case 149/85, Ct. of Justice.

3 See Leroy v HA [1964] CMLR 562. See also p. 296 post.

4 Eg Article 18 Merger Treaty 1965. These immunities are sometimes waived. See e.g. Report on Gaibisso's Case, EP Working Document A2-101/86/86.

5 Assembly members, through a combination of Articles 9 and 10 of the 1965 Protocol enjoy the same protection for extra as intra assembly activities if these can be said to be in performance of their duties. This could render invalid the qualified privilege conferred on an MEP in *Lindsay v Maher,* The Irish Times, 3 February 1984 when a member spoke publicly on a matter affecting his constituents. Official and unofficial reports of Community proceedings do not seem to be explicitly protected under Community law, but the former type at any rate would still be protected.

6 *More v Weaver* [1928] 2 KB 520.

7 *Minter v Priest* [1930] AC 558, at 574 per Viscount Dunedin, and at 586, per Lord Atkin.

8 The Report of the New Zealand Committee recommends at para 169 that the doubt whether this privilege still exists, be finally dispelled by legislation, and that instead such statements should only enjoy a qualified privilege.

This would be unequal treatment and would be difficult to justify in constitutional terms.

Finally, for reasons which are stated later,[9] it is not considered that an absolute privilege attaches to newspaper and broadcast reports of court proceedings under s18 of the Defamation Act 1961.

PARLIAMENTARY PROCEEDINGS

In order for the Houses of the Oireachtas to perform their constitutional duties effectively and for public confidence in the parliamentary process to be maintained, it is necessary that various utterances and acts can be done by certain persons without the fear of incurring liability before a court or other authority outside of parliament. The law recognises by the Constitution, by statute and by the common law a number of occasions, contained within the parliamentary process, in which the makers of defamatory statements enjoy an absolute immunity from legal liability. These occasions are fivefold — (1) utterances made in either House and (2) reports of these utterances, (3) utterances made in parliamentary committees and (4) reports of these utterances, and finally (5) the publication of official reports and publications.

Utterances in the Houses of the Oireachtas

Article 15.13 of the Constitution of 1937 provides that 'The members of each House of the Oireachtas . . . shall not, in respect of any utterance in either House, be amenable to any court or any authority other than the House itself.' This re-stated in substantial terms Article 18 of the Constitution of 1922, whose purpose was stated during the debate on that Constitution to be the privileging of statements made in the House, 'That is to say, an action for libel would not lie against a member making a statement in the House'.[10] While this may have been the intention, it is not clear, as will be seen shortly, that the words used, then and now, actually achieve this. The constitutional protection arises only in relation to the Houses of the Oireachtas, and would not therefore include any body, such as a local authority, which exercises delegated legislative power when, for example, making bye-laws.[11]

9 See p. 171 post.

10 Dáil Debs. vol. 1 col. 1078, Pres. of Ex. Co.; and see generally Note, 'Brewster, Gravel and Legislative Immunity' (1973) 73 Colum L Rev 125; Yankwich, 'The Immunity of Congressional Speech' (1951) 99 U Pa L Rev 960.

11 Common law is also against any more than a qualified privilege for local authority

The words in Article 15.13 differ, in important respects, from those used in the English Bill of Rights of 1688. This legislation formed the basis of the privilege enjoyed by the parliament of the United Kingdom of Great Britain and Ireland from 1801 to 1922, and it may also have formed the basis of the privilege of the Irish parliament prior to 1801. It continues nowadays to form the basis of the English privilege. Article 9 of the Bill of Rights provides that 'The freedom of speech and debates or proceedings in Parliament ought not to be impeached or questioned in any court or place out of Parliament.' Although not originally directed at the prevention of defamation actions, it was later accepted that this was one of the consequences of Article 9.[12] Thus, in *Dillon v Balfour* (1887)[13] where although a plaintiff claimed not to question that words spoken in parliament were privileged, yet the court considered that this was what his claim amounted to. Palles CB thought it 'impossible to deny that an action for words so spoken is a breach of the privilege of Parliament,' and for the source of this privilege 'we have but to open the Statute Book, for the Bill of Rights . . . declares its existence.'[14]

It is curious that Article 15.13 refers only to utterances, and not to statements or proceedings. It is unclear why this is so. Neither set of Dáil Debates cast any light on the matter. It might be that there was a desire specifically to include casual conversations between members during debates within the privilege because, in an early American decision,[15] it had been held that parliamentary privilege did not protect private conversations between members from defamation actions. An utterance is, most commonly, an expression with the voice, though it can possess a wider meaning embracing communication by document, with respect to criminal forgery and counterfeiting. However, the reference in the Irish version of the Constitution to "cibé caint" indicates that utterances here refers only to oral expressions. Thus, the immunity protects speeches made by members in the House, any interjections by members while the House in sitting and possibly private conversations involving members even while the House is not sitting. Article 15.13 does not, however, appear to protect members' defamatory statements which are not utterances, such as statements in written documents. Also excluded from

proceedings — see p. 164 post. Whether a larger privilege should be recognised for certain council meetings does not seem to have been considered here. In the US, according to Eldredge 388-92 both authority and principle support an absolute privilege and he queries Prosser's suggestion that a scant majority of cases support only a qualified privilege.

12 See references by Crampton J at 1 ICLR at 194 and 5 ICLR at 171.

13 (1887) 20 LRIr 600.

14 At 611 et seq.

15 *Coffin v Coffin* (1808) 4 Mass 1.

protection would be defamatory signs and gestures. And, if the common law rule[16] that reading a document out loud is a libel rather than a slander is adhered to in this context, it might further reduce the scope of the privilege in Article 15.13 to utterances that do not consist of reading aloud from a script or document. It seems doubtful, however, that such a strained construction would be put by the law on the meaning of constitutional words which already bear a common sense meaning.

If this interpretation of Article 15.13 is correct, then the scope of its immunity from liability in defamation is surprisingly narrow, and one may turn, as one is entitled to, to examine the law existing before the enactment of the 1937 and the 1922 Constitutions to see if a wider protection existed then. That law consisted, as was already stated, of the protection contained in Article 9 of the Bill of Rights. That protection is recognised[17] as extending to the entire process by which a House of Parliament takes actions, and includes any necessary act such as voting, giving written notice of questions and presenting reports. Any written statement made in the course of a parliamentary proceeding is clearly protected.

The immunity contained in Article 15.13 applies only to statements by members, and not to statements by civil servants or to persons who have been invited, ordered or authorised to attend before the House. However, the immunity contained in the pre-existing law appears to have been wide enough to include within it statements by non-members such as witnesses or petitioners or others who are ordered or authorised to attend.[18] When a member of the Dáil or Seanad speaks in the other House he is also protected.

The immunity contained in the Constitution applies only to statements made in either House. Contrasting this with another immunity also contained in Article 15.13 — the immunity from arrest of members who are, inter alia, 'within the precincts of either House' — suggests that only statements made inside the building or chamber of each House are protected, and not statements made in nearby corridors or offices.[19] Statements made by members outside the House while performing their political and constituency duties enjoy only a qualified privilege.

While members themselves are not liable for their defamatory utterances and statements, it is a separate question whether any use may be made of these utterances and statements in the course of legal proceedings. The question could arise in an action against a member

16 See p. 81 supra.
17 May *Parliamentary Practice* 19th ed., 87.
18 At 83.
19 See Williams 75 fn 26a.

for a statement made outside the House where the plaintiff would wish to defeat the defence of qualified privilege by showing as evidence of malice a statement made inside the House. In England,[20] the privilege was held to possess the indirect effect of preventing absolutely any reliance on a parliamentary statement in legal proceedings. Here, it is more likely that the contrary applies and that reliance could be made on a parliamentary utterance or statement in legal proceedings. This is because of the difference which exists in the Irish text of the Constitution on the meaning of the terms 'privileged' which is used in Article 15.12 and 'not . . . amenable' which is used in Article 15.13. The former refers to a complete freedom from legal proceedings, whereas the latter refers only to a person not being tried in respect of the statement.[21] This suggests that a plaintiff here could rely on a parliamentary utterance or statement to defeat a defence of qualified privilege, and also as evidence of the fact that a statement was made.

The reform bodies[22] have recommended major extensions to the range of statements connected with the parliamentary system that are absolutely privileged. According to these, a statement between one member and another, or an officer of parliament, or a minister, ought to be immune from action no matter where it is made, so long as it is relevant to the member's position and is not published any wider than is necessary. It seems clear that at present such statements are not absolutely privileged. Should the Oireachtas wish to make them so it would have to ensure that the serious alteration in the balance between the constitutional right to a good name and other rights does not result in the former being denied. For assuming that the Oireachtas can create valid absolute privileges, it is still possible that the creation of these particular absolute privileges would be unconstitutional. They do involve drastic restrictions on the right to a good name, and, being at least one step removed from the essential working of the Oireachtas, the justification for such a move is much reduced. These extensions could be balanced, however, by empowering each House to waive a member's privilege if it thought fit to do so.

20 *Church of Scientology v Johnson-Smith* [1972] 1 QB 522.

21 'Privileged' is translated as 'táid saor ar chúrsaí dlí' whereas 'not . . . amenable' is translated as 'ní inchúisithe é.' On the other hand Morgan *Constitutional Law of Ireland*, 162 fn 15 suggests that the Church of Scientology case would probably be followed here because our wording is similar to that of the English provision in the Bill of Rights.

22 Faulks Committee Report para 203; NZ Committee Report paras. 184-7.

Article 15.12 of the Constitution of 1937 provides that 'utterances made in either House wherever published shall be privileged.' This restated Article 19 of the Constitution of 1922. Although the nature of this privilege is not identified in the English text, it is clear from the reference in the Irish text — 'táid saor ar chúrsaí dlí' — that the privilege is an absolute one. The Irish text also indicates that reports of parliamentary utterances cannot ever be relied on for any purpose in legal proceedings.

The privilege applies to *all* reports of utterances. Article 15.12 does not, it seems, allow any distinction to be made between the various media in which the reports are published. This interesting feature ignores the distinction which is usually made between official and unofficial reports, according to which the former are absolutely protected while the latter enjoy only a qualified privilege. The law, then, is different from that in other jurisdictions, and, so far as unofficial reports of parliamentary utterances are concerned, is a change from the pre-1922 law. All of the media are similarly protected. So, if and when the proceedings of the Houses of the Oireachtas are broadcast, all reports of utterances made therein will be absolutely privileged. The distinction which the reform bodies seek to make between live sound broadcasts and recorded sound broadcasts — in which the former would be absolutely protected while the latter would only enjoy a qualified protection[23] — could not be applied here.

However, a distinction which Article 15.12 does seem to require is one between reports of utterances and reports of other statements, such as would be visible to the eye via televised broadcasts. The use of the term utterance might leave unprotected the broadcasting by pictures of parliamentary proceedings for which it has been suggested the common law offers only a qualified privilege to members and broadcasters.[24] The reform bodies agree that recorded film broadcasts should only enjoy a qualified privilege,[25] but they differ on whether live film broadcasts should be absolutely privileged.[26] It is interesting to note that in Australia, the broadcasting of any part of parliamentary proceedings has been absolutely privileged since 1946.[27]

23 Faulks Committee Report para 222; NZ Committee Report para 193.
24 Davis, 'Parliamentary Broadcasting and the Law of Defamation' (1948) 7 U of Toronto LJ 385, 394.
25 Faulks Committee Report para 227; NZ Committee Report para 193.
26 The Faulks Committee favoured conferring only a qualified privilege on the picture part of live television broadcasts — para 221. The New Zealand Committee favoured an absolute privilege for the same — paras. 191, 192.
27 Parliamentary Proceedings Broadcasting Act 1946, s15.

There is no requirement in Article 15.12 that the report of the utterance be either whole or impartial.[28] A report in a newspaper which consists of an account of parliamentary proceedings interspersed with comment could not, it seems, be made the subject of a defamation action insofar as there would be any reliance on the utterances quoted in the report.

Utterances in parliamentary committees

The immunity contained in Article 15.13 of the Constitution extends only to utterances made by members in either House of the Oireachtas, and does not cover utterances made by members in parliamentary committees. Sometimes, however, when debating legislation, the House may constitute itself into a committee of the House, and utterances made then are within the constitutional protection, but only because the committee is an alter ego of the House. When a parliamentary committee is separate from either House, utterances made by its members are not protected by Article 15.13. In 1967, the Committee on the Constitution recommended, after noting the view that this sub-article 'might not provide privileges, in respect of utterances by the Public Accounts Committee and its members in the course of their duties,' that 'Privileges should be extended to the utterances and publications of all committees of the Oireachtas.'[29] Although the constitutional protection may seem limited, one may still have recourse to the pre-1921 law, and there it seems that all of the actions of properly constituted committees sitting in parliament, including statements made by members, were viewed as parliamentary proceedings and so within the Bill of Rights privilege.[30] Indeed, there were two nineteenth century cases, one English[31] and one Irish,[32] in which the evidence of witnesses before

28 The statement made during the Dáil Debates on Article 19 of the 1922 Constitution that no protection would be conferred on garbled or malicious accounts of the proceedings of parliament by journalists — does not appear to be correct. Morgan at 164 states that a fair and accurate report, and not a selective account is necessary. In an English case *Cook v Alexander* [1973] 3 AER 1037 it was held that a parliamentary sketch involving selective quotations. had to be fair. The text of Art 15.12 however contains no reference to either fairness or impartiality.

29 *The Report of the Committee on the Constitution*, 1967, Annex 27, 143.

30 May's *Parliamentary Practice*, 83. Morgan 160 disagrees with the view that pre-1921 common law can be resorted to, and argues that the constitutional provisions are exhaustive. But these are no less susceptible to eccentricity than British law is and where obviously deficient must needs be cured, in this instance, by reference to the pre-1921 position.

31 *Goffin v Donnelly* (1881) 6 QBD 307.

32 *Kane v Mulvany* (1866) IR 2 CL 402.

select committees of the commons and lords respectively were held to be absolutely privileged. So the proceedings of parliamentary committees here probably are protected by statute and common law. Nonetheless, the omission from the Constitution of a privilege protecting utterances in parliamentary committees was considered to create a doubt,[33] and on two occasions in 1970[34] and in 1975[35] the activities of particular committees were inhibited because of fears expressed about the lack of privilege. Legislation was passed in 1970[36] but that conferred an absolute privilege on only one committee sitting for a particular purpose. When the problem arose again in 1975, it was finally decided to clarify the matter, and the Oireachtas passed the Committees of the Houses of the Oireachtas (Privilege and Procedure) Act 1976, s 2 of which states

> (1) A member of either House of the Oireachtas shall not, in respect of any utterance in or before a committee, be amenable to any court or any authority other than the House or the Houses . . . by which the committee was appointed.
>
> (2) (a) The documents of a committee and the documents of its members connected with the committee or its functions.
>
> (b) all official reports and publications of a committee, and
>
> (c) the utterances in a committee of the members, advisors, officials and agents of the committee,
>
> wherever published shall be privileged.

It can be seen, then, that not only members but also others as well, who are involved with the committee, are protected.[37] A significant omission in the section is that no privilege is conferred on witnesses, although conferring such a protection may have been one of the objects of the legislation.[38] This matter would remain governed by the

33 See the remark of John Kelly TD at Dáil Debates vol 289 col 322 'The status and function of these committees are very unclear and every time a crisis or difficulty arises we all look a little foolish and a lot of time is wasted before we can discover what are our entitlements.'.

34 For an account of this event, see *Report of Tribunal of Inquiry*, 31 July 1975. See also *In re Haughey* [1971] IR 217, 237 et seq. per O'Dalaigh CJ.

35 For an account of this event, see Dáil Debates vol 289 col 310 et seq.

36 Committee of Public Accounts of Dáil Éireann (Privilege and Procedure) Act 1970.

37 S. 2(2)(c). In the US the privilege of a member of Congress has been held to cover an aide participating in committee proceedings, and the member can waive it if he wishes — *US v Brewster* (1972) 408 US 501.

38 Dáil Debates vol 289 col 317. This omission appears also to have had the consequence of inhibiting the work of particular Committees, see the report in *The Irish Times*, 3 March 1984. It was also reported in the same edition that the government intended shortly to introduce legislation to remedy the

pre-1922 law and the cases referred to above where statements by witnesses before parliamentary committees were held to be absolutely privileged. Although s2 of the 1976 Act does not indicate the nature of the protection, the privilege conferred by this section is, one submits, an absolute one. This is because the pre-1922 law recognised that the proceedings of parliamentary committees were absolutely privileged, because witnesses are absolutely privileged, and because s2 is phrased in similar terms to Article 15.13 of the Constitution which contains an absolute privilege. It is curious, though, that the Irish version of s2(2) refers to 'pribhléid,' while in the Irish version of the Constitution the term 'privileged' is referred to as 'táid saor ar chúrsaí dlí.'

Official reports and publications

Article 15.12 of the Constitution provides that 'all official reports and publications of the Oireachtas or of either House thereof . . . wherever published shall be privileged.' This restated substantially Article 19 of the 1922 Constitution, which had itself replaced s2 of the Parliamentary Papers Act of 1840. This Act remains in force in England. Although none of these provisions have described the nature of the privilege the reference in the 1840 Act has been interpreted as meaning an absolute one.[39] This is because of other references in the 1840 Act to privileges that are dependent on the absence of malice. The 1922 Constitution evidenced no desire to change this and the Irish text of Article 15.12 in the present Constitution makes clear that the privilege is absolute.

In order to be an official one, the report or publication must be published under the authority of the Oireachtas or of either of its Houses. Because a committee drawn from either or both Houses might not come within this, the opportunity was taken, when enacting the Committees of the Houses of the Oireachtas (Privilege and Procedure) Act 1976, to provide in s2(2)(b) that 'all official reports and publications of a committee . . . wherever published shall be privileged.' This privilege, too, would seem to be absolute.

THE ADMINISTRATION OF JUSTICE

An absolute privilege from liability in the tort of defamation attaches to statements which are made in the course of the administration of justice. Greene B stated in *Kennedy v Hilliard* (1859), one of the

situation by conferring absolute and qualified privileges in respect of testimony by witnesses before parliamentary committees. But no such legislation has yet been introduced.

39 Gatley para 423; Fleming 550; Winfield and Jolowicz *Tort*, 12th ed., 333.

leading Irish cases, 'It cannot be disputed, as a general rule, that anything said, or published in writing, in the court and as part of legal proceedings cannot be made the subject of an action for defamation . . .'.[40] The clarity in the law which is suggested by this statement, and by many others like it, is, however, deceptive, for two reasons. Firstly, the statement implies that relevant and irrelevant statements are treated similarly. This, as will be seen, might not be correct. Secondly, the law in this area has developed in a haphazard manner in which the positions of judges, parties, witnesses and advocates have been treated separately with little reference to the common basis of the rules which apply to each. In the result, not all of these courtroom characters enjoy the same measure of protection, and the law is therefore more varied and complex than it might be.

Judges of record

The Constitution of 1937 does not confer an explicit privilege on the judiciary from any kind of legal action, including actions in defamation. It merely provides in Article 35.2 that 'all judges shall be independent in the exercise of their judicial functions and subject only to this Constitution and the law.' It might be that a privilege is implicit in the idea of judicial independence, or that it is a pre-condition to the obligation to administer justice. Failing this, such judicial privilege as there is will be found only in the common law, for there has not been any legislation on the matter. At common law, a judge of record[41] — and this includes judges of the Supreme Court, High Court, Circuit Court and District Court — is absolutely privileged from any action, including defamation, in respect of what he says or does while acting in the performance of his office.[42] Of course, for what he does outside of his office — as where he anonymously publishes libels in newspapers,[43] or explains to outsiders his proceedings in a particular case,[44] or where he sends a copy of part of the pleadings to an outsider,[45] the judge enjoys no absolute privilege.

40 (1859) 10 ICLR 195, 221. Whether the immunity is so complete as to preclude any use of privileged judicial statements in subsequent proceedings is not clear. English authority suggests that it may be — *Roy v Prior* [1971] AC 470.

41 Statements by jurors appear to enjoy the same privilege as judges of record — *Kennedy v Hilliard* supra 209 per Pigot CB.

42 *Floyd v Barker* (1608) 12 Co Rep 23; *Hammond v Howell* (1689) 2 Mod 218; *Garnett v Ferrand* (1827) 5 LJ OS KB 221; *Taafe v Downes* (1812) 3 Moore PC 36n; *Ward v Freeman* (1852) 2 ICLR 460; *Tughan v Craig* [1918] 1 IR 245; *Macaulay & Co v Wyse-Power* (1943) 77 ILTR 61.

43 *R v Mr Justice Johnson* (1804) 29 ST 1.

44 *Croke v O'Grady* (1830) 4 Law Rec 49.

45 *Little v Clements* (1851) 1 ICLR 194. Both Croke's case and Little's case concerned magistrates, but it is submitted that the position would be the same with judges.

There is no dearth of assertions for the judicial privilege.[46] The following statement of the privilege, and the reason for it, by Fox J in *Taffe v Downes* (1812), is representative

> It is necessary to the free and impartial administration of justice that the persons administering it should be uninfluenced by fear and unbiased by hope. Judges have not been invested with the privilege for their own protection merely; it is calculated for the benefit of the people, by ensuring to them a calm, steady and impartial administration of justice; it is a principle . . . founded on the very frame of the constitution; it is to be met with in the earliest books of law.'[47].

In the same case, Fletcher J stressed the impracticality of any other rule

> (It) would be absurd . . . to bring, not the doctrines they promulgate or their adjudications, before a Superior Court of Appeal for reconsideration and examination, but the Judges themselves before co-ordinate tribunals to answer in damages for such decisions as equally fallible individuals may pronounced erroneous . . . It would besides be infinite.'[48].

A multiplicity of actions could arise because 'even while I was restraining another judge I was preparing material for some other judge to restrain me.'[49] The privilege of judges of record applies to mistakes and errors of law or fact, to illegal acts and to wrongful commitments whether they are done innocently, deliberately or maliciously. An English judge put it thus 'I am at liberty by the law of England in delivering judgement to be as malicious as I like; the law protects me.'[50] The privilege extends to acts and statements that are made in the course of office both outside of court and outside of term.[51] It covers statements that are made in the course of the

46 *Taafe v Downes* at 60 per Lord Norbury; *Ward v Freeman* at 467 per Greene B, 485 per Moore J, 486 per Jackson J, 497 per Perrin J, 504 per Crampton J, 513 per Torrens J.

47 At 51.

48 The lengthy judgement of Fletcher J, occupying over seventy pages, is not quoted in this report. It is however contained in Hatchell's *Report of the Arguments in the case of Taafe v Downes*, Dublin 1815. The present quote is at 165, and was quoted by Perrin J at 495 in *Ward v Freeman* (1852) 2 ICLR 460.

49 *Tughan v Craig* at 257 per Dodd J.

50 *More v Weaver* [1928] 2 KB 520, 522 per Scrutton LJ; for a comparative survey of the extent of judicial immunity, see Miller 'Defamation by a Judge: Fixing the Limits' (1980) Juridical Rev 88.

51 *Taafe v Downes* at 70 per Lord Norbury.

hearing or when delivering judgement. Thus in *Macaulay & Co v Wyse-Power* (1943),[52] when an action was brought against a Circuit Court judge because he said while giving judgement in a case 'No person in Connacht should ever again have anything to do with this disreputable firm which earns its profits by battening on the lack of legal knowledge of the simple people of the West,' it was dismissed.[53] The privilege also protects statements which are made after a case has finished and while another is being heard, whether on the same day as the first case or on the following or, it seems, any subsequent day. In *Tughan v Craig* (1918),[54] when, on the day following a case in which the plaintiff solicitor had been involved, the defendant who was Recorder of Belfast and so a judge of record said, while hearing another case,

> 'He was addressing the jury in a case here last night, and he told them that he could twist black and make it white, and even, if he liked, he could twist white again and make it black . . . and a statement like that, unblushingly made . . . goes a long way to justify public opinion as regards some members of the profession . . .',

an action for the words was dismissed.

But one ought not to make too much of this privilege because, although it is a 'most useful principle in the administration of justice . . . there is also another principle equally, if not more, sacred in our constitutional jurisprudence, namely, that justice must not be denied to the suitor: *nulli negabimus justitiam*.'[55] The privilege of the judiciary does not in fact extend so far as it appears at first glance. There are two situations in which judges do not enjoy an absolute privilege from liability in defamation.

Firstly, it seems that where a judge acts only ministerially he enjoys no absolute privilege for what he says or does.[56] An English judge,

52 (1943) 77 ILTR 61.

53 *More v Weaver* [1928] 2 KB 520 suggests that when a judge makes entirely extraneous remarks during a case he has, in effect, abandoned his position as a participant in the legal proceedings, and may be sued. General pronouncements here on judical privilege might not agree with this. In logic, too, it seems a doutbful proposition. If a District Justice makes an extraneous remark, however irrelevant, it will surely be born from some issue before him, and therefore be made in the performance of his office. Whether such an extensive immunity is actually necessary for judicial independence and efficiency is questioned by Miller supra 108.

54 [1918] 1 IR 245.

55 *Ward v Freeman* (1842) 2 ICLR 460, 513 per Torrens J.

56 *Ferguson v Kinnoull* (1842) 9 CL & Fin 251; *Ward v Freeman* supra.

Lord Cottenham, stated in 1842 'Where there is a minsterial act to be done by persons who on other occasions act judicially, the refusal to do the ministerial act is equally actionable as if no judicial functions were on any occasion entrusted to them.'[57] It is difficult to distinguish between a ministerial act and a judicial one, or rather an administration of justice since the essential function of a judge under the Constitution is that of administering justice.[58]

The essence of a ministerial act appears to have been decided by the House of Lords in *Ferguson v Kinnoull* (1842) [59] to be the absence of any discretion in a judge as to whether he may or may not do an act. In other words, where by law he is under an obligation to perform an act, then he is acting ministerially. So, it was held in Ferguson's case that the refusal by a court of record in Scotland to hear a case, which it was legally bound to hear, was a refusal to perform a ministerial act, for which the court was held liable. In an Irish case, *Ward v Freeman* [60] — which came before ten judges of the Court of Exchequer Chamber in 1852 — where a judge of record, an Assistant Barrister, had refused, in breach of a specific statutory duty, to permit a litigant to take the steps necessary to make an appeal against his decision, the entire court accepted the distinction between a ministerial act and a judicial one, with the express or implicit understanding that in the case of a ministerial act, no privilege existed; '... all the judges in *Ward v Freeman* seem to have assumed that for a breach of ministerial duty imposed by statute an action would lie. The question always is: what is ministerial, and what is not?' [61] The court in Ward's case divided evenly on whether the act of permitting an appeal to be made was ministerial or judicial. It may be suggested that the better view is that the initial duty to allow the litigant take the steps before appealing was ministerial, but that the demand on the judge's discretion to see if the statutory requirements for making the appeal were met may have been judicial. [62] There would seem

57 *Ferguson v Kinnoull*, at 312.

58 In the cases 'ministerial' is used in opposition to 'judicial'. It seems better to eschew the latter term because of the different senses in which it is sometimes used. It can refer to everything a judge does while in office, or to when he acts according to natural justice, or to when he administers justice; whereas for Irish purposes, the latter is its true meaning. The term ministerial may seem an unfashionable way to refer to tasks which are not an administration of justice, yet it is used in the older cases in the present context and its value in marking the distinction is established. See also *Lynham v Butler* (No 2) [1933] IR 74, 80, and Miller supra.

59 (1842) 9 Cl & Fin 251.

60 (1852) 2 ICLR 460.

61 *Tughan v Craig* [1918] 1 IR 245, 249 per Dodd J.

62 Eg 512 Torrens J; 521 Monahan CJ.

to be many examples of ministerial functions being performed by judges, such as where a case is within a judges jurisdiction and he must hear it, or where a District Justice is obliged to send an accused forward for trial on being satisfied at a preliminary hearing that there is a case to answer, or when signing some document like a writ of habeas corpus. Whenever Rules of the various courts, or statute law generally, require an act to be done a ministerial function is probably involved, although since there will often, if not always, be an administration of justice preliminary to performing the ministerial task, the likelihood of a defamatory statement being pinned down to so fine a point as performing the ministerial task must be remote.

In identifying what acts involve an administration of justice, since there are no defamation cases in point, reliance must be placed on the body of case law based on Article 34.1 of the Constitution, which deals with, amongst other things, the functions of the courts.[63] In these cases various acts have been identified by the courts as involving an administration of justice with a view to resisting any legislative encroachments on the judicial sphere. From these it would seem that the administration of justice consists of the making of decisions that are final and binding. A decision can only be made if there is a choice between alternatives. If there is no choice, then there is no decision to make and so there is no administration of justice. Finally it may be noted that the legal duty on the judge to perform a ministerial act does confer a qualified privilege on him for the statements he makes while so acting.[64]

The second situation in which a judge of record will not be absolutely protected from liability in defamation is when he acts outside of his jurisdiction. Whiteside CJ stated in *O'Keefe v Cullen* (1873) 'Even a judge of a Court of Record, whose acts and language are challenged, is bound to show that what he did or said was in the exercise of jurisdiction lawfully committed to him. If he transgresses the bounds of that jurisdiction he is responsible for his acts.'[65] In the English case of *Houlden v Smith* (1850) [66] a judge of record who issued a summons against a person and committed him to prison for disobeying it, and who knew that in so acting he had no jurisdiction to do either, was held liable. It is not just the fact of an excess of jurisdiction which denies the judge of record the protection of an absolute privilege. The judge must also have been aware that he had no reasonable grounds for acting as he did.[67]

63 See generally Kelly *The Irish Constitution*, 2nd ed 232 et seq.

64 See p. 195 post.

65 (1873) IR 7 CL 319, 411.

66 (1850) 14 QB 841. *Beaurain v Scott* (1813) 3 Comp 388 is a case where a judge of an ecclesiastical court was held liable for an excess of jurisdiction.

67 *Sirros v Moore* [1975] QB 118, 140 per Buckley LJ.

There are very few cases in the reports where an actionable excess of jurisdiction has been identified. Buckley LJ thought, in an English case, that this was because 'where a judge of a superior court has been held to have acted beyond his powers, this has been regarded for the purposes of the rule of judicial immunity as an error of judgement of his part rather than an abuse of jurisdiction.'[68] Errors of judgement, it may be recalled, are absolutely privileged. This tendency makes it difficult to identify when a judge would be considered to be acting within or without his jurisdiction. Clearly when he hears a case or makes an order which he is aware that he has no reasonable grounds for thinking he is entitled to make, he is acting in excess. But merely making remarks about a case once it is over does not seem to be excess.[69] On this, the judge's privilege may be contrasted with that of the advocate. As will be seen shortly, the advocate's privilege does not protect him against liability for remarks made after the case is finished.

Parties and witnesses

A party or witness enjoys an absolute privilege from liability in respect of defamatory statements made in the course of the administration of justice. The privilege covers statements made orally during the hearing, or contained in affidavits,[70] or in matters which are done pending the action, such as supplying information to legal advisers,[71] or the making of a draft writ of a summons issued afterwards — of which there is almost invariably some publication before issue[72] — or contained in the pleadings; and it extends to necessary acts done after judgement in order for instance, to register the judgement.[73]

Pigot CB stated in *Kennedy v Hilliard* (1859), that 'for what is said by a party on his own behalf, or a witness in giving evidence in the ordinary course of a judicial proceeding, there is an absolute immunity from liability to an action for libel or slander.'[74] He added that this immunity was 'established by abundant authority both of ancient and modern times.' The basis of the privilege rests in the public policy that 'suitors or witnesses are not to be deterred by the fear of actions

68 *Sirros v Moore* at 141, also *Miller v Seare* (1777) 2 W Black 1141.
69 *Tughan v Craig,* supra.
70 For a consideration of the authorities, see *Kennedy v Hilliard* (1859) 10 ICLR 195, 202 per Pigot CB.
71 *Watson v McEwan* [1905] AC 480; see also Linden 699 fn 174.
72 *MacCabe v Joynt* [1901] 2 IR 115, 127 per Palles CB.
73 *McLoughlin v Doey* (1893) 32 LR Ir 518.
74 At 201.

from prosecuting claims or giving testimony in proceedings.'[75]

Although the privilege has usually protected statements properly and lawfully made in the due course of judicial proceedings, it is still unclear whether the privilege also includes irrelevant and malicious statements made during legal proceedings. Prior to 1971, the position here seemed to have been that neither irrelevance nor maliciousness lost the privilege. This was the result of two decisions in the nineteenth century — *Kennedy v Hilliard*[76] and *Gildea v Brien*, in 1821, which was an unreported decision cited in Kennedy's case.[77] Both of these cases were approved of in *MacCabe v Joynt*[78] in 1901. In Kennedy's case it was held that no action lies against a party for an irrelevant statement contained in an affidavit made by him as a witness in a case; Pigot CB stated that 'the immunity of a party ... attaches whether what he states be or be not material.'[79] In Gildea's case a similar decision was reached on broadly similar facts.

Despite all this authority, it should be noted that these decisions may not have emphatically dispelled an earlier doubt about the effect of an irrelevancy on the existence of the privilege. Leaving aside Gildea's case,[80] the authorities before Kennedy's case went both ways, with some support for the final decision,[81] but if anything, the better supported view was that irrelevant statements made in the course of judicial proceedings were not protected.[82] That must mean, then, that the weight of the decision in Kennedy's case rests more on the view of public policy taken by the court there than on authority. To quote again from the judgement of Pigot CB, as regards that policy

> If a party, in making ... a pleading or a statement [or] ... an affidavit ..., or if a witness ... shall be bound to determine, first, what are the exact questions at issue in the cause, and next, what is the exact line at which statement or evidence shall be material, and to determine this at the peril of an action for defamation if he be wrong ... the protection which the law professes to give to him

75 *Kennedy v Hilliard* at 223 per Greene B.
76 (1859) 10 ICLR 195.
77 (1821) mentioned at (1859) 10 ICLR 230.
78 [1901] 2 IR 115.
79 At 210.
80 It was hardly satisfactory that prominence should have been given to an unreported decision from almost forty years before, which was resurrected only by the memory of one judge and from which one cannot tell whether there was any discussion of the authorities in the area.
81 *Boulton v Clapham* (1640) Sir W Jones 431; *Astley v Young* (1759) 2 Burr 807.
82 *Ayres v Sedgwick* (1721) Palmer 142; *Hodgson v Scarlett* (1818) 1 B & Ald 232; *Buckley v Wood* (1591) Cro Eliz 230; *Chamberlain's case* (1721) Palmer 533.

would be nearly nugatory for its purpose. That purpose is to give him the courage ... as a party ... or, as a witness to give his evidence ... underterred by the fear of a prosecution or an action. It is impossible that he can be free from that fear, if his immunity must depend upon his not mistaking what is not material from what is ...".[83].

This view of the policy of the law was also accepted by Palles C B in MacCabes's case[84] when he quoted, approvingly, this passage. Even so, it must remain very much a matter of opinion whether a fear of liability would actually impede the use or efficacy of legal proceedings. Whether it was for this reason, or whether it was because of a reliance on the position in England — where an irrelevant statement maliciously spoken by a witness is, apparently, not protected[85] — one cannot tell, but in *In Re Haughey* (1971), Ó Dálaigh CJ expressed the view that an irrelevant statement loses a witness his privilege. 'It is salutary to bear in mind that even in the High Court, if a witness were to take advantage of his position to utter something defamatory having no reference to the cause or matter of inquiry but introduced maliciously for its purpose, no privilege or immunity would attach and he might find himself sued in an action for defamation.'[86] This view, which was expressed without reference to previous authority and was clearly obiter dictum, was nonetheless agreed with by two other Supreme Court judges.[87] Because of this, it is difficult to state what the law in this area is. Were it not for this remark the better supported view now is that maliciousness and irrelevancy do not lose a witness his privilege.

Advocates

Barristers, solicitors, and parties who appear on their own behalf enjoy an absolute privilege in respect of relevant statements made by them in the course of the administration of justice. The privilege 'is not the privilege of the advocate — it is the privilege of the client,'[88] though, as will be seen, the advocate's privilege may not be as

83 At 211.
84 [1901] 2 IR 115, 120.
85 Gatley para. 396, although Prosser 817 thinks it is.
86 [1971] IR 217, 264. In the US most courts do not privilege irrelevant statements — Eldredge 354, Prosser 817 — but they interpret relevance broadly, and not as in the law of evidence, so statements irrelevant to the issue but made with reference to the subject matter are protected.
87 Walsh and Budd JJ.
88 *R v Kiernan* (1855) 5 ICLR 171, 173 per Crampton J.

extensive as the client's. The privilege includes trial and pre-trial statements, whether contained in pleadings or in consultation with parties or witnesses when they are sufficiently connected with, or preliminary to, proposed judicial proceedings.[89] Other than this the lawyers' privilege is only qualified, and as such is discussed in Chapter 8.

It is not clear whether the privilege of the advocate goes beyond relevant statements to irrelevant and malicious ones. In England, since the decision of the Court of Appeal in *Munster v Lamb* (1881)[90] it has been taken that the privilege is an absolute one and is applicable to all statements made in an enquiry before any court of justice into any matter concerning the administration of law. However, before this there was a considerable body of opinion in Ireland to the effect that irrelevant and malicious statements made by advocates in legal proceedings were not protected.

In 1855, Crampton J expressed the law on the advocate's privilege in two propositions: 'The first is, that a Counsel, in the discharge of his duty, is not in an action answerable for words spoken by him in a case where those words were pertinent or relevant to the issue, however strong or severe ... The second position is, that if it be proved that the injurious words were not spoken *bona fide*, or if express malice be shown, there the words may be actionable.'[91] In the previous year, in *Higginson v O'Flaherty*,[92] the same judge restored a first instance decision in which a proctor in an ecclesiastical court was found liable for an irrelevant slander of the deputy registrar of the court uttered in the course of an action.

Three years later, in *The Queen v Hutchins*,[93] the Court of Queen's Bench made absolute a conditional order for leave to file a criminal information for a slander which was uttered by a person defending himself just after his case had ended. In delivering judgement Lefroy CJ stated 'This order must be made absolute, if for no other purpose than to put an end to any such idea of privilege existing in such cases ... and it is aggravated by the fact that the cause was then at an end; even pending the cause such language cannot be tolerated.'[94] There are in addition, dicta in a number of other cases to the same effect.[95] Whenever authority was cited in these

89 For a consideration of the extent of the absolute immunity, see *Saif Ali v Mitchell* [1980] AC 198, a negligence action. Eldredge 368-9 argues that lawyers should have an absolute privilege for statements unrelated to a judicial proceeding since so much legal work is of this type. See p. 118 supra.

90 (1883) 11 QBD 588.

91 *R v Kiernan* at 174.

92 (1854) 4 ICLR 125.

93 (1857) 7 ICLR 425.

94 At 426.

95 *Mitchell v Kerr* (1801) reported (1825) Rowe Rep 527 at 545 per Finnucane

cases reliance was made particularly on two earlier English cases — *Brook v Montague*[96] and *Hodgson v Scarlett*[97] — both of which certainly support the view that irrelevant statements are not protected. It is of interest to see how the Court of Appeal in the English case of *Munster v Lamb,* dealt with those cases and demonstrated their errors. In fact, though both decisions were mentioned in argument, they were not referred to in the judgements of the court, and those judgements reached their conclusion only be arguing on principle, and not on authority, and by analogy from the position of judges and witnesses. Further, in order to justify an absolute privilege for the irrelevant statements of advocates, Brett MR emphasised the difficulties which would otherwise be faced by counsel if they were to be liable for their irrelevant statements.[98] He did this by asserting, what is clearly not true, that it is not only as important to the administration of justice that an advocate be protected in the same way as judges and witnesses are, but also by asserting that it was actually more important that advocates should enjoy this absolute protection. Because of this, and because of the failure of the judgements to deal specifically with the previous authorities on this area — needless to say the Irish authorities were not mentioned — it might be that the decision in Munster's case does not overturn the well established view here that irrelevancy and malice do lose an advocate his privilege.[99]

If the view of Crampton J still represents the law here, then in each case the investigating court will have to consider the previous proceedings in which the advocate made the statement to see whether the sued-upon statement was relevant to them or not, and this in fact was done in a number of cases.[1] It is uncertain whether the burden of proof rests on the plaintiff to prove the irrelevancy of the statement, or on the defendant to prove that the statement was relevant to the occasion. It seems more probable, however, that the burden rests on the plaintiff because it is not to be presumed that what was said on such an occasion was impertinent or irrelevant.[2]

J; *Butt v Jackson* (1846) 10 ILR 120, 124 per Blackburne CJ; *Kennedy v Hilliard* (1859) 10 ICLR 195, 207 per Pigot CB, 224 per Greene B.

96 (1606) Cro Jac 90.

97 (1818) 1 B & Ald 232.

98 (1883) 11 QBD 588, 603 et seq.

99 Such a conclusion would also have the merit of harmonizing the position of advocates with that of witnesses — if one assumes that the remark of Ó Dálaigh CJ quoted earlier concerning the position of witnesses correctly states the law At the same time since the functions and positions of advocates and witnesses in a hearing are not identical, it does not have to follow that the privilege of each should be the same.

1 *Higginson v O'Flaherty* supra, *R v Kiernan* supra, *R v Hutchins* supra.

2 *Kennedy v Hilliard* at 226 per Greene B.

Finally, the fact that the advocate is identified with the client for the purpose of the privilege does not support the wider view of the privilege. There is this difference. A counsel cannot say anything that the client might say, nor anything that he was instructed to say. '[It] is the duty of counsel towards their clients to use their own judgement and experience and discretion; and as the result, whatever be their instructions, to exclude all topics and observations of which the case does not properly admit.'[3]

Bodies under Article 37 of the Constitution, and other bodies

Justice is administered in courts by judges appointed under the Constitution, and by persons or bodies who are not judges and exercise limited judicial functions and powers under law and according to Article 37 of the Constitution. From this alone one could conclude that proceedings under Article 37 are absolutely privileged, although there is a body of case law which also establishes this.[4] The protection extends, as in the case of proceedings in courts, not only to statements made during the hearing but also to statements necessarily preparatory to the hearing and to statements made afterwards that are necessary to give effect to the decision reached. The extent to which the proceedings of a body, established by law, are protected depends on whether there is an administration of justice. Identifying an administration of justice in this context is as difficult as it is when distinguishing between a judge acting ministerially and acting judicially. There are two views about when a body, established by law, should be deemed to administer justice.

Firstly, there is the view established by English authority which states that there can be an administration of justice whenever there is an authorized inquiry which, though not before a court of justice, is before a tribunal which has similar attributes and acts in a manner similar to that in which courts act.[5] According to this, one distinguishes between administrative and judicial functions. If the purpose of the body is of the former type then no privilege attaches to its proceedings regardless of the powers or procedures or attributes it enjoys or follows.[6] But if the function is judicial, then it seems that the body need only possess even one of the attributes of a court of justice for its proceedings to be absolutely privileged. And that

3 *Butt v Jackson* (1846) 10 ILR 120, 124 per Blackburne CJ.
4 For the English authorities, see Gatley para 409 et seq. There are no Irish cases on this area.
5 *Royal Aquarium v Parkinson* [1892] 1 QB 431, 442 per Lord Esher MR.
6 *O'Connor v Waldron* [1935] AC 76, 82 per Lord Atkin.

attribute need only be, for instance, the power to compel witnesses to attend on pain of punishment.[7] Their testimony need not be sworn,[8] nor need the conclusion reached at all affect rights, nor even be decisive.[9] It can be just the making of a report to another who may, but need not, act on it. However, conferring unusual powers in a judicial matter, such as powers of entry into premises and inspection of documents, may, though it is not clear, prevent proceedings from being privileged.

According to the second view, there is an administration of justice whenever a person authorised under Article 37 is required to make a final and binding decision in a dispute concerning rights and liabilities. To this may be added that the distinctive mark of state justice, as opposed to private or unofficial justice, is the ability to compel the executive power of the state to lend itself to the organisation of the hearing, to permit the hearing to run its course, and to assist in the production of evidence and the enforcement of decisions. This view requires a decisive adjudication affecting rights and also for executive assistance to be compellable. Those English authorities, in which proceedings possessing no decision-making capabilites were regarded as administrations of justice,[10] would, on this view, have been wrongly decided. Equally, those English authorities where proceedings, which did possess decision-making powers,[11] were not regarded as administrations of justice would also have been wrongly decided. By the same token, the Commission of the European Community might, when adjudicating on alleged breaches of competition law, be regarded as performing a judicial function because of the decisive nature of its adjudication, and because its decisions are enforceable in national courts, despite an English decision to the contrary.[12]

It would seem that the second view is much closer to the various Irish authorities on Article 37, although there is no case exactly in point. The second view recognises that the essential point about an administration of justice in any human society, must always be the power to make decisions. To ignore this and to consider the superficial features of a hearing, is to take much too broad a view. There may be grounds for absolutely privileging the proceedings of non-decision making bodies, but it is not clear whether the importance of these bodies is so great that, in constitutional terms, the protection of their

7 *Dawkins v Lord Rokely* (1873) LR 8 QB 255.
8 Supra.
9 *Dawkins v Lord Rokely* supra; *Barratt v Kearns* [1905] 1 KB 504; *Trapp v Mackie* [1979] 1 WLR 377.
10 Dawkin's case supra, Barratt's case supra, Trapp's case supra.
11 Eg Royal Aquarium case supra.
12 *Hassalbad v Orbinson* [1985] 1 AER 173.

proceedings demands an absolute rather than a qualified privilege.

There are a considerable number of persons or bodies, established by statute, that would appear to administer justice under Article 37. In certain instances, statute has specifically conferred privilege on various aspects of the proceedings of these bodies.[13] In others it has not,[14] although these bodies would, nonetheless, be absolutely privileged in their proceedings. There are too, a number of bodies that might not seem to administer justice, according to the second view, but which have yet had a privilege conferred on them by statute.[15]

The absolute privilege which is enjoyed by the proceedings of parties or bodies, established by law under Article 37, does not extend to private or domestic tribunals not so constituted, and would not either, it seems, extend to the Benchers of the Kings Inns,[16] unless the phrase 'law' in Article 37 is interpreted there to include the common law.

THE EXECUTIVE

Statements made by government ministers, civil servants and public officials in the course of their office and concerning acts of state are absolutely privileged from action in defamation. There was an implicit assertion of this in *McElveney v Connellan* (1864).[17] In this case, it was sought to compel the production of a report by the Inspector General of Prisons for the Lord Lieutenant for use as evidence of the making of a defamatory statement. The court, however, upheld the state's claim that it enjoyed an evidential privilege against producing the report. It was subsequently held in England that a

13 Eg Medical Practitioners Act 1978, s44 et seq; Industrial Relations Act 1946, s21(2). For such a body under the Land Purchase Acts, see *Madden & Others v Ireland*, HCt, unreported 1980.

14 Eg Dentists Act 1928.

15 Eg Solicitors Act 1954, Tribunals of Inquiry (Evidence) Act 1921.

16 Unlike in *Lincoln v Daniels* [1962] 1 QB 237. Some American authority supports recognising an absolute privilege for labour dispute settling process and arbitration proceedings on policy grounds of enhancing alternatives to the court system, although the limits and circumstances of such privilege are not clear — see Andrle, 'Extension of Absolute Privilege to Defamation in Arbitration Proceedings' (1984) 33 Cath UL Rev 1073. Here such proceedings would attract a qualified protection only, see Chapter 8.

17 (1864) 17 ICLR 55; see also *McSorley v Masterson* (1945) 79 ILTR 45, and *Forristal v Forristal* (1966) 100 ILTR 182. On executive privilege generally see Brecht, 'The Absolute Privilege of the Executive in Defamation' (1962) 15 Vand L Rev 1127; Huyett, 'Governmental Immunity' (1976) 50 Temple LQ 191.

previous decision[18] there on almost identical facts involved 'the conclusion that, even if such a document could be put in, it would be absolutely privileged and no action could be founded on it."[19] The immunity from liability in defamation is, therefore, related, in its origins, to privilege against producing certain evidence. The more recently recognised limitations on the state's evidential privilege[20] do not, however, affect the privilege in defamation. The consitutional basis of the government and its functions probably means that the privilege is now a constitutionally based one.

The privilege covers official communications that are made for purposes of state only, and not to statements made to friends or to the man in the street.[21] However, to deny a privilege for statements of executive policy contained in press releases is hardly to serve the public interest, which is the basis of the present privilege. It is well established in the US that press releases made by federal officials in the performance of their office are absolutely protected.[22] The absolute privilege also covers necessary and consequential publications that are made to clerks,[23] and presumably typists.

Statements which are made by the Taoiseach to the President, to Ministers and to subordinate officials, and by Ministers to the President, Taoiseach, Tánaiste and other Ministers[24] and subordinate officals[25] are all protected. Outside of these, it is difficult to be certain how far the privilege goes. It is clearly not limited to statements made by these persons,[26] but neither does it go so far as to protect everything which is done lawfully by a public official in the course of his duty.

There is no generally accepted test by which it can be ascer-tained whether a public official or civil servant is protected.[27] Statements made by higher public servants are generally considered to be within the privilege.[28] Some Australian judges have cast the

18 *Home v Bentinck* (1820) Brod & Bing 130. This was followed in McElveney's case.
19 *Chatterton v Sec. of State for India* [1895] 2 QB 189, 193 per Kay LJ.
20 See *Murphy v Dublin Corporation* [1972] IR 215.
21 *Peerless Bakery v Watts* [1955] NZLR 339, 353, per Barrowclough CJ.
22 Eldredge 396-8. See also p. 188 post.
23 *Isaacs v Cook* [1925] 2 KB 391, 399 per Roche J.
24 Chatterton's case, Isaac's case
25 Peerless Bakery case.
26 For instance, statements by officers in a force organised on a military basis in which discipline is essential to the effectiveness of the force, are protected — *Dawkins v Lord Paulet* (1869) LR 5 QB 94.
27 Conflicting views have been expressed in Australia over whether statements by a commissioner of taxation are protected — Jackson's case post.
28 *Gibbons v Duffell* (1932) 47 CLR 520, 526. *Peerless Bakery v Watts* at 353.

privilege more broadly to include communications made under an imperative statutory command,[29] and in the US a still broader protection covers all federal officials who are authorised to make statements in the course of performing their office.[30] The rationale for this is that nowadays the complexity of government has resulted in important functions being delegated to lower officials 'and we cannot say that these functions become less important simply because they are exercised by officers of lower rank in the executives hierarchy.'[31] Many American writers have, however, expressed unease over the broad scope of this privilege,[32] and many state courts have declined to apply it to state officials.[33] The difficulty arises over how the test for determining the extent of the protection should be formulated. A test which asked in each case whether the benefit to the public from protection outweighed the loss to the individual and the public from denial could render all public servants liable in some cases; while a test which focused on a statutory duty, and on those who had to execute it, or merely on whether an act was done in the course of a person's employment could protect all public servants in some cases. In Ireland a number of reasons suggest that the courts may incline towards or even beyond the former test. In a recent action[34] the Commissioner of the Garda Síochána was treated as having only a qualified privilege when transferring a number of police officers from one section to another, and not an absolute privilege, as his federal equivalent in the US would almost certainly enjoy.[35] This decision may raise doubts about whether even higher civil servants are absolutely privileged. Another reason is that a purported justification for the wider protection — encouraging public officials to communicate information to the public — seems inapplicable here where a centralised system of ministerial responsibility and a traditional civil service reticence result in a different public information climate from the US. If this reasoning is valid, the public servants's protection might only be a qualified one.

29 *Jackson v Magrath* (1947) 75 CLR 293, 310 per Starkie J and 317 per Williams J.
30 Eldredge 399.
31 *Barr v Mateo* (1959) 360 US 564, 572.
32 Eldredge 402.
33 Prosser 822, although Eldredge 405 regards the cases on this point as being in substantial conflict.
34 *Corliss and Diggin v Ireland*, HCt, unreported, 23 July 1984 — preliminary hearing; The Irish Times, 30 November 1984 — full hearing.
35 cf *Heine v Rans* (1968) 399 F 2d 785; Eldredge 400-402.

8

The Defence of Qualified Privilege

The law recognises a series of occasions, related for the most part to the exigencies of every day life, when a defamatory statement may be made and its maker immunised from liability in defamation. But because these other occasions are not considered to be as important as the occasions of absolute privilege, the balance of interest between the right to a good name and freedom of expression and other rights has been struck so as to allow a plaintiff to defeat the defence if he can show that when making the statement the defendant acted maliciously.

So established and accepted is this balance between the various opposing interests, that it is probably otiose to query whether the balance actually operates to deny the right to a good name instead of only regulating it. The effect of a successful reliance on the defence of qualified privilege is that although the statement is defamatory and untrue, a plaintiff still loses his case. His reputation may continue to be unfairly damaged because of this defeat. In return, nothing at all is asked from the defendant. No apology, expression of regret, facilitation of reply, retraction, or even a correction of the untruth is, in general, required. It is not surprising that there is some unease about this situation. In one case,[1] Hamilton P thought it regrettable that the operation of the defence had left the plaintiff without any remedy at law, and in another[2] the same judge chose to treat the plaintiffs' defeat by the defence as unreservedly establishing and vindicating their good names and reputations. It might be open to question whether the general failure of the law to attach some condition of retraction or reply to the operation of the defence results in a balance of rights that excessively denies good name. The state is obliged to vindicate good name and that necessity still exists even though a plaintiff might not obtain any damages. A proper vindication of good name might even require that the victim of defamation should have a pre-hearing right to demand an appropriate response from

1 *Lynch v Toland*, The Irish Times, 21 January 1984.
2 *Corliss and Diggin v Ireland*, The Irish Times, 30 November 1984.

a defamer in cases where it is likely that the defence of qualified privilege will succeed.[3] The one instance when something is required of a defamer arises under s.24 of the Defamation Act 1961, where a media privilege is made dependant on the publication of an explanation or contradiction. But the usefulness of this is diminished because it is only a reply, there is no right to insist on it, and it only applies to a restricted category of media reports.

The defence of qualified privilege can be defeated by proof of malice. This is a narrowly defined type of fault, and does not include carelessness, irrationality or prejudice.[4] This may also appear to suggest an imbalance in the law, but the reality of imbalance must depend on the defamer's position as well. It could be, for example, that the constitutional rights of the media may affect the law's balance. In this regard it is interesting to note that, with media defendants, the US Supreme Court has held[5] that the American Constitution requires that a broadly defined type of fault — interpreted by most courts as negligence[6] — should be the pivot on which a defence of qualified privilege stands or falls when the victim is a private individual; and that a more narrow basis of liability — akin to proof of lying — is necessary where the victim is a public official or figure, and the matter is one of public interest.[7] Whether good name and media constitutional protection here would necessitate a similar development is considered elsewhere in this chapter. One must asume that the general structure of the defence is constitutionally valid because of the absence of any suggestion that it is not; though, as will be seen when examining the defence, there are aspects of some privileges whose constitutionality seems more clearly doubtful.

In the defence of qualified privilege the law distinguishes between a privileged occasion and a privileged communication. A privileged occasion arises when a defendant establishes that the statement was made for a legitimate reason, and that there was no excess in the communication made, that is to say that the statement was not given an unnecessary circulation and that it was not grossly irrelevant to the occasion. When a statement is made on a privileged occasion it is presumed to have been made for the proper reason, and so it is

3 This potential remedy is considered further at p. 234 post 4 See p. 207 post.

5 *Gertz v Welch* (1974) 418 US 323; see Eldredge 228-97, 450-451, Prosser 807-8.

6 Eldredge 291-2, quoting Levine J in *Jacron Sales v Sindorf* (1976) 276 Md 580 'The adoption of a negligence standard in cases of purely private defamation hardly introduces a radical concept. The application of the negligence standard in tort cases is so well established that juries can safely be expected to comprehend the term when applied in defamation cases'. See also Hughes 'Defaming Public Figures' (1985) 59 Aust LJ 433; and generally Bloom 'Proof of Fault in Media Defamation Litigation' (1985) 38 Vand LR 247.

7 *New York Times v Sullivan* (1964) 376 US 254; for further consideration of this important American case, see p. 162 post.

presumed to be a privileged communication. But if a plaintiff can show that, when making the statement, the defendant's motive was not what it should have been, then the statement will not be privileged and the protection will be lost.[8] The defence may not be used for an attack. It is a shield and not a sword. Any disparity between the real and the proper motive for making a statement is called malice. The use of the term here is an unfortunate one, both because its meaning does not correspond exactly with the layman's understanding of the word and because the law of defamation already uses this term in another context but with a different meaning. Such a peculiar situation is due solely to the historical development of this area of the law. In order to distinguish between the different uses, the terms 'malice in law' and 'malice in fact' are used. Malice in law is the inference that is drawn from the fact that a statement is defamatory. It is rebutted by proving that a statement was made on a privileged occasion.

Malice in fact is the wrongful motive that impelled the statement, and it defeats the privilege. Nowadays, the term 'malice in law' is seldom used, and 'malice in fact' is often shortened to malice. In order to avoid misunderstanding, the reform bodies have recommended that, in future, the term 'malice' should be avoided and be replaced instead by a reference to 'spite', 'ill-will', or 'improper motive'.[9]

Traditionally, the defence of qualified privilege has required a duty — legal, social, or moral — on the part of the maker of the statement to make it to a recipient who has an interest in receiving it.[10] This formulation dates primarily from the early nineteenth century when it was stated by Parke B.[11] It emphasises the generality of the rationale underlying the multifarious occasions of qualified privilege. This is a positive emphasis and its frequent citation keeps before the judicial mind the basic principles underlying the defence. An emphasis on basic principle rather than on precedent accords, too, with the liberal approach that judges should adopt when considering new occasions of qualified privilege.[12] The list of occasions is not closed, and the courts do not wish to close them.[13] They will recognise new

8 *Jacob v Lawrence* (1879) 4 LR Ir 579, 582 per May CJ.

9 Faulks Committee Report para 240; NZ Committee Report para 199. According to Eldredge 509-510 in the US the 'slipperiness' of the term 'malice' has resulted in it being discarded for 'abuse of occasion' or 'abuse of privilege'.

10 This classification was used in the first edition of Odgers' *A Digest of the Law of Libel and Slander* in 1881, in the first edition of Fraser's *Principles and Practice of the Law of Libel and Slander* in 1893.

11 *Toogood v Sprying* (1834) 1 CM & R 181-93.

12 *Hamerton v Green* (1863) 16 ICLR 77, 106 per O'Brien J.

occasions, and the absence of a precedent is no barrier at all to success.[14] Furthermore there may be, as is argued later,[15] a constitutionally guaranteed privilege where in certain instances a person acts to protect the public. So numerous have the occasions of qualified privilege become, that one could assert that, nowadays, a person needs only to have had an acceptable reason for making a statement, and to then proceed to considering how the privilege may be lost.

At the same time, there is a tendency to read the duty and interest statement not as a particular and helpful judicial pronouncement but almost as a statutory definition, to be repeated at all appropriate times, and to be analysed as though duty and interest were rigid legal conceptions, so that, for example, if a reason for making a statement could not easily be classified as based on a legal, social or moral duty, then it might not result in the occasion being privileged. Nowadays, there is not such a need to emphasise the duty/interest idea because, unlike the early nineteenth century when the actual occasions were not so well known, there is now a huge body of case law identifying the various occasions of privilege. Another reason for discounting the duty/interest idea is that the terms are singularly unhelpful in enabling a presentation of the case law on this subject.[16] Both terms are vague and general, and are not informative, in light of case law, as to when the occasions of privilege arises. For these reasons, the rules and cases on qualified privilege are not presented here according to the traditional classification, but will instead be presented according to the relevant valid reason why the statement should be made.

The law recognises nine occasions of qualified privilege, although as will be seen, not all of these are mutually exclusive. These occasions arise when a statement is made by a person (1) while acting to protect himself, or (2) while acting to protect another, or (3) while acting to protect a group, or (4) while acting to protect the public, or (5) while reporting judicial proceedings, or (6) while reporting public meetings and other matters of public interest as defined by statute, or (7) while acting under a legal duty, or (8) while unofficially reporting parliamentary proceedings other than utterances, or (9) while

13 At 97 per Hayes J.

14 As was the case in Davis v Reeves (1855) 5 ICLR 79; *Buckley v Kiernan* (1857) 7 ICLR 75, and *Towell v Fallon* (1912) 47 ILTR 176.

15 See p. 167 post.

16 Aside from the incongruity of referring to a duty to make a statement when it is, usually, no more than a discretionary choice, the terms social and moral are particularly difficult to use because it is not clear whether they refer to the same or different ideas, and, if the latter, how the distinction between the two can be satisfactorily drawn. No judge has so far, it seems, explained the distinction between the two.

acting as lawyer, or possibly, a witness in a judicial proceeding.

These last two occasions were already considered in the chapter on absolute privilege and are mentioned here only for completeness. The various occasions of qualified privilege will now be considered, and reference will then be made to excess of communication and to malice.

ACTING TO PROTECT ONESELF

There are two occasions of qualified privilege on which a person may make a defamatory statement in self defence. The first arises where his reputation is attacked and the second arises where his property is threatened.

Where a person's reputation is attacked by a statement which is made to a particular audience, he is entitled in reply to place before that audience matters of rebuttal and explanation in order to ensure that it has all of the materials before it upon which it might reasonably make a judgement. In so doing, he will be acting on a privileged occasion, and if he also acts bona fide, and without malice,then he will be protected from liability in defamation. The initial attack can be either an explicit or an implicit one.[17] It should not, however, be too implicit, or be based only on rumours, or a fear of suspicion of wrongdoing that might arise because a person is a member of a group, one or all of whom is suspected of wrongdoing. Otherwise a defendant might respond to an attack which was not made or could not be proved. This happened in *Ede v Scott* (1858),[18] where one member of a party of at least four accused another member of having stolen a cable which was found to be missing after they had visited a ship. Rumours had been circulating in the area as to who was responsible and the accusation was made to remove whatever suspicion the speaker might attract because of his membership of the group. The court rejected a claim that the occasion was privileged. It would seem valid to deduce from this that a volunteered communication inspired because of membership of a suspected group can never give rise to a privileged occasion. This may seem a harsh outcome. If rumours are circulating and a person was being accused without being able to show by whom, and there was no doubt but that he was an object or suspicion because of his membership of a group, it seems unfair that the occasion of speaking should not be privileged simply because he cannot pinpoint any accuser.

The defamatory response, which is made the subject of an action, must be made to the same persons as the provoking statement was

17 Eg *Towell v Fallon* supra.

18 (1858) 7 ICLR 607; see also *Gillis v McDonnell* (1869) IR 4 CL 342.

made to, otherwise the occasion might not be privileged[19] That audience can be an individual,[20] or a group,[21] or the public in general, or the part of the public that reads a local newspaper,[22] or a national one.[23] While the audience must be the same, the medium by which it is reached need not always be, though in most of the cases it has been. In one case,[24] the attacks on the defendants were made at public meetings, in parliament and in the press generally, while the defendants responded with the defamatory statement in their own newspaper.

A wide latitude is accorded to the subject matter of defamatory statements that may be made in self defence. The subject matter of the reply will be determined by that of the attack, and as the attack can relate to any aspect of a person's life, so too may the statement which is made in reply. Thus, a plaintiff, may, by the mode of publishing his attack, give the public an interest which it might otherwise not have.[25] As Palles CB stated 'In general, no doubt, the right ... in the public is restricted to matters of public interest. But he who appeals to the public for their judgement upon a matter not public cannot, for the purpose of preventing his adversary's defence, be heard to say that the public have not the right to pronounce the judgement which he so asked'.[26]

A particular question which has arisen concerns when a plaintiff may be said to have resorted to the bar of public opinion, and so to have entitled a defendant to make a public statement of response. In one of the cases,[27] the plaintiff involved the public by writing letters and reports to a newspaper which published them, and in another,[28] the public became involved by the plaintiff publishing an election address in a paper; and in a third case — *Nevin v Roddy and Carty*[29] in 1935 — the public was involved by a councillor who, knowing the press was present, stated at a council meeting 'Councillor O'Connell has asked for it and he is going to get it, and so will the members of the council and the people of Sligo'. By contrast with these decisions, in *Murphy v Halpin* (1874),[30] where 'The plaintiff

19 As happened in *Murphy v Halpin* (1874) IR 8 CL 127.
20 *Jacob v Lawrence* (1879) 4 LR Ir 579; *Towell v Fallon* supra.
21 *Croke v O'Grady* (1830) 4 Law Rec 42, where the audience was the Bar of Ireland.
22 *O'Donoghue v Hussey* (1871) IR 5 CL 124; *Murphy v Halpin* supra; *Nevin v Roddy and Carty* [1935] IR 397.
23 *Dwyer v Esmonde* (1877) IR 11 CL 547 HCt, (1878) 2 LR Ir 242 CtA; *O'Brien v Freemans Journal* (1907) 41 ILTR 35.
24 *O'Brien v Freemans Journal* supra.
25 *See Murphy v Halpin* at 135 per Fitzgerald B.
26 *Dwyer v Esmonde* at 550.
27 *O'Donoghue v Hussey* (1871) IR 5 CL 124.
28 *Dwyer v Esmonde* supra.
29 [1935] IR 397.
30 (1874) IR 8 CL 127.

was a member of a public board. He addressed the board at a meeting at which the ... press attended. He knew that if he spoke at the meeting, his speech would be reported, ... if the proprietor or the editor of the newspaper thought fit to do so';[31] the court refused to regard this as an involvement of the public on the ground that the plaintiff had not intended to involve the public. The decision is misconceived, one submits, because, although the intention of the maker of a statement can sometimes be relevant, he is not allowed to assert a meaning for a statement which, according to the objectively judged circumstances, the statement cannot bear. Here was a case where, in fact, the public could hardly have had a better right to be involved, regardless of the speaker's intention. It seems clear from some of the judgements in this case that the court was unhappy with the very idea of a privilege in these circumstances, and the arguments that were addressed against what it viewed as an extension of the privilege were actually arguments against the existence of the privilege.[32]

The second situation in which an act of self defence is protected by a qualified privilege concerns a threat to a person's property. Where a person's property has been placed at risk, or has already been damaged, and he makes a defamatory statement in order to protect it, or while seeking its recovery, then, so long as the statement is made bona fide and without malice, he will be protected from liability in defamation. Property here may be broadly understood as including real property, or personal property like an investment,[33] or money[34] or turf,[35] or a debt,[36] and also the avoidance of a legal liability that would reduce one's property.[37] The threat to property, which causes the defamatory statement, may actually have materialised, as where property has already been stolen and it is sought to recover it.[38] Or the threat might not yet have materialised but is likely to if the statement is not made, as where a person will be sued for breach of contract unless he explains his refusal to perform the contract,[39]

31 At 138 per Dowse B.

32 See especially the judgement of Dowse B at 138; also Christian LJ in Dwyer v Esmonde at 261.

33 *Waring v McCaldin* (1873) IR 7 CL 282.

34 *Hyland v Clery & Co*, SCt, unreported, 9 April 1964.

35 *McFadden v Lynch* (1863) 17 ILTR 93.

36 *Robinson v Jones* (1879) 4 LR Ir 391.

37 *Hobbs v Bryers* (1878) 2 LR Ir 496; *Willis v Irish Press* (1938) 72 ILTR 238; *Hartery v Welltrade*, HCt, unreported, 15 March 1978; see also *Maxwell v Gavin Low*, SCt unreported, 11 January 1967.

38 *McFadden v Lynch*, *Hyland v Clery & Co.*

39 *Hobbs v Bryers.*

or where a person will be sued,[40] say, for a defamation[41] unless he apologises,[42] or where a businessman feels that he is being unjustly charged for a service.[43] It is not necessary that the statement which is made actually dispels the risk or remedies the loss. It is enough, as is later seen, that it is made to a person who can set in train events which may achieve these results.

Another particular question which has arisen here, on the privilege of self defence, concerns the motive with which a person may speak when accusing another of having stolen his property. In most of the cases the obviousness of the entitlement to speak — based on the theft of property and the desire to recover it — has rendered it unnecessary for the courts to consider exactly the issue of motive. These cases, nonetheless, assert that the wish to recover one's stolen property is a permissible motive for speaking. The legal propriety of this ought to have been unquestionable because it is based, and has been so held,[44] on the dictum of Parke B in *Toogood v Spryng* (1834),[45] that a qualified privilege protects statements about matters in which a person is interested. However, this motive has been questioned by the decision in *Coleman v Keanes Ltd* (1945),[46] where Haugh J held that an accusation that a woman had stolen some bacon from a butcher's shop was not privileged because it was made with the desire to recover the property, instead of a desire to bring a thief to justice. It is submitted that Haugh J was wrong to have held as he did. The latter motive, it is true, is also a recognised one,[47] though the authority which was cited is slim enough.[48] However, it is the only case of many, involving accusations of theft, in which a desire to recover stolen property was specifically held to be an insufficient basis for a privilege.[49] In all of these, a privilege was

40 In *Sayer v Begg* (1864) 15 ICLR 458, Monahan CJ stated at 465 'In more than one case in this Court we held that a letter written by a person threatened to be sued, to the attorney of the party about suing him, was a letter written on a privileged occasion'.

41 *Jacob v Lawrence.*

42 *Willis v Irish Press.*

43 *Fishbourne v Lord Lucan* (1865) 10 IJ NS 209.

44 *Padmore v Lawrence* (1840) 11 A & E 380; *Cutbush v Grove* (1901) 21 NZLR 67; *Norton v Hoare (No 1)* (1913) 17 CLR 310.

45 (1834) 1 CM & R 131.

46 (1946) IJR 5.

47 *Bowles v Armstrong* (1912) 32 NZLR 409.

48 He mentioned *Fowler v Horner* (1812) 3 Camp 294, in which two of the judges did not mention the point, a third — Lord Ellenburgh — did, but almost as an aside at the end of his judgement and apparently conflicting with some earlier remarks of his.

49 For the American cases clearly recognising a shop's privilege to accuse customers see Eldredge 452-3, 521-2; see also Reed, 'Stopping and Questioning Suspected Shoplifters without Creating Civil Liability' (1976) 47 Miss LJ 17.

found to exist without any suggestion that both motives were mutually exclusive. It is in a failure to appreciate this that, one submits, the decision in Coleman's case was wrong.

ACTING TO PROTECT ANOTHER

Where a person makes a defamatory statement in order to protect another, then depending on the relationship between the two, he may be acting on a privileged occasion and, if he also acts bona fide and without malice, he will be protected from liability. In determining whether such a privileged occasion exists, it is necessary to consider the sufficiency of the relationship between the maker of the statement and the person whose interest he seeks to protect, and also the nature of the risk which must be posed by the person who is defamed to the affairs of the person in whose interest the statement is made.

The relationship

There must be a sufficient relationship between the person making the statement and the person whom it is sought to protect by it before an occasion can be privileged. Such a relationship has been recognised in a number of instances, but these are so varied that there is really no single test which can identify when an occasion is privileged. It was suggested in England[50] that whether the great mass of right-thinking people would have done as the defendant did is a sufficient test, and a comment in the American *Restatement of Torts* refers to whether the act was 'within current standards of socially desirable or at least permissible conduct'. Both tests are so general as to be of little value. One must, instead, describe the particular relationships, and in some instances this is difficult because the sufficiency of certain relationships is unclear.

What also makes the task of stating the law difficult is that the sufficiency of a relationship can sometimes depend on how real the risk to the protected person's interest is. In order to present the law, one must first distinguish between statements which are made in response to a request, and statements that are volunteered.

Requested statements Where a person is enquired of to make a statement concerning another, and the enquirer has a valid reason for making the enquiry, then there will be a sufficient relationship between the parties as will justify the former in responding to the

50 *Stuart v Bell* [1891] 2 QB 341, 350 per Lindley LJ.

enquiry. Monahan CJ stated in *Owens v Roberts* (1850),[51] 'We are of opinion that if a person, having an interest in obtaining information as to the affairs of another person, makes a bona fide application to a third person for that purpose, and the latter, in reply to such enquiry, gives the information required, such communication is privileged'.[52] Thus, in that case, where the defendant had induced Carleton to become surety for the plaintiff, and Carleton had asked the defendant to inform him of any suggestion that the plaintiff might become insolvent, a communication to that effect by the defendant was held to be privileged.

This type of relationship, which was one of the first to be recognised as giving rise to a qualified privilege,[53] can also arise where the request for the statement comes, not from the person whose interests are at risk, but from someone else, who knows him and the danger to his interests. So, in *Davis v Reeves* (1855),[54] Bourke was a creditor of the plaintiff and the defendant was brought to him by an interested party and asked by him to tell Bourke what he knew about the plaintiff. The response was held to have been made on a privileged occasion. The enquirer may even delegate to an independent contractor the task of making enquiries, and the latter will then be possessed of a sufficient interest to make the communication.[55].

But it is not only the fact of a request by someone which gives rise to the privileged occasion. The enquirer must have a legitimate interest in the subject matter of the enquiry, and where he has not such an interest and the enquirer is aware of this, the response will not be protected because, with such knowledge, the defendant will not be able to show that he acted bona fide in making the statement. Where, however, there is nothing in the circumstances of the request which ought to suggest the lack of a legitimate interest by the enquirer, then a statement made in response will be protected. In the ordinary course of events, the fact of a request may imply a legitimate interest.[56]

In the cases, the enquirer's interest has been the likelihood that he may employ the plaintiff,[57] the fear of a financial loss,[58] and the incurring of a financial burden.[59]

51 (1856) 6 ICLR 386. For an obiter reference to this privilege, see *Waring v McCaldin* (1873) IR 7 CL 282, 288 per Fitzgerald B.

52 At 392.

53 See *Weatherston v Hawkins* (1786) 1 TR 110.

54 (1855) 5 ICLR 79.

55 *Fitzsimmons v Duncan and Kemp & Co* [1908] 2 IR 43.

56 See Prosser 818.

57 *Weatherston v Hawkins.*

58 *Davis v Reeves.*

59 *Owens v Roberts.*

Volunteered statements There are situations in which a statement might be made in order to protect another person without any prior enquiry or request to do so. The maker of the statement may have endangered the other by a previous act. He may be closely related to the other. Finally, he might be neither a friend nor a relation, and yet he might be aware of a danger to the other.

Where the previous act of a person has placed at risk the interests of another, then a statement which is made by the former in order to protect the latter is made on a privileged occasion. That risk can be the likelihood of incurring a legal liability. Thus, in *Halloran v Thompson* (1863),[60] a statement that was made by an employer in order to protect his employee, who had been threatened with litigation for carrying out his instructions, was held to have been made on a privileged occasion. The risk can also arise where a person endangers the reputation of another by making a defamatory statement about him. An apology issued in these circumstances will be made on a privileged occasion.[61] Another risk can arise where one person, having induced a second to become surety for a third, hears suggestions that the third is likely to become insolvent. A statement volunteered without request warning the surety of this would be protected.[62]

Where a person in a close family relationship with another preceives a threat to the interests of the other, then a statement which he makes to avert that danger will be made on a privileged occasion. Thus, in *Atkinson v Congreve* (1857),[63] a letter written by a first cousin and friend of E.D. with the object of preventing her intended marriage, by informing her of her fiancé's real character, was held to have been made on a privileged occasion. If a first cousin, or a son-in-law,[64] are closely enough related to the person whom they seek to protect, then so too would those in closer relation, such as parents, children, brothers and sisters, grandparents and grandchildren, uncles and aunts. The statement need not only concern marital or family matters. It can also concern the friends with whom the other associates.[65] It seems possible that the privilege which applies to statements concerning marital and family matters would now be based on Article 41 of the Constitution, under which the state pledges to protect marriage and the family.

60 (1863) 14 ICLR 335.
61 *Willis v Irish Press* (1938) 72 ILTR 238.
62 *Owens v Roberts* at 392 per Monahan CJ.
63 (1857) 7 ICLR 109. Fleming 537 cites an unreported Australian case where a daughter was held entitled to protect her deceased father's character.
64 *Todd v Hawkins* (1837) 8 C & P 88.
65 *Moffatt v Coats* (1906) 44 SLR 20.

Where two persons are just friends, it is less clear whether a statement, which is made by one in order to protect the other, is made on a privileged occasion. On balance, for contrasting views have been expressed,[66] it seems that they are. Where they are friendly because one occupies a position of trust towards the other, *Davis v Reeves* (1855)[67] held that a statement made in these circumstances was made on a privileged occasion. In that case the statement was made by a solicitor to his client about a non-legal matter — the supposed absconding of a debtor of the client — although the solicitor does not seem to have been retained to make such communications. Where a person employs another, then a statement made by him to protect his employee may be made on a privileged occasion — whether because of the employer's interest in protecting his servant or in protecting his own property. In *Cassidy v Kincaid* (1865),[68] an employer was found privileged in telling another employer that the latter's gardener was loitering about his house, intimidating his servant and inducing her to rob him.

Where there is no obvious connection between two persons, and one makes a statement because he perceives a risk to the interest of another, then it is probable that the statement is not made on a privileged occasion. For, while Pigot CB in *Davis'* case[69] thought that such a statement would be protected and there is support abroad for this view,[70] yet in two such cases, *Simmonds v Dunne* (1871),[71] and *Curneen v Sweeney* (1967),[72] statements of this type were held not to have been made on a privileged occasion. In the first case, a tenant told the land agent that the bailiff had not drained the lands of another tenant as he was supposed to have done. In Curneen's case, an auctioneer for the seller of land told his employee to warn the buyer of the land that the solicitor he was using was unsuitable and untrustworthy.

In the development of the privilege for volunteered statements,

66 In *Simmonds'* case post Fitzgerald B thought that it was not; in a New Zealand case, *Heimann v Meissner* (1936) NZLR Supp 56, Reid ACJ thought it 'no more than common sense' that it was. In Atkinson's case, the cousin was also a friend who had even quarrelled with her about the engagement.

67 (1855) 5 ICLR 79.

68 (1865) 10 IJ NS 176.

69 At 90, see also the wilingness of two judges — Keogh and O'Hagan JJ — in Cassidy's case to base the privilege not on the employers interest in his servant or his property, but on a moral duty.

70 In the US there are cases protecting volunteered statements by strangers — Eldredge 474-6, Prosser 827 — although the 'tale bearing friend' is not protected. Distinguishing between the two is acknowledged as a difficult problem.

71 (1871) IR 5 CL 358.

72 (1969) 103 ILTR 29; hesitancy in reaching this conclusion was, in fact, admittted by Lavery J who delivered the court's judgement. Privilege had been found in the High Court.

the rules applying to statements by family, friends, fiduciaries, employers and strangers have evolved separately, and there has been little enough recognition of the fact that the issues of policy underlying each are largely the same, aside that is from the probably constitutional dimension to the protection of statements concerning the family. The issue of policy, put simply, is whether the law ought to protect the good Samaritan who goes to the aid of one whom he honestly thinks is at risk. The courts have given expression to the helpful Samaritan idea, but that they have also rather pragmatically, preferred the related or connected Samaritan to the distant one in an attempt to confine the extent of the privilege. It is not clear, however, that the present cut-off point, whereby statements by strangers are not protected, can be sustained. Once the principle of protecting the good Samaritan is conceded, as it has been, then why should the law make distinctions between different types of Samaritans that have no relevance to the idea of helping others? Some judges have, for example thought that whether they are protected or not, statements by friends and strangers should be treated similarly.[73] It can be suggested that either decisions such as in Simmonds' and Curneen's cases cannot continue to stand, or else that all the other decisions recognising privileges should no longer represent the law.

The risk of damage to the person who is protected

Where a person acts to protect another whether as an individual or a member of a group, then, he must show that a third person posed a threat to the interests of the other person he seeks to protect in order that the occasion be privileged. Whether such a threat exists depends on whether there is, or is likely to be, any contact between the third person and the person it is sought to protect, and if there is, whether the latter would be likely to suffer a loss as a result. Where the two persons are already in contact, as in many of the cases already mentioned, then the only question concerns the damage that might result if the statement is not made.

Where, however, the third person and the person who it is sought to protect are not in contact and are not contemplating contact when the statement is made, then there is uncertainty as to whether the risk of damage is sufficient that a protective statement would be made on a privileged occasion. There is strongly expressed support for the view that where the parties do not expect any contact, such as making a commercial contract, and both are in the same area of activity, there

73 See views of Fitzgerald B in Simmonds' case, at 363, who considered that neither type of statement should be protected.

is not a sufficient threat as would create a privileged occasion. Palles CB stated in 1908, concerning communication by credit rating agencies 'I am not to be taken as holding that the communication to a client of a book, containing particulars as to the solvency of a number of persons, with many of whom the inquirer has no intention of dealing is within the privilege. I entertain a strong opinion that it is not'.[74] This view was reiterated, in lengthy and emphatic terms by Black J in the Supreme Court in two cases, *Reilly v Gill* (1946),[75] and *Green v Blake* (1948).[76] He even considered that to hold the opposite might well open the flood gates to a deluge of privileged defamation. His views may be summarised in four propositions –

a) If the only interest a person has in hearing a statement is an interest which he shares with everyone else, then a protective statement would not be made on a privileged occasion;
b) if that interest is shared generally with all other members of a cross section of the community, then the same is also the case;
c) if present or future dealings are contemplated, then a protective statement would be made on a privileged occasion; and
d) the fact that the defamed person and the protected person both belong to the same group, the members of which are more likely to have dealings with each other than non-members are, is not a proof of contemplated dealings.

It is not clear, however, that the views in propositions (b) and (d) represent the law. The view of Palles CB was an obiter dictum. In Reilly's case, the opinion of Black J did not form part of the ratio decidendi of the majority, as two of the three judges in the majority[77] expressly declined to comment on it. In Green's case, where the statement was contained in a horse racing newspaper and was intended for the racing public in general and not merely for those who had or who contemplated dealings with the plaintiff, a majority of the Supreme Court,[78] appear to have accepted, implicitly rather than explicitly, that had the statement been made only to the racing public in general it would have been protected, but because it was also made to the wider public – the paper could be bought by the public in shops – the statement was held not to have been made on a privileged occasion. It is also of relevance to note that in another

74 *Fitzsimmons v Duncan and Kemp & Co* [1908] 2 IR 483, 495.
75 (1946) 85 ILTR 165.
76 [1948] IR 242.
77 The majority consisted of Geoghegan, O'Byrne and Black JJ. A similar viewpoint operates in the US according to Prosser 829.
78 Maguire CJ, Murnaghan and Geoghegan JJ; a minority of cases in the US support this view – Eldredge 471-2.

case, *O'Keefe v Cullen,* (1873)[79], a statement made to all the parishioners in a parish about their priest was held to have been made on a privileged occasion, and no suggestion was made that only those who had dealt with, or contemplated dealing with, the priest, would have been sufficiently interested in having the statement made to them. All this might suggest that a sufficient likelihood of contact — and thus of risk — can be found, not only in actual and contemplated dealings, but also from the fact that the subject of the defamatory statement and the person whom it is sought to protect are members of a section of the community who would on that account be more likely to interact than if they were not members.

ACTING TO PROTECT A GROUP

Where a person makes a defamatory statement in order to protect a group and its members, then depending on the relationship between him and the group, he may be acting on a privileged occasion. If he also acts bone fide and without malice, he will be privileged from liability. There are three main issues to be considered here — how is the group defined? what must the relationship between the maker of the statement and the group be?, and what must the relationship between the person who poses the threat and the group be?

The group

There is no limitation on the type of group which can be the object of a privileged defamatory statement. The group can be broadly understood to include the membership of a formal organisation, association, or institution such as a credit union,[80] or a particular religion,[81] or the board of governors of a hospital,[82] or the membership of a profession, such as officers in the Defence Forces.[83] It can also include such loosely defined groups as the users of a service which is available to the public, like those who retain

79 (1873) IR 7 CL 319.
80 *Hayes v Board of Irish League of Credit Unions,* The Irish Times, 18 June 1977.
81 *O'Keefe v Cullen.*
82 *Lynch v Toland,* The Irish Times, 21 January 1984.
83 *Mitchell v Kerr* (1801), reported (1824) Rowe Rep 537; *Bell v Parke* (1859) 10 ICLR 279.

solicitors,[84] or simply those who pay rates,[85] or subscribe to charities,[86] or who share an active interest in a particular sport or pastime, like horse racing.[87]

The relationship between the maker of the statement and the group

The maker of the statement — the defendant in the action — must have some connection with, or interest in, the group before there can be a privilege in attempting to protect it. In some cases, this will come from membership and participation in the group and a desire to ensure that harm or discredit does not befall the group.[88] In others, it will come from membership and from holding, under the rules of the association, a position of supervision and discipline over the group, and also from an obligation to communicate to the group any decision that is reached.[89] An employee,[90] or agent,[91] of the group would also have a sufficient interest in protecting the group.

Generally speaking, statements by outsiders who have no connection with the group and are mere busybodies or intermeddlers will not be regarded as being made as a privileged occasion. In *Gillis v McDonnell* (1869),[92] one of the reasons why a housewife was not privileged in accusing another housewife of having fraudulently claimed malicious damage for a fire, was that she was not a ratepayer herself, although her husband was, and so did not have a sufficient interest in wishing to protect ratepayers. Some outsiders may, however, be sufficiently interested in a group that their accusations would be made on a privileged occasion. On an analogy with the privileged occasion where one person attempts to protect another — regardless of whether the statement is requested or volunteered — then non-members, such as those who had previously placed at risk the interests of the group, or who were sympathetic to the aims of the group, would be protected. The same might also be true of an ex-member of a group who was still interested in it.

The welfare and interest of some groups might be of such

84 *Hamerton v Green* (1863) 16 ICLR 77.
85 *McCarthy v Maguire* [1899] 2 IR 802; *Keaveney v Geraghty* [1965] IR 551.
86 *Clancy v Cahill* (1825) Sm & Bat 232; *Currigan v Ryan* (1865) 11 IJ NS 406.
87 *Reilly v Gill* (1946) 85 ILTR 165; *Green v Blake* [1948] IR 242.
88 As in Bell's case. In *Lynch v Toland* a group of radiologists in one hospital and a radiologist in another were held sufficiently interested in commenting on the application of a radiologist for a position in the hospital where the former group was employed.
89 As in O'Keefe's case, Reilly's case, Green's case and Hayes' case.
90 *McMullan v Mulhall* [1929] IR 470.
91 See also *Eglantine Inn v Smith* [1948] NI 29.
92 (1869) IR 4 CL 342.

importance to the community that an outsider, who is not a member of the group, would be acting on a privileged occasion when making a statement to protect the group. However, it is not clear how far this protection goes. It has been stated that only certain groups, like those who use the services of pre-eminent professions, such as solicitors, could be protected in this way. In *Hamerton v Green* (1863),[93] a complaint was made to the Law Society about a solicitor who was alleged to have started off in a case representing the defendant and then to have changed over to representing the plaintiff. The defendant in the previous case was the complainant here, but he expressly forbore relying on this as a reason why the complaint should be privileged, and instead relied on a community interest in the behaviour of solicitors. While the court held by three to one[94] that the complaint was privileged, different grounds were relied on by each of the majority. Only one of them, Hayes J, accepted that the privilege was based on the pre-eminence of solicitors. The obvious difficulty about this, as was pointed out by Fitzgerald B,[95] is that it is difficult to see how solicitors can be singled apart from the rest. If the privilege is to be recognised at all, it must apply to other professions as well. This appears to have been accepted in an English case — *Beach v Freeson* (1972)[96] — where, a complaint by a member of parliament to the Law Society on behalf of a constitutent about a firm of solicitors was held to be privileged. The court accepted that complaints about all professional people should be treated in the same light, and as being on the same footing as public officials, in whom everyone is interested.[97] The court also accepted that anyone can make the complaint on the privileged occasion but added, restrictively, that they must act as an agent of the victim. Presumably this means that some authorisation to make the complaint must first be given by the victim to the defendant. It is unclear, however, whether such a requirement can be validly maintained since it does not appear to coincide with the fact already referred to,[98] that a privileged occasion can sometimes exist where statements in protection of individuals are made to those individuals without any requests to do so. There is unequal treatment here, under which if the protective statement is made to the individual it is protected, but if it is made to the group responsible for the person causing the injury it is not.

93 (1863) 16 ICLR 77.
94 Lefroy CJ O'Brien, Hayes, JJ, Fitzgerald J dissenting.
95 At 94.
96 [1972] 1 QB 14.
97 At 22.
98 See p. 152 post.

The relationship between the person defamed and the group

Where a defamatory statement is made about a person in order to protect a group, it must be shown that the person posed a threat to the interests of the group before a privileged occasion can be found. The threat may come from the fact that the person is a member of the group and has broken its rules and may be likely to do so again.[99] It can also come from the fact that he is not a member of the group but provides services for it and in so doing has damaged the group's interests.[1] The threat may even come from a person who is neither a member nor deals with the group, but is a competitor, and the statement is made in order to show that he is not a member of the group, as where a trade union official in seeking to ensure a fully unionised work force points out to an employer that a particular employee is not a member of the union.[2] As regards this particular privilege, it must now be added that if the statement is made to coerce an employee to surrender his constitutional right not to associate in a union, then it is likely that such a privilege would be unconstitutional since the Constitution does not permit a 'closed shop' to be achieved in this way.[3]

Domestic disciplinary tribunals

Where a defamatory statement is part of the proceedings, deliberations, judgement or pronouncement of a domestic tribunal exercising disciplinary authority over a group, then certain additional proofs must be established before the occasion will be held to be privileged.

Firstly, the domestic tribunal must possess jurisdiction over the person whose conduct is the subject of investigation. This jurisdiction will always be based on the rules of the association and, most importantly, on the consent of the accused to be bound by those rules. That consent can be an express one, as where a person signs a document agreeing to be bound by the rules, and he knows or can find out what the rules are. In most cases, though, any consent will have to be implied, as can be done from the fact that a person participates in an event or activity which is governed by particular rules. For instance, in *Green v Blake* (1948),[4] where a tribunal

99 As in *O'Keefe v Cullen; Reilly v Gill; Green v Blake.*

1 As in *Hamerton v Green; Currigan v Ryan; De Buse v McCarthy* [1942] 1 KB 156, *R v Rule* [1937] 2 KB 375.

2 *McMullan v Mulhall* [1929] IR 470.

3 See Kelly *The Irish Constitution* 472 et seq.

4 [1948] IR 242.

adjudicated on a complaint that a jockey in a horse race had cheated both before and after the race about his weight, it was assumed on all sides that the fact of entry and participation in the race implied a consent to be bound by the rules governing it. The validity of an implied consent will not, generally speaking, be affected by whether the person whose conduct is investigated was actually aware that any rules existed or even whether he had seen a copy of the rules before the hearing.

Aside from questions of consent, it is not clear whether a tribunal's jurisdiction to act can be affected by whether the person accused attends and participates in the proceedings. Logically, once a valid consent is found and the rules of natural justice followed, then no significance ought to be attached to whether an accused person chooses to attend or not. In *O'Keefe v Cullen* (1873),[5] where a consent to the rules was established,[6] and where the accused had attended and participated at the hearing, only one of the four judges — Whiteside CJ, who dissented — thought that an enquiry into the reason for attending was still open. Where, however, a consent is less obvious and more implied, then it seems that some significance can be attached to the issue of attendance and participation in the proceedings In *Reilly v Gill* (1946),[7] where the accused person claimed only a slight knowledge of the tribunal, and none at all of its rules, and where an extract of the rules was only sent to him when legal proceedings were pending, a majority of the Supreme Court appeared to base the tribunal's jurisdiction, partly, on the accused person attending at and participating in its proceedings.

The second additional proof which is needed to establish the privileged occasion for the actions of a domestic disciplinary tribunal is that the domestic tribunal must be shown to have acted, both in its deliberations and in its decision, in accordance with the rules of the association. If it does not conform with its rules, then statements concerning its conclusions will not have been made on a privileged occasion. Thus, in Reilly's case, where the tribunal was competent only to decide whether a punter had made a bet of £90 with a bookmaker, and it decided instead that the punter should pay £45, it was held that the announcement of this decision was not made on a privileged occasion.

Thirdly, a disciplinary tribunal may set its own rules of procedure, but it must, in its proceedings, act in line with the requirements of natural justice. And this is so regardless of what the rules of the association provide. To act in disregard of natural justice is to prevent

5 (1873) IR 7 CL 319.
6 See Barry J at 361.
7 (1946) 85 ILTR 165.

an occasion from being held privileged. Natural justice, in this context, includes a variety of requirements. One of the essential ones 'is that an accused person should have notice of the charge to be made against him, and another of them is that he should know the evidence on which the case is going to be decided, and have an adequate opportunity of challenging it and of calling witness for this purpose'.[8] To this might be added, that the accused should also know when and where the investigation will take place. In Green's case,[9] the rules of the association allowed a preliminary hearing at which only evidence was to be gathered. The plaintiff attended and participated in this. However, the actual adjudication was made at a different hearing of which the plaintiff was neither notified nor given an opportunity to defend himself. The announcement of a decision in these circumstances was held not to have been made on a privileged occasion.

ACTING TO PROTECT THE PUBLIC

There is considerable authority to support the view that, where a statement is made on a matter of public interest to the public at large, it is not, for that reason, made on an occasion of qualified privilege, and so cannot be privileged from an action in defamation. Fleming, the most explicit of the textbook writers, states on this point 'A defamatory publication has no claim to privilege merely because it deals with a matter of public interest'.[10]

Thus, in *Doyle v The Economist* (1980),[11] when a news magazine published a story that some Catholic QC's at the Northern Ireland Bar considered that the plaintiff had been appointed to the county court bench as a token Catholic, Murray J in the Northern Ireland High Court held that the magazine had not acted on a privileged occasion. Courts in England,[12] New Zealand,[13] Canada,[14] and certain Australian states,[15] and up until 1964 in the USA[16] have

8 *Green v Blake* at 251 per O'Byrne J.
9 *Green v Blake* at 269 per Black J.
10 *Law of Torts* 6th ed 540.
11 [1980] NI 171.
12 *Purcell v Sowler* (1877) 2 CPD 215; *Hebditch v MacIlwaine* (1894) 2 QB 54; *London Artists v Littler* [1968] 1 AER 1075; *Blackshaw v Lord*[1983] 3 WLR 283; Anon, 'Privileged Communications in Libel' (1877) 11 ILT & SJ 118.
13 *Truth (NZ) v Holloway* [1960] NZLR 69; *Brooks v Muldoon* [1973] NZLR1.
14 *Banks v Globe and Mail* (1961) 28 DLR (2d) 343; for the other Canadian authorities, see Linden *Canadian Tort Law* 1982, 708 fn 243.
15 New South Wales — *Morosi v Minor Newspapers* [1977] 2 NSWLR 744; Western Australia — *West Australia Newspapers v Bridge* (1979) 141 CLR 535.
16 Prosser, 4th ed, 819.

reached similar conclusions. The position is one which is adverse to media interests, who have argued for such a privilege, and who would be the principal beneficiaries were it recognised.

The reasons given by the courts for this refusal to recognise a public interest qualified privilege have varied from denying that the reported matter was of real public interest,[17] or denying that the reporter was under any duty to report,[18] to the fear that, were the courts to recogise such a defence — and were journalists to continue refusing to reveal their sources — that 'it would give journalists a licence to print libel',[19] or that the recognition of the defence would render useless the defence of fair comment,[20] or would give protection for untrue allegations.

There is, however, some support in England,[21] in certain Australian states,[22] and in East Africa,[23] for the general principle of a public interest qualified privilege. Even before 1964 in the US Prosser writes that there was always 'a substantial and vigorous minority view that even false statements of fact were privileged if they were made for the public benefit with an honest belief in their truth because the public interest demanded that those who are in a position to furnish information about public servants be not deterred by fear of suit ...'.[24]

In 1964, in a landmark decision, *New York Times v Sullivan*,[25] the Supreme Court of the US signalled a substantial readjustment of the balance between the right to free speech and that of good name by holding that the constitutional protection of the freedom of the print and broadcast media created a constitutional privilege against actions in defamation. This privilege, it held, would protect all media statements concerning public officials, whether of fact or comment,unless a plaintiff could show malice in the defendant, and this malice was narrowly defined as akin to proof of lying in an action in deceit.

17 As in *Brooks v Muldoon*.
18 As in *Doyle v The Economist*.
19 At 176 per Murray J.
20 As in *London Artista v Littler* and *Blackshaw v Lord*.
21 See *Cox v Feeney* (1863) 176 ER 445; *Perera v Perera*[1949] AER 1; *Webb v Times Publishing* [1960] 2 QB 535.
22 In Queensland by virtue of s 377 Criminal Code, and in Tasmania by virtue of s 16 Defamation Act 1957 a media public interest qualified privilege is recognised. A privilege was formally recognised in New South Wales — *Calwell v Ipec Australia* (1975) 135 CLR 321 — but by virtue of Defamation Act 1974 s 22(1), this position may be changed. See generally ALRC Report para 143.
23 *Shah v Uganda Argus* [1972] EA 86.
24 4th ed. 820.
25 (1964) 376 US 254.

Since then, the privilege has been applied to statements about a wide range of public officials, and has been significantly expanded to protect statements about public figures, including even those who are merely involved in public controversies. Such a wide range for the privilege, however, gave rise to concern about the diminished protection of the right to a good name, and more recently the Supreme Court has adopted a stricter approach to the question of when a person becomes a public figure.[26]

The courts in Ireland have not had to decide yet between the divergent common law and American views as to which represents the position here, aside that is from Doyle's case, a Northern Irish authority of persuasive influence. But, although there might not be authority on the point, it is possible to comment on what the position may be by drawing inferences from certain privileges which already exist and which are based on public interest grounds. These are privileges which apply to statements made by public representatives, and to statements made during election campaigns. There is also a constitutional dimension to this matter because of the clear references to freedom of expression and to the rights of the media, or the organs of public opinion, in the Constitution, though, or course, there are countervailing principles referred to there as well.

Public representatives

When an elected public representative makes a defamatory statement while performing his duties, he is acting on a privileged occasion, and if he also acts without malice, he will be privileged from an action in defamation. For a member of the Oireachtas, this privilege protects statements which he makes while outside of the House to which he belongs, say, while addressing a meeting of his constituents. In *McCarthy v Morrissey*(1939),[27] a TD was held privileged when he condemned, before some journalists and constituents, the report of a local medical officer in which local children were accused of a lack of cleanliness; and in the *Lindsay v Maher*,[28] a member of the European Parliament, who represented a predominantly rural

26 See generally Eldredge 252-9; Prosser 804-8; Zillman, 'American Approach to Defamation' (1980)10 Anglo-Am L Rev 225; ALRC Report Appendix F; Faulks Committee Report paras 166-9.

27 (1939) IJR 82.

28 *The Irish Times,* 4 February 1984.

constituency, was held privileged in accusing the Master of the High Court of ignorance of the real conditions of farmers.

The privilege also protects statements by members of local authorities. The rule was stated by Pigot CB in 1856, in a case[29] concerning a statement by a member of a board of guardians: 'It is also, in my opinion, clear, that for what is said by any guardian at a meeting of the board, in the fair and *bona fide* discharge of his public duty, and without malice, he cannot be made responsible in an action for oral slander'.[30] In a recent case,[31] a member of Wexford County Council who was also a TD was held to have been privileged in respect of disparaging remarks he made about a caretaker of a dump at a council meeting. The privilege of local authority members also applies to statements made by them outside of the council chamber, while acting in the course of their duties. In *Crawford and Frame v Vance* (1908),[32] a member of Dublin Corporation was privileged when writing letters to the Local Government Board, and to a newspaper on matters affecting his constituents. The basis of the privilege of the public representative is his public representative capacity, and also that the statement is made on a matter which is relevant to the representative's constitutents. This permits him to speak on a wide range of issues. As Hanna J stated in McCarthy's case, the '[defendant] represents the people of Nenagh in a dual capacity both as a member of the Dáil and as a member of the Nenagh Urban District Council, and anything affecting the people whom he represented was a matter in which he was entitled, and, in fact, was bound, to take an interest'.[33] The privilege of a public representative is not limited to matters which are relevant to his constitutional or legislative duties. It also applies to statements which he makes on any additional matters that is is customary for him to be interested in. In a recent Northern Ireland case,[34] a member of Parliament was privileged when he complained to a housing authority about an alleged unfair allocation of jobs and houses in his constituency.

In the various cases the privilege has only been spoken of as protecting public representatives. It is a step from this, for which there is no express support, to state that a member of the electorate of the public representative would also be protected when commenting on a matter of importance to the constituency, or community.

29 *Pierce v Ellis* (1856) 6 ICLR 55, 65.

30 At 65.

31 *Long v Byrne* The Irish Times, 27 November 1984, see also *Dalton and Others v Dunne* The Irish Times, 20 March 1981.

32 [1908] 2 IR 521.

33 At 84.

34 *Kearney v McCusker* The Irish Times, 30 April 1983, see also *Beach v Freeson* [1972] 1 QB 14.

However, if one considers the reasoning behind the privilege — that it is essential for a healthy democracy that public representatives be able to speak freely on public matters, and without the fear of an action in defamation — then it is difficult to see how a healthy democracy can be achieved if the ordinary person, who makes up the democracy, is himself to be deterred from speaking on public matters.[35] Power under our Constitution comes from the people. In this situation, if a representative capacity can imply a privilege, it is inconsistent to say that an individual capacity cannot also do so. The British theory, by which a privilege devolving from the sovereign could, with some logic, stop at public representatives and fall short of the Crown's subjects, seems inapplicable here. There may be grounds, therefore, on which a judge so minded to could act to hold that, according to our constitutional theory and also in logic, a statement by a member of the electorate on a matter of public importance and made to the electorate, or community, ought also to enjoy a qualified privilege.

Elections

Where a statement is made about a candidate for public office to those who possess the power to decide whether or not to elect him to that office, then the statement is made on a privileged occasion, and if it is made bona fide and without malice, it is privileged from an action in defamation. The statement will often be made to the electorate by one candidate about another. But it can also be made about those who support or are behind the other candidate, because 'It appears to us to be impossible to draw a distinction between such a person and the candidate himself ... There is an old saying that "Those who play at bowls must expect rubbers"'.[36] Significantly, the privilege also protects statements which are made about a candidate by one elector to another,[37] or to those who support a candidate.[38] Whether the privilege applies to statements made during a campaign for a constitutional referendum is not clear. In principle since a referendum is part of the constitutional democratic process, statements might be protected, but since the debate concerns

35 See Weiler 'Defamation, Enterprise Liability and Freedom of Speech' (1967) U of Toronto LJ 278, 286 et seq.

36 *Braddock v Bevins* [1948] 1 KB 580, 591 per Lord Greene MR; the effect of this decision in England has since been reversed by s 10 of the Defamation Act 1952 for local authority and parliamentary elections.

37 *Bruce v Leisk* (1892) 19 R 482.

38 *Bradney v Virtue* (1909) 28 NZLR 828.

issues, and not personalities, that might suggest that there is theoretically no real need for a privilege.

The reason for the election privilege is 'the great importance that none but persons of good character should be elected to public offices'.[39] Both the obviousness of, and the necessity for, the privilege were mentioned by Lord Greene MR in an English case — *Braddock v Bevin* (1948):[40]

> In principle, and quite apart from such assistance as can be derived from authority, we should have thought it scarcely open to doubt that statements contained in the election address of one candidate concerning the opposite candidate, provided they are relevant to the matters which the electors will have to consider in deciding which way they will cast their votes, are entitled to the protection of qualified privilege. The electors clearly have an interest in receiving a communication of that kind. Indeed, the task of the electors under democratic institutions could not be satisfactorily performed if such a source of relevant information *bona fide* given were cut off by the fear of an action for libel.

Some uncertainty exists about where the protected statement may be made during an election campaign. In Braddock's case the statement was contained in an election pamphlet, but in another case no privilege was recognised because the statement was contained in a newspaper,[41] and it was feared would be received by uninterested persons. It is not clear if the same might apply where the statement is made at a large meeting.[42] It is difficult, however, to see how a distinction about location or medium may be made. Nowadays reliance by politicians on the media and on mass advertising is a fundamental part of an election campaign, and if the privilege is to have meaning at all, it must surely apply to statements so published and protect both politicians and the media.[43] The possibility that some uninterested persons may receive the statement will always exist, although considering that most people over eighteen will be entitled to vote, the risk may be slight.

39 At 839 per Edwards J.

40 At 590.

41 *Duncombe v Daniel* (1837) 8 C & P 222.

42 See *Pankhurst v Hamilton* (1887) 3 TLR 500.

43 It is interesting that the New Zealand Court of Appeal, when faced with this issue in *Templeton v Jones* [1984] 1 NZLR 484, conceded that the common law may need reform in this area, but it balked at doing so itself really because no one else had done so.

Since election campaigns give rise to privileged occasions, a question arises concerning the length of time for which the privilege will last. This does not seem to have been considered in the cases. It certainly lasts for the duration of the campaign, presumably from the date the election is called until polling day. Beyond this, the matter is unclear. But again, when one considers the nature of the democratic system, and such facts as that elections are inevitable, there is a maximum duration for each parliament or council, and especially that the performance of those in office will be relevant to their chances of re-election, it would seem difficult to restrict the privilege to the election campaign simpliciter. Further, there are some democratic systems where the length of elective office is fixed and immutable and the election is known well in advance, so that there is no formal length to the election campaign. If the extent of the privilege depended on the kind of electoral system used, statements about Dáil candidates would only be protected if made during the necessary thirty days after the dissolution of the Dáil and before polling day, but statements made about candidates for the European Parliament could be protected though made any time in its five year term. Assuming that the electorate are interested in all the facts necessary to decide who to vote for in an election, there is much in logic to support the submission that no significance ought to attach to the point in time at which a statement is made and that the occasion will be privileged for as long as the campaign lasts, and that may be as long as the previous parliament or council lasted.

Constitutional protection

There is much in our Constitution which allows of reasoning similar to that relied upon by the US Supreme Court in *New York Times v. Sullivan* when it found a constitutionally based qualified privilege for the mass media,[44] although the admonition here in Article 40.6

44 The enactment in Canada of the Charter of Rights and Freedoms has opened up parallel possibilities there. For an article based on quite similar grounds to those advanced below, and advocating a Canadian form of a public interest qualified privilege based also on the constitutional protection of fundamental rights, see Doody 'Freedom of the Press, The Canadian Charter of Rights and Freedoms, and a New Category of Qualified Privilege' (1983) 61 Can B Rev 124.

(1) against undue state interference with the rights of the media is not so assertively made. Our preamble indicates that here, too, sovereignty resides with the people and not with the government. Article 5 declares this to be a democratic state. In Article 40.6 (1), the state guarantees liberty for the right of citizens to the free expression of convictions and opinions, and, further, specifically mentions the rightful liberty of expression of the organs of public opinion, such as the press, including the right of criticism of government policy. If the US Supreme Court could then consider that the importance of free speech, and a free press, in a democracy required the recognition of a constitutional privilege for the media against liability in defamation, and assuming that the free flow of statements is no less vital to the health of Irish democracy than it is to the health of American democracy, it can be suggested that our Constitution, too, recognises a privileged occasion when the media publishes on a matter of public concern involving politicians, public officials or public figures.

But, the question of the nature of such a privilege, and when it may be lost are different matters. If our Constitution contained only the provisions outlined above, that would be a reason for suggesting that the privilege would only be lost when a plaintiff could establish a degree of malice akin to proof of lying in deceit, as was held in the *New York Times* case. However, our Constitution, unlike the American one, expressly recognises a right to a good name and obliges the state to vindicate it, if practicable. It goes further, too, and renders the citizen's, and the media's, rights of free expression subject to public order and morality, and the latter additionally to the status of the authority of the state. It seems likely that these provisions would be held to go some way towards limiting the variety of occasions when the privilege would arise, possibly so as to exclude non political public figures and thereby usefully avoid some of the difficulties raised in the aftermath of the New York Times case about who is a public figure. But the entire exclusion of reports about non-political figures from the privilege might be too restrictive of media rights, since such figures can, through economic, religious or other influence, possess great power. It may also be likely that the American definition of malice would hardly satisfy these provisions. A broader and less restrictive definition of malice would probably be required. Perhaps the present common law definition — that a defendant act honestly when making the statement — would do, though it is likely that a still broader one, involving compliance with certain conditions or absence of negligence would be required.[45]

45 See the recommendations of the NZ Committee Report at para 237; for whether the New York Times malice, and common law malice are mutually exclusive,

The law relating to public representatives and to election campaigns recognises two occasions of qualified privilege — when the public representative is performing his duties and when an election campaign is in progress. The rationale underlying these privileges suggests a wider application for them — one that would privilege statements made by members of an electorate about any matter affecting the electorate, or influencing how others would vote in an election. This would still fall short of a general public interest privilege for it would apply only to political matters and official affairs and not to matters of public concern generally. Any constitutional privilege for the media would probably cover reports of those matters also, and possibly beyond it as well to include reports on the activities of a narrowly defined class of public figures, since if it did not do so the media's constitutional protection would, aside from the definition of malice, be no greater than the individual's freedom of expression. The separate treatment in Article 40.6 appears to suggest a special position for the media. Whether media protection would go so far as to protect reports about private individuals momentarily thrust into the public light is, however, more problematic.

Whatever the extent of individual and media constitutional privilege, it would appear that to recognise them would subsume the two common law election privileges. This, at any rate, is the conclusion drawn by Prosser as to the effect which the decision in the New York Times case had on the pre-existing minority view there that there was a public interest qualified privilege.[46]

It is also worth noting that the recognition here of a constitutional privilege for the media would subsume a number of other media protections as well. At present, there is already a measure of protection for some statements that are made in the public interest. There is, for instance, both the common law and statutory protections conferred on various reports of judicial proceedings. There is also s 24 of the Defamation Act, which confers, in a complicated way, a qualified protection on a lengthy list of media reports of matters of public interest and concern. The defence of fair comment is another instance where certain comments on public matters are protected.[47] All these, which are considered later in the text, would, it seems fair

see Motlow 'The Constitutionality of Punitive Damages' (1979) 10 Cumb LR 498-508.

46 *Law of Torts* 4th ed, 786.

47 In *Blackshaw v Lord* (1983)3 WLR 283, Dunn LJ noted, at 310, that the recognition of a public interest qualified privilege woud have this effect on fair comment.

to assume, be subsumed in a constitutional protection for non-malicious statements.

Finally, it is worth noting how the reform bodies have considered this matter. Both the English[48] and Australian[49] bodies recommended against creating by statute a public interest qualified privilege, essentially because they felt that it would incline the balance of interest too much away from the protection of reputation. They also considered that a principal reason for changing the law — that the media were discouraged from investigative journalism by the lack of privilege — did not hold true in practice. By contrast, the New Zealand Committee recommended the creation of a public interest qualified privilege for the media subject to certain conditions — that reasonable care is taken, that an explanation is given to the aggrieved person, and a statement of explanation by him is facilitated, and that all his reasonable costs and expenses are paid.[50] The reason why the committee favoured a privilege was, it seems, that the New Zealand press was overcautious in its approach to publishing material. Of course, all these views, and in particular the rejection of the privilege by the English and Australian bodies, should have no bearing on the question whether our Constitution contains such a privilege or not. At the same time, it is conceivable that if the Supreme Court held that a public interest privilege did protect the media[51] the court could also conclude that the balance of interest would then be best struck by making the privilege dependent in the same way as the New Zealand committee has recommended.

REPORTS OF JUDICIAL PROCEEDINGS

Fair and accurate reports of the proceedings of courts that are administering justice, and also of the proceedings of bodies functioning under Article 37 of the Constitution, are privileged from an action in defamation if made bona fide and without malice.[52] The privilege

48 Paras 211-215.

49 Para 146; see also Hughes 'Defaming Public Figures' (1985). Aust LJ 433; Lloyd 'Defamation Law Reform' (1984) 58 Aust LJ 595.

50 Committee Report, Chapter 10; although the ALRC Report did not favour a wide privilege, it seems to have struck a middle ground by recommending a general fair report defence covering attributed statements only and not a reporters own allegations — paras 165-180.

51 The court could also cite the constitutional references in Article 40.6 to the organs of public opinion as supporting such a privilege, and it would thereby safeguard itself against private citizen complaints of unequal treatment.

52 A rare case where malice was actually found in *Stevens v Sampson* (1879) 5 Ex D 53 concerning a solicitor who sent a report of a case to a local paper; see Anon 'Libellous Reports of Judicial Proceedings' (1880) 14 ILT & SJ 207.

can be either a common law one or a statutory one depending on the type of report in question. The statutory protection is now contained in s 18 of the Defamation Act 1961, which restated, with some extensions, s 3 of the Law of Libel Amendment Act 1888. S 18 provides.

> (1) A fair and accurate report published in any newspaper or broadcast by means of wireless telegraphy as part of any programme or service provided by means of a broadcasting station within the State or in Northern Ireland of proceedings publicly heard before any court established by law and exercising judicial authority within the State or in Northern Ireland shall, if published or broadcast contemporaneously with such proceedings, be privileged.
>
> (2) Nothing in subsection (1) of this section shall authorise the publication or broadcasting of any blasphemous or obscene matter.

This privilege, as may be seen, covers only certain reports by newspapers and broadcasting stations. There are, of course, many other kinds of reports such as those contained in conversations, or letters, or pamphlets or leaflets, or documents, or books, like law text books and the various series of law reports, and, as the term 'newspaper' is earlier defined in s 2 of the Act as a paper published at least once every thirty-six days, then periodicals of longer time span would also be among these other reports that are not included in the statutory protection. For all these other reports recourse would need to be had to the common law protection, which exists regardless of the type of report. Besides this difference between the common law and statutory privileges, there are other differences as well. It should be noted, however, that these differences are important only if the common law privilege is qualified and the statutory privilege is absolute. Many of the text writers consider this to be the case.[53]

The nature of the statutory privilege

Those textbook writers who support the view that the statutory privilege is absolute rely largely on interpretative support. There is also a decision at first instance in which the privilege was held to be absolute.[54] The interpretive reasons are based on the title and preamble to the 1888 Act[55] — which are equivocal — and on the

53 For example, Fleming 550; Salmond and Heuston 153.
54 *McCarey v Associated Newspaper* [1964] 1 WLR 855.
55 Clerk and Lindsell *On Torts* 15th ed, 20-135 fn 88.

assumption that if the privilege is qualified, then it only restates the common law and so would have been unnecessary, thus its enactment must have meant that the privilege would be different and therefore absolute. There is also the reason that as another section of the 1888 Act, when creating a qualified privilege, specifically described it as such, then the absence of any qualifying term here would imply an absolute privilege.[56] These latter reasons would, it is clear, be compelling were it not for the fact that the legislature when enacting the 1888 Act actually intended that the privilege should be a qualified one. When introduced originally, the bill described the privilege as an absolute one, but by amendment 'absolute' was dropped because, according to the Attorney General, 'If the words "absolutely privileged" remained, reports published with malice would be protected, but according to the amendment the protection would only be given where no malice was shown'.[57] In light of this, it can only be out of a deference to the rule that the proceedings in parliament cannot be opened to a court in order to assist in ascertaining parliament's intention, that the suggestion is made that the privilege is absolute.

This rule, however, has not always been observed by judges,[58] and there appears to be a modern willingness to disregard it in cases where there is a reasonable doubt as to a provision and where, in the words of Lord Reid, 'examining the proceedings in Parliament would almost certainly settle the matter immediately one way or the other'.[59] That there is such a doubt is clear from the facts that one authority,[60] in opposition to the majority, regards the privilege as a qualified one, that the majority acknowledge the uncertainty, and that the Faulks Committee recommended that the matter be clarified.[61]

But, though the debates may, one submits, be opened, an additional question arises here. Which debates? Those on the 1888 Act or those on the 1961 Act? Perhaps the former may be opened in order to state the law as it existed before the 1961 debates. The privilege will then be clearly identified as qualified. In the debates on the 1961 Act, the nature of the proposed privilege was actually adverted to, and it was clearly the intention of the government that the privilege should

56 Carter-Ruck *On Libel and Slander*, 3rd ed, 116.
57 Hansard, 3rd Series, vol 326, col 1278.
58 For a list of some occasions, see Cross *Statutory Interpretation* 134.
59 *Warner v Metropolitan Police* [1969] 2 AC 256, 279. See also *Wavin Pipes v Hepworth Iron* HCt, unreported, 8 May 1981; considered by Casey in a Note, (1980) DULJ 110.
60 Odgers, 6th ed, 1929.
61 Para 191.

be an absolute one [62], despite its express refusal to use the term 'absolute' in the legislation.[63] That that intent could actually be achieved without using this term was doubted by the opposition, and in the result where the privilege is described in the same way as in the 1888 Act, it may be, although one cannot be certain, that the wording does not reflect the ascribed intent, and that the 1961 Act cannot be taken to have altered the pre-existing position. Thus the statutory privilege, one submits, is a qualified one only.[64].

Proceedings that may be reported

At common law the range of judicial proceedings, the reports of which are protected, would be as wide as the range of judicial proceedings that are themselves absolutely protected. Such proceedings include the making of pre-hearing statements necessary for litigation, the making of statements in the course of the hearing, and post-hearing statements that necessarily follow the decision. Some of the cases here have concerned reports under the latter heading.[65] It has been held that the records of judgements in judicial proceedings are part of the judicial proceedings so as to draw a privilege to reports of such judgements. As O'Brien J stated in *McNally v Oldham* (1863),[66] 'it is clear... that the privilege which exists of publishing the proceedings of a Court of Justice, includes the publication of the judgement of that Court'.

The reports of proceedings of bodies now coming under Article 37 of the Constitution are also protected, and their proceedings are, similarly, broadly defined to include necessary pre- and post-hearing statements. This privilege seems to have been recognised here as early as 1834 when, in a case,[67] where a witness at a commission of inquiry had reported his own evidence, two of the three judges[68] assumed a sufficient similarity between the commission and a court of justice, and thus a conditional privilege for the report, though the case was decided against the defendant on other grounds. The basis

62 Dáil Debates, vol 191, col 1980 et seq.

63 An amendment by the opposition to explicitly describe the privilege as absolute was defeated, Dáil Debates, vol 191, col 2537 et seq.

64 It could even be argued that because the 1961 Act debates are so difficult to interpret — since the judge has to interpret how deputies thought judges would interpret their words — that the debates ought not to be consulted at all, which should probably leave the pre-1961 situation still operating.

65 *McNally v Oldham* (1864) 16 ICLR 298, *Cosgrave v Trade Auxiliary* (1874) IR 8 CL 349, *Annally v Trade Auxiliary* (1889) 26 LR Ir 11, 394.

66 At 315.

67 *R v O'Brien* (1833) Cooke v Alc 128.

68 Jebb, Burton JJ.

of the privilege exists, as is clear from the leading English precedent,[69] in the degree of public interest in such bodies, and in the duties of such bodies towards the public.

The reported statement must have formed part of the proceedings. The law on this may be deduced both from cases on the point, and from cases[70] where it was attempted to sue the maker of an irrelevant statement that was made during the hearing of a case. From both it seems clear that reports of irrelevant statements by witnesses and parties would not be protected. So too with onlookers. In one of the cases,[71] where a bystander at an inquest volunteered that a witness had perjured himself, Dowse B remarked that 'It is an abuse of terms to call a slanderous observation of this description, volunteered by a bystander, a part of the proceedings at the inquest'.[72] Reports of irrelevant speeches by counsel would probably also not be protected. In another case,[73] a report of the speech of counsel before what was considered then a court of justice, made the day after the hearing had terminated but before a decision had been announced, was held not protected as it had been given 'without evidence, and ... without any object towards the prosecution of a cause...'.[74] Concerning reports of irrelevant remarks by judges, the trend of the decisions is to the effect that a judge cannot make an irrelevant remark. It would seem then that the only report of judicial remarks which is not protected would be when the remarks were made while the judge was knowingly acting in excess of his jurisdiction.

The statutory privilege contained in s 18 of the Defamation Act 1961 does not protect the reports of as many proceedings as the common law. It only applies to reports of proceedings publicly heard before any court established by law and exercising judicial authority within the state or in Northern Ireland. Neither privilege would apply to reports of cases heard in camera or in a judge's chambers, but would probably apply to ex parte proceedings.[75] Neither privilege would apply to reports of the pleadings of cases not yet before the court.[76] But the statutory privilege alone would not apply to reports

69 *Albutt v Gen Co of Medical Education* (1899) 23 QBD 400.
70 See p. 133 supra.
71 *Lynam v Gowing* (1880) 6 LR Ir 259.
72 At 268.
73 *Kane v Mulvaney* (1866) IR 2 CL 402.
74 At 420 per Monahan CJ.
75 See Anon 'Privileged Reports of Judicial Proceedings' (1878) 12 ILT & SJ 467.
76 See Hansard, 3rd Series vol 326 col 1272. The same is probably true, at common law, of pre-trial reports of litigation documents — Linden 700, Fleming 550. However, in the US the cases are in 'sharp conflict', and while Prosser 837 states that the prevailing view is against including reports of pre-trial documents

of any of the proceedings of bodies functioning under Article 37 of the Constitution, as these are not courts.

One area, though, where the statutory protection might be broader than the common law one concerns its extra-territorial dimension. S 18 privileges reports published here of proceedings of courts of law in Northern Ireland.[77] Whether the common law has any such dimension as to privilege reports of judicial proceedings in foreign states is uncertain. In England, it has been held that such reports may be protected if they would be of real interest to a reasonable person there.[78] Any recognition of such a qualified privilege would, of course, mean that a person's constitutional right to a good name is, in the circumstances, to be subordinated to a public interest in receiving the report. Since good name is a constitutional right, it can only be subordinated to another constitutional right. The question then arises — what is there in the Constitution upon which could be based such an imperative in reading foreign judicial proceedings as requires subordinating the citizen's constitutional rights? It would seem that the only such imperative is contained in Article 29.4 (3) whereby the state is committed to the consequences of achieving European economic union. It is possible then that there may be a privilege, and a constitutional rather than a common law one, for reports of the proceedings of the courts of the European Community and of the member states of that community when dealing with matters relating to the economic union. Beyond these, it is difficult to see any constitutional reason which supports a qualified privilege for reports on the proceedings of foreign courts. Indeed, it may be that the only ground on which the statutory privilege for reports published here of court proceedings in Northern Ireland is constitutional is the assertion in Article 2 of the Constitution that the national territory consists of the whole of the island.

within the privilege, on grounds of affording too great a scope for public defamation, according to Eldredge 427-31 the trends since a hallmark decision in 1927 is 'strongly' in favour of protection, partly because pleadings are obviously part of judical proceedings since they start them off, partly because the cut-off point is illogical in contrast to reports of ex-parte applications which are protected, and partly because the defamatory effect of such reports is diminshed by public awareness that accusations are to be expected in pleadings.

77 This is to be distinguished from the extra-territorial effect of s 18 which protects reports published inside Northern Ireland. Arguments about the constitutionality of a similar effect in s 24 of the 1961 Act can also be raised against this provision.

78 *Webb v Times Publishing* [1960] 2 QB 535; the same is, apparently, the case in Canada, see Williams 90-91 and in Australia, see Fleming 551.

Accurate and fair

The report must truly and accurately state the facts of the proceeding which is being reported. Generally speaking, whether the facts in the proceeding are themselves true is not relevant to this, and such facts may well be untrue. In *Annally v Trade Auxiliary* (1889),[79] a newspaper was protected in accurately reporting an entry in the register of judgements, although the entry in the register was itself inaccurate. But where it is known that the facts in the proceedings are untrue, then truth and accuracy requires the report to be published in such a way as to convey the real state of affairs.

The facts in the proceedings that are known to be untrue may be reported, but it must also be reported that these are untrue, as in *Cosgrave v Trade Auxiliary* (1874),[80] where it was conveyed by an asterisk that the correctly reported entry in the register of judgements was untrue. If prior knowledge of the untruth of the facts in the proceedings is not conveyed, then the privilege will be lost, as happened in *McNally v Oldham* (1864),[81] where an accurate report did not convey the reporter's prior knowledge that the facts in the report were untrue.

Besides the issue of the truth of the reported facts, the report does not have to be accurate in the entirety of the facts stated. It is sufficient if the report is substantially accurate and 'a mere *petitio principii*'[82] does not matter. In *Annally's* case, the inaccuracy in the report that the judgement had been recovered, when the register only stated that it had been registered, was held in the circumstances to be insignificant and so did not affect the privilege.[83]

In addition to being accurate, the report must also be fair. It should therefore not contain comments either in the text, or in the heading which is attached to it, as would render it partisan. Thus, in *R v O'Brien* (1834),[84] where a report of evidence, given at an enquiry into allegations that the Lord Mayor of Cork had obtained bribes from local bakers, was titled 'The Golden Loaf', it was held that the report was unfair. There were also comments contained in the body of the report, and Bushe CJ stated 'for nothing is a fair report, which

79 (1889) 26 LR Ir 11, 394.
80 (1874) IR 8 CL 349.
81 (1864) 16 ICLR 298; see also *Pierce v Ellis* (1856) 6 ICLR 55.
82 *Annally v Trade Auxiliary* at 403 per Fitzgibbon LJ; in *Bankole-Bright v Boston* (1920-36) ALR SL 410 it was suggested that a newspaper report by a trained lawyer might require a higher standard of accuracy than otherwise.
83 One of the judges, Barry LJ at 404 had doubts, though not to the point of dissent, about whether the occasion was privileged.
84 (1834) Cooke & Alc 128.

going beyond a plain narrative, indulges in comments or observations calculated to exhibit any individual as an object of scorn and contempt, and represents the evidence given in such a coloured manner as rather bespeaks the work of a partisan than a reporter; when we look at the heading prefixed to, and collateral observations accompanying this alleged report, we cannot (consider this to be) a fair report'.[85]

A fair and accurate report does not have to be a verbatim account of all the evidence and of the judgement delivered. It can be a fair summarized account of such of either, or both, as is given on a particular day. Fairness also relates to when a report is made, and not just to when the event occured. If made sometime after the event, a report must present a fair picture of the overall proceeding, and may not selectively quote from some witnesses evidence without referring to some relevant context, such as whether the evidence was accepted or rejected. If a decision is appealed a report of the trial might not be fair if it did not also indiciate the fact or outcome of the appeal because both trial and appeal may be regarded as one large proceeding.[86] In the US some courts impose a duty on a reporter to inquire into the existence and outcome of any post trial proceedings. Such a duty clearly requires more of a reporter of dated than contemporaneous proceedings. Failure to discharge this duty, even where the reporter was unaware of any intervening proceedings, can render the report unfair.[87]

When may the report be published?

At common law, there is no restriction on when a report of judicial proceedings may be published, and it may then be published during the continuance of the proceeding. Monahan CJ stated in 1866 that 'when the case is going on from day to day, you may report each day's proceedings'.[88] The report may also, of course, be published

85 At 136. A daily newspaper which contemporaneously reported the prosecution's evidence but not the defence's from a later date may probably be within the statutory protection, but is hardly fair to the accused, see Anon, 'Libelling by Report of Judicial Proceeding' (1890) 24 ILR & SJ 485. In the US according to Johnsen 1045, 'if a newspaper uses the privilege to publish daily reports of a trial it may not abruptly halt the pattern, leaving one sides evidence unreported.' A case to similar effect might possibly be made through reliance on the fairness dimension to good name protection cited in *In re Haughey* [1971] IR 217.

86 Johnsen 'When Truth and Accuracy Diverge: The Fair Report of a Dated Proceeding' (1982) 34 Stan L Rev 1041, 1051-3.

87 Johnsen argues that the present strict liability which is imposed when the duty is not discharged is too harsh on reporters, and suggests it should be replaced by a standard of liability based on a reckless failure to inquire.

88 *Kane v Mulvaney* (1866) IR 2 CL 402, 420.

after the proceeding. But the report of dated proceedings, perhaps years after the event, may unfairly resurrect the past misdeeds of an individual, and while the defence of justification or qualified privilege appears to protect the reporter, it may be open to question whether the Constitution in its protection of reputation, standing and privacy might require greater emphasis to be placed on an individual entitlement to live down his past,[89] unless some compelling reason justified the report, such as citation as a legal precedent.

The statutory protection in s 18 only applies to reports published contemporaneously with the proceedings. The meaning of contemporaneity here was well described during the debate on the 1888 Act by the Attorney General, who thought that it should be 'construed with reference to the issue of the paper ... Contemporaneous publication in the case of a weekly newspaper would mean the publication of proceedings which had transpired during the week prior to the day of publication, and ... in the case of a daily newspaper would be the publication of proceedings which had taken place on the day of publication or the day before....'[90] Presumably, therefore, a monthly newspaper would be entitled to report on proceedings which occurred in the month before it was printed.

REPORTS OF PUBLIC MEETINGS, AND OTHER MATTERS

In s 24 of the Defamation Act 1961, the Oireachtas conferred on newspapers and broadcasting stations a qualified privilege in respect of fair and accurate[91] reports concerning any of a lengthy list of subject matter set out in two parts in the second Schedule to the Act. One must assume that any such discrimination in favour of these media as against the rest of the community does not infringe rights to equal treatment before the law because of the differing social function of these organs of public opinion, or because of their express constitutional recognition. The exclusion of other media, such as cinema, books and magazines published less frequently than once every thirty six days may be constitutionally invalid since those may also be constitutionally recognised organs of public opinion.[92]

The privilege is dependent, in some instances set out in Part II

89 See p. 115 supra.

90 Hansard 3rd Series vol 326 col 1275.

91 For the meaning of fair and accurate here, see *Pierce v Ellis* (1856) 6 ICLR 55 and *Daly v Cork Herald* (1887) 31 ILT & SJ 165.

92 The Faulks Committee regarded the restriction to these media as 'difficult to understand', and recommended that books and other publications should also be protected — para 229.

of the Second Schedule, though not in the other instances set out in Part I, on a reporter publishing, at the request of a person conceiving himself defamed, a proper statement of explanation or contradiction. The privilege is also dependent, in all cases, on the subject matter of the report being of public concern, and its publication being for the public benefit, and not prohibited by law.

As will be seen, there are a number of areas of considerable difficulty in this defence. These include the issues of why some topics are included in the Schedule and others are not; why some topics are included in Part II rather than Part I and vice versa, and why some places, the reports of whose subject matter is to be protected, are selected while other places are not. As a result of these and other matters, and also as a result of an apparent ignorance of Irish law displayed in enacting a section that was substantially based on the recommendations of an English reform body — the Porter Committee — this is about the most complicated, least rational and constitutionally dubious area in the whole of the law of defamation.

The development of the statutory privilege

The statutory privilege was first created by s 2 of the Newspaper Libel and Registration Act 1881 and applied only to reports of lawful meetings that were open to the public. The privilege was created, it seems, at the behest of newspaper interests because by then the common law had still not recognised any privilege covering reports of public meetings.[93] The privilege was subject, even then, to the publication, if requested, of an explanation or statement similar to the present one. The setting of this condition, however, was peculiar. For instance, the condition might have gone further and required the publication of an apology. That it did not, it seems, was because newspapers did not like making public apologies for merely reporting the statements of others. They argued,[94] that the wrong, if any, would be principally that of the maker of the statement and not of the reporter. It was also argued that an apology would be inappropriate because, apparently, newspaper experience under the previous rule had shown a difficulty in verifying the facts in a report inside the permitted time to allow a reliance on an apology.[95] These were not very impressive arguments. The fact that a newspaper is a voluntary reporter for profit goes some way to diminishing the first point. The second point could be met with the view that a paper should not

93 See the account by Huddleston B in *Pankhurst v Sowler* (1887) 3 TLR 193, 195.

94 *Report of a Select Committee on the Law in relation to Libel in Newspapers and Journals* 1879, British Sessional Papers, 1878/9, vol XI, p 277.

95 At 270.

report a statement unless it knows it is true. But if that is too restrictive, a rule that the paper be given a reasonable time in which to make an apology would certainly have met the difficulty. That the provision was enacted with the condition as it stands now illustrates the one-sided view unduly favourable to newspapers taken by the legislature then and repeated since, of how the balance between good name and other rights should be struck.

In the Law of Libel Amendment Act 1888, s 2 of the 1881 Act was repealed and re-enacted in the same terms except that a list of occasions of various meetings of a public nature was given instead of the vague description in the 1881 Act. The reason for this change is not clear. A list had not been given in the 1881 Act so as to enable additional types of public meeting that might become of interest in the future to be included; but the courts had not, it seems, interpreted the 1881 Act in the flexible manner hoped for. The statement of the list in precise terms — intended to reflect what parliament thought then of public interest — meant of course that it would in time become anomalous, and that deserving occasions of recent origin would not be protected. Periodic reviews would then become necessary, inspired by the detailed and particular recommendations of reform bodies, each working on the labour of its predecessors and, in the process, greatly complicating the law. Thus the recommendations of the Porter Committee in England in 1948 led to the list being expanded, and the recommendations of the Faulks Committee will, if implemented, lead to another expansion in the lists; and for each period between which an anomaly is perceived and legislated upon, the law is rendered absurd.

Our s 24 is taken substantially from Porter's and these recommendations significantly introduced a variation concerning the condition of explanation or contradiction. Thenceforth, certain occasions involving reports of foreign matter were to be exempt from even this mild condition. This was an impressive tilt of the balance of interest away from the protection of reputation. The reasoning given by Porter for this had nothing at all to do with any need to make such reports available to the public. From the vague reasoning given,[96] it seems there was a fear [97] that foreigners would be able to force newspapers to publish contradictions of derogatory material about the foreigner contained in the report. At first glance, it might seem that the

96 Para 107, see also Wade 'Defamation' (1950) 66 LQR 348, 351.

97 This might be thought rather xenophobic since in the era of modern communications a newspaper could be able to resist the attempt by obtaining evidence of the true situation. It is interesting to note that in New Zealand, where reports of all foreign matter were made subject to an explanation or contradiction in their Defamation Act 1954, there is no suggestion that the procedure has been abused.

dropping of the condition in Ireland would be an unconstitutional denial of good name; but that would depend on whether non-citizens can avail of the Constitutional guarantee,[98] and on how media rights of expression are evaluated.[99]

Statements enjoying qualified privilege under the Second Schedule

Various statements are listed in Parts I and II of the Second Schedule which may be reported so as to enjoy the privilege contained in s 24 of the 1961 Act.

Part I Paragraph 1 refers to:

> A fair and accurate report of any proceedings in public of a house of any leigislature (including subordinate or federal legislatures of any foreign sovereign State or any body which is part of such legislature or any body duly appointed by or under the legislature of such State to hold a public enquiry on a matter of public importance.

By covering statements in all foreign legislatures, and not just some, the Oireachtas has sensibly avoided the difficult task of justifying any distinction between foreign legislatures on grounds that would be relevant to the balance between good name and other rights.[1] The legislatures referred to must possess legislative power. Thus, reports of statements in bodies like the former Northern Ireland Assembly or the Parliament of the European Communities would not be protected.[2] The requirement that the body holding the public inquiry be appointed by the legislature or executive of a foreign state would exclude, without reason, reports of public inquiries instituted under constitutional or judicial authority. It has been doubted [3] whether the term 'proceedings' includes the concluding reports of the foreign bodies. One suggests, however, that the act of a report and of authorising its publication would be every bit as much a proceeding as any other act of a body, and in that sense a

98 For whether a non-citizen can sue, see Kelly *The Irish Constitution* 2nd ed, 433.

99 See e.g. *Miami Herald Publishing v Tornillo* (1974) 418 US 241 which held that a right of reply statute violated a constitutional guarantee of a free press. See also p. 235 post.

1 Unlike the English Act.

2 Reports of the European Parliament woud also not be protected because the EC is neither foreign, nor a state nor sovereign, at least in the traditional sense. The Faulks Committee recommended, at para 231(a) (see also Appendix XI) that reports of the proceedings and publications of the Parliament and Commission of the EC should be included in the privilege.

report would be a proceeding. Asssuming that a report may be part of a proceeding, the only protected reports that may be reported are those of legislatures, their committees and certain public enquiries. There are however, many other types of official reports as well, and there seems no reason why these are not also included. The reference to the matter being of 'public importance' presumably refers to its importance to the foreign public, as it is elsewhere required that the report be of public concern and benefit here.

Paragraph 2 refers to 'A fair and acccurate report of any proceedings in public of an international organisation of which the State or the Government is a member or of any international conference to which the Government sends a representative'. It would seem that reports of proceedings at the United Nations or the Council of Europe would be protected by this. But the term 'organisation' might not refer to a mere part of it, especially when the institution or body in question is performing just one of many functions which the whole organisation is involved in.[4] It could be that none of the sub bodies of the U N or of the institutions of the European Communities would be included. The limitation that the international organisation consist of states or governments, of which Ireland or its government is a member, reflects a decidedly narrow view of what is of public interest. There are international organisations of which Ireland is not a member, like NATO and OPEC, yet their proceedings are clearly of importance.[5] It is also unduly restrictive to limit the protection to reports of official international organisations. Non-official international organisations can be of as much interest as official ones, witness the Red Cross and Amnesty International. The same narrow view is also evident so far as international conferences are concerned, and here even conferences which members of the judiciary or the legislature attend are not included.[6] Finally, it seems correct to conclude that conferences to which a government sends only an observer as opposed to being represented, would not be protected.[7] All of these exclusions are all difficult to justify.

Paragraph 3 refers to 'A fair and accurate report of any proceedings in public of the International Court of Justice and any other judicial

3 Duncan & Neill, 108.
4 Wade 352.
5 The New Zealand Act is slightly broader than this, in Para 6 of Part II of its Schedule, it includes also international organisations or conferences of which any commonwealth country is a member.
6 The Faulks Committee recommended an extension only to include UN organisations and agencies, see Appendix XI.
7 Gatley para 280 fn 91.

or arbitral tribunal deciding matters in dispute between States'. The limitation here of the privilege to reports of statements before tribunals hearing inter-state disputes seems unjustifiably narrow, for while reports of the proceedings of the Commission and the Court of Human Rights, and also of the Court of Justice of the European Community when hearing inter-state disputes are protected, reports of cases before these bodies involving individuals would not be protected.[8]

Paragraph 4 refers to 'A fair and accurate report of any proceeding before a court (including a court martial) exercising jurisdiction under the law of any legislature (including subordinate or federal legislatures) of any foreign sovereign State'. The reference here to courts that exercise jurisdiction under the law of a legislature is peculiar. The identical English provision was probably based on the British view of how courts there obtain jurisdiction. Its unthinking repetition here rather ignores the Irish view that courts can also obtain jurisdiction under a Constitution, as do the High and Supreme Courts, and there must be many other foreign courts who are similarly seized of jurisdiction. There can be no reason why reports of statements made on such occasions are denied the protection. The Oireachtas was, however, consistent in treating all foreign states equally.[9]

Paragraph 5 refers to 'A fair and accurate copy of or extract from any register kept in pursuance of any law which is open to inspection by the public or of any other document which is required by law to be open to inspection by the public'. It is doubtful if there was a need for this provision here because, already in *Annally v Trade Auxiliary* (1889),[10] the common law had recognised that a statutory right of access to information gives a qualified privilege to those who report it.

Paragraph 6 refers to 'Any notice or advertisement published by or on the authority of any court in the State or in Northern Ireland or any judge or officer of such a court'. In order to determine if this protection applies, it is necessary to consider the reason why the notice or advertisement is published. Where it is issued as a 'mere preliminary to setting a court in motion,'[11] and is not of essential

8 Under Faulks' recommendations, reports of the proceedings of all cases in public before any international court, the Court of Justice and the Commission of Human Rights would be protected.

9 Unlike the English Act but like the New Zealand Act, although the latter only provides Part II type protection for such reports.

10 (1889) 26 LR Ir 11, 394.

11 Clerk and Lindsell *On Torts* 14th ed, para 1730.

importance to the conduct of a case in progress, then the protection here applies. But where the notice is published in order 'to protect those who are to participate in proceedings from a flank attack',[12] then the notice may well be regarded as part of the judicial proceedings, and so enjoy at common law an absolute privilege, rather than the statutory qualified privilege.[13].

Part II — Statements privileged subject to explanation or contradiction
Paragraph 1 refers to a fair and accurate report of the findings or decision of any association formed for the purpose of encouraging or promoting (a) any art, science, religion or learning, (b) any trade, business, industry or profession, (c) game, sport or pastime, provided that the finding or decision relates to a person who is a member of, or is subject to, the control of the association.

The privilege conferred on reports of these statements is much wider than the common law privilege that applies to communications of the proceedings and decisions of domestic disciplinary bodies. The common law privilege, at its widest, is limited to where the report is made to members of the association or group. Under the statutory privilege, any recipient of the newspaper or broadcast would be deemed interested in the report. When it is further noted that this report may concern an association that is not a public one, or that the finding or decision may have been given in private, then the great ambit of this privilege will be appreciated. Were it not for the additional requirements in s 24 (3) that the report be of public concern and public benefit, it might be that an excessive intrusion by a report published under this paragraph could infringe constitutional protections in privacy and confidentiality.

The paragraph refers only to the reports of 'the findings or decision' of a body in contrast to the term 'proceedings' which is used elsewhere in the Schedule. Presumably, then, reports of the proceedings of hearings are not included here.[14] Why this should be so is not apparent, because whatever reasons exist for including or excluding the findings would equally operate for the proceedings.[15]

12 *Lincoln v Daniels* [1962] 1 QB 237, 263.

13 In including notices of courts in Northern Ireland, the Oireachtas went further than the English Act, but not as far as the New Zealand Act which gives Part II type coverage to the notices of courts from anywhere. Faulks recommendations on this are peculiar; aside from commonwealth countries, they would limit the protection to courts of states which are recognised by the UK.

14 The New Zealand protection, in para 10 of its Schedule, refers to proceedings.

15 Faulks recommended that an additional sub-paragraph be inserted which would include associations with charitable or other objects beneficial to the community and who enjoyed control over their members — Appendix XI. The ALRC Report — para 161 — considered it desirable to avoid the unneccessary demarcations involved in enumerating the various associations, and recommended the general category of 'associations'.

The list of subject matter which the associations mentioned in the paragraph must deal with before the report can be protected, reflects the Porter Committee's 1948 view of what the English public were considered interested in. The Oireachtas clearly saw such little difference between the societies that it considered us to be interested in the same matters the English had been interested in thirteen years earlier. This particular list also illustrates, as well as any, the disadvantages of so precisely and narrowly defining the protected reports. Clearly, as society does not remain static, the disciplinary affairs of associations active in matters of little interest in 1961, but of interest now, are excluded from its ambit, and so reports of these bodies do not enjoy the statutory privilege. Thus, among the unprotected reports would be reports on a wide range of special interest groups that are interested in family and social reforms, or the various charities that care for the disadvantaged at home and in the Third World, or those groups that are interested in environmental matters. Another notable exclusion from Paragraph 1 is reports on the disciplinary affairs of political parties, and these would not seem to be included under any other paragraph.

Paragraph 2 refers to 'A fair and accurate report of the proceedings of any public meeting held in the State or in Northern Ireland, being a meeting bona fide and lawfully held for a lawful purpose and for the furtherance or discussion of any matter of public concern whether the admission is general or restricted'. This, it will be recalled, was the original occasion which gave rise to this privilege. The phrasing of the paragraph makes clear that not only must the holding of the meeting be lawful, but it must also be held for a lawful purpose. This latter requirement presumably excludes meetings involving illegal intimidations, incitements and conspiracies. The paragraph has also been interpreted here to deny protection to reports of meetings which criticised lawful actions. In *McInerney v Clareman Printing and Publishing* (1903),[16] where a newspaper report described meetings of the United Irish League at which those who took land that was being boycotted were denounced as land grabbers, it was held that such reports were not protected, partly because 'the purpose of each [meeting] ... was to denounce a local trader for doing a perfectly lawful act. It would be a degradation of the English language to say that the section could apply to such a state of things ...'[17] Whether this was a correct decision then, it must be doubtful now

16 [1903] 2 IR 347.
17 At 387 per Wright J.

that a report of plain criticism of a lawful act could properly lose the privilege, because that might be to deny to a public medium its constitutional liberty to function as an organ of public opinion. The same case also illustrates the point that the protection will be lost if the meeting is not a public one. The police were constantly excluded at the various meetings and the interested parties were normally excluded from attendance.[18].

The paragraph clearly allows for reporting of restricted access public meeetings, although the logicality of this has been doubted.[19] On similar reasoning, reports of press conferences[20] might be protected. The meeting must be for the furtherance or discussion of matter of public concern. While the term discussion implies a two-way dialogue between speaker and audience,[21] the term furtherance seems wider and would allow for the protected reporting of mere speech-making without contributions from the audience so long as it advanced the speaker's cause.

Paragraph 3 refers to: A fair and accurate report of the proceedings at any meeting or sitting of:

(a) any local authority, or committee of a local authority or local authorities, any corresponding authority, or committee thereof in Northern Ireland;

(b) any Judge or Justice acting otherwise than as a court exercising judicial authority and any corresponding authority, or committee thereof in Northern Ireland;

(c) any commission, tribunal, committee or person appointed, whether in the State or Northern Ireland, for the purpose of any inquiry under statutory authority;

(d) any person appointed by a local authority to hold a local inquiry in pursuance of an Act of the Oireachtas and any person appointed by a corresponding authority in Northern Ireland to hold a local inquiry in pursuance of statutory authority;

18 See also Wright J at 386.
19 Hansard 3rd Series, vol 329 col 309.
20 Faulks recommended that these be expressly included in the Schedule, Appendix XI; while the New Zealand Committee considered that this would confer too wide a protection, and instead recommended that only press conferences held by persons, already included by the Schedule should be protected — Para 229.

> (e) any other tribunal, board, committee or body constituted by or under, and exercising functions under statutory authority, whether in the State or in Northern Ireland, not being a meeting or sitting admission to which is not allowed to representaties of the press and other members of the public.

Insofar as the paragraph refers to various meetings to which the press and public must have been admitted before the report can be protected, it is repetitious of Paragraph 2 above. The present list of occasions is much the same as the original list which made up the entire category of reportable topics in the 1888 Act. The specific reference to the press alone at the end of the paragraph is somewhat out of place in a privilege that protects both press and broadcasting, though no legal consequence would come from this as reports from broadcasting stations would be included within the reference to other members of the public.[22]

Paragraph 4 refers to

> A fair and accurate report of the proceedings at a general meeting, whether in the State or in Northern Ireland, of any company or association constituted, registered or certified by or under statutory authority or incorporated by charter, not being in the case of a company in the State, a private company within the meaning of the Companies Acts 1908 to 1959 or in the case of a company in Northern Ireland, a private company within the meaning of the statute relating to companies for the time being in force therein.

This paragraph seems wide enough to cover the proceedings of any body constituted under, or registered by, statute, and so could include building societies, credit unions and co-operatives. The exclusion of certain companies by reference to the nature of their legal constitution may be undesirable, since the private or public aspect of that nature can only be a crude and inaccurate test of public interest or concern in their affairs. Private companies can be of great economic importance. In whatever way it is defined, it might be that the impact of a business on the economy of an area would be the surest test of public concern in its affairs.[23] The term 'proceedings' could, on

21 *Heffernan v Regina Daily Star* (1930) 3 WWR 656.

22 Faulks recommended, nonetheless, that a specific reference to broadcasting be included here — Appendix XI.

23 Neither Faulks nor the New Zealand Committee considered this question.

analogy to proceedings in courts and bodies under Article 37 of the Constitution, be interpreted to include pre-meeting documents necessary to give notice of meetings, the agenda and other documents of information concerning matters to be discussed or decided at the meetings, such as auditor's reports and documents concerning the election of directors.[24] Insofar as any of these are not issued with a view to a meeting, then reports concerning them would not be protected. The meting need not, of course, be open to the public.

Paragraph 5 refers to 'A copy or fair and accurate report or summary of any notice or other matter issued for the information of the public by and on behalf of any Government department, local authority or the Commissioner of the Garda Síochána or by or on behalf of a corresponding department, authority or officer in Northern Ireland'. Excluded then from this paragraph are copies or notices issued by other statutory authorities, such as health boards. Where the local authority acts in another capacity, say as fire authority, it is unclear whether a copy or report of its notice is included within the protection. There seems to be little, if any, reason for these exclusions,[25] but this might not be so significant if, as was held in a Ugandan case,[26] there exists a general common law qualified privilege which protects reports carried by newspapers of statements issued to them by the government for circulation.

The paragraph applies to written notices that are issued, and to face to face or telephone statements made by departmental press officers to journalists.[27] The protection also covers statements issued in the discharge of specific duties for the guidance of the public, and it may also be wide enough to include announcements at press conferences

24 Faulks recommended that reports of any document circulated with the Board's authority, any document circulated by the auditors and any document concerning the office of director circulated apparently by any member of the company, regardless of the board's authorisation, should also be included in the Schedule para 231 (c). The New Zealand Committee's recommendations — para 229 (g) — broadly follow these, except that for reasons of balance — para 219 — the Committee did not approve of giving protection to reports of documents about directors which did not have the board's authorisation.

25 Faulks recommended the inclusion also of public authorities, nationalised industries and military and some police officers — Appendix XI.

26 *Shah v Uganda Argus* [1972] EA 86.

27 Fleming 552, doubts that 'mere political propaganda supplied to journalists by the publicity officer of a Minister' would be within the paragraph's 'intendment'.

by the political heads of departments of state about policies that are to be pursued in the future.[28] There seems to be a desire to construe rather narrowly the type of statement the report of which is protected. In a recent English case *Blackshaw v Lord*,[29] it was held that information extracted 'like a tooth' from a department public relations officer, or gossip, or statements that were neither official or authorised, or inferences drawn by journalists from the information given would not protect reports thereof. On the other hand, the range of persons protected seems quite wide, for it includes not only the reporter and the supplier of the information, but the person giving the information to the suppplier.[30]

Inconsistencies in the Schedule

The difficulty in justifying the inclusion of some reports in the list and the exclusion of others has already been noted and need not be repeated. There remain, however, other types of inconsistent treatment which are also difficult to justify.

Firstly, there is some inconsistency in the selection of the places wherein the subject matter of the reports occur. Paragraph 5 of Part I refers to matter in this state only, but both Paragraph 6 of Part I and all of Part II refer to the state and Northern Ireland. Again, the various reports in Part II of the Schedule, and also in Paragraph 6 of Part I, apply only to the state and Northern Ireland, but not to the rest of the world. Yet, certain reports from many other states, listed in Paragraphs 1 to 4 of Part I are included. The singling apart of Northern Ireland seems to have been done for political reasons, but if that is so, that could be reason to include other places as well.[31]

Secondly, the Schedule treats differently notices, or copies of notices published under judicial authority and under executive authority. In the case of the latter, the protection is subject to the condition of explanation, whereas with the former it is not. Notices by the legislature are not included in the Schedule, although these may well be official publications, and so under the Constitution enjoy absolute privilege.[32] Notices issued by parliamentary committees would also

28 *Blackshaw v Lord* [1983] 2 AER 311, 325.
29 See also *Campbell v Associated Newspapers* (1948) SR (NSW) 301.
30 *Boston v Bagshaw* [1966] 1 WLR 1126, where an auctioneer who convinced a police officer to make a television appeal for information concerning a theft of his property was held protected.
31 The New Zealand Report also referred to an inconsistency in the selection of the places whose subject matter is protected when reported.
32 Article 15.12.

be absolutely privileged, but by special statute.[33] It seems hardly satisfactory that the notices of the various powers of the state should be treated so differently.

Finally, it is not clear why Paragraphs 5 and 6 of Part I were placed there instead of in Part II. The Porter Committeee only gave reasons for including reports of certain foreign affairs in Part I. Paragraphs 5 and 6 do not concern foreign affairs. One could surmise that Paragraph 5 was included because the common law already conferred the ordinary form of qualified privilege on it,[34] though that might have been a reason for not mentioning the matter in the Schedule at all.

The statement of explanation or contradiction

Where a report is published which concerns any of the topics listed in Part II of the Second Schedule, then in order to be protected, the newspaper or broadcasting station must publish, on the request of the person conceiving himself defamed, a statement of explanation or contradiction, in a manner that is reasonable in the circumstances. The statement may be formally titled as an explanation or contradiction, but it need not be. In *Nevin v Roddy and Carty*,[35] the statement was contained in a letter written to the editor of a newspaper and published under the heading 'Sligo Town Clerkship. Recent Corporation Debate. Replied to by Mr Carty TD... We have received the following letter for publication from...'.

The statement is essentially that of the aggrieved person and not that of the newspaper or broadcasting station, although the paper or station may bear the expense of publication. This follows from the fact that the statement need not contain an apology, or even expression of regret, and that it need only be published if requested. The aggrieved person cannot insist on a correction. There is therefore no right of reply. The Australian Law Reform Commission has recommended, however, that there should be one.[36] That the

33 Committees of the Houses of the Oireachtas (Privilege and Procedure) Act 1976, s 2(2)(g).

34 See p. 183 supra.

35 [1935] IR 397. The requirement might even be satisfied where a journalist seeks out a person's response to a charge.

36 Para 178. The reply would have to be pubished at the earliest reasonable opportunity after the request is made — para 130. Although it might be thought that the media would be opposed to such a right, it is interesting to note that the Sunday Tribune, on its Editorial page, offers a general right of reply facility to its readers, subject to certain conditions. It may be that such conceded rights are enforceable entitlements under the contract of sale of the paper. See also p. 234 post.

statement of explanation is different from an apology was illustrated in an English case,[37] where a plaintiff was unable to show a refusal to publish an explanation because his letter had requested an apology. From this, the extraordinary result could follow that a newspaper which goes further than it needs to and publishes an apology — something of greater value than an explanation — would not be able to rely on the defence.

The statement of explanation or contradiction may itself amount to a libel on someone, and while there is nothing explicit in the section, or the Act, which would protect its publication, yet the Supreme Court held in *Nevin's* case where the statement was sued upon, that it was privileged.[38] The basis of this privilege would seem to be that where a person has previously endangered the reputation of another, an act by him — such as publishing the statement and intending to redress the wrong — ought to be protected.

Where a newspaper or broadcasting station refuses to publish an explanation or contradiction, or does so unreasonably, then the statutory defence is not available. No legal wrong is committed, however, and reliance may still be made on other defences, and an aggrieved person will still have to risk the uncertainties of an action.[39]

Prohibited matter, public concern and public benefit

Although a report may satisfy all of the requirements of the defence so far, subs 3 of s 24 contains some further conditions that must be met before the report is protected. One of these conditions requires that the publication of the report is not prohibited by law. The Offences against the State Acts and the Official Secrets Act contain examples of such prohibitions. The other conditions are that the report contain matter of public concern and that its publication is for the public benefit. The public concern test — essentially a privacy protection of a non specific type — may be anomalous as regards some categories of reports, such as meetings where the attendence will hear the statement but the media might not be able to report

37 *Khan v Ahmed* [1957] 2 QB 149.

38 Faulks recommended, in Appendix XI, that the statement be specifically included in the Schedule.

39 Whether the refusal may be evidence of malice seens an open question. It might be evidence, but on its own not sufficient evidence. According to Fleming 549, fn 6, such a failure is deemed by statute in the Australian code states to be merely evidence of malice.

it. Since meetings such as those of local authorities can go into private session, the requirement involves moving the task of applying the public concern test from the meeting to the reporter.[40] The double reference to public concern and benefit appears somewhat superfluous as the latter requirement is clearly the more stringent of the two. The 1881 Act referred only to public benefit, and the public concern requirement was introduced in the 1888 Act. The usage of both terms might, however, mean that public concern should be interpreted in an objective fashion, and not, as may have been done, in a subjective way. For instance, in *McInerney's* case [41] where the letting of land to an individual had caused uproar in a rural area, involving meetings and disturbances, the court held that this was a private matter. Fitzgibbon LJ remarked that 'this letting to the plaintiff, and his possession of this farm, must be regarded in a Court of Justice as matters of private concern affecting no one but the parties to a lawful transaction'.[42]

There have been few cases in this area in which the meanings of public concern and benefit have been discussed. Strangely, most of the cases have concerned the former. In addition to McInerney's case, it has been held in a number of English cases[43] that personal attacks made at meetings that are unrelated to the purpose of the meeting are not of public concern. The agenda of a local authority meeting is of public concern, and where the agenda recommended the dismissal of an employee, it was held, with some hesitation, that the publication of a report of this was for the public benefit.[44] Other instances where reports were published for the public benefit concerned the activities of a TD,[45] of political refugees,[46] and the embezzlement of property from an auctioneer.[47]

The statutory privilege and the common law

Section 24(4) of the 1961 Act provides that the statutory privilege is not to be construed as denying any other privilege that existed before the 1961 Act. This substantially repeated s 4(4) of the 1888 Act. Before the 1888, or for that matter, the 1881 Acts the common law had not

40 See ALRC Report para 160.
41 [1903] 2 IR 347.
42 At 390.
43 *Pankhurst v Sowler* (1887) 3 TLR 193; *Kelly v O'Malley* (1889) 6 TLR 62; *Ponsford v Financial Times* (1900) 16 TLR 248.
44 *Sharman v Merrit* (1916) 32 TLR 360.
45 Nevin's case.
46 Khan's case.
47 Boston's case.

recognised any qualified privilege for fair and accurate reports of meetings open to the public. There were, of course, various statements of the general policy underlying the law on qualified privilege. But these had not by then been applied to reports of public meetings.[48] The intention in the 1888 Act of not affecting any existing privilege appears to have been superfluous, as no such privilege was thought to exist at that time. The same might also be said about the present subs 4 because, since the 1888 Act had created privileges in this area, it might no longer have been open for the courts to create identical common law ones. However, because of an alteration in the definition of a newspaper — from something published at least once every twenty-six days in the 1888 Act to at least every thirty-six days in s 2 of the 1961 Act — subs 4 does have the effect of continuing any privilege developed by the common law between 1888 and 1961 for newspapers published less often than every twenty-six days but at least every thirty-six days.

It is important, then for that reason, and also to see if reports of any kind that are outside of s 24 are protected, to consider whether any common law privilege has been developed. There are divided opinions about this. Fleming considers that reports of public meetings enjoy no common law protection[49]. Gatley however, after citing a number of post-1888 cases, concludes that there may be such a privilege, and that it would apply to all types of reports. It would therefore overlap with the statutory protection.[50] It must be doubtful, however, that judges could develop a common law privilege that would overlap with a statutory one in a jurisdiction where the statutory one had been created because no common law one existed. It is nonetheless clearly correct to state that the common law has developed a privilege for reports since 1888 but that, as described by Clerk and Lindsell, it 'can give protection to reports outside the categories laid down in the Defamation Act ....'.[51]

Section 24 and the Constitution

If it were held that the Constitution recognises a general or news media qualified privilege for statements, and also reports, which are made on matters of political or official concern, as the Supreme Court

48 See p. 179 supra.
49 *The Law of Torts*, 6th ed, 552.
50 Paras 646 et seq. In Canada, according to Williams 92-3 it seems that some jurisdictions can be taken to have codified their law on this matter, whereas others, like here, have expressly preserved the common law.
51 Clerk & Lindsell *On Torts* 14th ed, para 1802.

of the USA has, in part, done,[52] a great deal of s 24 would be merely declaratory of a wider constitutional privilege protecting all kinds of reports, and no particular importance would attach to the various limitations and inequalities in the section. Reports not included in the section would still be protected. But because it is not certain that the Constitution contains such a privilege, it is necessary to consider the constitutionality of these limitations. In any event, the constitutionality of two particular features of s 24 — its extra-territorial effect and the division of the Schedule into two parts of different legal effect — would still remain to be considered.

On the question of the extra-territorial effects of s 24, which privileges here reports published inside Northern Ireland, whatever doubts there may be about the correctness of such an interpretation, it is now established,[53] that legislation possessing extra-territorial effect may be passed, although no equivalent to it existed before 1937. Thus, at least some reports published in Northern Ireland would, if sued upon here, enjoy the statutory protection. However, s 24 does not distinguish, as it should do,[54] between those relying on the privilege who are citizens of this state and those who are citizens of Northern Ireland. Since extra-territorial legislation can only affect the citizens of a state while outside that state, then insofar as the section purports to privilege here citizens of Northern Ireland for defamatory publications there, it might be unconstitutional.

There is also a second ground for querying the application of the privilege solely to the publication of reports in Northern Ireland. Where the publication in Northern Ireland deals with local matters, there may be some basis for the distinction made, and the constitutional imperative for equal treatment of plaintiffs defamed in reports from different countries might not be infringed. But, where the publication there deals with foreign matters that are of no greater concern here than if published in England or France, then unless reliance can be placed on some constitutional provision, such as Article 2 of the Constitution, there seems to be no basis for the special treatment of reports from Northern Ireland, and the Constitution might be infringed. The further issue of the validity of protecting reports published here concerning Northern Ireland might also turn on Article 2. If this is the case, the failure of s 24 to treat the EC states in the same way could be contrary to Article 29.4 of the Constitution which deals with the EC.

The failure to treat Part I and Part II type reports similarly might

52 See p. 163 supra.
53 *State (Devine) v Larkin* [1977] IR 24; *In re Article 26 of the Constitution and the Criminal Law (Jurisdiction) Bill* [1977] IR 129.
54 *State (Devine) v Larkin* at 28.

be open to constitutional attack by both individuals and the media on grounds of unequal treatment and undue restriction of the media's liberty of expression. But if the Constitution supports obliging the media to publish explanations or contradictions or retractions, as seems most likely, the serious constitutional issue will then concern the failure of the Schedule to attach the condition of explanation to Part I type reports, and that failure might not rest on sustainable grounds.

Finally, there are the various inconsistencies in the Second Schedule. Many topics are not included in the Schedule, and it is not clear why. Without repeating them all, one may note that reports concerning the institutions of the EC,[55] non-inter state disputes before international courts, foreign courts exercising constitutional jurisdictions, and the findings or decisions of bodies active in social, charitable and environmental matters are all excluded from the section. These exclusions may well be unconstitutional since they are based only on the failure of the Oireachtas to update the legislation.

ACTING UNDER A LEGAL DUTY

Where a person makes a defamatory statement while acting under a legal duty, then he will be acting on a privileged occasion, and if he also acts bona fide and without malice he will be privileged from liability. The duty to make the statement may be statutory in origin, as where an employer is obliged under the Unfair Dismissals Act 1977 to disclose the reasons for dismissal of an employee, if requested to do so.[56] In many instances the duty will be of a contractual nature, and may result from a contract of employment or from a contract for services. However, an employer or principal cannot by contract oblige another to make any statement he wishes, and thereby privilege the other. The law will only recognise the employee's legal duty and his privilege, where the employee can show that the employer had a legitimate interest in the employee making the statement. The recognition of an employee's privilege presupposes that had the employer made the statement, he would have acted on a privileged occasion. That occasion can be any of the other occasions of qualified privilege recognised by law.

Another type of legal duty which gives rise to a privileged occasion results from the possession of an office the holder of which is obliged

55 It is possible that Article 29.4 (3) dealing with the EC contains an implied privilege to report EC proceedings or that community law itself contains appropriate protestions. See also p 175 supra.

56 See *Lacarte v Board of Education of Toronto* (1959) 17 DLR (2d) 609.

or authorised by law to do certain acts and make certain statements. Thus, in the last century, the clerk of the markets of Dublin,[57] and a member of a grand jury[58] acted on privileged occasions while making defamatory statements. More recently, in *Corliss and Diggin v Ireland,*[59] the Garda Commissioner was held privileged when, acting in the performance of his office, he transferred two officers out of a section.

A number of instances of the contractual privilege have been found in the cases. The medical officer of a workhouse was protected when he commented adversely to a board of guardians about a tender to supply wine to the workhouse.[60] The supervisory engineer of a local authority was also protected when reporting to the council about an employee who had not maintained some machinery in a proper state.[61] The most common defamatory statement, however, which is made by an employee is an accusation of theft. So, a guard in a factory,[62] the secretary of a charitable institution,[63] and the manager of a shop[64] were all protected when accusing employees of theft. The managing director of a company was protected when accusing an employee who had just been dismissed of theft,[65] and the president of a university was protected when accusing a student of obtaining a cheque by false pretences.[66] Also probably protected are post office oficials when enquiring about forged postal orders,[67] and police inspectors when claiming that witnesses in hearings have perjured themselves,[68] although in particular cases statements of this type were not protected because they were made to the wrong people.

Similarly, statements made by independent contractors who are retained to provide a service are made on privileged occasions if made while performing their contractual obligations. A number of cases have concerned statements made by solicitors. A solicitor who writes a letter on behalf of a client in which he fairly rebuts the charges made against the client will be protected, but when, as happened

57 *Murray v McSwiney* (1876) IR 9 CL 545. See also *Keaveney v Geraghty* [1965] IR 551, *Little v Clements* (1851) 1 ICLR 194, and *Bennett v Barry* (1863) 8 IJ NS 167.
58 *Little v Pomeroy* (1873) IR 7 CL 50.
59 The Irish Times, 30 November 1984.
60 *Murphy v Kellot* (1862) 13 ICLR 488.
61 *Denvir v Taylor* (1936) IJR 4.
62 *Corcoran v W & R Jacob* [1945] IR 446.
63 *Wallace v Carroll* (1860) 11 ICLR 485.
64 *Hyland v Clery & Co* SCt, unreported, 9 April 1964.
65 *Dempsey v Wall & Co and Ryan* (1943) 78 ILTR 73.
66 *Kirkwood-Hackett v Tierney* [1952] IR 185.
67 *Sevenoaks v Latimer* (1919) 54 ILTR 11.
68 *Keenan v Wallace* (1916) 51 ILTR 19.

in one case,[69] he adds more and goes beyond the range of the privilege then he is not protected. A statement by a solicitor to his opposite number in a case concerning an affidavit sworn by the latter's apprentice in the course of litigation was held to be privileged,[70] and a statement by a solicitor to a client that his debtor was about to abscond was also privileged.[71]

There is some uncertainty about the extent of the privilege which is enjoyed by credit assessment agencies when providing credit assessments for clients. At first the position was quite clear. In *Fitzsimmon v Duncan, Kemp & Co.* (1908),[72] both the trial judge and the Court of King's Bench held that a statement by a credit assessment agency was privileged. No distinction was made between profit making and non-profit making bodies. In this case the defendant agency was a profit making one. When explaining the reason why such statements should, in general, be privileged, Palles CB stated, in the context of wholesalers and retailers.

> It is essential to the due carrying on of mercantile business that a wholesale trader, who contemplates selling on credit to a retail trader, should be entitled to make fair and reasonable inquiries as to the solvency of the latter; and if he has that right, so also must he be entitled to depute to another the duty of making those enquiries.[73]

Fitzsimmon's case was, however, appealed to the Court of Appeal, and just a few days before the court announced its judgement — it was apparently already written — the Privy Council in England held, in an Australian case,[74] that statements by credit assessment agencies were not privileged at all. When announcing the judgement of the Court of Appeal in Fitzsimmon's case, Fitzgibbon LJ referred, firstly, to the fact that the courts below had assumed that the occasion was privileged, and he than referred very shortly to the 'negation of privilege by the Privy Council' in the other case.[75] However, this remark belied the rest of Fitzgibbon LJ's judgement, because he then went on to consider the grounds of the appeal — which concerned proof of malice and whether it affected the agency's privilege — and he found that the agency was liable and that its protection was affected

69 *McKeogh v O'Brien-Moran* [1927] IR 348.
70 *Buckley v Kiernan* (1857) 7 ICLR 75.
71 *Davis v Reeves* (1855) 5 ICLR 79.
72 [1908] 2 IR 483.
73 At 494.
74 *MacIntosh v Dun* [1908] AC 390.
75 At 508.

by the malice of its employee. There would have been no need for such a finding and the issue of malice in fact would have been quite irrelevant, if no privilege had existed in the first place. Despite then his earlier remark, it seems that the court did consider the occasion privileged. It is interesting to note that in 1916 the House of Lords retreated somewhat from the decision by the Privy Council in McIntosh's case. It distinguished between profit orientated and non-profit orientated agencies and held that credit ratings by non profit orientated trade protection asssociations were privileged.[76] This is a particularly difficult distinction to maintain in logic, because it is hard to see how what is done by an agency — be it of either type — with any profits it earns, at the end of a year, can be of relevance to the question of balancing the interests involved. In the USA, although a few courts have applied this distinction, the majority have not and, instead, have recognised an equal privilege as protecting all credit assessment agencies.[77] In Australia, some state law ignores the distinction and protects profit orientated agencies, while some support it.[78] Two of the reform bodies[79] have criticised the distinction and have recommended its abolition. In the light of this, it may be that an Irish court would now interpret Fitzsimmon's case as conferring a privilege on all credit assessment agencies, regardless of their type.

EXCESS OF COMMUNICATION

When a person has a valid reason for making a statement, then in order for the occasion to be a privileged one, the statement must not be given a greater circulation than is reasonably necesssary, nor must there be any grossly irrelevant statements made, in addition to the relevant one. If either of these possibilities occur, the statement will not be regarded as being made on a privileged occasion, and its maker will not be protected from liability in defamation.[80]

76 *London Association for Protection of Trade v Greenlands* [1916] 2 AC 15.

77 Eldredge 467-71, Prosser 829. Eldredge considers that dicta of the US Supreme Court in *Virginia State Bd of Pharmacy v Virginia Citizens Consumer Council* (1976) 425 US 748 henceforth bases an agency's privilege on constitutional protection of free speech including economic speech; similar conclusions based additionally on private property could be reached here.

78 Fleming 536. The distinction is apparently followed in Canada, Linden 707-8. For whether communications to traders not contemplating any dealings with the person defamed are protected see p. 154.

79 Faulks Committee Report para 237; ALRC Report, para 142.

80 As happened in *Currigan v Ryan* (1866) 11 IJ NS 406; *Gillis v McDonnell* (1860) IR 4 CL 342; *Bell v Parke* (1859) 10 ICLR 279; *Keenan v Wallace* (1916) 51 ILTR 11; and *Sevenoaks v Latimer* (1919) 54 ILTR 11.

A denial of a privileged occasion on account of excess in the communication made is a quite distinct matter from denying protection to a statement made on a privileged occasion because it was made with malice. In the first situation, there is no privileged occasion at all, and, in the second there is, but the statement is made with the wrong motive. The separate findings, in a jury trial, of 'privileged occasion' and 'privileged communication' emphasise this. The issue of privileged occasion, and thus of excess, is a matter of law to be decided by the judge alone whereas the jury,[81] decides on privileged communcation. The two terms, then, are not interchangeable,[82] although the immediate consequence of a finding against a defendant on either point is the same the statement is not protected. As well, since many defamation actions should now be heard in the Circuit Court before a judge sitting alone, who will decide both questions, there will not be the same need to maintain the distinction, and it may well become blurred.

Irrelevant persons

It is only in some instances that an occasion might not be privileged because there was an excess of communication to uninterested persons. In the case of the statutory media privileges and the common law privileges which permit a statement to be made to the public, there is no question of this happening since the statement may legitimately be made to the public.

Whether the incidental presence of one or more persons who have no interest in receiving a statement, otherwise made for a good reason will operate to prevent the occasion from being privileged depends on the circumstances in which the statement is made. In general, if a statement is made to a number of persons, some of whom are interested in receiving it and some of whom are not, the receipt by those interested will complete the occasion of the privilege, but the presence of the disinterested may go to questioning the motives of the maker of the statement, and, thus, whether he acted maliciously.[83] It is thus possible for a disinterested person to receive a statement without destroying the occasion of privilege. 'The presence of strangers does not necessarily take away privilege...'.[84]

81 *Jacob v Lawrence* (1879) 4 LR Ir 579, 582 per May CJ.
82 See note on *Redmond v Kelly* (1894) 28 ILT & SJ 555.
83 *Keenan v Wallace* at 20 per Gibson J.
84 *Bell v Parke* (1860) 11 ICLR 413, 422 per Fitzgerald B.

On the other hand, there are some circumstances where the method of communication adopted is so 'intrinsically public'[85] that no privileged occasion will arise at all, even though there is a valid reason for the statement and some of the recipients are interested in receiving it. As Pigot CB stated in one case 'Suppose the words here charged had been uttered at a crowded mess, the defendant being at one of the table, and the plaintiff at the other, I would hold that, quite irrespective of any express malice, the selection of such a place and such an occasion, would, as a matter of law, take away the privilege'.[86] Thus in *Robinson v Jones* (1879),[87] the dispatch of a demand for payment of a debt through the post by open postcard 'visible to every person through whose hands it passes' was held not to be privileged; and in *Keenan v Wallace* (1916), an accusation of perjury by a police officer in open court after proceedings had ended and in the presence of public and reporters was also held not privileged.

A privileged occasion may also fail to be completed because although the defendant may have been interested in making the statement yet he made it too late after the reason for making it arose.[88]

Irrelevant statements

Where a number of statements are made on an occasion and only some of these are relevant to the reason why the occasion might be privileged, then whether the making of the irrelevant statements will prevent the occasion from being privileged at all depends on the degree of irrelevancy of the statements in question. If there is any doubt whether the statements are irrelevant, or at least if they are not overwhelmingly irrelevant, then the occasion will be held to be privileged, and such irrelevancy as there is may go to the jury as evidence of malice, if that issue is raised.

On the other hand, where a person, on an occasion that might be privileged, makes statements which are in the nature of affirmative and independent charges of misconduct, unconnected with, and having no reasonable or natural bearing on the conduct of the defamed person, then there is no privilege for such statements and the judge may proceed himself or direct the jury to so find. As Fitzgibbon J stated in Nevin's case in 1934 'So where the libelled defendant has replied with a torrent of manifestly outrageous or irrelevant charges,

85 *Keenan v Wallace* at 20 per Gibson J.
86 *Bell v Parke* at 429.
87 (1879) 4 LR Ir 391.
88 This would seem to be the ratio in *Echlin v Singleton* (1862) 7 IJ NS 225.

the Judge ought to advise the jury that they should find express malice, or ought himself to rule that such charges are not covered by the privilege...'.[89] Thus, in *McKeogh v O'Brien-Moran* (1927),[90] a solicitor was instructed by a midwife to rebut accusations made by a doctor of a lack of hygiene in her work. After doing this, the solicitor added in the letter that 'she will be able to prove when the time comes that there was greater reason for complaint against Dr McKeogh in his treatment of his patients than there was against her'. The court held that, while a solicitor acts on a privileged occasion when rebutting charges made against his clients, this unnecessary and irrelevant charge was not protected.

A court should not be very strict in determining that there is no reasonable connection between the statements in the defendant's response and the charges made against him.[91] May CJ stated in *Dwyer v Esmonde* (1878), '... I think a Court of Law should not overrule a plea of privilege on [a ground of irrelevancy] unless it found itself in a position to decide, without any doubt, that the statements ... had no reasonable connection with the charges brought against him'.[92] The reason for this latitude in construing irrelevant statements made on privileged occasions is twofold. Firstly, it is the acknowledged function of the jury to determine whether there is any evidence of impropriety that would defeat the defence. To quote May CJ again 'The question of libel or no libel is one for the jury, not for the Judge; and so I think the question of relevancy or irrelevancy ... will be much more satisfactorily decided by a jury under the guidance of a Judge, then by a Judge without the assistance of a jury'. The only occasion when a judge should decide himself that the irrelevancy is of such an order as to dispel the privilege would be where he would do so only to save time at the hearing, and with the certain knowledge that the jury could not have taken a different view. If he acts otherwise, he usurps the jury's function. The second reason why a judge should act slowly in deciding the matter is that if he is too easily encouraged to adjudicate upon an irrelevancy, and trained as he is in logical reasoning, he might bring unrealistically fine reasoning to bear on the question. Lord Diplock, in an English case, remarked on how persons may respond when attacked: 'as everyone knows, ordinary human beings vary in their ability to distinguish that which is logically relevant from that which is not and few, apart from lawyers have had any training which qualifies

89 [1935] IR 397, 421; see also *Dwyer v Esmonde* (1877) IR 11 CL 542 and (1878) 2 LR Ir 243; *Jacob v Lawrence*.

90 [1927] IR 348; see also *Fishburne v Lord Lucan* (1865) 10 IJ NS 209.

91 *Dwyer v Esmonde* at 285 per Deasy LJ; also Christian LJ at 259.

92 At 254.

them to do so. So the protection afforded by the privilege would be illusory if it were lost [upon objective logical analysis]'.[93] The judge, then, must strike his balance between too severe a test of relevancy, thus denying all hope of protection, and refusing to let logic and reason be altogether set aside.

The cases provide various examples of statements that have been held not to be completely irrelevant to a privileged occasion, and have therefore been left to juries to decide as to their effect on the defence. In Dwyer's case, a landlord's reply to an ex-tenant's accusation of oppressive conduct, in which the landlord accused the latter, of inter alia, fraudulently keeping from his sisters monies charged on the land to which they were entitled, was held not entirely irrelevant. In another case,[94] a reply to a letter from a solicitor threatening legal action advised the solicitor to look to his own costs because his client could probably not be trusted to pay them, was also held not entirely irrelevant. Other cases where the reply was similarly held not entirely irrelevant were where a letter to an employer pointing out a mistake made by his employee alleged that it had been made fraudulently rather than innocently,[95] and where a reply to a demand for a wider circulation of an apology assserted that the other's behaviour resembled more 'that of a freebooter than ... an honourable British merchant'.[96]

MALICE

A statement made on a privileged occasion will fail to become a privileged statement if the primary motive with which it was made was malice. Malice, in this context, means malice in fact, as opposed to malice in law which is merely a presumption from the defamatory nature of a statement. Malice in fact refers to any difference between the reason why the occasion is privileged and the reason why the statement is made. It has been variously described as a 'wrong or improper motive or feeling existing in the mind of the defendant at the time of the publishing and actuating that publication',[97] and as the actuation of 'feelings not accounted for by the exigencies of

93 *Horrocks v Lowe* [1975] AC 135, 151; Lord Diplock also seems to have implied that all relevant statements made on privileged occasions must be left to the jury to see if they are privileged, but this might not be correct. See also Gatley, para 582 fn 37.
94 *Jacob v Lawrence* (1879) 4 LRIr 579.
95 *Buckley v Kirenan* (1857) 7 ICLR 75.
96 *Sayer v Begg* (1864) 15 ICLR 458. Other examples are *O'Donoghue v Hussey* (1871) IR 5 CL 124 and *Hobbs v Bryers* (1878) 2 LR Ir 496.
97 *Kirkwood-Hackett v Tierney* [1952] IR 185, 203 per O'Byrne J.

the occasion — and ... not bona fide to serve the purposes of such occasions, but male fide, and in order to injure the complainant',[98] or quite simply as a 'want of good faith'[99] by the maker of the statement. Malice most often is spite or ill-will, but it is wider than this. The burden of proof in establishing malice rests on the plaintiff. This follows from the fact that when proof by the defendant of a privileged occăsion rebuts the inference of malice in law, it is then up to the plaintiff to establish malice in fact, in order to defeat the defence of privilege.[1] It is the function of the judge to decide whether there is sufficient evidence on which a jury could reasonably find malice. If there is, he leaves the matter to the jury to decide in fact whether or not malice actually motivated the statement.[2] 'Motive is, of course, a question for the jury but there must be some facts in evidence from which a jury is entitled to draw an inference of actual malice...'.[3]

The question of the sufficiency of the evidence by which the jury can be invited to find malice is of some importance. Clearly where there is no evidence of malice, then the judge ought not to leave the issue to the jury, and if he does he may be reversed on appeal.[4] It is also clear, according to O'Byrne J 'that you cannot get evidence of malice from a number of items of evidence, no one of which is, in itself, evidence of malice'.[5] It is not just any evidence of malice which will justify a trial judge in leaving the issue to the jury. To quote again from O'Byrne J 'It is not sufficient that the letter should be consistent with the existence of [an improper] motive. To enable the plaintiff to succeed, the letter must be more consistent with the existence of such a motive than with its absence',[6] and Haugh J stated to the same effect in another case 'In my view the burden of proving malice being on the plaintiff, it is not sufficient for him in the circumstances to leave the scales so finely balanced. At most the jury could only speculate as to malice being an actuating cause of the utterance of the words'.[7] Whether an irrelevant statement, which is held to be evidence of malice, can also be sufficient evidence of malice, depends it seems on the nature of the irrelevancy. Where

98 *Jacob v Lawrence* (1879) 4 LR Ir 579, 582 per May CJ.

99 *Kirkwood-Hackett v Tierney* at 199 per O'Byrne J.

1 *McMullan v Mulhall* [1929] IR 470, 485 per Fitzgibbon J.

2 The earliest reported Irish case in which this division of the function if apparent is *Mitchell v Kerr* (1801) reported (1824) Rowe Rep 537; see also *Black v Holmes* (1822) 1 Fox & Sm 28, 36 and *Clanchy v Cahill* (1825) Sm & Bat 232.

3 *McMullan v Mulhall* supra.

4 As happened in *Corcoran v W & R Jacob* [1945] IR 446.

5 *Kirkwood-Hackett v Tierney* at 204; *Sun Life Assurance v Dalrymple* (1965) 50 DLR (2d) 217.

6 At 208.

7 *Hyland v Clery & Co* SCt, unreported, 9 April 1964. See also *Hynes-O'Sullivan v Driscoll*, The Irish Times, 26 February 1987.

it is completely irrelevant to the privileged occasion then it can certainly destroy the privilege. Where, however, it is only slightly irreleant to the occasion, then it seems doubtful, if, on its own, it can establish malice.

Although these rules on the sufficiency of evidence of malice indicate that a restrictive view is taken of when there can be sufficient evidence of malice to go the jury, it is no doubt intended to prevent too facile a finding of malice by the jury. For there is hardly a case in which the possibility of malice does not exist.[8]

Evidence of malice

Exceptionally, a defendant may actually admit that the reason why he made a statement was different from the reason that ought to have motivated him. In an English case,[9] a defendant, who had been a candidate in an election, admitted that he had attacked another candidate in a different constituency for the illegitimate reason of furthering his own chances of election, instead of wishing to inform the elctorate of the other candidate's character. It is possible that an admission that the reason for publishing a defamatory statement was to amuse, or cause sensation or increase a newspaper's circulation would be regarded as malice.[10] Admissions are unusual, however, and in most cases, any malice will have to be found, either intrinsically from the making of the statement, or extrinsically.

The circumstances in which a statement is made may be relevant as extrinsic evidence. For instance it is 'very material that there should be evidence that the defendant was in an angry state when he spoke the words, for to establish that he was in an angry state was to establish the presence of a possible motive, which if it was the motive, would show malice',[11] although proof of anger alone is neither proof of malice nor recklessness. In *Kirkwood-Hackett v Tierney* (1950), a display of aggressiveness and a constant pacing up and down a room during which a College President accused a student of criminal pretence in obtaining payment of a grant was held not to be evidence of malice.

Circumstances occuring before a statement is made can be most material on the question of malice. In some instances 'The condition of mind of the defendant ... can best be ascertained by finding out

8 See Gatley, para 794 quoting Scrutton LJ in *Barber v Deutsche Bank* (1918) HL Printed Cases at 317.

9 *Pankhurst v Hamilton* (1887) 3 TLR 500.

10 Eldredge 512-3 cites some pre-New York Times cases where media privilege's were lost for such reasons.

11 *Kirkwood-Hackett v Tierney* [1952] IR 185, 213 per Black J.

from whom and in what manner he made enquiries before he published the defamatory statements...'.[12] In others, 'a long practice of libelling the plaintiff may show in the most satisfactory manner, that the defendant was actuated by malice in the particular publication...'.[13] — the frequency and remoteness of those going only to the weight of the evidence. In one case,[14] where malice was found, the plaintiff had been described in an earlier statement as 'a most deceptive, sneaking fellow', and in another case the previous statements had been made nine months earlier.[15]

A history of confrontation or opposition between the parties can also help establish malice. In *McCarthy v Maguire* (1899),[16] where the solicitor for Sligo Corporation was falsely accused of, inter alia, forging a certificate of taxation, evidence of malice was found in the fact that on five or six previous occasions the plaintiff had, on behalf of the Corporation, successfully prosecuted the defendant for breaches of various laws.

Circumstances arising after the making of the defamatory statement can also be evidence of malice, although the interval of time between these and the occurence of other events, such as the institution of poceedings, can affect the weight of this evidence. Thus, although a majority in the Supreme Court in Kirkwood-Hackett's case, considered that a letter written by the defendant to the grant-paying authority, which contained omissions and unnecessary restatements of the facts four months after the defamatory statement was made, could be evidence of malice, yet it also held that this was of insufficient weight to have been left to the jury. The demeanuor of the maker of the statement in the witness box and accusations that the other side was lying when testifying on points which contradicted his own testimony can also constitute evidence of malice, although in *Corcoran v W & R Jacob*[17] a majority of the Supreme Court held that they did not do so in that case.

Honesty of belief in the truth of a statement will, in many cases, prevent a finding of malice, although it is still possible for an honest statement to have been made with an improper motive, such as a desire to injure, and so be malicious.[18] On the other hand, the absence of an honest belief in the truth of the statement when making it, and even a reckless indifference to the truth of the statement, is

12 *Fitzgerald v Watson* [1918] 2 IR 411, 429 per Molony LJ.
13 *Barrett v Long* (1851) 3 HLC 395, 414 per Parke B.
14 *Fitzsimmons v Duncan and Kemp & Co* [1908] 2 IR 483.
15 *Campion v Mooney* (1945) IJR 72.
16 [1899] 2 IR 802.
17 [1945] IR 446.
18 *Cruise v Burke* [1919] 2 IR 182 is an example of such a case, although it was a malicious prosecution action.

always evidence by which malice can be established. In *Clarke v Roe* (1854),[19] a receiver in Chancery published in a lawful notice a statement which he knew to be untrue at that time — that criminal proceedings were then pending against the plaintiff. Malice was found. And in *Sevenoaks v Latimer* (1919),[20] it was found that, given the plaintiff's remarkable physical appearance, a false accusation against him by a postmaster of having fraudulently cashed a cheque, was maliciously motivated. It is often difficult to establish that a person did not honestly believe the truth of what he stated, and certainly 'a cross-examination suggesting there was room for mistake or misunderstanding is not a challenge to the defendant's honesty'.[21] Nor could such evidence arise merely on a clash of evidence as to whether a defendant was in error or not.

It is sometimes stated that there is an exception to the rule that absence of honest belief is always evidence of malice.[22] A man 'may believe a statement to be untrue and yet may be perfectly justified in publishing it to the persons whom he is in communication and with whom it may be his duty to communicate freely on the subject of the information he has received'.[23] Exact authority in support of this view is scarce and what support there is mostly obiter and academic. The exception was, however, applied in a Australian case,[24] when a qualified privilege was upheld for the distribution of copies of a report of a conference of an institute by the secretary to the members, even though the secretary knew that it contained falsehoods.[25] This exception seems open to question for a number of reasons. On principle, it appears to be fundamentaly unsound, because, if it does not encouraage the telling of lies, it at least facilitates them, and, what is more, it allows a person to escape responsibility for telling a lie although he knew he was doing so. The exception may also be based on too narrow view of the interests to be considered when deciding whether to privilege the telling of lies. Not only are good name and social intercourse relevant, but the protection of truth must also be considered and should at least require that the informer also communicate his knowledge that the statement is untrue. That

19 (1854) 4 ICLR 1.
20 (1919) 54 ILTR 11.
21 *Maxwell v Gavin Low* SCt, unreported, 11 January 1967, per Ó Dálaigh CJ at p 10 of his judgement.
22 For example Clerk & Lindsell *On Torts* 15th ed, 20-154, Street *On The Law of Torts* 7th ed., 134, *Carter-Ruck on Libel and Slander* 153.
23 *Botterill v Whytehead* (1879) 41 LT 588, 590 per Kelly CB.
24 *Hay v Australasian Institute* (1906) 3 CLR 1002. See also *BR Traffic v CRC* [1922] 2 KB 260.
25 The Australian Court also held that the secretary's knowledge of the falsehoods could not be imputed to the Institute so as to destroy its privilege, although the opposite was held here in Fitzsimmon's case.

the general policy of Irish law seems set against a narrow view of the interests at stake when creating a privilege, is clear from the remarks of Holmes LJ in a deceit action in 1905, when he stated 'In matters of truth and falsehood, of honesty and dishonesty, our law requires a man to judge for himself, and will not allow him to escape responsibility by pleading that he was carrying out the directions of another'.[26] Where an employee complies with this, and refuses knowingly to communicate falsehoods, he will be protected by the law against any adverse conequences that he may suffer.[27]

Acting carelessly, or rashly, in making a defamatory statement is not evidence of malice or improper motive. Pigot CB stated in 1854 that the 'courts do not enquire very minutely into the degree of conviction. If the party acts honestly, that is sufficient',[28] and in 1950 O'Byrne J stated 'It is not sufficient to show that the defendant acted rashly, improvidently or stupidly so long as he acted in good faith'.[29] So, proof that a person did not use due caution and did not make any enquiry before making the statement, despite having ample time to do so, is not on its own evidence of malice.[30] In *Pyke v Hibernian Bank*[31] (1950), a negligent omission by a bank manager to make a record of an overdraft arrangement with a customer was also held not to be evidence of malice. But carelessnesss allied with other evidence can establish malice, and in McCarthy's case,[32] in addition to the history of litigation between the parties, there was the significant fact that, in the words of O'Brien LCJ, 'The defendant brought this charge forward recklessly, relying on a perfunctory rush through the [Taxing] office in Dublin, without taking the trouble to consult anyone, though he himself was without experience or knowledge of the ways of the law'.[33] The rejection of all

26 *Delaney v Keogh* [1905] 2 IR 267, 290; the ALRC Report, paras 142, 148 ,took the view that the exception should not be abolished, and indeed that the redefinition of malice should include reasonable conduct in the circumstances. According to the Commission this was necessary for these 'rare cases' when a defendant felt it his duty to pass the statement onto someone in authority. The Hayes type situation might not be so rare, however. Besides, it may not be desirable to assume the risk of such broad phrasing for a situation where the problem could be adequately meet by communicating the statement to the person defamed who could then decide his own course of action; or perhaps, if the statement is accompanied by an assertion that it is not true, and is only made under a binding duty.

27 See Hepple and O'Higgins *Employment Law* 4th ed, para 617.

28 *Clarke v Roe* (1854) 4 ICLR 1, 10.

29 *Kirkwood-Hackett v Tierney* [1952] IR 185, 203.

30 *Clarke v Roe.*

31 [1950] IR 195.

32 [1899] 2 IR 802.

33 At 806.

imperfections in the mental process — such as irrationality or prejudice or carelessness — by which belief is arrived at and the consideration only of the honesty of belief in the conclusions reached,[34] does accord a wide latitude to the facility with which a defamation may be uttered. The exclusion of prejudice as evidence of malice may not 'recognise the psychological reality that the prejudice which gives rise to a belief may itself be the product of an improper motive'.[35] These exclusions, however, at least enjoy the merit of consistency, for they seek to ensure against too easy a finding of malice and thus a denial of the defence.

Proof of malice in the making of a statement can also be established by intrinsic evidence, that is to say, the defamatory statement itself may be evidence by which malice may be established. Such evidence will consist of irrelevant statements or parts thereof, made on the privileged occasion, whether the irrelevancy was great or slight. The question of when either kind of evidence can, on its own, establish malice was considered earlier.

34 See generally Lord Diplock et 149 et seq *Horrocks v Lowe* [1975] AC 135.
35 Gatley, Preface vii, 7th ed.

9

The Defence of Fair Comment

The defence of fair comment confers protection against liability for those who make defamatory statements which contain fair comments on matters of public interest. The burden of raising this defence rests on the defendant. He must establish a number of proofs. He must show that the statement consisted of comment and of facts supporting the comment, and, if the facts are not included in the statement, they must at least be discernible from it. The supporting facts must be shown to be true, and the comment must be shown to have been fair in the sense that there is some logical connection between the facts and the comment. Fairness thus has a different connotation to its ordinary usage. The subject matter of the communication must be shown to have been a matter of public interest. The defence is, conditional on the absence of malice, and if a plaintiff can show its presence when the statement was made then the defence will be lost. To this extent, the defence is similar to the defence of qualified privilege. Indeed the question of the relationship between the two, and whether the former is merely a species of the latter, has provoked some controversy.

The defence is a peculiar one, and is unlike any other in its application to comments only, and not all comments at that. The law treats various comments differently, depending on their truth or when they are made. If a comment is true, (i.e. correct) then under the defence of justification, there will be no liability in respect of it. If a comment is untrue, but is made on a privileged occasion, then under the defence of privilege, there will also be no liability. Thus comments which are true, or correct, and comments which are untrue but privileged, can be protected. There remain other types of untrue comment. A comment can be malicious or dishonest or can be based on falsehoods. None of these are protected by the law. But between these and privileged or true comments, there rests a type of untrue comment which can be about public or private matters and can be based on either true or untrue facts. The courts have decided that the balance of social interest in these instances between the right to a good name and the liberty of expression requires that only untrue comments, based on true facts, about public matters should be protected.

The defence of fair comment is predicated on a balance of interest that was originally struck in the nineteenth century by common law judges who, while refusing to recognise a qualified privilege for public comment — and so make the truth of the supporting facts irrelevant except on the question of malice — offered public debate the lesser protection of this defence.[1] The defence stands only at a half way or lesser point between protecting public debate and not protecting it. It is clearly less advantageous than the defence of privilege and hardly merits being 'regarded as a bulwark of free speech'.[2] The refusal to allow comment any privilege required the law to embark on the perennially difficult task of distinguishing between fact and comment.It can be suggested that the real issue with a defamatory statement is whether it is likely to be believed or not. Whether a statement is a fact or a comment is just one of a number of circumstances which can influence this, and hardly merits having an important distinction based on it.

As the defence has grown it has become complex and technical, and has been much criticised.[3] It can still give rise to serious confusion,[4] and is restrictive in nature. It leaves unfair comment unprotected, as well as comment based on untrue facts, or no facts, comment on private matters, malicious comments and unreasonable imputations of base and dishonourable motives. Such a wide range of unprotected comment constitutes a significant impediment to free speech, and one which may require constitutional support in order to be valid.

Interestingly, the Constitution is explicit in protecting comment. Article 40.6 (1) recognises the entitlement of citizens to 'express freely their convictions and opinions' and goes on to recognise the media's 'rightful liberty of expression, including criticism of Government policy'. The use of terms like 'freely' expressed in Irish by the even more emphatic 'gan bac' and 'rightful' lend particular force to what, between the English and Irish versions must be treated as a powerful assertion of the ideal of free speech in relation to comment, more impressive indeed than 'Congress shall make no law ... abridging the freedom of speech or of the Press' contained in the First

1 See the judgements of Cockburn CJ at 777, Crompton J at 778, Blackburn J at 780, and Mellor J at 783 in *Campbell v Spottiswoode* (1863) 3 B & S 769.

2 Faulks Committee Report para 151.

3 See Weiler 'Defamation, Enterprise Liability and Freedom of Speech' (1967) 17 U of Toronto LJ 278, 319 et seq; Keeton, 'Defamation and Freedom of the Press' (1976) 54 Tex L Rev 1221, 1240 et seq.

4 See p. 217 post for the controversy surrounding the Canadian Supreme Court decision in Chernekey v Armadale Publishers (1978) 90 DLR (3d) 321.

Amendment to the US Constitution. Significantly, it was through reliance on this provision that the US Supreme Court has made largely redundant the common law defence of fair comment, and has substituted in its place a general immunity from liability for pure comment by the media, and possibly non media as well, but not for comment which is really fact.[5] Such a development could have an obvious parallel here. The reasoning relied on was that since opinions are neither true nor false, but only accepted or not, it is wrong to impose a liability based on an implicit trial assertion that an opinion can be right or wrong. 'Under the First Amendment there is no such thing as a false idea. However pernicious an opinion may seem, we depend for its correction not on the conscience of judges and juries, but on the competition of other ideas'.[6] The European Court of Human Rights has also expressed similar views about national libel laws that make unlawful value judgements made in politicial debate.[7] Using reasoning like this, there is certainly scope in our Constitution for suggesting a wider protection for defamatory comment than is contained in the common law defence. The difficult question concerns how far that extra protection might go, and whether for example, it would protect any comment however unfair or unreasonable, or would include private comment, or would require a more narrowly defined type of malice, consisting only of a deliberate falsehood.

FACT AND COMMENT

Before the defence of fair comment can be established, it is necessary to show that the statement consists of fact and comment. If it consists only of fact, then the defence is not applicable.[8] The distinction, however, between a fact and a comment can often be a matter of degree, so that the task of separating the two may be a matter of difficulty[9] over which views may vary.[10] This difficulty can be compounded because comment can sometimes be expressed in the guise of fact and vice versa;[11] and because sensationalist journalism

5 *Gertz v Welch* (1974) 418 US 323; see Prosser 813-815.
6 At 339 per Powell J.
7 Lingens case, 1986, Series A, No. 103.
8 As happened in *Eglantine Inn v Smith* [1948] NI 29,37.
9 *Black v Northern Whig* (1942) 77 ILTR 5, 8 per Brown J.
10 As happened in Black's case and in *Campbell v Irish Press* (1955) 90 ILTR 105.
11 Terms such as 'I think' 'in my view' etc will often suggest a comment, but not always. Professional people often use expressions as 'in my opinion' to elevate an expression of opinion into an assertion of fact. Newspaper editorials, on the other hand, which contain much comment, will avoid reducing the authoritiveness of the views expression by the use of similar terms.

sometimes precedes the fact by comment,[12] and, at other times, so intermingles fact with actual or possible expressions of opinion 'because of the impossibility of achieving sensations, and still effecting a clear separation of facts from the defamatory expressions of opinion'.[13] It is hardly surprising that paradoxical language such as 'a sentence which is in form a statement of fact may in reality be, or contain, a comment',[14] or 'a matter of fact (may) be excused as comment on another fact'[15] is common enough in the cases.

A useful example of the difficulty that can exist in distinguishing between fact and comment is provided by two statements in *Campbell v Irish Press* (1955),[16] which were contained in a newspaper article about an exhibition game of billiards. The first statement -'The only thing that was missing was no table' — was held by the trial judge as being capable only of being a fact, whereas in the Supreme Court, Kingsmill-Moore J held that while it could mean as a fact that all the necessary apparatus of an exhibition, except the table, were missing, it could also be a comment in an attempt to express in a would-be smart and epigrammatic fashion, the opinion that the exhibition was run in a slovenly way.[17] Similarly, with the second statement — 'He failed to make a century break because the table told lies' — he disagreed with the trial judge's ruling that this could only be fact. The first part of the statement could, he held, be a comment on the ability of an allegedly great player who had failed to make a century; and the second part of the statement could, he held, have been a comment consisting of an inference from the fact that the ball had deviated.

There are no fixed rules in distinguishing between fact and comment. The courts rely on a variety of circumstances, such as the language used and its arrangement, the person who makes the statement, and the way he conducts his case.[18] There is, indeed, as much certainty on this question as there is about whether a statement is defamatory; and just as the same statement has in different cases

12 In Black's case, the trial judge called this 'journalese'.

13 *Smiths Newspapers v Becker* (1932) 47 CLR 279, 304 per Evatt J; it has been stated — see Gatley para 704 — that when there is a dense mixture of fact and comment, it may all be regarded as fact. But this does not seem correct. Either a reasonable person will remember the comment he noticed and treat the rest as fact, or he will persist and distinguish all comment, or seeing the deliberate confusion might disbelieve the whole thing.

14 *Campbell v Irish Press* at 110 per Kingsmill-Moore J.

15 *Lefroy v Burnside* (1879) 4 LR Ir 556, 566 per Palles CB; see also *Kane v Mulvaney* (1866) IR 2 CL 402, 418 per Monahan CJ.

16 90 ILTR 105.

17 At 110.

18 As in Campbell's case and in *London Artists v Littler* [1969] 2 QB 375.

been held both defamatory and non-defamatory,[19] so too in an English case[20] the term 'quack' was held to be a comment, while in an Australian case[21] it was held to be a fact. The one so-called rule which has been asserted is that 'If what is intended to be comment appears in the guise of a fact, and there is nothing to show on what it is based, then it must be treated as a statement of fact ... but [not as a comment]'.[22] Although the cases supporting this[23] were correctly decided, it is wrong to conclude from them that a mere assertion on its own without any supporting facts must always be a fact. These cases were peculiar for the way in which the sued-on statements were divorced from the contexts in which they were made. Ordinarily one does not find this happening. Rules of severance will apply[24] or the necessity to plead a general innuendo will prevent for example, suing on a newspaper headline without reference to the article.[25] Further, people tend not to burst out with a comment without there being some context to it. But even when they do, the absence of such a context is more likely to make the statement a personal opinion than not.

SUPPORTING FACTS

In order for a comment to be regarded as fair, it must be established that it was supported by facts, that the facts were largely true, that they were known or discoverable, and that there was some connection between them and the comment.

The truth of the supporting facts

The comment must be based on facts which are true, or as it is sometimes put, on facts which are truly stated or not mistated. Palles CB stated the rule in 1879 'A man may [not] invent facts and comment on the facts so invented, in what would be a fair and *bona fide* manner on the supposition that the facts were true'.[26] So, if the underlying

19 See p. 82 supra.
20 *Dakhyl v Labouchere* [1908] 2 KB 325n.
21 *Smiths Newspapers v Becker*.
22 *Crawford v Albu* [1917] 1 AD 102 at 105, cited in Gatley para 701, fn 46.
23 *Cooper v Lawson* (1838) 8 A & E 746; *Popham v Pickburn* (1862) 7 H & N 891; *Davis v Shepstone* (1886) 11 App Cas 187. See also *Templeton v Jones* [1984] 1 NZLR 448.
24 See p. 102 supra.
25 *Kemsley v Foot* [1952] AC 345 was an exceptional case where the headline was divorced from the article because the latter bore little relation to the former.
26 *Lefroy v Burnside* (1879) 4 LR Ir 556, 565.

facts are untrue, then the defence is not available.[27] Where there is an unsuccessful attempt to show that the facts are true, a jury is entitled to award aggravated damages against the defendant.[28]

Not all of the supporting facts need be proved true. If the facts contained in the sued-on statement are divisible into major and minor facts, then a failure by the defendant to show that the minor facts are true will not affect reliance on the defence. This is provided for in s 23 of the Defamation Act 1961. This provision was introduced on foot of a recommendation by the Porter Committee in 1948. The Committee was concerned that a failure of the entire defence, because minor facts were unproved, was causing 'continually growing rigidity' in the law.[29] S 22 of the Act also introduced a similar distinction into the defence of justification. Although the criticisms made earlier[30] are also applicable to this section, it may be noted that an effect of s 23, unlike s 22, is to increase the range of defamatory statements which are protected. S 23 does not apply to all cases in which the defence of fair comment is raised. It only applies to defamatory statements in which the comment and the supporting facts are contained therein. It does not apply to statements which contain comment whose supporting facts are elsewhere. This seems clear both from the wording of the section and from the report of the Porter Committee.[31] This ommission in the scope of s 23 does not apppear to have been accidental, although the Faulks Committee thought it might have been.[32] It seems clear from the judgement of Lord Porter, in *Kemsley v Foot* (1952),[33] that he considered that the law then treated differently statements in which the supporting facts were contained from those in which the supporting facts were not contained. The former were subject to the old rule outlined above,which was considered rigid and was relaxed by s 23, while the latter were not subject to it. In the latter instance, a defence could always succeed even though some of the facts were untrue. The explanation for this different treatment was that where the facts are contained in the sued-on statement, they could on that account, be derogatory. But where the facts were not in the sued-on statement, then they 'are not published to the world at large, they are not the subject matter of the comment, but facts alleged to justify that comment'.

27 As in *Fisher v Nation Newspaper and Rooney* [1901] 2 IR 465 and *Eglantine Inn v Smith* at 38.
28 *Campbell v Irish Press* at 112 per Kingsmill-Moore J.
29 Porter Committee Report para 87.
30 See p. 105 supra.
31 Porter Committee Report para 87.
32 Faulks Committee Report para 172.
33 [1952] AC 345, 358.

This reasoning was, however, valid only up to a point. It is true that if a statement only points at its supporting facts, then those who actually check them out may well be less in number than those who received the defamatory statement, and so less significance might attach to some untrue facts contained there. But that is only an assumption, and by the fact that the law requires, at the very least, that a statement point at its supporting facts it clearly envisages the possibility of there being an equality between those who receive the statement and those who know the facts. Although the Porter Committee might have thought it unnecessary to include within s 23 statements which did not contain supporting facts, some of the more recent reform bodies have considered this omission to be an error and, to rectify it, have recommended that the defence should still succeed in those cases where any untrue facts do not detract from the fairness of the comment.[34]

Mangena v Wright

It is sometimes stated that there is one exception to the requirement that the supporting facts must be true, and that this arises where the untrue facts are contained in a privileged document, such as a parliamentary publication.[35] If this is correct, then a comment could be protected although all of its supporting facts were untrue, unlike the rules discussed above which protect only minor untrue facts. An English judge, Phillimore J purported to establish this exception in *Mangena v Wright* (1909) when he stated.

> If by some unfortunate error a vote in Parliament recites, or a judge in giving the reasons for his judgement states, that which is derogatory to some person, and the charge is mistaken and ill-founded, and a newspaper reports such vote or judgement, and proceeds in another part of its issue to comment upon the character of the person affected in terms which would be fair if the charge were well-founded, the newspaper ... should be entitled to the protection of fair comment.[36].

Phillimore J also made it clear that this exception was not limited to privileged documents, and that it was but one example, albeit an especially good one, of another principle — that supporting facts need

34 Faulks Committee Report para 173; NZ Committee Report para 146; see also the ALRC Report para 130.
35 Linden 712, Fleming 556, not mentioned in Williams or Salmond and Heuston.
36 [1909] 2 KB 958, 977.

not be true 'when one person alleges and another comments'. Although he cited neither precedent nor principle in support of this view, a probable explanation for it is that it is wrong for the law to leave unprotected the large amount of public comment that consists of comments on facts that are stated by others.

Since this decision, no consensus has emerged about the extent of the principle in Mangena's case. On one view,[37] it is limited to comments on the findings or conclusions of parliaments, the courts and various statutory tribunals. On another,[38] it is not limited to findings or conclusions but can include, say, comments on the evidence of individual witnesses in judicial proceedings. However, on both principle and logic, it is difficult to see how the exception could validly stop at either of these. A third view, based on Phillimore J's own words, seems most likely — that the exception will apply whenever one person comments on allegations made by another about a matter of public interest. This, one submits, is the true extent of the principle in Mangena's case. If this submission is correct, then it will be immediately apparent that, at a stroke, Phillimore J has practically undermined the basis of the entire defence of fair comment and has all but in name created both a media and non media public interest qualified privilege. For, if in these cases, the underlying facts need no longer be true, then there is effectively little difference between this defence and the recognition of a qualified privilege for public debate. On the other hand the facts, that no-one has advanced this view in the cases since then and that the separateness of the defence of fair comment is still recognised, suggest that the principle of Mangena's case can hardly stand, even to the limited extent of forming the ratio of the decision there, and one could conclude that the rule was simply invented by Phillimore J to meet the case before him.[39]

The whereabouts of the supporting facts

Since a comment must be supported by true facts before it can be fair, it follows that there must, at the very least, be some indication in the statement of the factual basis relied upon. The recipient of the defamatory statement must be as well placed as a jury would be to judge for himself the sequence of progression from fact to comment.

37 *Bailey v Truth and Sportsman* (1938) 60 CLR 700, 717 per Starke J.

38 *Grech v Odhams Press* [1958] 2 QB 276, 285 per Jenkins LJ.

39 Dixon J at 724 in Bailey's case, thought that no such protection as is suggested by Mangena's case exists. If, however, constitutional support for the right to comment is recognised — See p. 210 supra — it seems likely that it would embrace such a principle as Mangena's.

Sometimes a person might neatly present his facts first and follow on with his comment.

Other times the reverse might be the case, or there might be a deliberate confusion of both throughout the whole statement. But in each of these instances, the supporting facts are located within the statement.

Where the maker of a defamatory statement omits to mention all or any of his supporting facts in his statement, he may still rely on the defence provided the statement contains some pointer or indicator to the source of the facts. Thus a critic need not cite an entire work before reviewing it. In one English case,[40] comments in a newspaper article were held protected, though the article only referred to a petition in which the facts supporting the comment were contained. Often, the source referred to will be a clearly identifiable reference,such as a book, or a letter. But the source can, now, be as vague and ill-definable as the public knowledge of some well-known facts. In a leading English case, *Kemsley v Foot* (1952),[41] where a comment in a newspaper article attacked, in an oblique way, a newspaper proprietor, but without citing any supporting facts, the court allowed the defendant to establish his supporting facts by referring to the public knowledge of how the plaintiff ran his newspapers. In the words of the defendants quoted by Lord Porter in the House of Lords 'We have pointed to your press. It is widely read. Your readers will, and the public generally can know at what our criticism is directed ... it is comment on a well-known matter...'.[42] It is possible that such a view could also enable a comment based on some generally understood context within a group to satisfy the supporting facts requirement.

The fairness of the comment

In order to be protected, a comment must be fair. But this only means that there must be some minimum basis in fact for the comment. It does not mean that a judge or jury must, as reasonable people, consider it to have been a reasonable or proper one to make. So, the comment can be 'exaggerated, unreasonable or even prejudiced'.[43] The burden of proof in showing the logical connection between the comment and the facts rests on the defendant.[44] He does not, at

40 *Grech v Odhams Press.*

41 [1952] AC 345.

42 At 357.

43 ALRC Report para 129.

44 *Cherneskey v Armadale Publishers* (1978) 90 DLR (3d) 221 majority judgement by Ritchie J.

least initially, have to show that his comment was an honest one, though if a plaintiff adduces evidence tending to show that the comment was malicious or not honest the defence might be lost unless the defendant can prove otherwise. It has been suggested, however, that fairness includes honesty, and that, at the outset, the defendant must prove the honesty of his comment. This opinion has been criticised[45] as needlessly introducing a doubly subjective stage to establishing the defence, and as a partly shifting the burden of proof as to honesty onto the defendant. Much of the difficulty surrounding this issue stems from the different senses in which the terms 'fair', 'unfair' and 'honest' are used. It may be better to avoid them all and, in the present context, to emphasise that a defendant need only show some factual basis for his comment, and to leave any question of his honesty to be raised and proved by the plaintiff when alleging malice. The law reform bodies appreciated the potential for confusion, particularly for juries,of the current terminology, and recommended that the term 'fair' be dropped, and that the defence be simply named 'comment'.[46] There may be one exception to the rule that fair does not mean reasonable, and this arises where the comment imputes base and dishonourable motives.

Although it may usually be easy to state the distinction between fair and unfair comments, it is not always easy to apply it. For instance, in *Lefroy v Burnside* (1879),[47] a newspaper reported from an official publication before it had been released. When another paper criticised this practice, a journalist on the first paper, who was also the manager of the state printing office, conceived himself defamed and brought an action. In his defence of fair comment, the defendant claimed that because the plaintiff had the means and because the wrongful disclosure actually occurred, it was fair comment to allege that the plaintiff had wrongfully disclosed the report. However, Palles CB found the link too tenuous. 'I can see nothing that would make it a fair inference, unless the fact of a man having the means of committing a crime, and the crime being in fact committed, will warrant the inference that he who had the means was the criminal'.[48] It is open to question whether this was a correct decision. There was clearly a minimum basis in fact supporting the comment. The comment might not have been one that reasonable

45 In a minority judgement by Dickson J in Cherneskey's case; see also *Hawke v Tamworth Newspaper* [1983] 1 NSWLR 699. For a detailed consideration of the issues, see Heerey 'Publishing the Defamatory Statements of Others' (1985) 59 ALJ 371, 372-7.

46 Faulks Committee Report para 152; NZ Committee Report para 142; ALRC Report para 129.

47 (1879) 4 LR Ir 556.

48 At 567. See also *Prior v Irish Press*, The Irish Times, 26 February 1987, where the defendant did not attempt to defend a similar type of inference.

person would have made but then it did not have to be reasonable. Even if the inference was an exaggerated one, as may have been the case, it should still have been protected.

A case in which a comment was held to have been fair is *Joyce v Monaghan* (1890).[49] A witness testifying before a parliamentary commission accused the defendant of being a land-grabber. In response, the defendant wrote letters to the *Tuam News* and *The Irish Times* in which he denied the accusation and stated that the plaintiff had perjured himself. At the trial, the defendant proved that he was not a land-grabber, and the jury accepted that the accusation of perjury was a fair comment based on that fact.

Imputations of base and dishonourable motives

When a comment imputes that a person was motivated by base and dishonourable motives in doing an act, then it is sometimes stated that in order for the comment to be protected, it must have been reasonable in addition to being fair. The originating authority for this view was the decision in the English case *Campbell v Spottiswoode*(1863).[50] In that case, a newspaper published letters written to the paper in order to increase its circulation and to promote interest in the conversion of China. The paper also printed the names of some subscribers to the paper and the number of copies for which they had subscribed. Another paper then commented that the subscribers were unreal and that the object of increasing circulation was private pecuniary gain. For these comments no supporting evidence was adduced, and it is clear that the comment could not have been fair because there was no connection at all between the comment and any facts. That alone would have been sufficient to decide the case, and would not have involved any departures, from, or exceptions to, the general rule. Unfortunately, whether by design or accident, the members of the court expressed their decision in terms which were at best ambiguous,[51] about whether such criticisms had also to be reasonable, and at worst openly indicated[52] that they had to be. Not only was any rule that a communication had to be reasonable not warranted by the facts of the case, but what is more the rule can be and has been criticised[53] as imposing too

49 (1890) 24 ILTR 100; other cases where a defence of fair comment succeeded are *Stannus v Finlay* (1874) IR 8 CL 264 and *Crawford and Frame v Vance* [1908] 2 IR 521.

50 (1863) 3 B & S 769; this principle was applied here in *Black v Northern Whig* (1942) 77 ILTR 5.

51 See Crompton J's reference at 778 to '[comments] not warranted by the facts'.

52 See Cockburn CJ at 777.

53 NZ Committee Report para 159; ALRC Report para 131. The line of authority

excessive a restriction on the defence and on free speech. Many comments in public debate do contain such imputations, and if each comment had also to be reasonable, the defence would often be of little use. In terms of balance of interest, the judgements involved a sharp leap backwards from protecting public debate. In a number of cases since then,[54] the principle of Campbell's case has been judicially approved of, and so one cannot, as one would like to, disregard it as merely obiter. The reform bodies have, not surprisingly, all recommended that the exception should be abolished because of its complexity, difficulty and restrictiveness.[55] It is also possible that the principle in Campbell's case infringes the constitutional protection for comment.

MATTERS OF PUBLIC INTEREST

In order for a defamatory comment to be protected, it is necessary to show, in addition to the proofs mentioned above, that the comment concerned a matter of public interest. The types of matter which may be the subject of fair comment are divided into two parts — matters which are inherently of public interest and matters which are submitted to the public for its attention. Under the first part are included matters of national and local government — 'the right to comment upon the public acts of public men is the right of every one'[56] — so that the voting activities of members of Belfast[57] and Dublin Corporations[58] were held to be of public interest. Other fit topics of public comment are the suitability of candidates for elected public office,[59] the behaviour of public servants[60] and the activities of police officers.[61].

The administration of justice is also a matter which is fit for public comment. Kenny J stated in the Supreme Court:

> The Court wishes to emphasise that criticism of the retention of

— mentioned in Faulks para 163 — which interprets Campbell's case as requiring that the comment be more than reasonable, and be true or correct, is even more unfounded and restrictive.

54 For a list of these cases, see Faulks Committee Report para 163, 164.

55 Faulks Committee Report para 169; NZ Committee Report para 160. According to Fleming 557, it has already been done in some Australian states.

56 *Kane v Mulvaney* (1866) IR 2 CL 402 per Monahan CJ.

57 *Black v Northern Whig* (1942) 77 ILTR 5.

58 *Crawford and Frame v Vance* [1908] 2 IR 521.

59 *Fisher v Nation Newspaper and Rooney* [1901] 2 IR 465.

60 *Lefroy v Burnside* (1879) 4 LR Ir 556.

61 *Clinton v Henderson* (1863) 13 ICLR App xliii.

> the death penalty, of the Offences against the State Acts, or of any of their provisions, and of the establishment of the Special Criminal Court are ... matters which may validly be debated in public even if the comments are expressed in strong language or are uninformed or foolish.[62].

In the cases, the evidence of witnesses in judicial proceedings have been commented on.[63] There is, however, a particular restriction operating where a comment is made on a judicial matter. The comment must not infringe the law on contempt of court.There appear to be three types of contemptuous statements.[64] Firstly, where a statement scandalises the courts, undermines peoples confidence in the judiciary or imputes improper motives to the judiciary. Secondly, where a statement seriously misrepresents a court's proceedings, and thirdly, where a statement is expressed about civil or criminal proceedings then pending in such a way as to prejudice the possibility of a fair and unbiased hearing of the case. Where a defamatory comment is also a contempt it seems likely, although there is no case in point, that it would not be regarded a fair comment, partly because it would not be on a matter of public interest.[65] It should be noted about the third type of contempt that not every comment on a case which is pending is a contempt, nor is it left unprotected by the defence of fair comment. 'It is a widely held fallacy that the issue of a writ automatically stifles further comment'.[66] The comment must possess 'a real and definite tendency'[67] to prejudice proceedings and, an appeal on issues of law is unlikely to do this.[68] In *Irish Provident Association v Hastings* (1904) an attempt to attach a newspaper proprietor for contempt for re-publishing statements after a writ in defamation was issued against him, failed because the court did not find in the mere fact of repetition any intention to interfere with the due course of justice.[69]

62 *In re Hibernia National Review* (1976) IR 388, 391.

63 *Kane v Mulvaney* (1866) IR 2 CL 402 and *Travers v Potts* unreported, mentioned in Kanes's case at 417.

64 For the law on contempt, see Kelly *The Irish Constitution* 2nd ed 249 et seq; McCormack 'Corrupting the Criminal Process' (1985) ILT & SJ 6.

65 See Gatley para 735, fn 78.

66 *Thomson v Times Newspapers* [1969] 1 WLR 1236, 1240 per Salmon LJ; 'Fair comment does not prejudice a fair trial' per Lord Denning MR in *Wallersteiner v Moir* [1974] 1 WLR 991, 1005.

67 *Fairfax & Sons v McRae* (1955) 93 CLR 351, 372, per Dixon CJ.

68 *Cullen v Tobin* [1984] ILRM 577.

69 (1904) 5 New Ir Jur Rep 10. The use of 'gagging writs' in an attempt to warn a paper off a story by issuing a writ and claiming high damages with little intent of pursuing the case, is an established tactic in many jurisdictions. By issuing the writ, a plaintiff hopes to invoke the sub judice rule, and to then threaten the paper with contempt proceedings. In New Zealand this tactic has, according

The second type of matter of public interest is matter submitted to the public for its attention. This would include commercial activities, sporting activities[70] and matters of literature and art submitted to the public, like the works of a poet, novelist, critic and journalist.[71] It should also be noted, that where something is pressed on the public, say, by a commercial enterprise, the resulting public interest need not be limited only to that matter, but can also be concerned with other aspects of the enterprise's affairs. Thus, in an English case,[72] the living conditions of a large number of people over a large area in dwellings owned by a coal mining company were held to be matters of public interest, as, also, in an Irish case,[73] were the employment practices of an intoxicating liquor licensee.

Different views have, in the past, been expressed about whether the issue of the possession of land is a fit matter for public comment. It will be recalled[74] that in *McInerney v Clareman Printing and Publishing*(1903),[75] the Court of Appeal held that private transactions involving land were not matters of public interest, although the public, or a part of it, in particular areas had interested themselves in it. By contrast, in *Stannus v Finlay*(1874),[76] a jury held, in opposition to the trial judge's personal view, that the management of a large estate of a lord, and the attitudes of the agent to the tenants, were matters of public interest. The possession of land was also held a matter of public interest when it was raised during the hearings of a parliamentary commission.[77]

Where a matter is of valid public interest, any comment which

to the Committee Report Chapter 19, been used and has inhibited journalism. Here, the media also receive from time to time what are perceived to be gagging writs, but the matter does not appear to be a major problem. The NZ Committee considered gagging writs an abuse of procedure, and recommended a number of ways of dealing with the matter — prohibiting plaintiffs from mentioning in their statements of claim the sum sought; enouraging judges to make a more deterrent use of the law of costs when sums awarded are grossly disproportionate to what is claimed at the trial; emphasising that solicitors who are knowingly party to the issue of gagging writs are guilty of unethical conduct for which disciplinary proceedings might lie. The intentional issue of gagging writs might also constitute the tort of malicious instigation of civil proceedings, see *Doreen v Suedes (Ireland)* [1982] ILRM 126. If juries were abolished in defamation cases the impact of gagging writs might be reduced, since judges would be less open to influence by pre trial comment.

70 *Campbell v Irish Press* (1955) 90 ILTR 105.
71 *Kavanagh v The Leader* SCt, unreported, 4 March 1955.
72 *South Hetton Coal v North Eastern News* [1894] 1 QB 133.
73 *Eglantine Inn v Smith* [1948] NI 29.
74 See p. 192 supra.
75 [1903] 2 IR 347.
76 (1874) IR 8 CL 264.
77 *Joyce v Monaghan* (1890) 24 ILTR 100.

is made therein must be careful to distinguish between the private and public lives of those involved. The private lives of these persons may not be commented on, though this is is subject to a right of public comment on the private lives or personal character of those involved where that is relevant to their involvement in public matters.[78] For instance, in one case,[79] criticism of a literary figure, which dealt with his 'poetry and journalism and his views and character as manifested in his output',[80] was held to be fair comment.

Notions about what is private or public will, of course, vary over time. Changes in society, affecting the range of public interest and curiosity, have, since the last century, been great. The state now plays a more active, and paternalistic role in the lives of its citizens. Whether for reasons of assistance, education, taxation or planning, there is almost no detail of the citizen's life that is not of public interest to the state, and so the general public, in some way. The existence of the entire framework of laws is ample testimony to at least an indirect public interest in all things.

The development of mass media technology, allied with higher levels of education, has resulted in the dissemination of more information of an ever-widening range of subjects. Against this kind of background, a contemporary reader may regard as anachronistic the customary classification of matters of public interest. He might consider that the emphasis should be reversed, and that all matter should be regarded as being of public interest unless it is shown that it is only of indirect public interest and did not require the identification of any particular person.

MALICE

Although a defendant may prove that he made a fair comment on a matter of public interest, he will still lose any protection which the law offers if a plaintiff can show that when making the comment, the defendant did not act bona fide, but acted maliciously. Malice here is defined, and proved,in the same way as with the defence of qualified privilege. It therefore retains its narrow meaning. Those who comment are entitled to great latitude in what they say.[81] The malice which is proved must have actually motivated the statement. One can have malice which does not do this, for it is 'possible for

78 See generally *Campbell v Spottiswoode* (1863) 3 B & S 769 and *Barrow v Carribean Publishing* (1971) 17 WIR 182.

79 *Kavanagh v The Leader*.

80 Per Kingsmill-Moore J at 1.

81 *Black v Northern Whig* (1942) 77 ILTR 5, 9 per Brown J.

a person to have a spite against another and yet to bring a perfectly dispassionate judgement to bear upon his literary merits'.[82]

Some of the authorities refer to there having once been a doubt about whether proof of malice actually displaces the protection of fair comment,[83] and the leading English authority[84] in which this was clearly dispelled dates only from 1912. It seems doubtful if there was ever a similar uncertainty here.

As far as one can tell from the reported Irish cases concerning fair comment in the nineteenth century, the defence always contained an averment that the defendant had acted bona fide,[85] and in two of the cases[86] judges expressly stated that a comment needed to be a bona fide one. The absence of doubt also seems clear from the judgements in *Stannus v Finlay* (1874),[87] where the Court of Queen's Bench had to consider whether a proper definition of a defamatory statement could refer only to the defamatory effect or whether it had also to refer to the absence of excuse or malice. In considering this, the court plainly thought that malice would defeat a plea of fair comment.

All of the reform bodies have criticised the continued use of the term malice. In its place, they have recommended that the defence should be lost if the criticism was not the maker's genuine opinion.[88] Surprisingly, the reform bodies are divided on whether this will merely simplify the law or will also change it. At present, an honestly believed criticism which is made for spiteful or ulterior reasons is not protected. Under this recommendation, it will be. The Australian Law Reform Commission clearly intended this because it thought the present law could produce odd results as between two critics writing the same honestly-held comment but one also desiring to injure. Only the former is currently protected. The Faulks Committee, in using a similar example, did not find this odd at all, and did not intend that its recommendation should prevent it from happening.[89]

If malice in the defence of fair comment is redefined, questions arise as to whether the resulting difference between malice in that defence and malice in the defence of a qualified privilege is

82 *Thomas v Bradbury, Agnew* [1906] 2 KB 627, 642 per Collins MR.
83 Eg Gatley para 763.
84 *Thomas v Bradbury, Agnew*.
85 *Clinton v Henderson* (1863) 13 ICLR App xliii; *Hort v Reade* (1873) IR 7 CL 551; *Kane v Mulvaney* (1866) IR 2 CL 402; *Lefroy v Burnside* (1879) 4 LR Ir 556.
86 *Kane v Mulvaney, Lefroy v Burnside*.
87 (1874) IR 8 CL 264.
88 Faulks Committee Report para 159; NZ Committee Report para 151; ALRC Report para 130.
89 At para 154.

constitutionally permissible. The suggestion was made earlier that the latter type was too narrowly defined, and the effect of the reform body recommendations would be to define the former type even more narrowly. It might be thought that since fair comment concerns public matters that different definitions would be justified. Yet it is not clear that this is so. There is no greater reason to protect a person's motives when speaking publicly than when speaking on a privileged occasion, especially when many privileged occasions concern public matters. It may also be that constitutional protection for the media would effectively nullify any attempted distinction between the two definitions of malice anyway. Whether the two defences are actually separate entities is another matter, and is considered below. If they are not, and if fair comment is really only a species of qualified privilege, there would be less reason to differentiate between the two types of malice.

FAIR COMMENT AND QUALIFIED PRIVILEGE

The question of whether there is any significant difference between the defences of qualified privilege and fair comment has received some consideration from the various writers in this area.[90] A number of differences between the two defences have been suggested. Firstly, it has been stated that findings of privilege 'proceed on the hypothesis that the writing in question is prima facie a libel if not privileged or excused', whereas 'a finding of fair comment stands on a somewhat different footing, because that which is a fair comment is not a libel at all'.[91] It is peculiar that a fair comment is regarded as not a libel, because the defence only needs to be raised, as in the case of privilege, where a statement is prima facie defamatory. The distinction hardly seems a real one, and the reference to fair comment being no libel probably has more to do with the fact that in the last century, in England, the defence of fair comment could be raised under the plea of no libel — which plea also disputed the defamatory nature of the statement — while the defence of qualified privilege had to be specially pleaded. This was not the case here,[92] where fair comment also had, for a time, to be specially pleaded, although, as in other instances, later Irish judges[93] were apparently unaware of this, and

90 Gatley para 694; Winfield & Jolowicz, 311; Clerk and Lindsell para 1772; Salmond & Heuston 169.

91 *McInerney v Clareman Publishing and Printing* [1903] 2 IR 347, 374.

92 This rule was established in *Dixon v Franks* (1855) 7 IJ OS 239, 384 and approved of by Whiteside CJ at 293 in *Stannus v Finlay* (1874) IR 8 CL 264; however, both Fitzgerald J at 276 et seq and Barry J at 289, 292 in Stannus' case were inclined to disapprove of it, and to follow the English practice.

93 Eg Barton J — in his statement of the distinction, quoted above.

so repeated here the English expressions of the distinction.

Secondly, it is stated that a privilege is a concession required by the exigencies of a special occasion whereas a right to comment is an entitlement enjoyed by all.[94] A variation on this is to state that a privilege benefits only one person while anyone can make a fair comment.[95] This seems also to be no more than a verbal difference. A fair comment can only be made when a matter is of public interest. Similarly, a privilege can only arise when a proper occasion exists. Once properly entitled, anyone can act on a privileged occasion, just as anyone can make a comment. Further, with some qualified privileges — such as during election campaigns — anyone can make a statement, and a privileged statement can also sometimes be made to the whole world.

Thirdly, the burden of proof is said,[96] in some unclear way, to be different in the case of each defence. But this is not so. For, with each defence, the burden rests on the defendant to raise it and on the plaintiff to defeat it.[97]

Fourthly, it is stated that there are differences in detail between the two defences.[98] This is quite true, but then there are also differences in detail between the various occasions of qualified privilege. Indeed one might as well ask if there is a similarity between the occasions of qualified privilege as ask if qualified privilege is different from fair comment. The predominant difference between the two defences is, of course, that the facts supporting a fair comment must be true while a comment made on a privileged occasion may be based on true or untrue facts. But even this is not so significant. The absence of true facts to support a defamatory comment made on a privileged occasion might well be evidence of malice, the practical effect of which is the same as where a comment on a public matter is based on untrue facts — no defence available.[99] In conclusion, one submits that the remark of Gibson J, in 1908, that 'Fair comment is a species of privilege'[1] accurately states the relationship between the two defences.

94 See generally *Merivale v Carson* (1887) 20 QBD 275, 279, 280 per Lord Esher MR, also referred to in Winfield & Jolowicz 311; Gatley para 694.

95 *Campbell v Spottiswoode* (1863) 3 B & S 769, 778 per Crompton J and 780 per Blackburn J.

96 *Thomas v Bradbury Agnew* [1906] 2 KB 627, 640 cited in Salmond & Heuston, 169.

97 See also Gatley para 790, 792; Street, 329.

98 Salmond & Heuston, 169.

99 If the principle in Mangena's case is a valid one, then that also diminshes the difference between qualified privilege and fair comment, because it allows protected comments to be based on untrue facts.

1 *Crawford and Frame v Vance* [1908] 2 IR 521, 567.

10

Other Defences

CONSENT

Where a defendant in an action for defamation establishes that the plaintiff validly consented to the act of publication, then that is a complete defence to the action. The consent can arise from the terms of a contract between the parties,[1] or it can exist as a result of an agreed waiver of his right to sue, made by the plaintiff before the act of publication, and expressly communicated by him to the defendant. The consent must be real and valid; a plaintiff either must have had or ought to have had a sufficient idea of what he was consenting to. Where a person is shown a statement before it is published because he fears he may be defamed by it, that is not a consent to publication, nor is any attempt to discuss with an author the reason for any adverse publication.[2]

So far as the first type of consent is concerned, the terms of the contract between the parties leading to the agreed publication must have been properly observed, and if they were not, then the defence will not rise.[3] If the contract is tainted by illegality, and both parties are equally to blame, that need not prevent a defendant from raising the defence.[4] The type of situation in which a defence of consent based on contract is likely to arise will be where a plaintiff joined a group, or participated in an activity, and by that fact, or else expressly, undertook to abide by various rules that provide for

1 As in *O'Keefe v Cullen* (1873) IR 7 CL 319; *Reilly v Gill* (1946) 85 ILTR 165; *Green v Blake* [1948] IR 242

2 See generally Boberg 'Defence of Consent in a Defamation Action' (1961) 78 SALJ 54

3 *Reilly v Gill*

4 *O'Keefe v Cullen*

5 *Green v Blake*

6 There has been some academic discussion as to whether the immunity conferred by consent means that no tort was committed at all, or that it was committed and that a defendant is absolutely protected — see Eldredge 316, Gatley para 851; see also *Tadd v Eastwood* [1985] ICR 132 where a court refused to imply

disciplinary proceedings if the rules are thought to be broken, and for the publication of the decision of the adjudicating body. In their proceedings these bodies must observe natural justice and, if they do not, that may vitiate any consent to the defamatory publication.[5] In the cases, the element of general consent has been used to help establish a qualified privilege; and while it may be that consent on its own does not create a qualified privilege, where real and valid it does more by conferring an absolute immunity, akin to absolute privilege, which is not vitiated by malice.[6]

The second kind of consent, which arises outside of a contract, is also embodied in the maxim volenti non fit injuria, which 'lays down that a man cannot ask a Court to treat as an injury that to which he has himself assented'.[7] Since the enactment of s 34 (1) of the Civil Liability Act 1961, this maxim has been replaced by the defence of agreed waiver of rights. This defence is somewhat narrower than the protection provided by the maxim, since an implied consent does not constitute the defence of agreed waiver.[8] The consent must now be an express one. Still, this might, in fact, not mean any change on the pre-1961 position, because even then if a plaintiff could show that he had encouraged the publication for the good reason of obtaining evidence of publication on which to bring an action, when there was no other way of getting it, the courts did not regard this as an implied consent. In *Irish People's Assurance v City of Dublin Assurance* (1929),[9] the Supreme Court rejected the argument that a publication induced by sending an agent to encourage it, with a view to bringing an action, was not actionable. In some cases, such a practice has been deemed a consent.[10] However, that is only a court imputed and not a genuine consent, and if the courts really wish to safeguard against manufactured evidence, some less unreal approach should be used. It seems that an invitation or challenge to 'Repeat that outside the House' or 'Repeat that in front of witnesses' if made in order to secure evidence of publication where no other evidence is available, or if made in circumstances which 'indicate that it was intended and understood as a request that the other would by the repetition ... abandon the protection ... and give the person defamed an opportunity to vindicate his reputation by an action at law',[11] that the defence cannot be raised.

a waiver of a right to sue by participation in domestic tribunal proceedings, but still held that the statement was made under qualified privilege.

7 *O'Keefe v Cullen* at 362 per Barry J; see also Fitzgerald J at 374, and O'Brien J at 398

8 *O'Hanlon v ESB* [1969] IR 75; *McComiskey v McDermott* [1974] IR 75

9 [1929] IR 25; see also p. 74 supra

10 Boberg loc cit

11 *The Second Restatement of Torts* s 583, quoted by Eldredge 321

Section 21 of the Defamation Act 1961 granted unintentional defamers a defence to an action for defamation if they made an offer of amends involving a retraction and an apology within a certain time, and also satisfied some other conditions. In doing this, the Oireachtas was just one of many legislative bodies who acted upon recommendations made by the Porter Committee in England in 1948.[12] These recommendations may have been intended primarily to safeguard media interests, but, for a variety of reasons referred to later, including the restrictive scope of the section, they have not achieved that objective. The section has been little relied on by the media.

Until 1961, the fact that a person did not intend to defame another did not affect his liability, if he was otherwise liable. Innocent and unintentional defamers were treated alike. In this sense, defamation was a strict liability tort. The law concentrated on damage to good name In the early stages of the development of the action, real malice, or intent, was, for a while, considered an essential ingredient of liability.[13] But in time this view was replaced by a purely formal and meaningless use of the term,[14] and by the nineteenth century it was settled that intent was irrelevant to liability.[15]

The change, then, involved readjusting the common law balance between good name and other rights, using intent as the pivot of liability. Section 21 is part of a general trend in tort law to use some type of fault as a criterion of liability. Being a post-1937 provision, the section also enjoys a presumption of constitutionality. There are, however, certain aspects of the defence whose constitutionality may be debated.

Section 21

Section 21 may be summarised as follows: an innocent defamer may make an offer of amends which, it it is accepted, will constitute a bar to any further proceedings. If it is not accepted, it will constitute a complete defence to an action, provided the offer was made as early as practicable after receiving notice of the wrong and has not since been withdrawn.[16] The offer must be expressed to be made under

12 The same provision was enacted in England, Northern Ireland, Tasmania, New Zealand, and New South Wales

13 See Prosser 771

14 See Napier 'Lecture on the Law of Defamation' (1840) 1 Leg Rep 128, 130; see also p. 144 supra on the distinction between malice in law and malice in fact

15 *Brommage v Prosser* (1825) 4 B & C 247; *Fox v Broderich* (1864) 14 ICLR 453

16 Subs 1

the section, and it must be accompanied by an affidavit stating the facts on which innocence is claimed. No facts, other than those stated in the affidavit, can be relied on in any subsequent action.[17] The offer of amends must consist of an offer to publish a correction and to make a sufficient apology. If the defamation was contained in a widely distributed mass medium, the defamer must also offer to take reasonable steps to inform the original recipients of the defamatory statement that the words are alleged to be defamatory of the person aggrieved.[18] Where the offer is accepted, the High Court has power to decide any disputes about its implementation, and to order a defamer to pay the aggrieved person's costs and expenses.[19]

Subsection 5 defines the types of necessary innocence. It arises where '(a) ... the publisher did not intend to publish them of and concerning that other person, and did not know of circumstances by virtue of which they might be understood to refer to him; or (b) ... the words were not defamatory on the face of them, and the publisher did not know of circumstances by virtue of which they might be understood to be defamatory of that other person, and in either case that the publisher exercised all reasonable care.' If a servant or agent of a publisher involved with the contents of the defamatory publication is not innocent, the publisher will not be either.[20] Finally, if special damage is proved to have resulted, or if the publisher, not being the author, cannot show that the author acted without malice, the defence is not available at all.[21]

There have been very few cases anywhere in which this section has been considered.[22] One may, however, on the question of what would be reasonable care for a newspaper, cite the old cases on the, now abolished,[23] defence of apology contained in s 2 of the Libel Act 1843, in which the paper had to show an absence of gross negligence in the publication. Thus, gross negligence was established when a paper was shown to have published similar attacks, over a period in the past on a plaintiff,[24] or where a morning edition asserted the opposite to what the previous evening's edition had asserted and was published without checking on the accuracy of the previous story,[25] or where an untruth was published in a column

17 Subs 2
18 Subs 3
19 Subs 4
20 Subs 7
21 Subs 6
22 Gatley at para 838 mentions two English cases — *Ross v Hopkinson*, The Times, 17 October 1956, and *Solomon v Simmonds*, The Times, 10 April 1954
23 Defamation Act 1961, s 4
24 *Barrett v Long* (1846) 8 ILR 331; (1848) 3 HLC 395
25 *Harris v Arnott* (1889) 26 LR Ir 55

headed 'all such announcements must be authenticated' when no check on the accuracy of an announcement was made.[26]

The most convenient way to consider the various provisions in s 21 is by referring to the many criticisms that have been made of it. The Faulks Committee found the section practically 'unworkable'[27] and the Australian Law Reform Commission stated that 'nowhere has the section been extensively used',[28] although the New Zealand Committee found, from its research, that it was used eleven times in a five year period by the press there.[29] The principal defects cited by the reform bodies are the practical difficulty and expense of arranging the necessary affidavit in time, the ban on the later use of facts discovered after the affidavit is served, and the need for the publisher, where he was not the author, to prove that the author acted without malice.[30] The Faulks Committee recommended replacing the affidavit with a mere statement, removing the ban on the subsequent use of newly discovered facts, and immunising a publisher, who was not the author, from the author's malice, except where he was the employer or principal of the latter.[31]

The New Zealand Committee favoured renaming the offer of amends an 'offer of apology',[32] and replacing the affidavit with a statement.[33] But it did not favour removing the ban on the subsequent use of newly discovered facts to establish innocence, because it believed that 'the facts surrounding the innocent publication should be known to the publisher at once'.[34] This seems the better view, since a publisher who wanted to rely on facts discovered later might have difficulty showing that he acted innocently, and with reasonable care, at the time of publication.[35]

26 *Bell v Northern Constitution* [1943] NI 108; see also *Tait v New Westminster Radio* (1985) 15 DLR (4d) 115
27 Faulks Committee Report para 281
28 ALRC Report para 87
29 NZ Committee Report para 301
30 Faulks Committee Report para 281; ALRC Report, para 87
31 Supra. For the infectious malice rule, see p. 269 post
32 NZ Committee Report para 298
33 At para 304
34 At para 305
35 The failure of the section to impose a duty on the defamed person to inform the defamer of any relevant circumstances connecting the statement to the defamed person has been criticised — see Gatley, para 834 — as unfair to the defamer who, presumably might not be aware of how the link was made. However, if the latter has acted with reasonable care, as he must have, then he ought to be aware of the facts showing an honest ignorance of how any link could be made. Both the NZ Committee and the ALRC emphasised that the publisher will know of the facts on which innocence, or lack of it, will be established.

Subsection 5 of s 21 has also been criticised. The use of the phrase 'might be understood' in both parts of the subsection whereby the defamer needs to show his ignorance of the possibility of connection between the circumstances and the defamed person, suggests a test of connection that is more onerous than the usual test of whether the circumstances would be reasonably understood to connect the publication to the defamed person.[36] Another criticism,[37] is that part (b) of subs 5 might not extend as far as was originally intended, since it does not cover a situation where words are defamatory on their face, but not of the person complaining. However, in that case, the statement would then come within part (a) of subs 5.[38]

From these criticisms of s 21, and from the infrequent use made of the defence, it will be apparent that this attempt, prompted by reform body recommendations, to allow some leeway to unintentional defamers has not been a successful one. Both the recent English and the New Zealand reform bodies have sought to resolve the difficulties by an improved s 21, but one cannot be too hopeful of the efficacy of these attempts in the light of previous experience. The response of the Australian Law Reform Commission to the situation has, however, been different, and deserves some attention because of its simplicity and practicability. After observing that unintentional defamation was not a great problem anyway, and that other recommendations allowed corrections to be ordered to reduce defamatory effects, the Commission recommended against enacting any provision dealing with unintentional defamation.[39] The position then would be that all defamers — innocent and unintentional alike — could have damages awarded against them, but that if a correction was promptly published, and an unintentional defamer would be likely to agreed to that, the damages would normally be no more than nominal. These proposals possess considerable merit, but they depend for their efficacy on a judicial power to order corrections, which presupposes some judicial hearing to determine whether, and in what way the power ought to be exercised. Courts, at present, do not possess or claim to possess such a power, although they could legitimately make such a claim.

There remains as a singular and positive feature of s 21 the offer of amends, which consists, essentially, of an offer to correct and

36 Gatley para 834

37 Gatley para 836

38 A further criticism is made by Delany 'Civil Proceedings for Defamation — The Defamation Act 1961' (1962-3) 28-9 IJ 1, 3 concerning the use in part (b) of the phrase 'did not know' instead of 'ought not to have known', though as he later acknowledged, this point is covered by the general obligation that the plaintiff exercise all reasonable care.

39 ALRC Report para 88

apologise. This is the only recognition in Irish law of the value which a correction or retraction possesses for rehabilitating reputation. The type of retraction envisaged by the section is a voluntary one, while the type recommended by the Australian Law Reform Commission refers to a judicial order to correct. Neither therefore involves a legal right to demand a retraction, and yet a case may be made for the recognition of such a right.[40]

Whenever a valid defence is maintained against a claim for defamation, the injured person's reputation is left damaged. It can be argued that there is a moral onus on the defamer, which should be reinforced by legal sanction, to ameliorate that harm by retracting the statement to those to whom it was made. Failure to publish a retraction could be treated as a criminal wrong punishable by a nominal fine, although in separate civil action for damages the defamer should still have a complete defence. Possibly a retraction could not be demanded where a defamer proposed to prove that the statement was true, and possibly also in the case of media defendants whose constitutional rights might safeguard them against enforced retractions prior to some judicial hearing. In the latter instance, an aggrieved individual could assert the quite different right to enforce an opportunity for reply, which would not require any admission from the media defendant that the statement was untrue.[41]

Constitutional issues

In its present form, s 21 raises a number of constitutional issues. Firstly, the section is unique among defamation defences in making a defence turn on the publication of a correction and apology. A plaintiff gains something from the provision, and his reputation may be rehabilitated. But a plaintiff faced with other defamation defences, such as qualified privilege, gains no such benefit when faced with defeat in a contemplated action. There is unequal treatment in this of different plaintiffs for which it is not easy to see constitutional justification; indeed, it might be that only some arrangement offering either a general reply or retraction, such as suggested above, would satisfy constitutional provisions.

Secondly, s 21 defines unintentional, or innocent, defamation very narrowly, so that over a wide range of other innocent defamations strict liability is, in the absence of other defences, still imposed. For

40 See pp. 265, 290.

41 Despite apparent judicial support for the idea, no such right to demand a retraction exists in the US, although there are retraction statues relating to malice and damages — see Sperenza 'Reply and Retraction in Actions against the Press for Defamation: The Effect of Tornillo and Gertz' (1974) 43 Fordham LR 223, 235/6

instance, s 21 does not cover such common instances as where an error is made due to a misprint or omission, or the use of a wrong photograph, or a mistake in reporting,[42] or where a person intended publishing in relation to a particular person and appreciated that the words were disparaging, but honestly thought that they were true. The failure of the section to prevent strict liability operating in this wide category of publication especially affects media defendants, to whom constitutional provisions appear to offer protection. In the US, since 1964, recovery against media defamers has been conditional on proof of fault of one type or another, depending on whether the plaintiff is a public or private figure.

Finally, the denial of the defence in subss 5 and 6 in s 21 where special damage is proved, or where a defamer is unable to prove that an author for whom he was responsible did not act maliciously raises a number of constitutional questions in relation to media protection. If, as seems likely, constitutional protection of the media prohibits the imposition of strict liability in defamation actions, and allows only some form of fault liability, then the denial in s 21 of fault liability to media defendants in these cases might be unconstitutional. The particular difficulties posed by ss 6 in relation to infectious malice are further considered in the Chapter 12.[43]

REPLY

Reply does not exist as a remedy in Ireland yet. However, arguments favouring the adoption of such a remedy, in one or other of its forms have been advanced, and sometimes rejected, in many jurisdictions.[44] Since it seems likely, for reasons outlined below, that this remedy will, in some form, find its way into Irish law, it is necessary to consider the matter.

The truest form of the remedy of reply arises when a person is granted a legally enforceable right to compel a media defamer to publish his reply to a defamatory publication without any hearing to determine truth, in circumstances as close as possible to the original publication in order to reach the same audience. Publication of a reply would not bar a subsequent action for damages, although it could

42 Eg *Doyle v Irish Press,* The Irish Times, 6 December 1984; *Latham and Byrne v Independent Newspapers,* The Irish Times, 9 May 1986; *Bowen v Connaught Telegraph,* The Irish Times, 16 May 1986

43 See p. 269 post.

44 See ALRC Report para 178-81; also Chafee‘ Possible New Remedies for Errors in the Press’ (1946) 60 Harv L Rev 1; Donnelly ‘The Rights of Reply: An Alternative to an Action for Libel’ ’(1943) 34 Va L Rev 867; Fleming ‘Retraction and Reply: Alternative Remedies for Defamation’ (1978) 12 UBC L Rev 15

mitigate the amount of damages awarded. Refusal to publish the reply would be a legal wrong. Other forms of reply provide for a statutory defence to an action for damages conditional on facilitating a reply, or a statement of explanation or contradiction, as it is put in s 24 of the Defamation Act 1961. But s 24 confers no enforceable right of reply, and is of limited use in applying only to the media and only in relation to restricted categories of matters of public interest, Many common law jurisdictions use the same, or a variant, of this type of reply, whereas civil law jurisdictions, including most EC states, have adopted the purer form.[45]

The particular advantage which the remedy of reply affords is that it enables a tailor-made response to be put directly to the audience of the first communication which attempts to negative the damage caused by it. Furthermore in dispensing with the need for a judicial hearing beforehand — on the basis that whoever provides the forum for attack should, at least, provide a forum for response — the remedy may be exercised quickly, and is thereby more likely to diminish the damage done.[46] The main disadvantages are that the exact same audience is unlikely to be reached, the reply may be seen as only the defamed person's view of the matter and might consequently not enjoy the authoritativeness of an admission of wrongdoing or a judicial determination of such. Still, as a purposive attempt to redress damage, reply is clearly an apt remedy, and in appropriate cases could be enhanced into an entitlement to demand the better remedy of retraction, and thereby avoid the possible shortcoming of reply, which is that it might only alert the public to a dispute and not redress damage. But, as is suggested later, a right to demand a retraction might only arise in some cases, and might not be applicable where a defamer definitely indicated he would plead and maintain justification, and also where media defamers were involved; the latter since it seems likely that constitutional protection of the media could not compel an involuntary retraction without prior judicial determination.

Many commentators, notably the Australian Law Reform Commission[47] have argued for a more widely used reply remedy. In 1974, however, the US Supreme Court struck down as

45 EC Commission *Television without Frontiers: Green Paper on the establishment of the common market for broadcasting, expecially by satellite and cable* 14 June 1984, Com (84) 300 final, 294-8

46 A particular advantage of a pre-hearing right of reply, is the avoidance of a major obstacle to a speedy reputation rehabilitation, which is the delay involved in preparing cases and in having them heard, NZ Committee Report para 369.

47 At paras 178-81

unconstitutional a state statute of the pure reply type.[48] It did so on grounds of onerous economic impact, excessive editorial intrusion, undue restriction on media contribution to public debate, and a general constitutional trend against compulsion to print. In principle however none of these arguments is especially convincing, and the constitutional climate here would be much more favourable to protecting good name and to permitting statutory intervention along the lines outlined. In addition to this, the EC Commission has recently suggested in a Green Paper on a proposed common policy for broadcasting that there may be a competence under community law to enact a directive requiring member states, in the context of such a policy, to afford a pure right of reply remedy in national law for persons defamed in broadcasts.[49] Although this proposal was subsequently dropped because it did not seem necessary,[50] the broad elements which such a right might involve were clear.[51] The right would arise where any juridic person's honour or reputation was damaged in any broadcast. It would be exercisable only on foot of a written application delivered within thirty days of the broadcast which identified the complainant and the offending broadcast, showed how the broadcast caused the damage and stated the text of the reply which would normally last no longer than three minutes. The broadcasting station would be obliged, at its own expense, and within thirty days of application, to broadcast the reply in toto without comment or contradiction in the next broadcast of the same type and to the same audience, unless the reply was tortious or criminal.

APOLOGY

The making of an apology for a defamatory publication does not, on its own, affect a publisher's liability in respect of the statement. However, if made in certain circumstances, an apology can help establish a defence to an action. Firstly,an apology may be contained in an accord and satisfaction, whereby an injured party agrees, in exchange for an apology and valuable consideration, not to institute or continue with proceedings. Such an agreement is a bar to further proceedings. The apology must, however, not be retracted, and, if it is, proceedings may be brought.[52] Secondly, an apology may be part of an offer of amends which is made to avail of the defence of

48 *Miami Herald Publishing v Tornillo* (1974) 418 US 241
49 At 288
50 Explanatory Memo para 25 to Com (86) 146 final 12
51 At 299
52 As in *Eiffe v Jacob* (1838) 1 Jebb & Sym 257

unintentional defamation contained in s 21 of the Defamation Act 1961.

There was, formerly, another situation in which an apology assisted in establishing a defence to an action, and that was under the Libel Acts of 1843 and 1845, whereby an apology, made in certain restrictive circumstances and coupled with payment into court, constituted a defence available to the periodic press. But these Acts were repealed by s 4 of the 1961 Act.[53] At present, the offering or making of an apology by anyone, under s 17 of the 1961 Act, only constitutes evidence in mitigation of damages. By the same token at common law, the absence of an apology, or the lack of a full one, can constitute evidence in aggravation of damages.[54]

Finally, it should be noted that an apology made to persons other than the defamed person, is made on a privileged occasion.[55] This is because a defamer is under a moral or social duty to set right any injury to the person's reputation which he may have caused by an earlier statement.[56] But if a validly-made apology is defamatory of someone else, and an action is brought in respect of the apology, the apologising party may be advised to plead justification, since if he pleads any other defence which involves accepting that the statement in the apology is untrue, then, he might be effectively retracting the apology, and leave himself open to be sued by the person he had apologised to. In *Willis v Irish Press* (1938), where an apology was unsuccessfully sued on, this possibility was not mentioned.

PERIODS OF LIMITATION

The law which determines the period of time within which actions of defamation must be brought is now contained in the Statute of

53 For cases on this defence, see p. 230 supra, and also *Barry v McGrath* (1868) IR 3 CL 576

54 On both these points, see p. 251 post; how effective a mitigating factor an apology may be is doubtful. Ideally a full and prompt apology ought to have at least a considerable impact, yet little account is taken of it in settlements. According to the NZ Committee Report para 368 only one-third is allowed. It does not seem as though any rule of thumb has emerged here. Litigants sometimes complain about the lack of a media apology. This might not however be due to bad grace, rather it may be due to a tactical desire not to hinder any defence by having previously apologised. Even where the media do apologise, there is a belief that it can actually encourage a litigant to persist; although it is also the case that many people consider their reputations adequately repaired by a media apology.

55 *Willis v Irish Press* (1938) 72 ILTR 238

56 At 240 per O'Byrne J

Limitations 1957. Libel and slander are treated differently. An action for libel must be commenced within six years from the date on which the cause of action accrued, that is to say, when the actionable publication was made.[57] An action for slander of any kind — whether actionable per se or only on proof of special damage — must be commenced within three years from the date on which the cause of action accrued.[58] In the case of slander actionable per se, the cause accrues when the words are spoken, and in the case of slanders actionable on proof of special damage, the cause accrues when the special damage occurs; which may be some time after the words are spoken.[59] If either of those limiting periods is not observed, then the action is statute barred, and may not be brought. This, however, is subject to certain exceptions, such as cases of disability, fraud, mistake, and some other instances. Longer period apply in these cases, but since these are general to most wrongs, they need not be considered here.[60]

Before 1957, the limitations periods, as set out in s 20 of the Common Law Procedure (Ireland) Act 1853, were six years in the case of libels and slanders actionable on proof of special damage, and two years in the case of slanders actionable per se. When the Statute of Limitations Bill was first introduced in the Dáil, in 1956, it was proposed that all slanders should be treated alike, and that the limitation period should be two years. The reasons given for this was the need for uniformity, and because 'It must be very seldom, indeed that slander actions are brought after two years. Further, a person's recollection of the exact words spoken in a particular instance is likely to be uncertain as time goes on'.[61] The period was later changed to three years in response to concern that two years might be too short in the case of slanders actionable of proof of special damage. The reason why a longer period was applied to libel is that 'what is written is permanent and there will be no doubt as to its exact content', and also because 'libel is a more serious tort generally

57 Statute of Limitations, s 11 (2) (a); it was suggested, in *Keaveny v Geraghty* [1965] IR 551, 559 per Lavery J, that tardiness in bringing an action even within the limitation period might be material in deciding whether the action is vexatious. But the majority in the Supreme Court do not seem to have agreed with this, and Ó Dálaigh CJ stated at 551 'while stale suite are bothersome they are not by reason only of delay necessarlly vexatious'.

58 Statute of Limitations, s 11 (2) (c)

59 The only case in which the issue of limitation periods was raised was a slander action — *Quinn v Wilson* (1850) 13 ILR 381

60 See McMahon & Binchy, 596 et seq

61 Dáil Debates vol 154 col 1166; whether this was a valid fear — in view of the fact that slanders actionable per se only become actionable once the damage has occurred or can be presumed — seems doubtful.

and, being often printed, can have a very wide circulation'.[62]

The reform bodies have recommended some new limitations periods. The Faulks Committee suggested three years for all defamations.[63] The New Zealand Committee recommended two years,[64] and the Australian Law Reform Commission recommended six months, or if a person was unaware of the publication at the time, then up to three years.[65] The Australian recommendation is so low because of the additional remedy of correction orders, which would only be effective if made promptly after the defamatory publication. The possibility of multiple actions resulting from the multiple publication of a defamation was the reason why the Faulks Committee suggested three years, although it had earlier recommended another measure to obviate this possibility — a ban on further actions without judicial consent.[66]

62 Dáil Debates, vol 160 col 1105 per Attorney General
63 Faulks Committee Report para 538
64 NZ Committee Report 129; this is the period in many Canadian jurisdictions, Williams 129
65 ALRC Report para 281
66 Faulks Committee Report para 291; see also p. 76 post

11

Remedies

The law recognises that a successful plaintiff is entitled to some damages.[1] This is the principal remedy for defamation and little has been done to wean the defamed away from it, although there are other remedies as well. After a verdict for the plaintiff, a court may award an injunction, either in addition to or instead of damages, in order to restrain any future publications of the defamatory statement. Even before the hearing, a court may award interlocutory injunctions to restrain any further publications until the hearing. Moreover, a plaintiff is free in an action, if he wishes, not to seek damages at all but to seek only a declaratory judgement against a defendant.[2] Reply and retraction are other defamation remedies but in Ireland these exist in an emasculated form, and are no more that conditions to be satisfied by a defamer should he wish to avail of statutory protections. There is no legal right to either. An apology is not a remedy. It is only an expression of regret for damage done, unless it contains an express or implied retraction of the charge.

DAMAGES

Damages can be either compensatory or punitive, nominal or contemptuous, general or special. Compensatory damages are awarded in respect of the actual injury caused to the reputation of a plaintiff and for any emotional distress, and also in respect of any further hurt which is caused to the feelings and dignity of the plaintiff. In this

1 *Campbell v Irish Press* (1955) 90 ILTR 105, 109 per Maguire CJ, and 115 per O'Daly J.

2 O 19 r 29, Rules of the Superior Courts; *Doyle v Griffin* [1937] IR 93 was a case where a 'shadowy' claim for libel damages was not made out, but declaratory relief against a warning-off was still obtained. All of the reform bodies — Faulks Committee Report para 378, NZ Committee Report paras 401-405, and ALRC Report para 274 — have recommended that this entitlement be given greater publicity by a specific reference in any defamation statute. For a consideration of the effect of a declaratory action on defamation law and on the relevance of the traditional defences in such a case, see Weiler 'Defamation, Enterprise and Freedom of Speech' (1967) U of Toronto LJ 278, 339 et seq.

latter guise, they are known as 'aggravated compensatory damages'. Punitive damages are awarded in an exceptional case where, because of a defendant's conduct, the judge and jury do not feel that compensation alone will signify their disapproval of that conduct, and so they may award an additional sum as a form of punishment. Whether damages of this type ought to be awarded in a civil action has been the subject of some debate.

Nominal damages are awarded 'where the plaintiff has a proper case but merely wants to vindicate his character'[3] and does not want 'to make money'.[4] They are usually awarded where the plaintiff has not requested compensatory damages, though they may also be awarded where he does not press his case. Contemptuous damages such as 'a farthing or some trivial sum' are awarded as 'a mark of contempt'[5] to indicate the judge or jury's disapproval of the action being brought, although the plaintiff may have been able to establish some damage to his reputation.

Compensatory damages can be divided into general or special, or presumed or actual damages. General damages in the law of defamation are the sum awarded in respect of the general injury to reputation, or good name, which is assumed by the law to follow from the publication of all libels and those slanders which are actionable in themselves.[6] Since this loss is assumed, it need not be proved, and in one case,[7] where a trial judge instructed a jury that the plaintiff had obtained a new job since the defamatory publication (which concerned his old one) was made, and that the plaintiff had not lost any money to that extent, it was held that the judge misdirected the jury because the plaintiff was entitled to compensation without reference to his other sources of income.[8] A plaintiff is also entitled, should he wish, to give evidence which will show the loss and damage which the law presumes for him. That is his choice, but since it is only showing what the law presumes, this evidence will not increase the amount of compensation.[9] In the US an award

3 *McDonagh v Tarpey* [1933] IR 666, 673 per Hanna J.

4 At 674; see Anon 'Costs in Actions for Libel' (1876) 10 ILT & SJ 103 mentioning an unusual case where although only nominal damages were awarded by a jury, the judge on the issue of costs found malice.

5 At 673; an example of contemptuous damages is *Keenan v Wallace* (1916) 51 ILTR 19, where the plaintiff was awarded one farthing; another example is Dawson v Mclelland [1899] 2 IR 486 where, on a second trial, the plaintiff and the defendant, in a successful counterclaim were awarded a farthing each.

6 There is another distinction which is made in pleading between general and special damage, but that is not of interest here.

7 *Campbell v Irish Press* (1955) 90 ILTR 105.

8 At 109 per Maguire CJ.

9 See Gatley para 1321.

of presumed damages against media defendants is now prohibited as a result of the Supreme Court holding that constitutional protection for the media requires that proof of actual harm be established unless the publication was a deliberate, or recklessly, made falsehood.[10] The purpose of this limitation was to prevent juries giving awards far in excess of what would be reasonable. The Second Restatement of Torts has suggested that this limitation should even apply in non media cases. The idea is by no means a radical one since actual harm is more broadly defined than special damage, and simply involves all the elements of presumed damage except that some proof must now be tendered. Where media interests are concerned, the limitation serves a useful protective function without unduly inconveniencing a deserving plaintiff. Whether a similar constitutional development might follow here is considered in Chapter 5.

Special damages are awarded for the loss known as special damage, which is what must be shown before all slanders — other than imputations of criminal wrongdoing, female unchastity, occupational discredit and possession of contagious illness — can be sued upon. As these types of slanderous imputation are only actionable because of the loss which is shown to have actually occurred, it might follow that the special damages awarded cannot include a sum for any future damage which might result from the same publication. It has been suggested that future actions could be taken for the same statement.[11] With libels and other slanders, compensation in an action is awarded for all foreseeable damage caused by the publication.

Before considering in greater detail compensatory and punitive damages, it is necessary to outline the duties of judge, jury and appellate court on the question of awarding damages. If a judge hears a defamation action while sitting alone, he will determine the amount of damages to be awarded. If the trial is by judge and jury, then the jury determines the amount of damages.[12] The size of an award to be made is, in cases of presumed damage, entirely discretionary, unlike the cases where special damages are claimed. Because of this, and because each defamation action is unique in its circumstances 'in truth, [other] cases are of little or no value in reference to the question of amount ..Each case must depend emphatically upon its own peculiar circumstances'.[13] For all this, the sum awarded must be in 'fair'[14]

10 *Gertz v Welch* (1974) 418 US 323; see Eldredge 537-9, Prosser 843.

11 See Gatley para 1460.

12 For an approving reference to this, see Reilly v Gill (1946) 85 ILTR 165, 178 per Black J.

13 *Harris v Arnott* (1889) 26 LR Ir 55, 67 per Palles CB.

14 *Harris v Arnott* at 70 per Lord Ashbourne.

or 'reasonable'[15] proportion to the particular case, or, what is the same thing, the sum must be such that twelve reasonable men would give.[16]

Where appropriate, help should be given to a jury as to how to assess compensatory damages. Henchy J suggested in *Barrett v Independent Newspapers* that the jury should, in some cases, be asked to reduce the allegation complained of to actuality, then to fit the allegation into its appropriate place in a scale of defamatory statements to which the plaintiff might have been subjected, and to measure damages accordingly.[17] This is a useful suggestion, although it could give rise to discussion about how comparative scales of abuse are to be set. It might not be appropriate where the charge made was the only one possible in the circumstances.

Where there is no proper proportion between what a jury awards and what could reasonably have been awarded, then an appeal will lie against the assessment of damages. An appellate court has power to examine and if necessary to overturn the verdict of a jury.[18] 'It cannot now be doubted that the Court has jurisdiction, even in an action of libel, to set aside a verdict for excessive damages'.[19] But an appellate court is 'cautious in meddling with verdicts,'[20] and should be slow to interfere,[21] and should require some abnormal circumstances before doing so,[22] particularly 'where there is clear evidence that the libel was published with actual malice... it requires an extremely strong case to upset a verdict'.[23] All of this is because of the 'large discretion'[24] enjoyed by the jury in assessing damages, although because the governing principles are the same as in other tort actions,[25] it does not seem an unusual discretion.

15 *Harris v Arnott* at 64 per Palles CB; *McCarthy v Maguire* [1899] 2 IR 802, 809 per O'Brien LCJ.
16 *Harris v Arnott* at 68 per Dowse B.
17 [1986] ILRM 601, 608.
18 *Edwards v Harding* (1787) Vern & Scriv 99, 103 per Power B; this was done in *Harris v Arnott* supra, and in *Higgins v Monaghan and O'Reilly* (1939) 74 ILTR 56, where the appeal judge increased the award from £2 to £40.
19 *Harris v Arnott* at 64 per Palles CB.
20 *Cosgrave v Trade Auxiliary* (1874) IR 8 CL 349, 358 per Whiteside CJ. 'The law reports abound with judicial tributes to the particular respect that must be accorded to the verdict of a jury in a libel action', *Barrett v Independent Newspapers* SCt, unreported, 12 March 1986 per McCarthy J at p 4 of his judgement; also Finlay CJ at p 9 of his judgement.
21 *Reilly v Gill* (1946) 85 ILTR 165, 173 per O'Byrne J.
22 At 178 per Black J; in *Kavanagh v The Leader* SCt, unreported, 4 March 1955, a jury verdict for a defendant was overturned because, inter alia, the presence of irrelevant questions on the order paper might have confused the jury.
23 *Kenny v Freeman's Journal* (1892) 27 ILTR 8, 9 per Palles CB.
24 *Dawson v McClelland* [1899] 2 IR 486, 500 per Holmes LJ.
25 See McMahon v Binchy *Irish Law of Torts* 565, et seq.

An appeal court will, however, interfere where the damages awarded are 'perverse'[26] or because 'the jury have been guilty of misconduct' or 'have made a gross blunder'[27] or have acted 'under some plain misapprehension'[28] or were 'misled into awarding the amount which they have found'.[29] More generally, the court will interfere where there is no reasonable proportion between the award and the facts, or where the award is 'unreasonably large'.[30] In deciding whether the damages are excessive, an appellate judge 'is not called on to say what sum, if I had been in the place in the jury, I should have given,' or to set aside the verdict simply because the amount found by the jury was greater than the court have found,[31] but rather to consider whether there was any basis in reason for the size of the award.[32]

Continuing use of juries

The continuing use of juries in assessing damages in defamation actions has been the subject of some debate[33] although not so much in Ireland, both because of the size of awards made[34] and costs incurred, and because of the great variations in the amounts awarded.[35] A number of reforms have been suggested, such as the

26 *Bell v Parke* (1860) 11 ICLR 413, 423 per Fitzgerald B.

27 *McCarthy v Maguire* [1899] 2 IR 802, 811 per Kenny J; *McDonagh v Tarpey* [1933] IR 666, 674 per Hanna J.

28 *Bell v Parke.*

29 *McCarthy v Maguire.*

30 *Bolton v O'Brien* (1885) 16 LR Ir 97, 131 per Johnson J.

31 *Reilly v Gill* at 173 per O'Byrne J; *McDonagh v Tarpey.*

32 The Supreme Court can substitute its own assessment of damages for that of a jury on a jury appeal should it wish to — *Holohan v Donahue* [1986] ILRM 250; see also *Higgins v Monaghan and O'Reilly*; the dissenting judgement of O'Daly J in *Campbell v Irish Press*; and *Broome v Cassell* (1972) AC 1027, 1087 per Lord Reid.

33 Eg See Hayes 'The Jury Verdict in Defamation: Commonsenses or Conniption' (1978) 11 U West Aust L Rev 140.

34 For some examples of high awards, see fn 90. The problem of high jury awards against media defendants is not a new one. In 1936 Hanna J stated extrajudically 'I agree in condemning the extravagance and unreasonableness of many of the verdicts in libel actions against newspapers' reported Anon 'Newspaper Libel' (1939) 73 ILT & SJ 68; as for remedying the situation 'My view is that all libel actions against newspapers should be tried by a judge. He would of course, give damages in a proper case, but within reasonable computation. Juries are sometimes erratic and unreliable and many of their decisions the result of compromise. No one can foretell what their decision will be.'.

35 Contrast *McDonnell v Preece,* The Irish Times, 21 November 1985 where a jury awarded £50,000 in an undefended action of a libel of a civil servant in a letter to his superior, and *Doyle v Irish Press,* The Irish Times, 6 December 1984 where

development of alternative remedies to damages,[36] the restriction of, or abolition of, presumed[37] and punitive damages, more explicit and comparative guidance on award sizes, the abolition of the jury,[38] and even the development of further, or easier, defences.[39].

Any consideration of the role of the jury in assessing damages cannot be done in isolation, but must be set in a wider context of the overall use of juries in defamation and tort law generally, and the type of remedies appropriate to a defamation claim. Three points may be made. Firstly, if all defamation jury rules enabled a jury to function without being subject to preliminary rulings by a trial judge then it might be an appropriate instrument by which the law could determine a community reaction to a statement, and what response was merited. But, the jury has only a limited role in many of the issues that arise,[40] and as the ability of the jury to justify the rationale for its existence is diminished, so also is the logical necessity for the jury role diminished. Secondly, many tort actions are not heard by juries. With the recent abolition of the jury in personal injury cases, the question arises whether the defamation action is so unique that the different treatment of various tort plaintiff's is constitutionally justified. One commentator has doubted that a distinction can be made.[41] There is only a limited validity in the community response argument, and so largely does the issue of damages loom in this as in other tort actions, and so much do issues of law intrude on the action that the case for exceptional treatment of a defamation might

£5,000 was awarded for the erroneous depiction in a national newspaper of the plaintiff as guilty of a huge fraud.

36 See p. 265 post.

37 See p. 241. Current restrictions on liability for presumed damages are ineffective. Appellate review is only useful if an appeal is taken, with its attendant risks and costs. Payment into court is not available under O 22 r 1(3) unless liability is admitted. There are mixed views on the appropriateness of another restriction on award sizes, that of applying modified personal injury general damages ceiling limits to presumed defamation damages; dismissive — Stephenson LJ in *Riches v News Group Newspapers* [1985] 2 AER 845, 858, approving — Owen JA in *Synder v Montreal Gazette* (1984) 5 DLR (4d) 206, 214.

38 None of the reform bodies recommended outright abolition. Neither the NZ Committee or the ALRC could reach a consensus on the matter, being equally divided betweem retention, and trial by judge only. The Faulks Committee suggested judicial control of the choice of jury trial, and where selected, that the jury's damages assessment role be limited to deciding between substantial, moderate, nominal or contemptuous. In Australia, where jury and non-jury systems operate in different states, the ALRC Report states at para 288 'It is impossible to demonstrate that one method of trial is more satisfactory than another'.

39 ALRC Report, para 252; Hayes supra 159.

40 See p. 40 supra.

41 Keeton, 'Defamation and the Freedom of the Press' (1976) 54 Tex L Rev 1221, 1226.

not be compelling. Thirdly, whether a jury ought to be used in defamation cases depends, obviously, on damages being the only remedy available. If damages are inappropriate, as a remedy in most cases perhaps to be replaced by an arrangement of retraction, reply or correction, as is suggested later, then the issue becomes whether there is any particular necessity for a jury to decide which is the most appropriate way of restoring a person's reputation; and if some of these remedies existed as pre-hearing legally enforceable entitlements the matter becomes whether an impermissible refusal was made. Neither task particularly requires a jury.

ASSESSMENT OF PRESUMED COMPENSATORY DAMAGES

'Damages are awarded by a jury principally in order to compensate the injury inflicted on the reputation of the Plaintiff — so far as such injury can be compensated by money'.[42] There can be a variety of factors involved in the computation or assessment of that compensation, such as the status of the plaintiff's reputation, the extent of the damage which is caused, and the existence of any aggravating or mitigating circumstances.[43]

THE PLAINTIFF'S REPUTATION

'The character, reputation, and position of a plaintiff ... must naturally constitute a material element for the consideration of a jury in estimating damages'.[44] Since the law presumes that everyone has a good reputation, and also that defamatory statements cause loss to that reputation, it might not in theory be necessary for a plaintiff to give evidence of that reputation when damages are being assessed. However, there may be a number of reasons why it can be incumbent on a plaintiff to produce evidence of his reputation. The damages awarded are more likely to be small than large if the jury does not appreciate the true position of a person in the community. A plaintiff might have given evidence in the course of the hearing, and it may be prudent to obviate the effects on the jury of any doubts that were cast on his credibility as a witness by the defence during cross-examination. Strictly speaking the credibility of a witness is not related

42 *Bolton v O'Brien* (1885) 16 LR Ir 97, 110 per May CJ; see also Heuston 'Recent Developments in Defamation' (1966) IJ NS 245.

43 See Griffin J in *Barrett v Independent Newspapers* [1986] ILRM 601 at 614.

44 May CJ supra.

to his reputation. 'It is however very easy for a jury, unless carefully and explicitly directed ... to regard a successful cross examination as to credit in the same light as if it was a successful attack on the general character of the plaintiff'.[45] Finally, it is open to a defendant, on the assessment of damages, to produce evidence showing that a plaintiff has a bad reputation, or at least not the one which he implicitly claims, in relation to the imputation in question. But a defendant will not be allowed tender in chief such evidence of the plaintiff's character, without the judge's consent, unless he has provided particulars of the evidence to the plaintiff at least seven days before the trial.[46]

Where a defamed person is reluctant to initiate an action because he has a bad reputation and fears that this will come out as evidence on the amount of damages — even if he could avoid testifying himself — his reluctance might, on one view, be misplaced. In two interesting cases in the US, one plaintiff successfully claimed compensation only for mental anguish resulting from a libel, and the other plaintiff successfully claimed only for punitive damages.[47] Since neither claim involved any reference to the size of the plaintiff's reputation evidence of that reputation was inadmissible. Similar reasoning could possibly allow a plaintiff who can prove specific loss to claim only for that loss, and thereby render evidence of his reputation inadmissible. Although this reasoning appears to stand up — since there is nothing exceptional about allowing a plaintiff choose which particular head of damage he will claim for, in the defamation context, it appears to be illogical because it allows a plaintiff to move away from the logic of his right to compensation. This right is based on the law's generous presumption of defamatory effect from a statement's tendency to defame. It should follow from this that some relied-on head of claim be related to that right.

Where a plaintiff's reputation is in issue on the quantum of damages, it is for the trial judge to decide whether the evidence tendered is capable of constituting evidence of reputation, and it is for the jury to decide whether it does so. There are, in theory, three types of evidence by which a person's reputation can be proved. Firstly, there can be evidence of his general reputation in relation to the conduct in question. It is established that evidence of this general type — whether produced by the plaintiff or the defendant — is admissible as proof of reputation because, obviously, of its great logical relevance

45 *Kavanagh v The Leader* SCt, unreported, 4 March 1955, per Kingsmill Moore at 2 of his judgement.

46 O 36 r 35, Rules of the Superior Courts.

47 *Time v Firestone* (1976) 424 US 448; *Rogers v Doubleday* (1982) Tex Civ App 644, mentioned in Prosser 847.

to the issue.[48] Secondly, a defendant might wish to tender evidence of specific acts of misconduct by the plaintiff so as to show a poor or bad reputation. In *Scott v Sampson,*[49] an English case decided in 1892 on the basis of previous authority the rule was stated that evidence of this type is not admissible to prove a plaintiff's reputation, because it is only evidence of disposition which 'At its most it tends to prove not that the plaintiff has not, but that he ought not to have, a good reputation'.[50] It was also reasoned that, if such evidence was admitted, a plaintiff would have to show a uniform propriety of conduct during his whole life, and that this would be too onerous a task. However, this was something of an overstatement. It would only be a plaintiff's conduct in relation to the particular charge that would be in issue and, anyway, an unsympathetic disclosure of a plaintiff's past misdeeds could rebound on a defendant in an increased damages award against him. Moreover, the logic relied on to support this exclusionary rule of evidence is doubtful. It suggests, rightly, that a court is concerned only with the reputation a person has, as opposed to what some think he ought to have. But, the rule can actually have the opposite effect, because by preventing the admission of clearly material evidence, and allowing a plaintiff establish by his friends his opinion of his reputation, it increases the likelihood that the reputation established will be the one the plaintiff ought to have, instead of his real one. Further, in the fact that a judge decides that all evidence of specific incidents, by its nature, is only disposition and not reputation, he is usurping the jury's role, whose function is to decide what the reputation is, and so the damages to be awarded.[51]

Scott's case was approved of by Kingsmill-Moore J in 1955, and

48 For a review of the authorities, see Cave J 498 post.

49 (1882) 8 QBD 491. Also, *Hobbs v Tinling* [1929] 2 KB 1; *Plato Films v Speidel* [1961] AC 1090; American authority supports this view — Eldredge 569-71, Prosser 847.

50 *Scott v Sampson* at 505 per Cave J; disposition refers to that which is observed in a person, and which explains individual acts of behaviour, but which is not of sufficient standing or frequency to have become part of his reputation. It can be reputation in embryo. Evidence of reputation can sometimes be relevant where justification is pleaded on the issue of liability.

51 The existence of this rule also involves the law in asserting, paradoxically, that single incident disposition evidence cannot show good reputation, but that single incident evidence can damage good reputation. The rejection of this exclusionary rule would end the tactical struggle between the parties — which worried the Porter Committee para 151 of its Report — in which a defendant would attempt to manoeuvre a plaintiff into the witness box so as to give in cross examination as to credit specific incident evidence which would not be given in chief by the defendant as reputation evidence. Hence the warning by Kingsmill-Moore J at 218. In favour of the rule is the general policy of defamation law of rejecting the views of the suspicious and unreasonable.

it is referred to by the text writers. But, it might not always have been applied here. For in one case, at any rate *Bolton v O'Brien* (1885),[52] where the defamatory statement alleged certain unnatural felonies, and the plaintiff had given evidence himself, the defendant was permitted to establish in cross-examination as to credit and with a view to damaging the plaintiff's character and 'reducing the amount of damages', certain evidence of specific incidents such as that twelve years previously and while married, the plaintiff had had an affair with a maid-servant, and also that on the occasion of his marriage to a wealthy lady, he had as a solicitor, executed the marriage settlement which was very favourable to himself, but which was subsequently set aside for that reason.

The third type of evidence by which a person's reputation might be attempted to be established is by evidence of rumours of misconduct. In Scott's case, it was also decided that this type of evidence was inadmissible because, if admitted, it might too easily facilitate those who have grudges against a plaintiff, and because such evidence might come from disreputable sources.[53] The Irish practice appears to have accorded with this. In *Bell v Parke* (1860),[54] the court refused to allow the defendant to adduce, as evidence of general reputation of the act imputed, rumours that the plaintiff had committed the imputed offence. Pigot CJ dissented strongly from this,[55] on the ground that such evidence is clearly highly relevant to the question of reputation, and because its omission would enable reputed wrongdoers to be treated the same as honourable people. He asked: 'Is it just or reasonable that a man so covered with the reputation of ... an atrocious crime should be entitled to as large a measure of damages, for being called a murderer, as a person of unblemished fame, upon whose character the breath of slander has never been blown?'[56] It is also a consequence of the exclusion of evidence of rumours that a defendant is denied the opportunity of having the jury's opinion as to whether his evidence actually constitutes evidence of reputation or not.

Exceptionally, evidence of specific misconduct may be admissible if it is such that it can actually constitute a person's reputation —

52 (1885) 16 LR Ir 97; see also *Goody v Odhams Press* [1967] 1 QB 333.
53 At 504 per Cave J.
54 (1860) 11 ICLR 413.
55 At 423 et seq.
56 At 425. In the US while Prosser 847 states that such evidence is not usually admissible, Eldredge 567-9 states that the case law is in sharp conflict, and he advocates the exclusion of rumour and gossip evidence. Some of the American cases, also according to Eldredge, have sought to find a middle ground, and admit evidence of general rumour, report or community belief, but exclude mere rumour or gossip.

'If these rumours and suspicions have, in fact, affected the plaintiff's reputation, that may be proved by general evidence of reputation'.[57] But this seems only to twist further some already knotted reasoning, because if both evidence of specific misconduct and rumours, when tendered as evidence of reputation, are inadmissible following the rule in Scott's case, how can a defendant ever establish a reputation by this evidence? In other words, if courts in the first instance refuse to consider rumour, how can they ever know that there is enough of it to make up reputation?

In 1948, the Porter Committee[58] criticised the exclusion of evidence of rumour and specific misconduct, and recommended that such evidence should be admissible. This was not acted on, however, because pressure of time on the day the English Defamation Bill was being given its third reading.[59] It is all the more extraordinary, then, that the recommendation was never even included in the Defamation Bill here. The Faulks Committee,[60] more recently has also recommended that such evidence should be admissible.

EXTENT OF ACTUAL DAMAGE

Once the status or content of a plaintiff's reputation has been established, the next matter to be considered is the extent to which the reputation has been damaged. The jury determines this from any relevant circumstances attaching to the publication, such as the extent of the publication and whether it was published 'in the most prominent and public manner',[61] and to whom it was published, as where a libel was published of a Catholic doctor in order to injure his practice among Catholics,[62] or where the statement would only cause damage in the eyes of those who did not know the plaintiff because 'those readers to whom the named meant anything regarded the notice from the beginning as a hoax'.[63] The jury may also consider the seriousness of the misbehaviour imputed to the plaintiff, as where the defendant had 'branded him with a crime so abhorrent and so loathsome ... that if committed, it would ..."force his sturdiest official friends to shrink from the wretch in public as from a leper"'.[64]

57 *Scott v Sampson* at 504 per Cave J.
58 Para 156.
59 Faulks Committee Report para 368.
60 Para 372; so too NZ Committee Report para 394 concerning specific incident evidence.
61 *Bolton v O'Brien* (1885) 16 LR Ir 97, 112 per May CJ.
62 *Kenny v Freeman's Journal* (1892) 27 ILTR 8.
63 *Bell v Northern Constitution* [1943] NI 108, 117 per Andews LCJ.
64 *Bolton v O'Brien* at 131 per Johnson J.

Aggravating circumstances

Besides being compensated for the extent of the damage to his reputation, a plaintiff is also entitled to aggravated compensatory damages for any hurt to his feelings and dignity caused by any particularly distressful conduct on the part of the defendant. Such conduct includes where 'a charge of forgery is made against a professional man, maliciously ... without a shadow of foundation...',[65] or where one of the defendants offered a considerable sum to settle the case 'accompanied by the threat that if it was not accepted, he would produce evidence either of justification, or to depreciate the plaintiff's character... especially when he did not present himself as a witness',[66] or where the defendant 'aggravated the offence by publishing other felonious charges of the grossest description' at the time of withdrawing the defamatory statement,[67] or where an apology is not a full one.[68] In the case of newspapers, an apology drafted by the defendant's solicitors in short and technical terms might also cause aggravated damages to be awarded.[69]

The manner in which a defendant behaves before proceedings are instituted, or makes his defence can be an aggravating circumstance, like where he 'put a justification on the records of the Court, and persisted, to the last stage of the trial, in insisting that he had made it good' although the defence failed,[70] or where the defence of fair comment is pleaded but fails,[71] or where 'the defendants, however, have attempted to attack her character in this case'.[72]

Mitigating circumstances

A defendant is entitled to produce in evidence matter which shows that the actual damage caused to the plaintiff's reputation by his publication was not as great as it might have been, and also matter, which while not showing that he had not done wrong, shows that he was not as culpable as he might otherwise have been. He may,

65 *McCarthy v Maguire* [1899] 2 IR 802, 809 per O'Brien LCJ.
66 *Tait v Beggs* [1905] 2 IR 525, 534 per Fitzgibbon LJ.
67 *Bolton v O'Brien* at 112 per May CJ.
68 *Harris v Arnott* (1889) 26 LR Ir 55, 66 per Palles CB.
69 *Harris v Arnott* at 74 per O'Brien LCJ and 77 per Barry LJ: in many instances apologies carried in newspapers are drafted by the lawyers of the defamed parties.
70 *Bell v Parke* (1860) 11 ICLR 413, 423 per Fitzgerald B; see also Johnson J at 131 in Bolton's case.
71 *Campbell v Irish Press* (1955) 90 ILTR 105, 112 per Kingsmill-Moore J.
72 *Higgins v Monaghan and O'Reilly* (1940) 74 ILTR 56, 57 per Johnston J.

for instance, present evidence to show that the plaintiff does not have a good reputation. This has already been considered. For other evidence in mitigation, the general principle was stated by Barry LJ in 1890.

> It is quite settled that, whilst, of course, the plaintiff is entitled to reasonable compensation for the injury he has sustained, the defendant .. may show in mitigation of damages that the injury was unintentional, or was committed under a sense of duty, or through some honest mistake, or that the defendant acted in good faith, and with honesty of purpose, and not maliciously.[73].

In one case,[74] a mitigating circumstance was the fact that the defendant had reported, at the earliest possible time a denial by the plaintiff of the charge against him. But, such a view may be generous to a defendant since a report of a denial is not a retraction or apology, and without a retraction hardly deserves to reduce damages by much. Where a person fails to take up an offer of reply in a newspaper he might seem to be doing less that he should to reduce his losses, but the beneficial effect of this failure on the amount of damages should still be small both because the paper may have attached conditions to the offer, and because the reply will not involve any retraction by the newspaper. In another case,[75] a defendant was able to show that in his report, which was defamatory of the plaintiff, he had not used many 'very strong and severe expressions' which were made about the plaintiff at the reported meeting. A defendant may show that he acted in response to a libel which the plaintiff had published about him and which provoked him.[76] Retracting a charge, or publishing a requested correction is, to a lesser extent, a mitigating circumstance. The making of an apology is also a mitigating circumstance. 'Readiness to apologise is generally relied on as a mitigating circumstance in actions for defamation'.[77] Both of these circumstances are now provided for in s 17 of the Defamation Act 1961, which re-enacted s 1 of the Libel Act 1843, and provides that an apology made or offered to the plaintiff either before the action or as soon afterwards as possible, is admissible in evidence in mitigation of damage, provided the defendant gives notice in writing

73 *Harris v Arnott* at 76; mitigation evidence in some American cases — Eldredge 563, 574 — is limited to actual damage to reputation and, unlike the Irish cases, excludes evidence of the defendant's state of mind.

74 *Harris v Arnott*.

75 *Creighton v Finlay* (1842) Arm Mac & Og 385.

76 *Dawson v McClelland* [1899] 2 IR 486.

77 *Tait v Beggs* [1905] 2 IR 525, 539 per Holmes CJ; another possible ground of mitigation might be a defamer's drunkeness — Eldredge 576.

of his intention to do this when filing or delivering his plea in the action. The conduct and attitude of the plaintiff can also have a bearing on damages, as where he wrote a moderate letter of protest to the paper hoping it would publish his letter, and did not even ask for an apology.[78] Another ground of mitigation unrelated to any act of the defendant is provided for in s 26 of the 1961 Act. This allows a defendant to show that the plaintiff had recovered, received, or agreed to receive compensation for other publications of words to the same effect, or has brought actions for them. Whether this provision requires a jury to firstly decide on a total figure for the damage caused by the publication, and then make a deduction, or credit allowance, for the other amounts, or whether the jury should simply determine a figure on the basis of all the relevant evidence, is uncertain. American authority suggests the latter because the jury in the present case cannot be aware of the many unmitigating and unknown factors which influenced the other sums.[79].

The admissability of certain mitigation evidence is, by O 36 r 35 of the Rules of Superior Courts,made conditional on a minimum of seven days pre-trial notice to the plaintiff of the details of evidence to be adduced in mitigation. That evidence relates to the circumstances of publication or the character of the plaintiff. The failure to observe the condition can, however, be dispensed with by the judge, and, in any case, the rule does not apply where the defence of the justification is asserted by the defendant.

PUNITIVE DAMAGES

Punitive damages are awarded against a defendant in an action where the judge or jury consider that the award of compensatory damages does not also mark their sense of outrage at the behaviour of the defendant. Effectively, these damages are awarded as a punishment. Punitive damages have a special relevance to defamation law on account of a perceived willingness by Irish juries to mark emphatically their disapproval of media transgressions, in particular, and also because the focus on malice in some defamation cases can be a positive encouragement to a jury to act punitively.

The propriety of punitive damages has become, in recent decades, a matter of controversy both in defamation and in tort generally. Their existence has been criticised for a variety of reasons, such as the large number of occasions in which they are awarded, the imcompatibiity of

78 *Barrett v Independent Newspapers* per Griffin J at 614.
79 *Goodrow v New York Times* (1934) 241 App Div 190.

punitive damages with compensatory proceedings, the absence of fixed limits on the amounts which can be awarded, the excessive threats which such awards pose to the self-confidence, even viability, of media activities, the absence of criminal trial procedural and evidential safeguards in the making of awards, the fact that juries and not judges, make the awards, and the irrelevance of the punitive award to a plaintiff's presumed or actual loss. In opposition to all this is the simple feeling, enlivened by long experience, that a punitive element in civil proceedings is appropriate in order to express a juries disgust at a defamer's behaviour by hitting his pocket. This desire for vengeance finds expression in money terms, rather than some other form, because of the traditional common law emphasis on damages.

The continued propriety of punitive awards in Ireland would hardly be in issue were it not for developments in England in recent times, where the movement against the existence and extent of the power to make such awards has been strongest.[80] In England, the House of Lords has limited the occasions on which punitive damages can be awarded to three situations — where there was oppressive, arbitrary or unconstitutional action by government servants, where a defendant actually calculated to make a profit in excess of any compensation he might have to pay, and where an act of parliament expressly authorised punitive damages.[81] These categories were not logically based and were only a compromise forced on a court which, it seems, would have liked to abolish punitive damages in tort law altogether, but which considered that the precedents supporting the power to award in some cases was so strong that only the legislature could abolish it.[82] The House of Lords, lacking the constitutional power to invalidate the precedents possessed by the Supreme Court here, was obliged to retain these exceptions; accordingly there can hardly be any self-evident merit in these categories which would recommend itself to courts functioning under the Irish Constitution. Courts in Australia[83] and New Zealand[84] have explicitly refused to adopt these restrictions, Canada probably likewise.[85] Such courts prefer a power of wide ranging application for appropriate cases. The restrictions have, however, been accepted in Jamaica.[86] American developments

80 *Rookes v Barnard* [1964] AC 1129; *Broome v Cassell* [1972] AC 1027; the Faulks Committee Report para 360, and the ALRC Report para 263 both favoured abolition of the power in defamation actions, but the NZ Committee Report, paras 387-391 favoured retention of the power, but to be exercised only by a judge.

81 *Rookes v Barnard.*

82 *Broome v Cassell* at 1086 et seq per Lord Reid.

83 *Australian Consolidated Press v Uren* (1966) 117 CLR 185.

84 *Taylor v Beere* [1982] 1 NZLR 81.

85 Williams 141.

86 *Ying v Richards* (1972) 12 JLR 754.

are of particular relevance given the constitutional basis of defamation law there. The US Supreme Court has held in a number of cases that not only are punitive damages lawful in defamation cases, but also that such awards are not incompatible with the media constitutional rights. Considerations of the proper protection of reputation, and judicial control of jury awards were central to these decisions.[87].

The validity of punitive awards here will ultimately depend, as it has done in the US, on the provisions of the Constitution. No clear guidance is to be found in either the text of the Constitution or in case law. The most explicit reference would seem to be contained in Article 40, in which the state is placed under a duty to defend and 'vindicate' personal rights. Unless it is a tautology, vindicate must mean more than defend, and with abundant authority for the use of vindictive damages to describe punitive damages,[88] there could be a positive across-the-board duty to award punitive damages in deserving cases. But, the neatness of this conclusion urges caution. The Irish translation of vindicate — 'a shuíomh' might not support this view, and there is, in addition, the established use of vindictive to refer merely to the defeat of a wrong and the assertion of a right — thus, Hanna J in 1943, when he stated that nominal damages were awarded 'where the plaintiff has a proper case but merely wants to vindicate his character'.[89]

The existence of the criminal law of libel may also have a bearing on the constitutionality of punitive damages in certain defamation actions. A criminal prosecution for libel can be initiated by private as well as public prosecutors in respect of quite a wide range of libellous publications, although restrictions exist concerning proceedings against newspapers. If the law of criminal libel exists to further society's interest in suppressing defamatory publications, then is it constitutional for exactly the same purpose to be served by punitive awards in some civil actions, either with or without the stricter standards required by the criminal law? The state's obligation to safeguard society's interest in reputation through punishment could be satisfied by a single proceeding, which might well be the more appropriate criminal proceeding. It is true that the availability of criminal proceedings is restricted by s 8 of the Defamation Act which

87 See Motlow 'The Constitutionality of Punitive Damages' (1979) 10 Cumb LR 487; Eldredge 541-2, Prosser 845.

88 *McCarthy v Maguire* (1899) 2 IR 802, 807 per O'Brien LCJ; *Uren v John Fairfax* (1966) 117 CLR 118, 158 per Owen J; *Australian Consolidated Press v Uren* (1966) 117 CLR 185, 233 per Lord Reid; *Broome v Cassell* at 1073 per Lord Hailsham; see also McGregor *On Damages* para 309; Kelly 'The Inner Nature of the Tort Action' (1967) 2 IJ NS 279.

89 *McDonagh v Tarpey* [1933] IR 666, 673.

requires judicial permission before criminal proceedings against newspapers can be initiated. But this may perhaps be explained by reference to constitutional protection given to the print media, although if this is so, then the absence of similar obstacles to proceedings against the broadcast media, or to jury awards of punitive damages, may possibly be unconstitutional.

On balance, it is more likely than not that the power to award punitive damages in defamation actions is not unconstitutional. The predominant international trend favours the power to award such damages. The practise here to date has been to make such awards where necessary.[90] And in the US it has been accepted that constitutional media and non-media protection does not preclude such damages. But though in general the use of the power might not be unconstitutional, its exercise in certain circumstances might be, as where there is an inadequate or even non-existent judicial instruction to a jury on such damages, and possibly where no segregation is made of the punitive element in the sum awarded so to enable identification of the amount awarded.[91]

It remains now to consider the grounds on which punitive damages may be awarded, and the type of judicial instruction that should be given in appropriate cases. The US Supreme Court has considerably narrowed down the range of such occasions to where a defendant actually knew the statement was untrue or was recklessly indifferent to its truth.[92] In Australia, a much wider test operates where 'the defendant has been high-handed, insolent, vindictive or malicious or had in some other way exhibited a contumelious disregard of the

90 There may have been a suspicion of a punitive element in the following jury awards: *Doyle v The Economist* [1980] NI 171 — £50,000; *Egan v BBC*, The Irish Times, 12 December 1980 — £50,000; *Barrett v Independent Newspapers*, The Irish Times, 18 April 1985 (retrial ordered on all issues [1986] ILRM 601) — £65,000; *McDonnell v Preece*, The Irish Times, 21 November 1985 — £50,000; *Keating v Sunday Tribune*, The Irish Times, 17 December 1985 — £65,000. Settlements for lesser sums were later agreed in some of these cases. See also such earlier cases as *Edwards v Harding* (1789) Vern & Scriv 99 — £250, and *Bolton v O'Brien* (1885) 16 LR Ir 97 — £3,000. Whether some juries in making high awards assume that a media defendant is covered by an insurance policy is not known. In fact much of the print media does not have libel cover for a variety of reasons, such as prohibitive premia, insurer unwillingness to cover more than a percentage of an award, say a quarter, media disquiet over settlements they disagreed with, and conversely insurer suspicion that liability cover may encourage journalists not to be cautious.

91 Although non segregation of punitive awards is favoured in England, it is difficult to see how that might be valid here if it is the case that it is the effectiveness of judicial control of jury awards that ensures their constitutionality, as it is in the US.

92 *Gertz v Welch* (1974) 418 US 323; for an argument that this might not be narrow enough, see Note 'Punitive Damages for Libel' (1985) 98 Harv LR 847.

plaintiff's rights'.[93] This is broad enough to include all three of the English categories and also many of the circumstances usually thought to give rise only to aggravated damages, as redefined in *Rookes v Barnard.* It is a test which seems preferable to the American test which might be unduly narrow. One particular ground, therefore, on which punitive damages may be awarded, and one of special relevance to the media, arises where a defendant calculated to make from his publication a profit in excess of any compensation he might have to pay for a libel. Since the media always publish for profit, and could thus be invariably exposed to punitive awards, the courts require some further element of blameworthiness before a proper award can be made.[94] Whether any satisfactory statement of this element — which would not in effect confer a near total immunity against punitive damages -can be found remains to be seen.[95]

The burden of proof in establishing a case for punitive damages rests with the plaintiff. He must show to the trial judge that there is evidence on which the jury could be satisfied on the balance of probabilities that the defendant possessed the necessary degree of fault. He must then satisfy the jury that this was the case. The trial judge in instructing the jury should emphasise that such awards are rare, and if made are to be reasonable, but that account can be taken of the defendants resources and of the width of publicity given the statement. Of essential importance is an instruction by the trial judge that punitive damages can only be awarded if a *supposed punitive dimension* to compensatory damages is not sufficient to punish the defendant, and that matters of aggravation are to be clearly disregarded on this question since they are covered under compensatory damages.[96].

93 *Uren v John Fairfax* at 129 per Taylor J; a similar test was favoured by the NZ Committee Report — 'flagrant and contumelious disregard of the plaintiff's rights'.

94 *Manson v Associated Newspapers* [1965] 2 AER 954; *Riches v News Group Newspapers* [1985] 2 AER 845.

95 In Riches case Parker LJ, at 862, had doubts about whether a valid differentiation could be made, and thought that henceforth only in the rarest cases might a paper be exposed to punitive damages. Heuston 'Damages in Libel' (1965) 1 DULJ 23 thought that this element 'imposed a very heavy burden of proof' on a plaintiff.

96 *Riches v News Group Newspaper*. An additional issue in this case concerned the awarding of punitive damages where there is more than one plaintiff. Whether a punitive dimension to compensatory damages arises only where there are aggravating circumstances, or where there are none is not clear. In either case, the selective perception of compensatory damages as possessing a punitive dimension in this circumstance, but not others, may weaken the usual view that defamation damages are compensatory.

An injunction is an order of a court, which may be granted at the court's discretion before, during or after the hearing in a defamation action, and which restrains a defendant from either publishing, continuing to publish or re-publishing a defamatory statement either for a period of time or indefinitely.[97] The granting of injunctions in defamation proceedings before the trial is a serious matter, because it involves the denial of the individual's and the media's liberty of expression. In fact the jurisdiction to grant injunctions in defamation actions is of relatively recent origin.

Prior to the Common Law Procedure Amendment Act (Ireland) 1856, injunctions were not granted in defamation actions. Courts of law did not grant them because this was a remedy which they were not competent to grant. Courts of equity did not grant them, because a libel was regarded as a crime and thus beyond its jurisdiction. Since Fox's Libel Act 1792 and its Irish equivalent of 1793 injunctions were also not granted because, juries were regarded as the arbiters of defamatory meaning and it was desired not to usurp their function by granting an injunction; also, more generally, because defamation was an action properly belonging to a Court of law.[98] The 1856 Act granted the power to issue injunctions to the common law courts in various cases, which seemed to include defamation actions, although the power does not seem to have been much used. The first reported case was an English one in 1878.[99] The 1856 Act did not affect courts of equity — despite various attempts to establish an equity jurisdiction based on viewing a defamatory publication as tending to the destruction of property, including character[1] — the predominant view remained.[2] Thus, Chatterton VC was able to state, in 1876, that 'it is settled law of the Court of Chancery .. that it has no jurisdiction to grant an injunction to restrain a publication merely because it is a libel'.[3] This view was, however, changed by the enactment of the Judicature (Ireland) Act 1877[4] which conferred on the High Court the power to grant injunctions in all cases where

97 See generally, Pound 'Equitable Relief against Defamation and Injuries to Personality' (1915) 29 Harv L Rev 640; Hayes, 'Injunctions before Judgement in Defamation Cases' (1971) 95 Aust LJ 125; Martin 'Interlocutory Injunctions in Libel Actions' (1982) 20 U of W Ont L Rev 129.

98 For a review of the reasons and authorities, see *Dunlop v Dunlop Rubber* [1920] 1 IR 280, 293 et seq per Powell J.

99 *Saxby v Easterbrook* (1878) 3 CPD 339.

1 *Springhead Spinning v Riley* (1868) LR 6 Eq 551; *Dixon v Holden* (1869) LR 7 Eq 488.

2 Eg *Prudential Assurance v Knot* (1878) LR 10 Ch 142.

3 *Hammersmith Skating v Dublin Skating* (1876) IR 10 Eq 235, 237.

4 S 28.

it appeared just and convenient to do so, and on such terms as the court thought fit. Thus, in *Punch v Boyd* (1885),[5] May CJ in the Court of Queen's Bench granted an interlocutory injunction, on the basis of the 1856 and 1877 Acts, to restrain the publication of certain libels until the trial, even before delivery of the statement of claim. And, in another case in 1892, the same court acknowledged that while it had the power to grant interlocutory injunctions pending a trial, that power did not apply to statements not complained of in the writ of summons.[6] At present, 0.50 r.6 of the Rules of the Superior Courts authorises the grant of interlocutory injunctions.[7].

Injunctions can be classified either by their nature or by their length of application. According to the first classification, an injunction may be a *quia timet* injunction, a prohibitory injunction or a mandatory injunction. The former type is issued in respect of a defamatory statement which is not yet, but is about to be, published and is calculated to injure a person's reputation. A prohibitory injunction is most appropriate to the defamation action since it can restrain future wrongful publications, whereas a mandatory injunction compels the doing of an act so as to remedy a wrongful state of affairs. When classified according to their length of application, there are also three types of injunction. A perpetual injunction, which may be granted after the trial, will last indefinitely. An interlocutory injunction, which is granted before the hearing, lasts until the determination of proceedings. It is granted on notice to the defendant. The third type of injunction is known as an *interim* injunction, although it is also a type of interlocutory order. It is granted *ex-parte* for a short period until the hearing on notice of the motion for an interlocutory injunction. Both types of interlocutory order are heard on affidavit.

Interim injunctions

'There is jurisdiction to grant an injunction in a libel action *ex parte* where a writ is issued'[8] But an interim injunction ought not to be lightly granted, and if it is wrongly granted, it will be dissolved on appeal.[9] The principles on which a court relies when deciding on

5 (1885) 16 LR Ir 476.

6 *Smith v McHugh* (1892) 27 ILT & SJ 388.

7 A separate jurisdiction to grant injunctions to restrain defamations of parliamentary candidates exists under s 11 of the Prevention of Electoral Abuses Act 1923; this was applied in *Cullen v Stanley* [1926] IR 73.

8 *Fitzgerald v Clancy* [1902] 2 IR 207, 217, per Walker LJ; see also O 52 r 2,3 of the Rules of the Superior Courts; such an order was made in *Gallagher v Touhy* (1924) 58 ILTR 134, and in *Scott v Eason & Son,* The Irish Times, 9 August 1980.

9 As happened in *Fitzgerald v Clancy.*

applications that are made *ex parte,* that is without notice to the other side, are similar to those that govern applications on notice, which are outlined below, with the additional considerations that the interim order will last only a matter of days,and the plaintiff should show reason why the application is made *ex-parte* and not on notice.[10] It does not appear that a plaintiff has an absolute right to insist on an *ex-parte* application. One reason for such an application would be that to proceed by notice would or might entail irreparable or serious mischief to a complainant. Where, in a media case, a person hears only late in the day of a proposed publication, then whether an emergency *ex-parte* application is the appropriate proceeding must depend on the circumstances and on the medium in question. Such a proceeding might be more appropriate with the broadcast media than with the print media. But, in any case, where there is sufficient time for a hearing, a court should be slow to proceed *ex parte* because of the greater difficulty facing the applicant, of convincing the judge of the likelihood that no defence can be made, when the judge has no idea what the defendant's view is.[11] Paradoxically it may actually be easier to succeed in *ex parte* proceedings because rules of evidence may be more laxly applied, and because judges may interpret wrongly the defendant's absence to the plaintiff's advantage rather than his disadvantage.[12] A court should be even slower to prohibit any public reference to the application, or even that it had taken place.[13]

10 In a recent case *ACC v Bedstone* HCt, 1 August 1985 — described The Irish Times, 5 August 1985 and Magill, September 1985 — a plaintiff was allowed successfully to proceed ex-parte even though the defendant news magazine knew beforehand about the application, and the editor and his lawyers were permitted attend the hearing, but were not allowed participate in it. Such a situation is hardly satisfactory, though it is not unknown. The necessity for the court to have proceeded ex-parte was surely reduced by the presence of the person in whose power it lay to stop publication, and if it was a case that procedure rules did not allow the hearing to be treated as on notice because formalities had not been observed, that is surely a reason for allowing greater flexibility in the implementation of the rules.

11 According to Martin 134 'The basic problem with issuing such injunctions ex parte is that they make much of the law on the subject meaningless. The rule is that if the respondent avers that he plans at trial to attempt to make out one of the recognised defences there will be no injunction. But if the respondent is not present at the time application is made, how is the judge to make a finding on the question?'.

12 Hayes 137; Martin suspects that another reason is that judges might not be aware of the special circumstances and rules governing interlocutory injunctions in defamation cases.

13 Such an order was made in *ACC v Bedstone*, but in the end did not prevent the news from coming out. In any event the order could be rendered ineffective at the interlocutory stage, see Note 'And Be Damned' (September 1985) Incorp Law Soc Gazette.

In 1902, Fitzgibbon LJ stated that 'under the Judicature Act, the power to grant injunctions ... exists, but its exercise is very strictly limited'.[14] Indeed so much so, that the grounds on which injunctions are issued in defamation actions are narrower than in the case of other tort actions in Ireland. For, apart from questions relating to adequacy of damages and balance of convenience, the general test appears to require a plaintiff to establish merely that a fair or serious question exists[15] but the test in defamation requires a plaintiff to establish that it is very unlikely that the defendant will succeed in the action. To quote Fitzgibbon LJ again; 'I believe that we all agree that an injunction to restrain a publication merely because it is defamatory or injurious is unknown. The publication must be proved to be also false and malicious and if it be a question reasonably open for trial whether the alleged libel, although defamatory, is true or privileged, or is "no libel", the granting of an injunction would be wrong in principle'.[16] Of course, it need only be *prima facie* proof of its falsity'[17] because as O'Connor J stated in 1926, the court acts 'on the evidence before it at the time the injunction is applied for. No doubt, at the trial further evidence may be given, and on that further evidence the verdict may rightly differ from the view entertained by the Court on the hearing of the injunction motion. That possibility ought not ... to prevent the Court from acting on the only evidence presented to it at the time'.[18]

Since a court will require a high degree of proof before granting an interlocutory injunction, it appears to follow that, where a defendant raises a claim or plea of justification or qualified privilege or fair comment the court will examine his affidavit to see if there are any grounds for the claim.[19] It seems, then, that when Murnaghan J in 1924[20] refused to grant an injunction simply because the defence of justification was raised, that he was wrong,

14 *Fitzgerald v Clancy* 212.

15 For the criteria relied on in other tort actions; see McMahon and Binchy, 588 et seq.

16 *Fitzgerald v Clancy.* A case where an interlocutory application for an injunction against a newspaper was refused in *Penny Bentley v Sunday World,* The Irish Times, 18 November 1976.

17 *Cullen v Stanley* [1926] IR 73 at 83 per Kennedy CJ.

18 *Cullen v Stanley* 84.

19 As the Court of Appeal did in Fitzgerald's case, and as O'Connor J did in Cullen's case. In Australia, according to Fleming 561, there must be on this point 'no real ground for supposing that the defendant may succeed with a defence'. Martin implies that Canadian courts will examine the matter to some extent when he states that an injunction will not be granted where a defendant indicates an intent to raise a defence, unless is manifestly without foundation.

20 *Gallagher v Touhy* (1924) 58 ILTR 134.

although some English authority appears to support his view.[21]

The court must also, at the interlocutory stage, be satisfied that the defendant intends publishing or republishing the statement before the full hearing. In addition, the plaintiff must establish that the balance of convenience in granting or refusing the injunction favours the plaintiff. A court should be careful lest it too easily finds that the grant of an injunction would cause little loss to a media defendant, but that its refusal would cause great loss to a plaintiff; otherwise media liberty may be seriously diminished. It is easy to foresee where the granting of an injunction would cause serious harm to a media defendant while damages would adequately compensate an injured reputation. The court may make it a condition of any injunction it grants that a plaintiff undertakes to abide by any order about damages it makes at the full hearing, if the defendant succeeds,[22] though the court should also be satisfied that the plaintiff is in a position to abide by such an undertaking.[23]

The granting of interlocutory injunctions — both *ex parte* and on notice — in defamation proceedings is of major consequence because of the effect which it has, particularly in preventing the media from exercising its constitutional liberties of expression. The common law courts have traditionally recognised this, as already indicated, in the greater certainty of plaintiff correctness that is required in defamation actions than in other tort actions. This was, or is, unequal treatment of different tort plaintiffs, but can be justified by reference to the media's constitutional protection. The real issue, however, is whether that protection goes further and invalidates interlocutory orders in defamation cases, as it has been held generally to do in the US.[24] An interlocutory injunction is nothing short of a total denial of free speech, which is based on meagre, uncertain, opinionated, hearsay, untested, and in the case of *ex parte* orders one-sided, evidence. This is a shaky basis for constitutional validation. Further, any restriction on free speech, and not just speech, is usually taken to mean facing the consequences after speaking. Given the human condition, it is hard to see how any valid balance of rights involving free speech could actually mean not speaking at all. The very need to assert free

21 See Gatley para 1574; *Herbage v Pressdram* [1984] 2 All ER 769. According to Hayes there might be an exception with pleas of justification whereby the court does not examine the grounds of the defence.

22 *Sinclair v Gogarty* [1937] IR 377.

23 Hayes 133.

24 See Pound supra, and Prosser 772-3. In *Near v Minnesota* (1930) 283 US 697, 713 per Hughes CJ 'In determining the extent of the constitutional protection [of the liberty of the press] it has been generally, if not universally, considered that it is the chief purpose of the guaranty to prevent previous restraints upon publication'.

speech comes from the historical desire of democracies to invalidate denials of it; and while interlocutory orders might only be granted rarely, the unsettling and inhibitory effect which their granting has is out of all proportion to any benefit thereby gained, especially when it is remembered that self help or legal redress is still available to a plaintiff. There is a case for declaring interlocutory relief in defamation proceedings unconstitutional, but it is strongest in relation to *ex parte* injunctions..

Perpetual injunctions

A court has jurisdiction to award a successful plaintiff after the hearing of an action a perpetual injunction restraining the defendant from ever repeating the defamatory publication where the likelihood of repetition is established.[25] Since the entitlement to do this is discretionary, a court may take into account in the case of works of a literary or educational value, whether any loss which a plaintiff would suffer if the injunction was granted. If this was the case the in proportion to the loss which the community, and the defendant, would suffer if the injunction was granted. If this was the case the judge could take that into account in assessing damages, and so refuse to grant an injunction. The Australian Law Reform Commission was sufficiently convinced of the merit of this, that it recommended that this discretion should be made explicit by statute.[26] If a perpetual injunction is granted, that may reduce the amount of any compensatory damages awarded since the court will assume that granting the injunction will reduce the amount of future damage to reputation.

REFORM

One of the leading writers, Fleming,[27] has criticised the common law's 'preoccupation' with the remedy of damages as a 'crippling experience over the centuries', since the existence of damages as the only remedy in most cases has reduced the number of options in an action to an award of damages or nothing. This has resulted in great emphasis being placed on the various defences. The plaintiff and defendant are both placed in an all-or-nothing situation; if a defendant

25 Such a situation arose in the Circuit Court action of *Trustee Savings Bank v Kirby*, Irish Independent, 2 October 1987 where a perpetual injunction was granted, in addition to damages, because the defendant refused to promise to desist from distributing defamatory leaflets outside the plaintiff's premises.

26 Para 237.

27 'Retraction and Reply: Alternative Remedies for Defamation' (1977) 12 UBC L Rev 15.

can show privilege or excuse the plaintiff will obtain no redress from the law, although the sued-on statement was actually defamatory and untrue. If the plaintiff can establish liability, there is no option but a possibly hefty award of damages.

This is a valid criticism. The object of any civil remedy for defamation should be to rehabilitate reputation, and it is difficult to see not only any automatic relationship between damages and rehabilitating reputation, but also how an award of damages can satisfy the state's constitutional obligation to protect 'as best it may' the individual's good name, which is the criterion of a tort remedy. For, if as is the case, a plaintiff is free to do with his damages whatever he wants, and does not have to apply them to inform those who received the defamatory statement of its falseness, then how can it be said that damages protect reputation?

Any chance publicity attendant on a trial or settlement, often a year or more after the publication, is too haphazard to count as an adequate means of rehabilitating reputation, and may even be, at best, irrelevant, and at worst, counterproductive. Furthermore, the fact that damages are neither purposive, efficient or rehabilitative suggests that they are also not even civil in nature; and the manner in which juries often award what are nominally compensatory damages adds weight to this.[28] When punitive damages, as commonly understood, are then awarded,there is a doubly punitive dimension to the action satisfying, firstly, the plaintiff's desire for vengeance, and, secondly, the juries.[29] It is true that some aspects of defamation damages are compensatory, such as mental anguish, and actual loss. But the theoretical basis of these is rather opposed to the idea of rehabilitating reputation, and it is somewhat incongruous that they are compensated for in a defamation action, and not as some separate wrong.[30] Damages can also be unduly unfair to a defendant, especially a media

28 A similar view is expressed in the Second Restatement of Torts, S 620, Comment C: 'the common law doctrine of damages invited damages by way of punishment rather than true compensation'. See also the remark of Hanna J in a speech to journalists in 1936 reported Anon, 'Newspapar Libel' (1939) 73 ILT & SJ 67, in the context of libel awards: 'The damages, if assessed on any basis, are not dealt with as a measure of the damage to the plaintiff, but are meted out as a punishment, which, of course, is primarily wrong'. See also Hayes, 'The Jury Verdict in Defamation: Common sense or Conniption' (1973) U West Aus L Rev 140, 150, 155. Could it also be that an award of compensatory damages in the not unusual case — where a plaintiff informs a court in advance of his intention to give any awards made to a charity — can not be really compensatory?

29 For punitive damages see p. 252 supra; so long as damages remain the principal remedy and serve a punitive function, it is quite logical to even argue that the civil action be replaced by criminal prosecutions, with fines being paid to victims in appropriate cases.

30 See Day 'Mental Suffering as an Element of Damages in Defamation Cases' (1966) 15 Clev Mar L Rev 26, 36 et seq.

defendant, because of the disproportionate financial impact which a single award of damages can have, and because of the impermissible deterrent effect which the fear of an award may have on the exercise of free speech. Reputation is not like an arm or a leg, and, remedy-wise, should not be treated like one.

There are a number of remedies which may be set in opposition to damages, and which are much more purposive in design. Since the effect of a defamatory statement is to influence the opinions of a number of people, it seems obvious that the best way to remedy that is by promptly making to the same audience one or more counteracting statements possessing the prestige of accuracy and correctness — either from the defamer's acknowledgment of his wrong, a retraction, or from the pronouncement of an independent arbiter, a correction, or, as a minimum, from the defamer facilitating a reply by the aggrieved person.

A retraction, in particular, seems to offer a more effective means of rehabilitating reputation. It could, too, have a much broader scope than damages; for, even where a defamer has a complete defence to damages liability, since it was his act that caused the damage, there is some onus on him to redress that by making a retraction. Transforming that moral onus into a pre-hearing legally enforceable right to demand a retraction would be a logical and purposive step for a law which seeks to be founded on rational grounds to take. A retraction is, however, a serious step to expect a person to take, especially if he maintains the truth of the statement; and it may be proper to deny the right in such a case, though to permit an award of damages should a defence of justification fail at the trial. Imposing a retraction remedy on the media may cause particular difficulties. Given the scale and nature of media output, it might be unfair to require the publication of a pre-hearing retraction. In any case, it seems doubtful that the constitutional recognition of the importance of the media would permit such an obligation. Yet some speedy pre-hearing redress could still be expected of the media since, again, it is their act which has caused the damage. A legally enforceable right of reply by the injured person might be a minimum that could be expected.[31]

In relation to corrections, the absence at present of any power in a court after a hearing to order a defendant, whether found liable or not — aside from those who justify — to publish either in the court's name or in his own name a correction of the mistaken impression caused by his publication is surprising. So potent with beneficial effect

31 For further consideration of the retraction and reply remedies see p. 290 post. See also the similar 'vindication action' suggested by Hulme 'Vindicating Reputation: An Alternative to Damags as a Remedy for Defamation' (1981) 30

would the judicial pronouncement, in particular, be that one may wonder whether such a power must not inure in the judiciary's constitutional obligation to administer justice, or in the state's constitutional guarantee to vindicate good name 'as best it may'.

The Australian Law Reform Commission devoted considerable attention to the issue of correction orders,[32] and recommended that courts should have a discretionary power in appropriate cases to order a defendant to correct a false defamatory statement. It suggested that this power would be as an addition to, and not instead of, damages, and the amount of damages should reflect the likely effect of the correction. The Faulks Committee considered a similar suggestion involving advertisements in newspapers,[33] but felt it unworkable for, what must be considered doubtful reasons. Firstly, it thought the cost of the advertisement might be in addition to ordinary compensatory damages. In fact, if appropriate, the advertisement would reduce the damage to reputation, and so reduce the ordinary compensatory damages. Secondly, it thought that if the cost of the advertisement could be set against the compensatory damages, that it would be wrong for a court to, effectively, tell a plaintiff how to spend his damages. That view, however, reflects a misconception of what a defamation remedy should do. Success in an action should not be like a sweepstake for the winner.The remedy is intended to set right a wrong. A correction will often do that far better than damages. In any event, the cost of a correction would hardly be regarded as part of the damages, although the amount of damages would be influenced by a correction; and under the Australian proposal, it is specifically stated[34] that a plaintiff who does not seek a correction order should not thereby increase his damages.

Amer U L Rev 375, in which the court would merely declare the statement untrue and order the publication of a correction.

32 Paras 254-9.

33 Para 383; see also NZ Committee Report para 367.

34 Para 258.

12

Parties

JOINDER OF ACTIONS AND PARTIES

In general, the principles which determine whether more than one wrong can be litigated in an action, whether there may be more than one plaintiff or defendant in an action, and the liability of the various defendants both as against the plaintiff and among themselves, are the same in the law of defamation as in other areas of tort law.[1] However, there are some particular rules which deserve mention.

Where a person has been defamed by more than one publication, he may unite in the same action the several causes of action if this is a convenient way to dispose of the matters.[2] Where the same, or substantially the same, defamatory statement is published by different persons, then, to the extent that the different publications reach the same audience, the different publishers may be treated as concurrent wrongdoers and so be sued in the same action.[3]

Where more than one person in injured by a defamatory statement, then the application of O 15 r 1(1) of the Rules of the Superior Courts, dealing with joinder of plaintiffs, would seem to permit all of those who claim relief in respect of the same defamatory publication, or those in whose actions common questions of law or fact are involved, to maintain an action in respect of the publication, either jointly or severally. Thus in a number of cases, where two persons, whether husband and wife,[4] employer and employee,[5] fellow partners,[6] fellow workers,[7] were allegedly defamed in the same way in the

1 For the general position, see McMahon & Binchy, Part II.

2 This is the application of O 18 r 1 of the Rules of the Superior Courts to defamation actions. For a case where the joinder of actions was not permitted, see Stewart v Sefton [1964] IR 36.

3 Civil Liability Act 1961, s11 (5).

4 *Hewson v. Cleeve* [1904] 2 IR 536.

5 *Bell v Northern Constitution* [1943] NI 108.

6 *Gallagher and Shatter v Independent Newspapers*, The Irish Times, 10 May 1980; *Latham and Byrne v Independent Newspaper*, The Irish Times, 9 May 1986.

7 *Thorpe and Lee v Kildare Report*, The Irish Times, 23 November 1978; *Hogan*

same statement, they were permitted to maintain joint actions. One case, however, which is difficult to reconcile with this line of authority is *Peddie v Kyle,*[8] which was decided by the Court of Queen's Bench in 1899, and approved of by the Court of Appeal. In this case, a letter, alleged to be defamatory, was written referring in the same way to a number of workmen, and two of them who worked for the same employer sought to maintain a joint action in respect of it. This was refused, Johnson J in the Court of Queen's Bench remarking 'What community of interest is there between the plaintiffs? They have separate causes of action, and the circumstances and measure of damages of each individual would be different'. However, it does not seem necessary that the measure of damages should be the same. In one case[9] where the court ordered the payment out of a sum lodged in court to two plaintiffs, the sums were different, although in recent actions,[10] plaintiffs were awarded equal amounts. Moreover, the wording of O 15 r 1(1) requires only that the relief sought be the same. It does not require that the extent of relief granted should be the same.[11]

A plaintiff may join as defendants all or any of those whom it is claimed were responsible for the defamatory publication. Where the action is in respect of a slander, care should be taken to ensure that the claim is not presented as to suggest that the words were spoken by all of the defendants, unless that is what happened, for as was stated in one case where a claim of joint liability for slander was struck out '... the speaking of one is not the speaking of the other, and the idea the paragraph complained of in this case conveys to me is that the words were spoken by all the defendants...'.[12] It has been held that there cannot be joint liability in cases of slander,[13] but this does not seem correct. An employer is surely jointly liable for a slander by his employee.[14] Two can speak in unison, and similar slanders

and O'Neill v Sunday World, The Irish Times, 20 March 1981; *Corliss and Diggin v Ireland,* The Irish Times, 30 November 1984. In another case, *Black and Others v Northern Whig* (1942) 77 ILTR. 5, ten members of Belfast Corporation were successful in a joint action.

8 [1900] 2 IR 265. See Note 'Joinder of Parties in Actions of Libel and Slander (1899) 33 ILT & SJ 234.

9 *Bell v Northern Constitution* supra.

10 Thorpe and Lee's case supra; Hogan and O'Neill's case supra; Latham and Byrne's case supra. In Black's case, supra, each of the plaintiffs also received the same damages.

11 A possible explanation for Peddie's decision is that the defendant proposed different defences in relation to each plaintiff, although it is still conceivable that a joint action would be an appropriate one.

12 *Bannigan v Callaghan* (1897) 33 ILTR. 58,59 per Madden J.

13 *Chamberlain v White* (1623) Cro Jac 647.

14 As happened in *Dempsey v Wall & Co. and Ryan* (1943) 78 ILTR. 73. In

spoken by different people to the same audience can now be sued for in the same action.[15].

Where joint defendants are found liable, judgement may be given against them jointly or separately, and if it is given against them jointly, it is to take effect as though given against them separately.[16] Each of the defendants is, in respect of the damage for which they are concurrent wrongdoers, liable for the entirety of the plaintiff's damages,[17] except where a particular defendant can show mitigating circumstances applicable only to him and then the amount of his contribution will be reduced.[18] These rules, which are contained in the Civil Liability Act 1961, have reversed decisions in such defamation cases as *Dawson v McClelland* (1899),[19] and *Johnson v Larkin and Gaelic Press* (1926),[20] where new trials were ordered because juries had awarded separate damages against joint defendants.[21].

JOINT PUBLISHERS AND INFECTIOUS MALICE

Where a defendant is sued, either jointly or severally, as being responsible for the defamatory publication of another and he relies on a defence — personal or derived — which is conditional on the absence of actual malice, the question arises whether proof of malice in the other deprives him of the defence. The defence may be a common law privilege, or a statutory one under s 24 of the Defamation Act 1961, or it may be the defence of fair comment, or unintentional defamation, under s 21 of the 1961 Act.

In the first instance, this issue depends on whether the defendant in question is vicariously liable for the act of the other. If he is, then proof of malice by the other will be fatal to the defendant's protection. This was recognised in *Fitzsimmons v Duncan and Kemp & Co* (1908)[22] where the malice of the first-named defendant employee

Corcoran v W. & R. Jacob (1945) IR 446, and in *Coleman v Keanes* (1946) IJR 5, employers alone were validly sued for slanders by their employees. This suggests that had the speakers themselves been joined, this would have made no difference.

15 Civil Liability Act 1961, s 11 (5).

16 Civil Liability Act 1961, s 14 (1).

17 Civil Liability Act 1961, s 12 (1).

18 Civil Liability Act 1961, s 14 (6).

19 [1899] 2 IR 486.

20 [1926] IR 640.

21 The old rules still apply in England, and the Faulks Committee Report para 350 did not recommend their abolition, considering that this was a question for tort law in general, and not only defamation. The arguments against those rules, which may have influenced the legislature here are set out in Williams, *Joint Torts and Contributory Negligence*, at pp 67, 72.

22 [1908] 2 IR 483.

was held to destroy the privilege of his employer, the second-named defendants. Where, however, the defendant is neither employer or principal of the other, and is not vicariously liable for his acts, then proof of malice by that other will not, now, affect the former's privilege. This is provided for in s 11 (4) of the Civil Liability Act 1961 which states that 'Where there is a joint libel in circumstances normally protected by the defences of qualified privilege or fair comment upon a matter of public interest, the malice of one person shall not defeat the defence for the other, unless that other is vicariously liable for the malice of the first'. This provision altered the previous law, except in relation to slanders,under which all the defendants responsible, in whatever way, for a publication could be infected, and so have their defences annulled, by the malice of one of their number.[23] The absence of any reference in s 11 (4) to the defence of unintentional defamation in s 21 of the Defamation Act is not accidental, for subs 7 of s 21 requires, say, a newspaper defendant wishing to avail of the defence where the words are stated by a contributor, actually to prove that the author stated the words without malice. This may be impossible when a letter writer cannot be traced.[24] Broadcasts are included within s 11(4) by virtue of s 15 of the Defamation Act 1961 which equalled defamatory broadcasting with libel for the general law of libel and slander.

The protection contained in s 11 (4) depends on whether one person is vicariously liable for the act of another. Clearly employers and principals are responsible for the acts of their employees or agents, but it is not clear whether the publisher of a newspaper, magazine or broadcast is vicariously liable for contributors to the paper or programme, who are not his regular employees. In one English case,[25] it was stated that a magazine was responsible for the malice of a reviewer since he was considered its agent, although, he was not an employee. In the Canadian case of *Cherneskey v Armadale Publishers*, a majority of the Supreme Court in Canada held a newspaper liable for a letter to the editor, and certain obiter dicta suggested that a writer's malice could infect a newspaper's defence

23 There is no corresponding provision in England, although a somewhat similar position exists there now since the decision in *Egger v Viscount Chelmsford* [1965] 1 QB 248 noted by Newark, 'Joint Publishers, Privilege and Malice (1965) 2 NILQ (ns) 90; 'Libel, Qualified Privilege' (1964) 98 ILT & SJ 463.

24 See Delaney, 'Civil Proceedings for Defamation' (1962/3) 28/29 IJ 1. Where a number of persons are joint authors of a defamatory statement, and they wish to rely on the defence of unintentional defamation, s 11(4) does not immunise one person against the malice of another because it omits to cover this type of unintentional defamation. But since imputed malice might not prevent reliance on the defence of unintentional defamation anyway, the omission might be without significance.

25 *Gros and Another v Crook and Times Newspapers* (1969) 113 SJ 408

of fair comment.[26] But the finding that the reviewer was an agent has been doubted,[27] as has the aptness of the term 'agency' in relation to contributors,[28] and there was a vigorous dissent in *Cherneskey's* case, supported by academic opinion.[29] Some of the reform bodies have recommended that the publisher should not be vicariously responsible for the malice of either independent contractors or unsolicited correspondents, anonymous or otherwise.[30] If the user of an independent contractor is not vicariously liable for his malice, then the decision reached in *Eglantine Inn v Smith*,[31] in which a printer's privilege was infected by his client's malice, could not be reached here now. In Ireland, however, there appears to be a tendency to view as the test of vicarious liability whether one person has a sufficient degree of control over another.[32] If he has, then he is vicariously responsible and thus the mass media would be responsible for the malice of both its employed and non-employed contributors. At the same time the difficulty which this would pose for the media could be avoided if the reference to vicarious liability in s 11 (4) of the Civil Liability Act 1961 was interpreted so as to exclude liability for the malice of non-paid contributors, as it could be.

The operation of the infectious malice rule is not the only way in which a publisher responsible for the contributions of others might be denied a defence on the grounds of malice. Where differing views are expressed by contributors to a broadcast or by letter writers to a newspaper, a plaintiff suing in respect of one of these views might attempt to show actual or non-infectious malice in the publisher by arguing that the sued on statement was a contradiction of other views expressed in the medium; or he might argue that since the publisher disagreed with the sued on statement, that statement had not been honestly made. Of course the paper might not have supported either view, or may have taken a view for the purpose of the action. It would only have been providing a forum for debate among its readers. If a judge or jury decided to interpret malice by what could be inferred from the media's actions, malice might often be found against the media. One judge has concluded 'If the defendant is not the writer or commentator himself but a subsequent publisher, obviously

26 (1978) 90 DLR (3d) 321, 330, 336.

27 Faulks Committee Report para 272.

28 See judgement of Dickson J. For consideration of this case, see Heerey, 'Publishing the Defamatory Statements of Others' (1985) 59 ALJ 37; Rogers, 'Some Probems of Fair Comment and the Press', (1981) 10 Anglo-AmLR 225; Martin, 'Libel and Letters to the Editor' (1983) 9 Queens LJ 188.

29 Rogers supra.

30 Faulks Committee Report para 272; NZ Committee Report 125.

31 [1948] NI 29.

32 *Moynihan v Moynihan* [1975] IR 192. See also McMahon & Binchy, 97 et seq.

[defendant personal belief] is an inappropriate test of malice'.[33]

It will be apparent from the foregoing that the media's position in this area is a difficult one. Not alone can it lose any protection it has because its employed and non employed contributors acted maliciously, it can conceivably also lose it when opposing views are expressed in its columns, or when it disagrees with the views expressed. Depending on how broadly or narrowly media malice is defined, and on how frequently employed or non employed contributor malice can be shown, much of the protection of the media against defamation liability can thereby be rendered nugatory. Such a possibility could raise a question of whether media constitutional protection permits this since that protection by clearly referring to the media in addition to individuals seems to assume that there are aspects of media liberty of expression which are different from the individual's, and for which particular media protection is required. The operation of the contributor malice rule seems to be one of these. Furthermore, the manner by which Article 40.6 of the Constitution refers to the media as 'organs of public opinion' presumes that the media reflects public opinion, and therefore anything which prevents the media functioning as an organ or forum for the expression of opinion may conflict with that provision.

INFANTS

An infant, that is a person under eighteen years of age, can both sue[34] and be sued [35] in an action in defamation, as he can generally in tort. To that extent, the matter hardly merits particular attention here.[36] There are, however, a number of points that should be made. When suing as a plaintiff, an infant must sue by his best friend, and if he does not, then the writ will be set aside.[37] Whether a statement is defamatory of an infant depends on how the judge or jury, as the case may be, consider a reasonable exponent of the standard of opinion would react.[38] The standard of opinion must be

33 *Cherneskey v Armadale Publishers*, supra, 346 per Dickson J.

34 *Smith v Corr* [1937] IR 248; *Purcell v Irish Press* [1944] IR 217. See generally, Stevens, 'The Reputation Rights of Infants' (1975) 9 Family LQ 435. Whether an infant could sue the parent who gives out to him or her in front of his friends seems doubtful. 'But if a parent exceeds his authority or reaches beyond the home to defame his child, an action might lie': Stevens 439.

35 *Defries v Davis* (1835) 7 Car & P 112.

36 For the general position of infants in tort law, see McMahon & Binchy, 65 et seq.

37 *Lindsay v McCord* (1897) 33 ILTR 71.

38 Since an infant's reputation is unlikely to bring an action within the High Court jurisdictional limits, most cases will be heard by judges sitting alone. The difficulty for any judge in interpreting adverse infant reactions is relieved somewhat in

acceptable to the law. For this reason, an accusation of squealing to the teacher is unlikely to be actionable.[39] But an accusation of the larceny of a saw,[40] or of using bad language, or having a bad school report, or being expelled from school, or having venereal disease, or being pregnant has been found so.[41] Publication of slanderous words to parents has been an issue in some American cases, and although there may be a valid publication in such a case, recovery has been denied where the parents did not think less of their child as a result of hearing the charge.[42]

The extent of a child's reputation may well influence the amount of damages awarded. The reputation might be of a lesser dimension than an adult's, or any damage may well be less because of limited publication or a diminished likelihood of lasting effect. The younger a child is, the greater the likelihood that damages will only be nominal.

An infant can be sued in an action, not on his own, but through his guardian *ad litem*. Again, whether a reasonable standard of opinion would interpret a charge made by an infant as being defamatory must depend on each case. If the charge involves sexual misconduct, it may well be defamatory and an action will lie.[43] Infancy may assist a defendant in maintaining the defence of unintentional defamation, or, in a case where he relies on a qualified privilege, in rendering it difficult for a plaintiff to prove actual malice.[44].

BANKRUPTS

Bankruptcy does not affect a persons right to sue in defamation.[45] 'There is no doubt that the right to bring an action for an injury to the person, character, or feelings of a bankrupt, does not pass to the assignees ...'.[46] Nor is bankruptcy a defence to an action in defamation.[47] Any damages which are awarded to a bankrupt

jury actions where persons as young as 18 years of age may sit — Juries Act 1976, s 6.

39 See p. 19 supra and the reference in *Berry v The Irish Times* (1973) IR 368, 382 per McLoughlin J.

40 In *Smith v Corr* supra, an infant recovered £1 for a libel and £1 for a slander to this effect.

41 Stevens 437, 440.

42 Stevens 438.

43 *Woolworth v Meadows* (1804) 5 East 463, 472 per Lawrence J.

44 According to Stevens 443 some American Courts have adopted irrebuttable and rebutable presumptions of malicious incapacity for infants below 7, and between 7 and 14, respectively.

45 *Dowling v Browne* (1853) 4 ICLR 265.

46 *Beckham v Drake* (1849) 2 HLC 579, 621 per Maule J.

47 Bankruptcy Act 1914, s 30 (1).

plaintiff for damage to his reputation may be retained by him and do not vest in his trustees in bankruptcy.[48] Where, however, additional injury is sustained by a bankrupt's estate, then only the trustee may recover damages in respect of this, whether joined with the bankrupt's claim in defamation or separately.[49]

TRADING AND NON-TRADING CORPORATIONS

A trading corporation or a non-trading corporation, such as a local authority, can sue[50] and be sued[51] in respect of a defamatory publication. The trading corporation will have a reputation in respect of its trading activities, and it may have a general reputation in respect of other activities, such as its treatment of its employees or its sponsorship of cultural and civic events. A non-trading corporation will have a general reputation for the non-profit making activities it engages in and a particular reputation over whatever segment of its affairs, which if it is defamed, would produce some financial loss. It seems clear that, at present, the law recognises all these types of reputation and will protect them. Thus, in one English case,[52] a coal mining company received compensation in a case where its housing policy towards its employees was criticised; and, in an Irish case, *Eglantine Inn v Smith* (1948),[53] a company which ran a public house recovered compensation for a defamation of its policy towards its employees joining trade unions. In another English case [54] a local authority received compensation for a defamation which, since it was unlikely to result in financial loss, appears to have damaged the authority's general reputation.

Satisfactory though this situation may seem, there is a substantial body of opinion which would limit the legal protection given to corporate reputations, and in certain circumstances effectively deny this right to a good name.[55] Regarding a trading corporation, it has,

48 *Ex parte Vine* (1878) 8 ChD 364.

49 *Wilson v United Counties Bank* [1920] AC 102.

50 For trading corporations eg — *Praeger & Co. v Shaw* (1885) 4 ICLR 660 and *Eglantine Inn v Smith* [1948] NI 29. For non-trading corporations, eg — *Bognor Regis UDC v Campion* [1972] 2 QB 169 and *Church of Scientology v Globe & Mail* (1978) 84 DLR(3d) 239; *City of Prince George v BC Television* (1979) 95 DLR (3d) 577; *Windsor R.C. Separate School Bd v Southam* (1984) 9 DLR (4d) 284.

51 For trading corporation eg — *Kenny v Freemans Journal* (1892) 27 ILTR 8. For non-trading corporatios eg — *O'Hea v Guardians, Cork Union* (1893) 32 LRIr 629.

52 *South Hetton Coal v North Eastern News* [1894] 1 QB 133.

53 Supra.

54 *Bognor Regis UDC v Campion* supra.

55 *Mayor of Manchester v Williams* [1891] 1 QBD 94, 96 per Day J.; *Lewis v Daily*

for instance, been stated that its reputation is a narrow one because there are many activities which it is incapable of, such as having indecent or vulgar manners or committing assault or murder or incest or adultery[56] or corruption.[57] This would leave only imputations that impinge on the trading capacity of a corporation to be the subject a proceeding, such as imputations of insolvency, near bankruptcy, lack of trustworthiness, insecurity, bad management and fraud. This, however, appears to involve unjustifiably selective reasoning which is based on an inaccurate view of corporate capacity, and also on the role of a jury, where there is one, in a defamation action. If it is desired to make a distinction between human and corporate capacity, it must be immediately apparent that there really is no such thing as corporate capacity since a corporation is only a legal abstraction that can do nothing on its own. Therefore, any reference to corporate capacity must, in fact mean the capacity which is attributed to a corporation in ordinary linguistic usage. If this is so the judge should leave it to the jury as the arbiters of defamatory meaning and effect, to determine this question. Any jury would find it commonplace to refer to a company as being late, slow, lazy, inefficient or unmannerly, or that it could commit a wide range of crimes and torts. Thus a number of imputations, in addition to those of purely trading relevance, would be actionable.

A related argument which is used against protecting the wider aspects of a trading corporation's reputation involves actually denying that it can have a reputation apart from a trading reputation. This is a legalistic view based on the nature of the corporation.[58] It ignores the fact that, public usage may comprehend such a wide reputation, and while this question is clearly one of law for the judge, public usage must bear on his reasoning. Another, and perhaps stronger, point against the narrow view is that some companies do clearly have reputations in addition their trading reputations, because they are involved in other activities as well, such as subscribing to charities and political parties, or sponsoring sporting, cultural or civic activities. Of course, it can be said that these may, indirectly, affect a trading reputation. But, if indirect effect is to be given such a meaning, then the question becomes one of semantics only since the imputations would then be actionable.

The argument against protecting the entire reputation of non-trading corporations is based on the view that the only kind of

Telegraph [1964] AC 234, 262 per Lord Reid; All of the reform bodies have recommended that corporate reputation should mean only that estimation which if lowered can be shown to result, or be likely to result, in pecuniary loss.

56 *South Hetton Coal v North Eastern News* supra 138,141 per Lord Esher M.R.

57 *Metropolitan Saloon Omnibus v Hawkins* (1859) 4 H & N 87,90.

58 *Lewis v Daily Telegraph* supra 262 per Lord Reid.

reckonable loss is financial damage, and thus only imputations which have that effect should be actionable.[59] Since those imputations would have to affect the corporation's material property, it will be apparent that the entire range of activities for which the non-trading corporation was established would be left unprotected from attack. Thus, a local authority could be libelled with impunity merely because the libel had no effect on its financial position. This seems unjust, and it is hardly an answer, in the case of local authorities, to assert that they should put up with it,[60] since that ignores the fact that these corporations too must have rights that deserve to be weighted against the critic's right to free speech. Any restriction on what the non-trading corporation could sue for would also fail to appreciate that, in the public eye, its reputation would still be as wide as 'the nature of its trade or calling. Where the trade or calling, as here, is one of 'religion' the scope, for injury in the trade or calling may be very broad indeed'.[61] .

UNINCORPORATED ASSOCIATIONS

As a general rule an unincorporated association does not possess, in the eyes of the law, sufficient personality that it can sue or be sued in a defamation action in its own name.[62] Exceptions to the rule arise in the case of trade unions and partnerships, which will be considered shortly. The only way, then, that an unincorporated association can, effectively, sue is through the individual members of the group. In this regard, there are two possibilities — all of the members suing together, and an individual member suing on behalf of the other members. Concerning the first possibility, O 15 r 1 of the Rules of the Superior Courts allows, it will be recalled, different persons to join in one action as plaintiffs where there are common issues of law or fact in question arising out of the same context, whether they sue jointly or severally or in the alternative. However, it has been argued that this would not be a practical procedure in the case of associations with large memberships.[63] Concerning the second possibility, r 9 of O 15 provides 'Where there are numerous persons having the same interest in one cause or matter, one or more

59 Faulks Committee Report para 340.

60 Weir supra. See also ALRC Report para 94. The Report did, however, recommend that injunctive and declaratory relief should be available even where there was no liklihood of financial harm.

61 *Church of Scientology v Globe & Mail* supra 241 per Cory J.

62 *London Association for Protection of Trade v Greenlands* [1916] AC 15, 20.

63 Lloyd, 'Actions Instituted by or against Unincorporated Bodies' (1949) 12 MLR 409, 411.

of such persons may sue or be sued... in such cause or matter, on behalf, or for the benefit, of all persons so interested'. For an action to be maintained in these circumstances, the plaintiff and all of the class which he represents, and not just some, must have been individually able to maintain the action. Each member will thus need to have been sufficiently identified from the statement, and where only the class is named, the larger it is the less likely will the courts regard its members as being sufficiently identified. Further, the injury of which each complains must be the same, the defences available against each must be the same and the damage awardable in each case must be the same.[64] Such a precise identity of elements in the action would seem quite unlikely in a defamation case where the quality or nature of the reputations of the members may well vary. R 9, however, might facilitate a declaratory action more easily since no claim for damages is made, and so the extent of the injury to each reputation, so long as there was injury, would not matter. So far as being sued is concerned, since the unincorporated association may not be sued in its own name, a plaintiff may join the various members as joint defendants in an action, but only on the basis that each member is individually liable, and mere membership of an association does not necessarily imply consent to the publication of the defamatory statement. A plaintiff may also sue a defendant on a representative basis under r 9 of O 15, but, again, the members must all be equally liable, and if some have defences which others have not, then the procedure is not available.[65].

It is open to question whether the law is right to refuse to allow unincorporated associations to sue in their own names, particularly if the possibility of a representative action is so remote. For, despite the weight of authority, an unincorporated association may, in reality, be viewed by the public as a distinct entity in exactly the same way as a corporation. As one commentator has argued 'they appear to occupy premises, own funds, act through duly appointed officers, describe themselves by a collective name and purport to engage in transactions... under that name'.[66] The unincorporated association is obviously open to defamatory attack and the refusal of the common law to protect its reputation will not alter that fact. On that account it is difficult to see why the members should be put to the difficulty of trying to arrange a joint or representative action simply because the legal system has not yet got around to recognising the importance of these bodies as the community views them. Some types of association — partnerships and trade unions — are already recognised,

64 *Seafarers International v Lawrence* (1979) 97 D.L.R. (3d) 324.
65 *Mercantile Marine v Toms* [1916] 2 KB 243.
66 Lloyd supra 410.

as will be seen. So also are corporations that comply with the Companies Acts. There is unequal treatment in this and it is not clear that the function or capacity of unincorporated associations is so different that this is justifiable treatment.

Trade unions

Since a trade union is not a legal corporation, one might expect that it could not be a party to litigation in its own name, and that its position would be the same as with other unincorporated associations. However, it is now established that trade unions possess enough of the attributes of personality to be a 'near corporation'[67] and so are able to sue[68] or be sued[69] in their own names. This conclusion was not an obvious one, and the reason why it was reached was that the courts were impressed by the detail of statutory regulations governing trade unions, and concluded that these rested sufficient attributes of personality in the union enabling it to litigate in its own name.[70] As O'Connor J stated in a recent English case 'If the statute, when looked at seems to give the unincorporated body powers which are only attributable to a person or a corporate body, then it is apparent that such an unincorporated association has got the necessary personality and that was the basis on which trade unions could sue for libel'.[71]

Before the judicial recognition that trade unions could litigate in their own names, the trustees of a union could, under s 9 of the Trade Union Act 1871, 'in all cases concerning the real or personal property of [a] trade union, sue and be sued ... in their proper names, without other description than the title of their office'. This provision still applies and would seem appropriate where a defamatory statement causes or is likely to cause the union pecuniary loss, although since the union can also litigate in its own name, it may not be relied on much. Both the availability of the union, and of its trustees, to litigate in a defamation action appears to depend on the union being an authorised one in possession of a negotiating licence. This could mean that unions who are not in this position would have to be treated as ordinary unincorporated associations. This would be because such unions, in not complying with statute, would not possess the attributes of personality that compliance with statute gives.[72]

67 *NUGMW v Gillian* [1946] KB 81,88 per Uthwatt J.
68 As in *NUGMW V Gillian* supra; *Willis v Brooks* [1947] 1 AER 197.
69 As in *Daly v ITGWU* [1926] IR 118.
70 See *Taff Vale Rly v ASRS* [1901] AC 426, and NUGMW case supra at 85, 89.
71 *EETPU v Times Newspapers* [1980] 3 WLR 98, 102.
72 The availability of the trustees depends on the union being registered or

Where a trade union or its trustees are sued in a defamation action, two particular provisions need to be referred to to see if the action even lies, regardless of its merits. In the case of a trade union, s 4 (1) of the Trade Disputes Act 1906, provides that 'An action against a trade union ... in respect of any tortious act alleged to have been committed by or on behalf of the trade union, shall not be entertained by any court'. This immunity from liability is indeed a wide one.[73] It is not limited to acts done for the purpose of a trade dispute, as other immunities in that Act are, and it has been specifically held to include immunity from actions in defamation.[74] It is difficult to see how such a broad immunity does not infringe a number of constitutional requirements. Firstly, the immunity completely denies the right to a good name for no better reason than that the defendant is a trade union. Important as trade unions are, they are not so overridingly important that there can be any justification for this. Secondly, this immunity gives rise to unequal treatment of defendants in defamation actions, and since it is hard to see in the capacity or function of trade unions anything which is so unique or different, as compared with other legal persons and their activities, that would merit them this unequal treatment, the inequality might be unconstitutional.

Another immunity is conferred on the trustees of the union by s 4 (2) of the 1906 Act according to which they are not liable for any tortious act committed by or on behalf of the union in contemplation or in furtherance of a trade dispute. This immunity is not so extensive as the previous one, since it can only arise in the context of trade disputes, and the question of its constitutionality seems less problematic. Of course, it remains a matter of balancing the interests of trade unions and the right to a good name, and since the Supreme Court has effectively held[75] that even a trade dispute does not permit a complete denial of the right to trade, it seems possible that the same could be the case with the right to a good name. But trade and reputation are not the same, and there may be grounds for regarding this immunity as not infringing the Constitution.

A trade union's reputation seems to consist in the perception of how it represents the employment interests of workers. In view of the fact that trade unions engage in other activities as well, such as being employers themselves, representing the unemployed, and the

authorised, see s 9 of the 1871 Act. The availability of the union's name for litigation depends also on this, and on the union possessing a negotiating licence and complying generally with the Trade Union Acts.

73 Although it apparently does not prevent the courts granting injunctions against trade unions — McMahon & Binchy 78.

74 *Vacher & Son v London Soc. of Compositors* [1913] AC 107.

75 *Talbot Ireland v ATGWU*, The Irish Times, 1 May 1981.

economically weaker sections of the community,[76] subscribing to political parties and promoting political ideologies, there seems to be no reason why they should not also have a reputation for these activities. However, there does not appear to be any case on the point.[77]

Unincorporated partnerships

An unincorporated partnership is entitled to sue in respect of a defamatory statement affecting its reputation.[78] Though not a body corporate, it is recognised as possessing legal personality. This personality rests upon the existence of some matter or concern common to, and separate from the individuals who comprise the partnership. Blackburne CJ stated in 1846 that 'to enable and entitle [several persons] to sue together, they must show that the slander is injurious to them through the medium of a common right and interest, which is prejudicially and directly affected by it. It is for this reason, held, that partners in trade may join in an action for slander, written or oral, concerning them in the way of their joint business'.[79]

Equally, a partnership may be sued in respect of a defamatory statement[80] whether as a result of a joint wrong or an individual wrong, and individual partners too are severally and jointly liable for their own and the partnership's wrongs.[81]

An unincorporated partnership may, by virtue of O 14 r 1 of the Rules of the Superior Courts, sue or be sued in its own name. This also applies to friendly societies 'I see no reason why a friendly society, like other unincorprated partnerships, should not be permitted to bring an action in its "firm name" ...',[82] although statute may provide that it is sufficient that the action be brought in the name of an authorised officer.[83]

76 Witness the non-pay and non-employment aspects of the now defunct National Understandings.

77 The recommendations of the reform bodies — that trade union defamation actions be limited to where real or likely pecuniary loss is shown to result: Faulks Committee Report para 341, NZ Committee Report para 363 — prompt the same response as when made in the context of corporate bodies. They seem, again, to be based on an unrealistically narrow view of the reputation of these bodies.

78 *LeFanu v Malcolmson* (1848) 1 HLC 637; *Irish People's Assurance v City of Dublin Assurance* [1929] IR 25.

79 *LeFanu v Malcolmson* (1846) 8 ILR 410, 426.

80 *Meekins v Henson* [1946] 1 QB 472.

81 Partnership Act 1890, ss 10,12.

82 *Irish People's Assurance v City of Dublin Assurance* supra, 31 per Fitzgibbon J.

It is the accepted view[84] which is reflected by the reform bodies,[85] that an action in defamation is not maintainable in respect of a statement defamatory of a person who was not alive at the time of publication. The only clear authority for this apears to be American.[86] However, if an imputation on a dead person also has the effect of defaming a living person, then an action does lie but only for the damage which is caused to reputation of the living person. Thus, in *White v Tyrrell* (1856),[87] a jury found that a charge, that a person was descended from another who had amassed his wealth by fraudulent means, was defamatory of the son, and although on appeal the court refused to express an opinion on this,[88] one of the judges at least appeared of the opinion that such actions could be maintained.[89] According to Prosser,[90] there are similar authorities in the United States, and Fleming,[91] is of the opinion that to call a man's dead mother a whore is actionable by the son. It seems questionable whether these views can be right, because if the standard of opinion which is used to determine defamatory effect consists of reasonable people,[92] it appears unlikely that they would think less of a person merely because he was unfortunate enough, through no fault of his own, to be connected with whoever is criticised. A charge of illegitimacy should hardly be more actionable than an accusation

83 In the Irish People's Assurance case it was s 94(1) of the Friendly Societies Act 1896.

84 Eg *Street on Torts,* 7th ed. 305 fn 8; *Carter-Ruck on Libel and Slander,* 3rd ed, 65; Walker, *Delict*, 2nd ed 750. See also *Broom v Richie* (1904) 6 F 942; *Small v Glove Printing* [1940] 2 CLR 670.

85 Porter Committee Report para 27; Faulks Committee Report para 417; NZ Committee Report para 436; ALRC Report para 99. See also Zellick, 'Libelling the Dead' (1969) New LJ 769; Symmons, 'New Remedies against Libellers of the Dead? A Look at the Recommendatins of the Faulks Committee on Defamation' (1980) 18 U of W Ont L Rev 521.

86 Prosser 778/9; Williams 133. In the past a criminal prosecution lay for a libel of the dead, although so scant is modern authority that it is not clear if one would lie now. A separate matter from defamation of the dead is defamation by the dead, as where defamatory statements contained in a will are publicised when the will is probated. In the US which again appears to have the only case law on the subject, the majority of decisions favour actionability, primarily so as to provide some redress for a plaintiff, see Eldredge 225/30.

87 (1856) 5 ICLR 477, 498.

88 Supra 507 per Monahan CJ.

89 Ball J at 505.

90 Supra.

91 501.

92 As it must do, here at any rate. See p. 18 supra.

of having been raped,[93] although in some American cases, the word 'bastard' was actionable.[94] If such views as these are correct, then, by allowing such a latitude in determining when the living can be defamed by a libel on the dead, the separate question of whether the dead can be defamed is almost rendered nugatory, and the formal prohibition recited above is only a hollow one.

Even this is now under attack, because all of the reform bodies are agreed that the formal prohibition on suing for libels of the dead should go.[95] They have concluded that, within limited circumstances, the distress which can be caused to the families of deceased persons by defamations of the dead ought to outweigh any restrictions which might thereby be placed on the discussion and writing of history. The limited circumstances are, that the action must be brought within a definite period after the death of the defamed person — which as is clear from the various times suggested, six years, five years and three years, can only be arbitrarily fixed — and that only declaratory and injunctive relief, but not damages, be available.

These are radical recommendations, which if implemented would involve the law of defamation in a new departure, and on fundamental matters, from its existing concerns. Heretofore, the defamation action has protected only the extant — natural, juristic or quasi-juristic — and at their own initiative. If altered, the law would then also protect the dead through the extant. It would involve a quite new element of liability — damage to a person's remembrance as perceived by his family, and,necessarily, a new basis for any redress since there would be no formal or extant reputation to be damaged. The redress suggested is, in itself, logical enough; however, the displacement of damages as the central remedy merely emphasises the novel nature of what is involved in the recommendations. Indeed, the Faulks Committee admitted that what is involved here is'an entirely new cause of action'.[96] If this is so, why then should it be treated as a species of defamation when it is essentially different from it? The recommendations, if at all valid, might better have been directed at inclusion in the action for injurious falsehood. That it was not is, one presumes because, in that action, a plaintiff would have to prove that the statement was untrue, whereas in defamation this is presumed for him.

93 For whether an imputation of having been raped is actionable here, see p. 91. supra.

94 Prosser 776.

95 Faulks Committee Report paras 417-422; NZ Committee report para 441; ALRC Report paras 99-102. See also Note '... And be Damned' (September 1985) 79 Incorp Law Soc. Gazette. Two state reform bodies in Australia recommended against changing the law — ALRC Report para 99.

96 Para 419

There is little evidence to support the suggested need for this change in the law. Only slight evidence was cited by any of the reform bodies to show that the present prohibition worked injustice to the families of deceased persons,[97] although there was also little evidence of mixed value about whether the changes would unduly restrict discussion of the past.[98] One would think, however, that an action for libel on the dead would be bound to excessively inhibit historical discussion not least because it might be difficult to ensure that the public at large properly understood the rule. There may well be truth in the dissent of a member of the Faulks Committee, who felt that such an action could 'deal a paralysing blow the writing of recent history'.[99]

The provisions of the Constitution may also be cited against the recommended changes. To restrict any constitutional right, in this case the right to free speech, there must be an opposing constitutional right or policy. Dead people have no right to protection of their reputation because they are neither alive nor citizens. They have no personal rights. It is also doubtful, if less obviously so, whether the injured feelings of the surviving family — based as they would be on attacks on the dead — could be of sufficient weight to merit a restriction on the right to free speech that would not amount to a denial of that right.

SURVIVAL OF THE DEFAMATION ACTION

A cause of action in defamation, which subsists against a person who dies, does not survive his death.[1] Presumably, when a verdict or judgment is entered against a person, and he dies afterwards, that will not have any effect on the plaintiff's rights since the action is then complete and no longer subsists.[2] The rule is an exceptional one, for most other civil actions do survive the death of the wrongdoers. It also appears to be unjust to the plaintiff in an action, for clearly the damage to his reputation will continue after the defamer's death.[3] The rule may well be an unconstitutional restriction on a person's right to a good name and his right to litigate,

97 Faulks Committee Report para 420; ALRC Report para 100 fn 92
98 ALRC Report paras 78, 100.
99 Faulks Committee Report, Minority Report 205.
1 Civil Liability Act 1961, sections 8 (1) and 6. 'As one commentator has suggested, the present law licences the terminally ill to safely defame who they will': De Grand post 431.
2 The death of a defendant in a defamation action between verdict and judgement will also not affect a plaintiff's rights — O 17 r 1 of the Rules of the Superior Courts.
3 Faulks Committee Report para 401.

and may also produce unjustifiably unequal treatment among plaintiffs in different tort actions.[4] The reasons for the rule — that the absence of a wrongdoer could prejudice his personal representatives in presenting any defences, particularly those based on the absence of malice[5] — are not especial to the defamation action, and yet the ban on survival of actions has been abrogated in the case of most other wrongs. All of the reform bodies have recommended that the exceptional treatment of defamation actions should be ended,[6] and that the action should survive the death of a defamer.

Where a person is defamed and he dies before an action is started, or where an action is started and he dies before a verdict is given, then the right of action does not survive his death and it does not vest in his personal representatives.[7] But, where the hearing has concluded and judgement has been reserved, a plaintiff's death ought not affect the validity of the judgement.[8] It is arguable here, also, whether this ban on the survival of defamation actions, which does not exist in the case of most other civil wrongs, is constitutional. The reform bodies are agreed in recommending that a defamation action should survive the death of the defamed person,[9] but they express quite different views about what kind of damages should then be recoverable.[10] Only one aspect of this need be commented on.

4 In the US according to De Grand, 'Challenging the Exclusion of Libel and Slander from Survival Statutes' (1984) U Ill L Rev 423, 436 one state court in *Meyer v Philips* (1975) 462 Pa 395 has held that the exclusion of defamation actions is unconstitutional on equal protection grounds.

5 As outlined in the Faulks Committee Report para 402.

6 Faulks Committee Report para 407; ALRC Report para 104; NZ Committee Report para 432. There was a dissent to the Faulks Committee recommendation — Minority Report D, 204 — which was based on the view that the difficulties of the personal representatives of deceased wrongdoer in defending the action would, in fact, be too great to allow the action survive. The NZ recommendation, unlike the others, would limit the damages recoverable to special damages.

7 Civil Liability Act 1961, sections 7 (1) and 6. This provision is occasionally relied on by the media to avoid liability.

8 Williams 133.

9 Faulks Committee Report para 415; NZ Committee Report para 435, although this Committee recommended against allowing personal representatives start an action where the deceased has not started one; ALRC Report para 107.

10 The Faulks Committee also distinguished between where a deceased has started an action and had not. In the former case, both general and special damages would be recoverable. In the latter case, only an injuction and actual or likely pecuniary damage would be recoverable. The NZ Committee was against awarding general compensatory damages and would only award injunctions and special damages. The ALRC made no specific recommendations on remedies, feeling that the question could be left to the discretion of the court to adjust damages for each case. It particularly did not agree with the idea of basing distinctions on whether the deceased had started an action before his death or not, as the other two did, since it felt that this was too haphazard — para 106.

Both the English and the Australian recommendations would allow for general compensatory damages to be awarded in certain circumstances, while the New Zealand Committee saw no merit in awarding compensatory damages for damage to reputation after a person has died. Since a person's reputation is different from his memory, it would be a major extension of the action to award compensation for damage to memory. It even contradicts, to some extent, the reform bodies other recommendations that permit only injunctions and declarations for libelling the dead. At the same time, there is no reason why compensatory damages for injury suffered before death should not be allowed.

13

The Future Development of the Irish Law of Defamation

A predominant issue for the future development of the law of defamation concerns whether damages should continue to be the main, if not the only, remedy for a defamatory publication. Many suggestions for reform turn, or depend, ultimately on that. If, as seems likely for some time at least, damages are to continue in that role, then most attention in the reform or development area will naturally concentrate on the circumstances in which damages are awardable. Most of the suggestions for reform and constitutional arguments in previous chapters were presented in that context. A considerable number of the common law rules examined appear to need reform, or at least some constitutional re-interpretation; and it may be helpful at this point, briefly to recall the main points that were made.

Individuals should be able to take actions for group defamations and recover damages, except in the case of a large group when only declaratory or criminal proceedings should be available. The protected range of innocent and careful distributors of defamatory material may be unduly narrow. Restrictions should be placed on the volume of litigation that the media can be exposed to for the multiple publication of a defamatory statement. All types of slander and libel should be treated similarly in terms of their actionability. The defence of justification could be re-adjusted to require a plaintiff prove that a statement is true, and to require a defendant establish, in appropriate cases, that the publication was the public benefit. The defence of unintentional defamation is open to much criticism. In its place proof of the absence of some broadly defined fault requirement could be made a condition of the defence of qualified privilege and comment. A restricted type of public interest qualified privilege should be recognised, and the defence of fair comment should be considerably enlarged to protect a greater range of comment. The use of interlocutory injunctions should be greatly restricted, if not altogether abolished. When publishing the statement of others, the media should be afforded greater protection against the loss of a defence through proof of certain types of malice.

Some of these suggestions will increase the risk of an award of damages, whereas others will decrease it. Their general importance lies in attempting to ensure a more rational and fair method of determining whether damages should be awardable or not. Constitutional support has been suggested for a number of these, so it is not clear to what extent they can stand or fall according to the view taken of their merits.

The future development of the law of defamation will also be influenced by a number of particular matters. These are, firstly, whether the emotional distress or good name aspect of the action becomes paramount; secondly, a clear perception of the appropriateness of alternative remedies; thirdly, an awareness of the hazards of statutory reform; and, fourthly, an awareness of external constraints on the law's development.

REPUTATION AND EMOTIONAL DISTRESS

The estimation which an individual enjoys before others is the pre-eminent value served by the present law of defamation. But it does not seem to be the only one. The relief of emotional distress caused by the publication is becoming increasingly recognised as a further object of the law's protection. However, this secondary purpose does not rest comfortably with the first. Indeed, it has enveloped the action in such a cloud of uncertainty that now it is open to question just which of the two is the purpose which the action seeks to further.

Quite often, from the way a plaintiff and his counsel bemoan his situation in court, and from the sympathetic way which the jury is encouraged to, and often does, respond, and from the fact that the legal presumption of damage to reputation avoids any necessity to show actual damage, it appears that the action is really about satisfying the plaintiff's hurt feelings, and not vindicating his standing in the community. This suspicion is greatly strengthened by the fact that is is money — and not some rehabilitating redress — which is awarded to a successful plaintiff, and which he can do with as he pleases.[1] In one American case a plaintiff successfully sued in defamation not for damage to reputation, but for emotional distress.[2] However, the suspicion cannot harden into a complete truth because at least where a plaintiff loses, he receives nothing at all for the undoubted emotional distress which can be caused to him by a defamatory but non-actionable or privileged, or otherwise protected publication. The

1 See p. 264 supra.
2 *Time v Firestone* (1976) 424 US 448; see p. 247 supra.

position reached then is a stand-off. One cannot accurately say that the action is about protecting reputation or about compensating for subsequent emotional distress. It both protects both and protects neither.

In this unsatisfactory state, the development of the separate tort of intentional and, increasingly, negligent infliction of emotional distress raises further questions. Could a plaintiff sue in that action rather than in defamation, where he could win in defamation? Even more importantly, could a plaintiff sue for infliction of emotional distress where a defendant could claim the statement was not defamatory or was non-actionable publication, or was privileged, or fair comment? If he could then many of the present boundary markers of the defamation action would become irrelevant. Plaintiffs would increasingly sue for emotional distress only, and as was made plain in the case cited above what is now often suspected as the real purpose of a defamation action would become overtly established. Damage to reputation could then be viewed as just one of the proofs necessary to establish the wider tort of unnecessary infliction of emotional distress, and the defamation action might cease, in time, to be recognised as a separate tort. This will remain a possibility for as long as defamation law continues to use what is essentially an emotional distress remedy, and not some purposive remedy of its own suitable for rehabilitating reputation.

REPUTATION AND GOOD NAME

The correct interpretation of the reference in Article 40.3 of the Constitution to the right to a good name may have a number of important consequences for the future development of defamation law, aside that is from the extensive use already made of constitutional references when considering the reform suggestions outlined at the start of this chapter. Firstly, the gradual subsuming of reputation within an enlarged action for emotional distress would involve a shift in focus for the law away from reputation, as an aspect of good name to emotional distress. However, the explicit citation of good name in Article 40.3 possibly means that imperilling a good name must remain as an actionable wrong in its own right. Secondly, although good name seems likely to include reputation — and the constitution-based criticism of the common law action in previous chapters has assumed that it does — the terms are not necessarily similar. Good name may well have a wider meaning. If it does then there are a number of implications for other areas of tort law, not least of which would be whether there would then have to be a uniform basis for all good name remedies, which could be based on the remedy's effectiveness in correcting a false impression given. For this reason it may be useful to consider what the phrase 'good name' may mean.

Since a good name is only relevant in a social context, one may hazard that the citizen has a constitutional right to a benevolent, benign, approving view from those who know him, and to a non-critical view from those who do not know him. If left at that, since the term good is not the same as truthful, this right could enable people to protect lies about themselves, in addition to past or dated truths about themselves. However, the right is not left unqualified. It is made subject to a number of personal and public rights. Truth may not be one of the ideals expressly mentioned in the Constitution, but it may be taken that in a christian democratic society, the pursuit of truth would actually qualify the right to a good name. So, good can hardly mean good in the face of all the evidence, but rather a meritorious and accurate name or assessment. If truth can thus qualify good, so also must relevance, privacy and charity, not because the idea of truth requires the latter two — it does require the former[3] — but because the Constitution implicitly recognises that the individual is entitled to a space and realm of his own, and because the Preamble to the Constitution requires charity to inform the application of its provisions. One might then describe good name in terms of an individual's right to be considered to act in accordance with the established accurate but relevant perception of itself, or with whatever general standard of perception is appropriate to a particular activity or condition.

Looked at in this light, the scope of the constitutional protection may actually be much broader than the common law's concern with defamatory statements. It could include merely injurious non-defamatory statements, or even non-injurious non-defamatory statements. It might be that any statement which reflected any inaccurate or irrelevant perception of an individual could be actionable, and could cut across the present lines between wrongs like defamation, deceit, injurious falsehood, and negligent misstatement.

Moreover, such a development would strongly suggest that similar remedies would have to be employed to address what would merely be different forms of the same wrong. Another consequence could be that the law of defamation might have to be renamed the law of good name, and the text of a work on defamation expanded to include these other areas as well.

3 Walsh J has suggested — 'The Judicial Power and the Protection of the Right to Privacy' (1977) DULJ 38 — that good name could protect against the disclosure of irrelevant past truths. This assumes that good has to be qualified by truth, which in turn has to be qualified by relevance since truth is a changeable concept which can be determined over time by relevance. See also p. 116 supra.

Whether or not the remedies of reply, retraction and correction orders should be introduced into the law of defamation will be one of the major issues of debate in the law in the future. Much has already been stated of the reasons for dissatisfaction with the present use of damages. It certainly seems inevitable that there will be a greater use made of these alternative remedies. A variety of factors supporting such a trend can be suggested — general dissatisfaction with the operation of juries and in particular the making of excessive awards, the imtimidating and disproportionate effect which the possibility of awards and settlements have on media activities, the state's constitutional guarantee to protect good name 'as best it may', the intrinsic merit of these remedies, and a growing international acceptance of these remedies. At the same time, the public and professional perception of damages as providing an acceptable, if imperfect, solution for defamatory publications is a deeply held and long standing one. Accordingly, much of the debate in the future seems likely to concern the extent to which these other remedies will co-exist with, or supplant, damages, and the circumstances in which they will operate. There are too many imponderables for it to be worthwhile to assay what pragmatic arrangement may eventually be arrived at, but each of the remedies already discussed[4] does have its own essential logic.

Since a right of reply merely facilitates an attempt by a victim to limit the amount of damage done by certain publications, and would not be able to redress the damage caused — since no admission of wrong by the publisher is involved — it could not in any circumstances constitute an exclusive defamation remedy, and would have to operate at the victim's option, with some other remedy. It would also have to operate prior to any other remedy, and since its value lies in the speed with which it is made, it would have to be available as of right in all circumstances without any recourse to a court and within a fixed time.

A retraction possesses a considerable force for restoring a damaged reputation, because it involves the admission by the accuser that his statement was untrue. It can apply in all circumstances, and as a complete remedy in itself, and could not logically exist as an optional alternative to damages. Unless it is proposed to show the statement was true, a victim should possess a legal right to demand a retraction without going to court, and independently of any legal proceedings,

4 For reply, see p. 234 supra; for retraction, see p. 265 supra; for correction, see p. 265 supra.

but again it would be essential that the right be exercisable speedily, and within a fixed time.

Since a judicial order correcting a defamatory publication could only be made after a court determination that an appropriate case existed for such an order, the making of a correction order would not imply either that damages could or could not also be ordered. Nor would its use imply either that damages liability should be established before an order could be made, or conversely that it could be made merely when it was shown that a defamer made an untrue defamatory statement. The order would only be a consequence of some proceeding. Its use would not compel any particular set of pre-conditions.

A number of further general points may be made about the use of alternative remedies. A major objection which can be made about the efficacy of these remedies is that they may fail to effect the attitudes of suspicious or unreasonable minded people. A number of points may be made about this. Firstly, it is not clear that the law must take account of this possibility when devising appropriate remedies, since if it ignores them when deciding if a statement is defamatory, why should it not also ignore them when deciding if damage has been redressed? Secondly, the reference in the Preamble to the Constitution to the virtue of charity, and the consequent necessity for the state and its laws to reflect the virtue may possibly require that no account be taken of suspicious or unreasonable minded people on this point. Thirdly, if as a practical matter it is felt that some notice must be taken of those who might not believe a counter-acting statement, the most consistent approach to take would be to attach a legal presumption of credibility to every such statement — in the same way as defamatory statements are effectively presumed credible. This presumption could only then be rebutted by substantial first hand evidence of disbelief. Even where the presumption was successfully rebutted compensatory damages might still not be awardable — because of their irrelevance to the issue — and instead some form of criminal prosecution should ensue on the basis that such a proceeding best reflects the wider public concern at the inadequacy of the civil remedy. Finally, if it is argued that, say, a retraction lets a defamer off too lightly, and that damages at least make it expensive for him to defame, that is effectively advocating the use of damages for punitive reasons. A criminal proceeding is the more appropriate expression for such a view. It should be appreciated, incidentally, that the use of alternative remedies would not at all affect the entitlement to seek compensatory damages for emotional distress caused. There is every reason why that right should continue, although the size of awards could be expected to be much lower than present defamation awards.

Many of the substantive rules of the law of defamation would be seriously affected by the adoption of the alternative means of redress, and particularly by the remedy of retraction. A large part of the law at present consists of liability avoidance rules, such as the defence of qualified privilege that would have no relevance to the making of counter-acting statements, since part of the basis for their use rests on the simple idea that whoever causes or is responsible for causing damage to reputation should repair it. On the other hand, some rules such as those determining what is defamatory and who is responsible for defamatory publications would remain valid.

Where there are intentional, aggravated or punitive circumstances attaching to a defamatory publication, the ordinary form of a counter-acting statement might not, on its own, fully meet all the elements of public concern at such a situation. Either of two options, both of which are consistent with the idea of counteracting statements, could then be available to the victim. Either he could have the right to demand that the counter-acting statement should include an admission by the defamer that his — the defamer's — own credibility has been damaged by his actions and that similar future accusations made by him may be less credible as a result; or, a criminal proceeding with a clear punitive dimension could be institutionable. The former option, by drawing the taint of disgrace onto the maker of the statement, would give to the retraction remedy the extra force which the circumstances would warrant.

The role of juries in defamation law could be seriously reduced by the use of alternative remedies, and also, incidentally, if the constitutional protection of good name was found to extend over an area wider than that of reputation. Most defamatory publications would thenceforth be remedied outside of court by reply and retraction. However, if there was an increased involvement of the criminal law in punishing a wider range of defamatory publications — as the introduction of reply and retraction remedies would suggest — juries could have a role in the proceedings to the same extent as in any other criminal prosecution. Also, if damages were no longer an option in most defamation cases, the remaining principal jury function would be as arbiter of defamatory meaning. However, if it was found that the right to a good name involved an entitlement to have a false impression of whatever sort corrected then the crucial feature of an infringement of that right would be the incorrect impression caused, and not that the impression related to reputation. Determining incorrect impression is not a task which especially requires the use of a jury; nor, indeed, would selecting an appropriate form of correction require a jury.

There is a further and particular merit about the use of reply and retraction remedies. The use of these remedies could in many cases do away with the necessity of having any civil proceedings for defamation. At present, where the individual can only be assured of redress by suing, there is a great air of unreality and irrelevance about the whole trial and appellate process of slowly examining a statement long after it was made, and often forgotten about. Quite unnecessarily much intellectual energy goes into such questions as — What did the statement really mean? What did people really think of it? How is the trial to be divided up between judge and jury? — and lots of time, effort and money is expended in deciding the law's response to the statement when its impact on the minds of those who heard or read it was often no more than one of hundreds of fleeting impressions created every day. The victim is forced into a highly demanding, combatative and adversarial process before the law will grant him or her anything. The whole point of what the law should be doing to fairly help a defamed person becomes quite lost. The availability and use of retraction remedies would, at least, help redeem that.

THE MANNER OF REFORM

There are three ways by which the two broad categories of reform suggestion — those where damages remain the principal remedy and those where it does not — can be incorporated into the law. The first is by judicial development or re-interpretation of the common law, the second is by judicial interpretation of constitutional provisions, and the third is by statutory enactment. In other common law jurisdictions the manner of reform has been by statutory enactment preceded by some reform body report. This is partly because the judiciary in those jurisdictions possess no function of constitutional interpretation, and partly because the report of a reform body set up to examine and report on the law has been considered a good approach to legislative action. It may be that reform here will follow a similar path, although one can be critical of this approach for a number of reasons. It seems appropriate then to examine how reform body involvement has affected the general development of defamation law. Firstly, one may refer to the Defamation Act 1961.

The Defamation Act 1961 closely followed the recommendations of an English reform body report in 1948[5] and the subsequent English Defamation Act of 1952; as indeed did the legislation of many other common law jurisdictions. No reform body was established here to undertake a general review of defamation law, or even to report

5 This was the *Report of the Committee on Defamation*, referred to as the Porter Committee Report, after the committee's chairman Lord Porter.

on whether English developments first recommended thirteen years previously should be followed. One may wonder how much full or independent consideration was given to the law in whatever review was undertaken by the government of the day, which prompted it to follow the English pattern. Despite a few noticeable differences[6], the 1961 Act not only repeated the shortcomings and even omissions[7] of the English legislation. It assumed, wrongly, that no more was needed here than was done in England. Furthermore, there are parts of the 1961 Act which appear both unsuitable[8] and invalid[9] in light of the 1937 Constitution. This experience of the 1961 Act makes one fearful of another copycat exercise, given that another English reform body has reported in the meantime.[10] However, Australian[11] and New Zealand[12] reform bodies have also reported on the law, often with different perspectives and conclusions to the English one. Together these constitute a useful corpus of reform analysis and recommendation.

Whether all this should lead to the establishment of some Irish defamation reform body to plan the reform of our law in light of the local environment remains doubtful. There are three broad reasons for these doubts. Firstly, defamation reform bodies tend to produce unnecessarily complicated law, or law whose only merit is that it reflects a compromise,[13] or law which is stated in such detail that it only reflects current needs and does not allow for subsequent needs.[14] This detail results in built-in obsolescence, and,

6 Such as a writer's infectious malice destroying a publisher's defence of unintentional defamation, certain differences in the type of reports covered by media qualified privilege, and the inclusion of Northern Ireland in a number of provisions.

7 The Porter Committee's recommendation that evidence of rumour and specific misconduct be admissible as evidence of reputation when assessing damages — which had originally been in the English Defamation Bill but was lost apparently merely because of a rush at the end of the debate to have parliament pass the bill — was not even included in the Irish bill. See p. 250 supra.

8 The outstanding example of this is contained in para. 4, Part I, Second Schedule of the 1961 Act which, adopting the British model, privileges reports of foreign courts exercising jurisdiction under a legislature, but not, as here, when exercising jurisdiction under constitutional authority.

9 S. 24 of the 1961 Act conferring various media privileges seems riddled with constitutionally dubious provisions — see p. 193 supra.

10 This is the *Report of the Committee on Defamation* 1975, referred to as the Faulks Committee report, after the committee's chairman Faulks J.

11 This is titled *Unfair Publication* 1979 by the Australian Law Reform Commission.

12 This is the *Report of the Committee on Defamation in New Zealand*, 1977.

13 S. 21 of the 1961 Act describing the defence of unintentional defamation exemplifies both these points.

14 This is exemplified by the extraordinary detail of s.24 of the 1961 Act in describing various media privileges.

incidentally, in ensuring a rationale for future reform bodies.

Secondly, the value of reform body is crucially dependant on the merit of the analysis and recommendations made. Since the establishment of such a body and the making of recommendations does somehow imply that the right solutions to the right problems have been found, an unimpressive report if acted on can compound the situation it was supposed to resolve.[15] In the case of the three reports already mentioned, some issues were addressed that did not need to be[16], some were not addressed that should have been[17], other recommendations were ill-judged.[18] In general terms, it can be said that the Faulks Committee, which produced the relatively recent English report, did not examine the fundamental premises of the law, and merely concerned itself mainly with altering some existing provisions, which in some instances by codifying de facto situations would introduce a new rigidity into the law.[19] The New Zealand report followed the Faulks' one to an unnerving extent, except that its recommendations occasionally differed sharply from Faulks' and it did not always provide an adequate explanation for these.[20] The Australian report, produced by the federal law reform commission, is much better than the other two. It adopts a generally critical approach and produced a number of interesting and imaginative proposals.[21]

Thirdly there is a clear tendency in all the reform reports over the last hundred years[22] to alter the balance of interest in defamation law more and more in favour of free speech, and especially in the media, and less in favour of protection of personal reputation. No

15 See, for example, the recommendations of the Faulks Committee on the English equivalent of s.22 of the 1961 at p. 104 above.

16 Examples of this are recommendations on the reputation of corporations and defamation of the dead.

17 An example of an omission concerns the principle in Mangena's case at p. 215. supra which effectively nullifies a major distinction between the defences of qualified privilege and fair comment.

18 An example of this was the Porter Committee's recommendations which produced ss. 22 and 23 of the 1961 Act.

19 A good example of this are Faulks' recommendations for remedying the defects in the two previous sections.

20 A particular aspect of these disagreements concerns the criticisms made by the subsequent reform reports of the Porter Committee Report. There may be an important general lesson to be drawn from this. If, as it is suggested, Porter was wrong in many of his recommendations that were enacted into law, does this mean that we have had bad law all along which will be remedied by recent recommendations? If so, why should it not happen that thirty years hence we will be told that the present recommendations enacted into law were also bad?.

21 Relating, for example, to unintentional defamation and correction orders.

22 Dating from the *Report of a Select Committee on the Law in relation to Libel in Newspapers and Journals* in 1879, which led to the enactment of the Newspaper Libel and Registration Act 1881.

doubt this is more the result of social and economic change than an excessive media influence in obtaining reform,[23] though media demands have been influential in having reform bodies established. Even now, there is good reason to think that the law ought, in some respects, to favour the media far more than it does.[24] But it should not always have to happen at the complete expense of the defamed. Unfortunately, reform bodies do not often perceive how, or that, this can be done; and when this failure is repeated a number of times, or when unimpressive arguments are advanced against requiring even a minimum from the media in return for greater protection,[25] one may become concerned whether a reform body can actually secure a fair and adequate protection for reputation.

EXTERNAL CONSTRAINTS

There remain two influences which may affect the future working on Irish defamation law, and which may be shortly mentioned. These are European Community law and the European Convention on Human Rights. While it is too early to judge the nature and extent of the influence of EC law,[26] whatever that influence is it will have the major effect of constraining all other sources of, and influences on, defamation law. At first it may be wondered what concern EC law has with the protection of reputation. The concern is an indirect one, at present, though nonetheless real for that. Divergent national defamation laws can assuredly function as impediments to the freedom of the media to provide services across the community. The Community can be sued under community law for defamatory publications for which it is responsible. There is also the reliance by the Court of Justice on the Convention on Human Rights, and the Court's general attachment to common notions of justice, rights and obligations prevalent in the Community's member states. Already the European Commission has proposed to compel broadcast media to grant defamed persons rights of reply on the continental model to charges made against them in broadcasts. Subsequently the Commission dropped its right of reply proposal, though only because it was not satisfied that present divergences in national laws had any appreciable effect on media activities.[27] It is also quite clear from

23 Indicative of the ineffectiveness of media influence was the refusal of the Faulks Committee to recommend a protection which media interests would very much like — a public interest qualified privilege. See p. 170 supra.
24 See pp. 169 and 210 supra.
25 As, for example, with the arguments made against attaching a public benefit requirement to the defence of justification. See p. 115 supra.
26 Some effects can, however, be described. See p. 169 and 221 supra.

reading the Commission's rationale on the subject that it could have — had it considered it propitious — remodelled large areas of defamation law as it affects the media, or indeed other businesses like supermarkets and banks, in order to produce uniform defamation rules throughout the Community. The creation of EC rules of defamation law could have far-reaching effects on Irish defamation law. These effects rest too much in the future to be considered here, though one in particular may be mentioned. Our Constitution would offer little protection against the capriciousness of many Community rules. For example, if an EC directive had introduced enforceable rights of reply against broadcast media, a person defamed by print media would have no comparable right of reply, and yet he could not claim impermissibly unequal treatment under the 1937 Constitution, since it would be required by Community law.

Although the European Convention on Human Rights does not explicitly recognise a right to a reputation, it does effectively recognise such a right and the national laws which protect it in Articles 8.1, 10.2 and 6.1 which protect, respectively reputation as it relates to privacy, as it restricts freedom of expression, and as it affects right of trial and access to the courts. There have been cases concerning the relationship between national defamation laws and the Convention. In one case parliamentary immunity was upheld as not infringing the Convention,[28] and in another refusal under national law to allow a group maintain an action for defamation was also upheld.[29] On the other hand, a criminal libel rule which punished

27 See p. 236 supra. Another instance where a community measure showed a concern to safeguard reputation and good name was the draft directive published in 1978 — Com (77)724 final — prohibiting misleading and unfair advertising. The latter was defined so as to include discrediting an individual's or a business' good name. The 16th Report of the Joint Committee on the Secondary Legislation of the European Communities (Misleading and Unfair Advertising) Prl 7275, expressed concern about the implications of the proposed directive for the laws of defamation and injurious falsehood, and called for an examination of the issue. Essentially the proposal involved making available an extra procedure and remedy for a particular type of defamatory publication. This would not give rise to impermissibly unequal treatment of defamation plaintiffs in relation to remedies for reasons outlined below. The similar treatment of defamation and injurious falsehood by the draft directive did raise the question whether the domestic distinction between the two actions is a valid one. The proper interpretation of the phrase 'good name' in the Constitution may answer this question affirmatively — see p. 289 supra. As adopted in 1984 the proposal relating to unfair advertising was dropped from the directive, and deferred to a later date, because of lack of agreement on how to define unfair advertising.

28 *X v Austria*, 3374/67, Yearbook XII at 246; *X v UK*, 7966/77 unpublished.

29 *Church of Scientology v Sweden*, 8282/78, D & R 21 at 109.

the expression of political opinion was held to infringe the Convention.[30]

The general view seems to be that if a finding or denial of liability under national law is one which is in accordance with national law, and is necessary in a democratic society for the protection of reputation or free speech, then the finding will not be disturbed. Although Irish courts are not bound by the Convention, it is interesting to speculate on whether successful actions could be taken against the Irish state because, say, there is no public benefit condition attached to the defence of justification, or because Irish law grants no automatic right of reply to those defamed by the media. It seems plausible to suggest that the existence of such rules could be seen as necessary in a democratic society in order to protect reputation.

30 Lingens' case, 1986, Series A, No. 103. See p. 211 supra.

APPENDIX

Defamation Act, 1961

Number 40 *of* 1961

AN ACT TO CONSOLIDATE WITH AMENDMENTS CERTAIN ENACTMENTS RELATING TO THE LAW OF DEFAMATION. [17*th August*, 1961.]

BE IT ENACTED BY THE OIREACHTAS AS FOLLOWS:—

PART I

PRELIMINARY AND GENERAL

1.—This Act may be cited as the Defamation Act, 1961.

2.—In this Act—

"local authority" has the same meaning as in the Local Government Act, 1941;

"newspaper", except in section 27, means any paper containing public news or observations thereon, or consisting wholly or mainly of advertisements, which is printed for sale and is published in the State or in Northern Ireland either periodically or in parts or numbers at intervals not exceeding thirty-six days;

"proprietor" means, as well as the sole proprietor of any newspaper, in the case of a divided proprietorship, the persons who, as partners or otherwise, represent or are responsible for any share or interest in the newspaper as between themselves and the persons in like manner representing or responsible for the other shares or interests therein, and no other person.

3.—(1) This Act shall come into operation on the 1st day of January, 1962.

(2) Part III of this Act shall apply for the purposes of any proceedings begun after the commencement of this Act, whenever the cause of action arose, but shall not affect any proceedings commenced before the commencement of this Act.

4.—The enactments specified in the First Schedule to this Act are hereby repealed.

PART II

CRIMINAL PROCEEDINGS FOR LIBEL

5.—(1) On every trial of an indictment for making or publishing any libel to which a plea of not guilty is entered, the jury may give a general verdict of guilty or not guilty upon the whole matter put in issue on the indictment, and the jury shall not be required or directed by the court to find the person charged guilty merely on the proof of the publication by him of the paper charged to be a libel and of the sense ascribed to such paper in the indictment.

(2) On every such trial the court shall, according to its discretion, give its opinion and directions to the jury on the matter in issue in like manner as in other criminal cases.

(3) Subsections (1) and (2) of this section shall not operate to prevent the jury from finding a special verdict, in their discretion, as in other criminal cases.

6.—On the trial of any indictment for a defamatory libel, the person charged having pleaded such plea as hereinafter mentioned, the truth of the matters charged may be inquired into but shall not amount to a defence, unless it was for the public benefit that the said matters charged should be published; and, to entitle the defendant to give evidence of the truth of such matters charged as a defence to such indictment, it shall be necessary for the person charged, in pleading to the said indictment, to allege the truth of the said matters charged, in the manner required in pleading a justification to an action for defamation, and further to allege that it was for the public benefit that the said matters charged should be published, and the particular fact or facts by reason of which it was for the public benefit that the said matters charged should be published, to which plea the prosecutor shall be at liberty to reply generally, denying the whole thereof; and if, after such plea, the person charged is convicted on such indictment, the court may, in pronouncing sentence, consider whether his guilt is aggravated or mitigated by the said plea and by the evidence given to prove or to disprove the same: provided that—

(a) the truth of the matters charged in the alleged libel complained of by such indictment shall in no case be inquired into without such plea of justification;

(b) in addition to such plea of justification, the person charged may enter a plea of not guilty;

(c) nothing in this section shall take away or prejudice any defence under the plea of not guilty which it is competent to the person charged to make under such plea to any indictment for defamatory libel.

7.—Whenever, upon the trial of an indictment for the publication of a libel, a plea of not guilty having been entered, evidence is given establishing a presumption of publication against the person charged by the act of any other person by his authority, it shall be competent for the person charged to prove that the publication was made without his authority, consent or knowledge and that the publication did not arise from want of due care or caution on his part.

8.—No criminal prosecution shall be commenced against any proprietor, publisher, editor or any person responsible for the publication of a newspaper for any libel published therein without the order of a Judge of the High Court sitting *in camera* being first had and obtained, and every application for such order shall be made on notice to the person accused, who shall have an opportunity of being heard against the application.

9.—A Justice of the District Court, upon the hearing of a charge against a proprietor, publisher or editor or any person responsible for the publication of a newspaper for a libel published therein, may receive evidence as to the publication being for the public benefit, as to the matters charged in the libel being true, as to the report being fair and accurate and published without malice and as to any matter which, under this or any other Act or otherwise, might be given in evidence by way of defence by the person charged on his trial on indictment, and the Justice, if of opinion after hearing such evidence that there is a strong or probable presumption that the jury on the trial would acquit the person charged, may dismiss the case.

10.—If a Justice of the District Court, upon the hearing of a charge against a proprietor, publisher, editor or any person responsible for the publication of a newspaper for a libel published therein, is of opinion that, though the person charged is shown to have been guilty, the libel was of a trivial character and that the offence may be adequately punished by virtue of the powers conferred by this section, the Justice shall cause the charge to be reduced into writing and read to the person charged and shall then ask him if he desires to be tried by a jury or consents to the case being dealt with summarily, and, if such person consents to the case being dealt with summarily, may summarily convict him, and impose on him a fine not exceeding fifty pounds, and the Summary Jurisdiction Acts shall apply accordingly.

11.—Every person who maliciously publishes any defamatory libel shall, on conviction thereof on indictment, be liable to a fine not exceeding two hundred pounds or to imprisonment for a term not exceeding one year or to both such fine and imprisonment.

12.—Every person who maliciously publishes any defamatory libel, knowing the same to be false, shall, on conviction thereof on indictment, be liable to a fine not exceeding five hundred pounds or to imprisonment for a term not exceeding two years or to both such fine and imprisonment.

13.—(1) Every person who composes, prints or publishes any blasphemous or obscene libel shall, on conviction thereof on indictment, be liable to a fine not exceeding five hundred pounds or to imprisonment for a term not exceeding two years or to both such fine and imprisonment or to penal servitude for a term not exceeding seven years.

(2) (a) In every case in which a person is convicted of composing, printing or publishing a blasphemous libel, the court may make an order for the seizure and carrying away and detaining in safe custody, in such manner as shall be directed in the order, of all copies of the libel in the possession of such person or of any other person named in the order for his use, evidence upon oath having been previously given to the satisfaction of the court that copies of the said libel are in the possession of such other person for the use of the person convicted.

(b) Upon the making of an order under paragraph (a) of this subsection, any member of the Garda Síochána acting under such order may enter, if necessary by the use of force, and search for any copies of the said libel any building, house or other place belonging to the person convicted or to such other person named in the order and may seize and carry away and detain in the manner directed in such order all copies of the libel found therein.

(c) If, in any such case, the conviction is quashed on appeal, any copies of the libel seized under an order under paragraph (a) of this subsection shall be returned free of charge to the person or persons from whom they were seized.

(d) Where, in any such case, an appeal is not lodged or the conviction is confirmed on appeal, any copies of the libel seized under an order under paragraph (a) of this subsection shall, on the application of a member of the Garda Síochána to the court which made such order, be disposed of in such manner as such court may direct.

PART III

CIVIL PROCEEDINGS FOR DEFAMATION

14.—(1) In this Part—

"broadcast" has the same meaning as in the Wireless Telegraphy Act, 1926 (in this section referred to as the Act of 1926) and "broadcasting" shall be construed accordingly;

"broadcasting station" has the same meaning as in the Act of 1926, as amended by the Broadcasting Authority Act, 1960;

"wireless telegraphy" has the same meaning as in the Act of 1926.

(2) Any reference in this Part to words shall be construed as including a reference to visual images, gestures and other methods of signifying meaning.

(3) Where words broadcast by means of wireless telegraphy are simultaneously transmitted by telegraph as defined by the Telegraph Act, 1863, in accordance with a licence granted by the Minister for Posts and Telegraphs, the provisions of this Part shall apply as if the transmission were broadcasting by means of wireless telegraphy.

15.—For the purposes of the law of libel and slander the broadcasting of words by means of wireless telegraphy shall be treated as publication in permanent form.

16.—Words spoken and published which impute unchastity or adultery to any woman or girl shall not require special damage to render them actionable.

17.—In any action for defamation, it shall be lawful for the defendant (after notice in writing of his intention so to do, duly given to the plaintiff at the time of filing or delivering the plea in the action) to give in evidence, in mitigation of damage, that he made or offered an apology to the plaintiff for such defamation before the commencement of the action, or as soon afterwards as he had an opportunity of doing so, in case the action shall have been commenced before there was an opportunity of making or offering such apology.

18.—(1) A fair and accurate report published in any newspaper or broadcast by means of wireless telegraphy as part of any programme or service provided by means of a broadcasting station within the State or in Northern Ireland of proceedings publicly heard before any court established by law and exercising judicial authority within the State or in Northern Ireland shall, if published or broadcast contemporaneously with such proceedings, be privileged.

(2) Nothing in subsection (1) of this section shall authorise the publication or broadcasting of any blasphemous or obscene matter.

19.—In an action for slander in respect of words calculated to disparage the plaintiff in any office, profession, calling, trade or business held or carried on by him at the time of the publication, it shall not be necessary to allege or prove special damage, whether or not the words are spoken of the plaintiff in the way of his office, profession, calling, trade or business.

20.—(1) In an action for slander of title, slander of goods or other malicious falsehood, it shall not be necessary to allege or prove special damage—

(a) if the words upon which the action is founded are calculated to cause pecuniary damage to the plaintiff and are published in writing or other permanent form; or

(b) if the said words are calculated to cause pecuniary damage to the plaintiff in respect of any office, profession, calling, trade or business held or carried on by him at the time of the publication.

(2) Section 15 of this Act shall apply for the purposes of subsection (1) of this section as it applies for the purposes of the law of libel and slander.

21.—(1) A person who has published words alleged to be defamatory of another person may, if he claims that the words were published by him innocently in relation to that other person, make an offer of amends under this section, and in any such case—

(a) if the offer is accepted by the party aggrieved and is duly performed, no proceedings for libel or slander shall be taken or continued by that party against the person making the offer in respect of the publication in question (but without prejudice to any cause of action against any other person jointly responsible for that publication);

(b) if the offer is not accepted by the party aggrieved, then, except as otherwise provided by this section, it shall be a defence, in any proceedings by him for libel or slander against the person making the offer in respect of the publication in question, to prove that the words complained of were published by the defendant innocently in relation to the plaintiff and that the offer was made as soon as practicable after the defendant received notice that they were or might be defamatory of the plaintiff, and has not been withdrawn.

(2) An offer of amends under this section must be expressed to be made for the purposes of this section, and must be accompanied by an affidavit specifying the facts relied upon by the person making it to show that the words in question were published by him innocently in relation to the party aggrieved; and for the purposes of a defence under paragraph (b) of sub- section (1) of this section no evidence, other than evidence of facts specified in the affidavit, shall be admissible on behalf of that person to prove that the words were so published.

(3) An offer of amends under this section shall be understood to mean an offer—

(a) in any case, to publish or join in the publication of a suitable correction of the words complained of, and a sufficient apology to the party aggrieved in respect of those words;

(b) where copies of a document or record containing the said words have been distributed by or with the knowledge of the person making the offer, to take such steps as are reasonably practicable on his part for notifying persons to whom copies have been so distributed that the words are alleged to be defamatory of the party aggrieved.

(4) Where an offer of amends under this section is accepted by the party aggrieved—

(a) any question as to the steps to be taken in fulfilment of the offer as so accepted shall, in default of agreement betwee the parties, be referred to and determined by the High Court or, if proceedings in respect of the publication in question have been taken in the Circuit Court, by the Circuit Court, and the decision of such Court thereon shall be final;

(b) the power of the court to make orders as to costs in proceedings by the party aggrieved against the person making the offer in respect of the publication in question, or in proceedings in respect of the offer under paragraph (a) of this subsection, shall include power to order the payment by the person making the offer to the party aggrieved of costs on an indemnity basis and any expenses reasonably incurred or to be incurred by that party in consequence of the publication in question;

and if no such proceedings as aforesaid are taken, the High Court may, upon application made by the party aggrieved, make any such order for the payment of such costs and expenses as aforesaid as could be made in such proceedings.

(5) For the purposes of this section words shall be treated as published by one person (in this subsection referred to as the publisher) innocently in relation to another person if, and only if, the following conditions are satisfied, that is to say—

(a) that the publisher did not intend to publish them of and concerning that other person, and did not know of circumstances by virtue of which they might be understood to refer to him; or

(b) that the words were not defamatory on the face of them, and the publisher did not know of circumstances by virtue of which they might be understood to be defamatory of that other person, and in either case that the publisher exercised all reasonable care in relation to the publication; and any reference in this subsection to the publisher shall be construed as including a reference to any servant or agent of the publisher who was concerned with the contents of the publication.

(6) Paragraph (b) of subsection (1) of this section shall not apply where the party aggrieved proves that he has suffered special damage.

(7) Paragraph (b) of subsection (1) of this section shall not apply in relation to the publication by any person of words of which he is not the author unless he proves that the words were written by the author without malice.

22.—In an action for libel or slander in respect of words containing two or more distinct charges against the plaintiff, a defence of justification shall not fail by reason only that the truth of every charge is not proved, if the words not proved to be true do not materially injure the plaintiff's reputation having regard to the truth of the remaining charges.

23.—In an action for libel or slander in respect of words consisting partly of allegations of fact and partly of expression of opinion, a defence of fair comment shall not fail by reason only that the truth of every allegation of fact is not proved, if the expression of opinion is fair comment having regard to such of the facts alleged or referred to in the words complained of as are proved.

24.—(1) Subject to the provisions of this section, the publication in a newspaper or the broadcasting by means of wireless telegraphy as part of any programme or service provided by means of a broadcasting station within the State or in Northern Ireland of any such report or other matter as is mentioned in the Second Schedule to this Act shall be privileged unless the publication or broadcasting is proved to be made with malice.

(2) In an action for libel in respect of the publication or broadcasting of any such report or matter as is mentioned in Part II of the Second Schedule to this Act, the provisions of this section shall not be a defence if it is proved that the defendant has been requested by the plaintiff to publish in the newspaper in which the original publication was made or to broadcast from the broadcasting station from which the original broadcast was made, whichever is the case, a reasonable statement by way of explanation or contradiction, and has refused or neglected to do so, or has done so in a manner not adequate or not reasonable having regard to all the circumstances.

(3) Nothing in this section shall be construed as protecting the publication or broadcasting of any matter the publication or broadcasting of which is prohibited by law, or of any matter which is not of public concern and the publication or broadcasting of which is not for the public benefit.

(4) Nothing in this section shall be construed as limiting or abridging any privilege subsisting (otherwise than by virtue of section 4 of the Law of Libel Amendment Act, 1888) immediately before the commencement of this Act.

25.—An agreement for indemnifying any person against civil liability for libel in respect of the publication of any matter shall not be unlawful unless at the time of the publication that person knows that the matter is defamatory, and does not reasonably believe there is a good defence to any action brought upon it.

26.—In any action for libel or slander the defendant may give evidence in mitigation of damages that the plaintiff has recovered damages, or has brought actions for damages, for libel or slander in respect of the publication of words to the same effect as the words on which the action is founded, or has received or agreed to receive compensation in respect of any such publication.

27.—(1) The proprietor of every newspaper having a place of business in the State shall, where such proprietor is not a company registered under the Companies Acts, 1908 to 1959, and is not required under the provisions of the Registration of Business Names Act, 1916, to be registered under that Act in respect of the business of carrying on such newspaper, be registered in the manner directed by that Act, and that Act shall apply to such proprietor in like manner as it applies to a firm or individual referred to in section 1 thereof.

(2) Every reference in the Registration of Business Names Act, 1916, to that Act shall be construed as a reference to that Act as extended by subsection (1) of this section.

(3) In this section "newspaper" means any paper containing public news or observations thereon, or consisting wholly or mainly of advertisements, which is printed for sale and is published in the State either periodically or in parts or numbers at intervals not exceeding twenty-six days.

28.—Nothing in this Part shall affect the law relating to criminal libel.

FIRST SCHEDULE

ENACTMENTS REPEALED

PART I

Acts of the Parliament of Ireland

Session and Chapter	Title
28 Hen. 8, c. 7 (Ir.).	An Act of Slaunder.
2 Geo. 1, c. 20 (Ir.).	An Act to limit the time for Criminal Prosecutions for words spoken.
33 Geo. 3, c. 43 (Ir.).	An Act to remove doubts respecting the functions of juries in cases of libel.

PART II

Acts of the Parliament of the late United Kingdom of Great Britain and Ireland

Session and Chapter	Title
60 Geo. 3 & 1 Geo. 4, c. 8.	Criminal Libel Act, 1819.
3 & 4 Vic., c. 9.	Parliamentary Papers Act, 1840.
6 & 7 Vic., c. 96.	Libel Act, 1843.
8 & 9 Vic., c. 75.	Libel Act, 1845.
32 & 33 Vic., c. 24.	Newspapers Printers and Reading Rooms Repeal Act, 1869.
44 & 45 Vic., c. 60.	Newspaper Libel and Registration Act, 1881.
51 & 52 Vic., c. 64.	Law of Libel Amendment Act, 1888.
54 & 55 Vic., c. 51.	Slander of Women Act, 1891.

SECOND SCHEDULE

STATEMENTS HAVING QUALIFIED PRIVILEGE

PART I

Statements privileged without Explanation or Contradiction

1. A fair and accurate report of any proceedings in public of a house of any legislature (including subordinate or federal legislatures) of any foreign sovereign State or any body which is part of such legislature or any body duly

appointed by or under the legislature or executive of such State to hold a public inquiry on a matter of public importance.

2. A fair and accurate report of any proceedings in public of an international organization of which the State or the Government is a member or of any international conference to which the Government sends a representative.

3. A fair and accurate report of any proceedings in public of the International Court of Justice and any other judicial or arbitral tribunal deciding matters in dispute between States.

4. A fair and accurate report of any proceedings before a court (including a courtmartial) exercising jurisdiction under the law of any legislature (including subordinate or federal legislatures) of any foreign sovereign State.

5. A fair and accurate copy of or extract from any register kept in pursuance of any law which is open to inspection by the public or of any other document which is required by law to be open to inspection by the public.

6. Any notice or advertisement published by or on the authority of any court in the State or in Northern Ireland or any Judge or officer of such a court.

PART II

Statements privileged subject to Explanation or Contradiction

1. A fair and accurate report of the findings or decision of any of the following associations, whether formed in the State or Northern Ireland, or of any committee or governing body thereof, that is to say:

(a) an association for the purpose of promoting or encouraging the exercise of or interest in any art, science, religion or learning, and empowered by its constitution to exercise control over or adjudicate upon matters of interest or concern to the association or the actions or conduct of any persons subject to such control or adjudication;

(b) an association for the purpose of promoting or safeguarding the interests of any trade, business, industry or profession or of the persons carrying on or engaged in any trade, business, industry or profession and empowered by its constitution to exercise control over or adjudicate upon matters connected with the trade, business, industry or profession or the actions or conduct of those persons;

(c) an association for the purpose of promoting or safeguarding the interests of any game, sport or pastime, to the playing or exercise of which members of the public are invited or admitted, and empowered by its constitution to exercise control over or adjudicate upon persons connected with or taking part in the game, sport or pastime;

being a finding or decision relating to a person who is a member of or is subject by virtue of any contract to the control of the association.

2. A fair and accurate report of the proceedings at any public meeting held in the State or Northern Ireland, being a meeting *bona fide* and lawfully held for a lawful purpose and for the furtherance or discussion of any matter of public concern whether the admission to the meeting is general or restricted.

3. A fair and accurate report of the proceedings at any meeting or sitting of—

(a) any local authority, or committee of a local authority or local authorities, and any corresponding authority, or committee thereof, in Northern Ireland;

(b) any Judge or Justice acting otherwise than as a court exercising judicial authority and any corresponding person so acting in Northern Ireland;

(c) any commission, tribunal, committee or person appointed, whether in the State or Northern Ireland, for the purposes of any inquiry under statutory authority;

(d) any person appointed by a local authority to hold a local inquiry in pursuance of an Act of the Oireachtas and any person appointed by a corresponding authority in Northern Ireland to hold a local inquiry in pursuance of statutory authority;

(e) any other tribunal, board, committee or body constituted by or under, and exercising functions under, statutory authority, whether in the State or Northern Ireland;

not being a meeting or sitting admission to which is not allowed to representatives of the press and other members of the public.

4. A fair and accurate report of the proceedings at a general meeting, whether in the State or Northern Ireland, of any company or association constituted, registered or certified by or under statutory authority or incorporated by charter, not being, in the case of a company in the State, a

private company within the meaning of the Companies Acts, 1908 to 1959, or, in the case of a company in Northern Ireland, a private company within the meaning of the statutes relating to companies for the time being in force therein.

5. A copy or fair and accurate report or summary of any notice or other matter issued for the information of the public by or on behalf of any Government department, local authority or the Commissioner of the Garda Síochána or by or on behalf of a corresponding department, authority or officer in Northern Ireland.

Index